# THE
# GREAT FOREST
# OF THE
# ADIRONDACKS

# THE
# GREAT FOREST
# OF THE
# ADIRONDACKS

Barbara McMartin

Maps, charts and graphs by W. Alec Reid

Research and editing by Edward Comstock, Jr.

NORTH COUNTRY BOOKS

Utica, New York

Published by North Country Books, Utica, New York 13501

First Hardcover Printing 1994
Second Hardcover Printing 1998
Hardcover ISBN 0-925168-29-7

First Paperback Printing 2005
Paperback ISBN 1-59531-003-7

**Library of Congress Cataloging-in-Publication Data**

McMartin, Barbara
  The great forest of the Adirondacks / Barbara McMartin
    p.  cm.
  Includes bibliographical references and index.
  ISBN 0-925168-29-7
  1. Forests and Forestry—New York (State)—Adirondack Mountains
Region—History. 2. Forest products industry—New York (State)—
Adirondack Mountains Region—History. 3. Forests and forestry—Eco-
nomic aspects—New York (State)—Adirondack Mountains Region—
History. 4. Adirondack Forest Preserve (N.Y.)—History. 5. Adirondack
Park (N.Y.)—History. I. Title.
SD144,N7M38  1994
33.75'09747'5—dc20                        94-13354
                                                 CIP

Printed in the United States of America
Cover design by Richard Loomis
Book design by Barbara McMartin

# Acknowledgments

Libraries and research collections form the basis of this book. To those institutions and especially to their librarians and archivists goes a special note of gratitude. The Adirondack Museum, Blue Mountain Lake; the Archives of the New York State Library, Albany; the Division of Rare Books and Manuscripts Collection, Carl A. Kroch Library, Cornell University; the Albert R. Mann Library at the College of Life Sciences, Cornell University; and the F. Franklin Moon Library, State University of New York, College of Environmental Sciences and Forestry, Syracuse were the principal research sources. Jerold Pepper, Librarian, Adirondack Museum; James D. Folts, Associate Archivist, New York State Archives; Flora Nyland, Archivist, Moon Library; and the staff of Carl A. Kroch Library were especially helpful. Kathryn Vreeland of the Northeast Regional Climate Center at Cornell also helped. The research at Syracuse and Cornell could not have been done without the efforts of Ted Comstock.

The collection of the Real Property Office of the New York State Department of Environmental Conservation was a major resource and John Keating of that office not only made it available, he shared his insights into some of the unpublished background of the rare documents in the State's collection. The office supplied copies of the 1950 Blowdown Map.

Robert Staph of the Office of General Services made early Land Office records available.

James C. Dawson, Ph. D., of SUNY Plattsburgh, deserves a special mention because he loaned the author a large part of his collection of commission reports, land acquisition records, numerous doctoral dissertations, and copies of magazine articles from the turn of the century. The fact that these books and documents were available throughout the research and writing of the book made it possible to consult them readily, as new questions arose. Robert Youker's gift of an early land map was very helpful.

Jim Dawson's help was also much appreciated for helping me understand the Adirondack iron industry. In addition, he read and commented on the text. Michael Kudish, Adirondack railroad expert, corrected both text and the map relating to his specialty.

Richard Nason of Finch, Pruyn and Co. was most generous with records of the Hudson River Boom Association. He shared information on Finch, Pruyn and Company and read the manuscript to check the correctness of details from a forester's point of view. Several other foresters were very helpful: T. D. Schlachter of Whitney Industries; John Stock, formerly at Litchfield Park, offered a chapter from his contemplated book on that park; Joe Hanley and Pat Flood of International Paper Company; Daniel McGough, formerly of Lyons Falls Pulp and Paper Company; and Tom Lucey of Domtar. James Rogers IV shared J. and J. Rogers Company land ownership records.

Jim Goodwin let me use his unpublished paper on Keene Valley logging and helped with Adirondack Mountain Reserve history. Edie Pilcher also helped with AMR's history as well as introductions to the uncut portions of the Webb lands. Winthrop Aldrich of the Department of Environmental Conservation shared his research on Santanoni Preserve. Mary McKenzie, Town of North Elba Historian, shared copies of old surveys and information on the area west of Street and Nye. Ray Masters shared notes on Huntington Preserve. Norman J. VanValkenburgh, Adirondack historian, answered several questions. Philip G. Terrie, Adirondack historian, discussed the general plan for the book.

Edwin H. Ketchledge, Ph. D., helped me understand forest history and read chapters relating to foresters as well as the author's conclusions. Charles Cogbill, Ph. D, helped me understand old growth forests and ways of assessing them.

For the actual search for old growth forest, Paul Capone introduced me to the stereo photographs used by the Department of Equalization and Assessment. The Saranac Office loaned me photographs to study carefully at home. John Banta shared satellite photos and Adirondack Park Agency maps; he made available copies of DEC's map for me to use as base maps when I tried to assimilate the wealth of information from tax, trespass, fire, and other records.

My husband, W. Alec Reid, and Stanford Pulrang accompanied me on my many walks to view potential old growth sites.

John A. Koetteritz loaned photos of his grandfather. My thanks to Carlene Lankton for putting me in touch with him. The Adirondack Museum was generous in giving permission to copy the rest of the book's pictures from their collection. Jim Meehan was most helpful in their selection.

Ted Comstock did a meticulous job of editing this book, a service that was most important to my work. Carlene Lankton proofread the final version.

I am indebted to all of them for their help, but most importantly, I am indebted to my husband, W. Alec Reid, for the countless hours he spent putting all sorts of data on his computer and creating from it the results summarized in the maps, charts, and graphs. The whole subject is so complicated, that it would be impossible to understand without these visual summaries, which, in contrast to their apparent simplicity, took so long to prepare.

# Contents

# Illustrations

## Photographs

## Maps

Maps 2 through 13 created and copyrighted by W. Alec Reid

# Charts and graphs

The data used in these charts and graphs came from numerous disparate sources: the New York and United States Census for various years, reports of the Forest Commission and successor commissions, forest industry documents, particularly those of the Empire State Forest Products Association, the Hudson River Boom Association, and industry publications such as *Lumber Camp News* and its successor, *Northeastern Logger.*

Methods of reporting varied according to sources and the time periods in which they were made and because of the different units of measurement used, they are not initially comparable. Nor are the modes of calculating always sufficiently explicit that conversions from one method to another could be made. Nevertheless, an attempt was made to reconcile the boundaries of the regions and to translate the different quantities into one so that trends over time would appear. The results, in most cases, do not yield absolute statistical information, but do confirm trends.

If charts and graphs have been compiled from one consistent source, that source is cited in the text. If it was necessary to make calculations to combine information given in different units in order to show trends over time, no source is cited. Calculations have been made using one or more of the above sources and the following conversions:

2.92 Standards = 1 cord*
1 cord = 549 board feet**

Using these figures gives a slightly smaller number of board feet per standard (188) than the 195 quoted by Graves or the 200 board feet used by Fox.

* H. S. Graves, *The Woodsman's Handbook*, Part I, United States Department of Agriculture, 1903.

** Forest, Fish and Game Commission, *Annual Report for 1909.*

# Introduction

*In the four years since I completed* The Great Forest of the Adirondacks *the book has generated discussion, questions, controversy, and excitement. None of this was surprising because my approach questioned and refuted established ideas about the forest. The idea that there is so much old growth forest has inspired many people to view the Adirondack Forest Preserve in a new light. I have taken many forest researchers to my favorite sites and their exclamations of sheer pleasure have spurred me to find more special places. E. H. Ketchledge, Charles Canham, Charles Cogbill and others have joined me on forays to virgin spruce stands. Professors have sent graduate students to me so I could help them identify sites for their research. Some are now looking at old growth hardwood stands with many different questions in mind. I have led trips to accessible old growth stands for the Adirondack Museum and my lectures have encouraged many others to look at the places I have singled out. The interest in my book has been most rewarding.*

*I have used the historical material my research uncovered to discover other places to visit and every walk I have taken has brought me new insights into the wonders and complexity of the forest stands. I am amazed by the diversity of stands where we know that no logging ever occurred. I found a few places with very old stumps and I wondered if I had been mistaken about their histories. Then I found and used a list of permits the Conservation Department had granted for salvage after the 1950 blowdown. The sites with stumps were all within the permit areas. Nothing has happened to change my basic belief -- that there is upwards of a half million acres of forest land that either was never logged or logged minimally because it was inaccessible or contained only hardwoods.*

*The way hardwoods dominate the southern Adirondacks becomes more and more obvious. I tried to understand how much logging would have to occur to eliminate softwoods and concluded that it would take repeated clearcuts of softwoods for this to happen. Where there might have been logging, none of the acreage I have identified as special was logged more than once for softwoods.*

*Someone should be studying the recovery of the forests that were logged. After a hundred and twenty or thirty years or more, the kind of logging that occurred before 1890 has left these stands virtually indistinguishable from stands I know were virgin. For all the interest, research is very limited and long-range studies are virtually nonexistent. So are funds for basic forest research.*

*The northwest Adirondacks experienced a major windstorm in 1955 that has prompted new questions about the role of violent weather in the Adirondacks. Even the stands where most trees have long life expectancies have few older trees still standing. Nature, not man, has shortened their lives.*

*Responses to the book have been gratifying. Many have written that my hypothesis has merit and that its value is just emerging.*

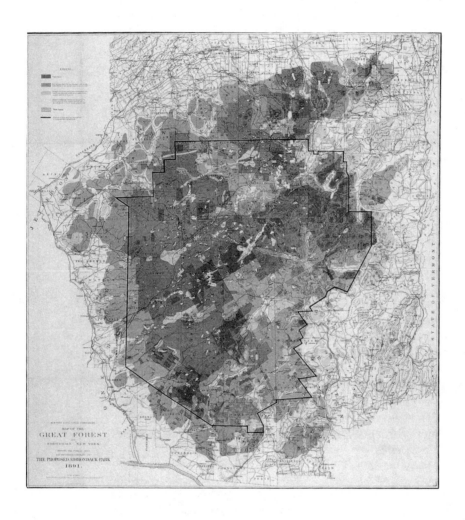

# I

# The Quest for the Great Forest

The map reproduced on the cover[1] has long intrigued me. What was the Great Forest really like? How much of it still exists? Do any of the forest tracts I wander through resemble the Great Forest? I have long suspected that they do, for some patches of forest inspire awe with their quiet magnificence. Like John Muir, I would choose to worship in nature's cathedrals, and although those in the eastern United States are less grand than their western counterparts, they are nevertheless wonderful structures of tall pillars with leafy canopies providing a fenestration that filters light and subdues worldly penetration.

These forests, by their slow-growing habits, provide a sense of immutability and stability in a world where man's ever-increasing dominance seems to impel the human race toward natural destruction. The solace I have found in many decades of walking through great forest tracts lies at the center of my being. I am entranced by their beauty. This mystical affinity impelled me to begin an aesthetic search for the remnants of the great forest, to start a journey of discovery that encompassed both historical and scientific inquiries. This book records that search. Research for it not only gave me a new appreciation for the parts of the great forest I hurried to revisit, it enabled me to find new treasures in that forest.

The natural history of Great Forest of Northern New York State, which became part of the Adirondack Park, can be traced from the recession of the last ice age to the present time. The history of the last two centuries has many milestones, most of which are represented by waves of assaults--flooding by dams, harvesting by charcoal makers and lumbermen and producers of pulp, and new methods to remove and transport lumber. One milestone--the creation of the Forest Preserve--stands out as a way to restore and protect the forest. From near rapacious harvesting to proposals for scientific forestry, the methods that altered the forests delineate the chapters in the forest's recent history.

One important aspect of this history has always been missing--a quantitative analysis of what happened to the forest and a comparison of the impacts on the forest of the different phases of exploitation over the decades. The lack of quantitative analysis has created many myths. In the year of the Adirondack Park Centennial, several writers noted the horrors of logging and the way destructive practices influenced the creation of the Park. The inference was that the damage done before the creation of the Park was horrendous and, by implication, that the Park's formation stopped much of the bad practices. Nothing could be farther from the truth. Although conspicuous, local examples of extreme damage to the forest were far from universal; pristine forest covered the heart of the Adirondack region a century ago.

The raw data needed for quantitative analyses are difficult to amass and almost impossible to make consistent in a way that leads to meaningful comparisons throughout the past two centuries and across the entire Adirondack region, but patterns do emerge from the information available.

First, early nineteenth century logging did very little to change the character of the forest since only pine and spruce were originally sought by lumbermen. For that matter, logging for lumber alone did remarkably little to change the forests until the last decade of the past century--until after the Park had been established. Focus on spruce, lack of transportation, cutting only large size timber (spruce above 10 or 12 inches diameter at breast height), and lack of mechanized means of bringing logs to mills or waterways, all limited the areas that were selectively cut to the region's river valleys where permanently flowing waterways served as the public highways of the day. The lumbermen ventured from these valleys only when they were tempted to build roads to stands that were predominantly spruce.

Agriculture played a much greater role in the early demise of the forests, but only on the edges of the region, particularly in the eastern Adirondacks. Ironmining and the concomitant charcoal production did destroy the forests in the eastern portion of the region; and the lands cleared for charcoal were available for more farmland. Although agriculture persisted only in the Champlain Valley and in the St. Lawrence lowlands to the north, it was locally responsible for more clearing of forest lands than was harvested to make charcoal.

The logger's axe became the dominant factor in the northern forest in the decades between 1850 and 1890 when floating logs to mills was the only available transportation. Dams were built so that the waters they harnessed could convert rivers and streams into highways. Hemlock trees were felled for their bark to supply the tanneries that ringed the Adirondacks. Hemlock stands on the periphery of the region and near the Schroon and lower Hudson rivers were stripped away.

Throughout the last half of the nineteenth century, spruce was king. The role of spruce is central to understanding today's forests, but the vision of spruce contrasts sharply with that role. Spruce is rarely a tree of grand proportions. This realization changed the perspective with which I viewed the great forest. I had to look closely to see even the largest of the tall, narrow specimens with scrawny tops, their dark spires disappearing above hardwoods stands. Their presence among so many of the species' fallen giants brought me to a new appreciation of old forests where the subtle role of death and decay should really be viewed as rebirth and renewal.

Returning to the exploration of the historical record, I found that the years around 1890 marked dramatic changes.

Railroads that ringed the Park had exerted a minor impact on the forests except on the periphery of the area until the 1890s, but after that date they began to play an important role in the lumber business. In 1892, a railroad penetrated the heart of the northern forest, crossing it from north to south, thereby facilitating the shipment of sawn lumber from newly-built mills in the interior. Shortly after, railroad spurs became an important means of transporting logs to mills.

Changing markets also affected the timber harvest. The market with the greatest single impact on the northern forests was the emerging paper industry with its voracious demand for pulp wood, for it allowed loggers to cut ever-decreasing diameter round logs of both softwoods and, later on, hardwoods. The pulp and paper industries appeared slowly after 1880, and their full effect was not felt until after 1890, but that effect was so great that by 1920 it had exhausted much of the resources of the region, not just the spruce but even the balsam, which was being harvested to supplement the dwindling spruce supplies.

Attempts to preserve the forests culminated in the decade from 1885 to 1895. Public lands were declared to be Forest Preserve in 1885; the State's acquisition of land was concentrated within the Blue Line boundary determined by the 1892 creation of the Adirondack Park; the Forest Preserve was given Constitutional protection in the closing days of 1894. But as I looked beyond these milestones I was surprised to learn how much of the forest was protected as early as 1870. The decades between 1870 and 1890 saw the beginning of the patchwork of mixed State and private ownership that persists to this day. This book does not merely retell the steps in forest preservation, but it explores what effect evolving preservation efforts had on the forest.

From the writings of Verplanck Colvin to those of Charles Sprague Sargent, the impassioned pleas and colorful prose of those who sought to protect the forest are best remembered and have served as the basis for later histories. Theirs is the record most easily found. Behind these sources is evidence of individuals whose contributions were equally important. My historical search led me to foresters, legislators, and members of organization who argued for forest preservation, but I was most fascinated by the untold story of the preservation work by people who had direct responsibility for the forest. Stories of individual efforts by State agents and people in the Comptroller's office emerge as highlights in forest preservation. A digression into the way the State acquired or reacquired forest land reveals just how much was protected even before the Constitutional amendment of 1894. From the perspective of what really happened to the forests to which the State had title before 1885 or 1890, it will be possible to conclude that the conditions of upwards of half a million acres in the Adirondacks were so little disturbed that today they appear as the great forest of long ago. In other words, what happened to the forest before 1890 presents a strong argument for my assertion that those half million acres appear today much as they did when first observed by the earliest white visitors to the Adirondack region. Strangely enough, the initial preservation of much of those half million acres was more an accident than the result of acts by the legislature or Constitutional Convention.

During the two decades following the establishment of the Park, the northern forests produced greater amounts of lumber and pulp wood than was harvested in any other period. After 1905 production levels began to fall. Part of the decline can be attributed to competition from new midwestern and western sources of timber, but the real cause was the failure of the local supply.

A close look at the years from 1890 to 1910 shows just how much lumber was extracted in those decades. From different sources, enough statistical information is available to make a comparison between the harvest of those years and that of previous decades as well as with twentieth century harvests. At the time of the forest's greatest decline, there was a decrease from nearly two million acres of virgin or untouched forests in 1885, to a bit more than a million acres in 1902, to just a few hundred thousand acres in 1910.

My quest prompted me to ask some pertinent questions, but regrettably it did not lead to all the answers: Was any part of the landscape damaged beyond natural recovery and how much of it was significantly impoverished? How extensive was the cutting in those critical decades? Was the heavy cutting limited to the tracts recently opened up to railroads? How did the private preserves respond and did their harvest practices improve? Did the large lumber companies, in particular Finch, Pruyn and Company and International Paper Company put into action harvest practices that would assure future yields? Were lumbermen concerned for future harvests? What effect did marketplace economics have on scientific forestry?

What has been the effect of mechanization on timber harvests? It can be seen clearly that modern techniques and hard-surfaced roads, as exemplified by the Gould Paper Company lands in the Moose River area, permitted much heavier harvest levels than earlier logging. How do modern logging practices compare with those of earlier times?

Some of the questions about forest preservation led me far afield. Why did the State not spend the money to add to the Forest Preserve in those critical early decades when land was cheap and the forest so little disturbed? This failure is particularly glaring in light of the fact that foresters knew that most fires that swept the northern forests--almost all of those that occurred before 1913 with the exception of the devastating fires of 1903 and 1908--affected only the cleared or previously harvested lands on the periphery of the Park or the lands adjacent to the railroad that cut through the Park. Even then, uncut forests and the Forest Preserve lands that would not easily burn, escaped the fires. The Forest Preserve land included those tracts that either had never been cut, such as in the Raquette Lake vicinity; or had been cut only for a meager amount of large soft woods, such as the lands in the present Silver Lake Wilderness.

The book records my search. Its format divides the forest history into loose time frames: the period from the last ice age to about 1800; the first half of the nineteenth century, with its focus on agriculture; the decades from 1850 to 1890 when the forests served the charcoal and tanning industries, but primarily served the lumbermen who sought spruce sawlogs; the period from 1870 to 1895 when forest protection was accomplished; the two or so decades after 1890 when logging was most severe; and the interval from 1920 to the present when logging practices first adjusted to a shrinking resource and later the industry found new ways to use the forest. The two chains of events that peaked around 1890 are so complex that they are necessarily dealt with separately, even though the chains--the revolution in the logging industry after 1890 and the culmination of preservation acts around 1894--interacted and influenced each other.

Certain individual tracts of land have histories that span a century and a half; similarly most of the region's modern companies have origins in the nineteenth century. Examples from the way tracts were treated or the way companies dealt with the forest are used to corroborate several themes. The stories of the tracts and the companies are sufficiently interesting in themselves that their entire recorded spans are summarized in two appendices.

Before looking at what happened to the forests, it is necessary to establish a conceptual base line with a description of what was in the forests, of what trees existed. Thanks to recent research, there is now a fairly accurate picture of what the forests were like before white man came on the scene. It is possible to compare descriptions of virgin forest from the 1890s and early 1900s with observations of scattered stands of virgin forests that for various reasons escaped attempts at exploitation. Early production records show what various tracts could yield. Several valuable sets of statistics, including the detailed timber cruise reports made on virgin tracts in the heart of the Adirondacks, complete the picture of the forests of the Park before Europeans arrived.

After looking at all the things that changed the forests, after exploring the synergism of natural forces and man's exploitive acts, I returned to the descriptions of the original forests to ask how much remains untouched today or only lightly disturbed, and how much resembles those stands that greeted the region's first visitors. Armed with new historical insights, I was able to find the answers in first-hand observations. I know how much of the great forest still exists. In this year of the centennial of the amendment that gave constitutional protection to the Forest Preserve, I can exult in New York's forest heritage and marvel at the extent and quality of the forest New Yorkers have been able to protect. I invite you to share with me the history that led to that conviction.

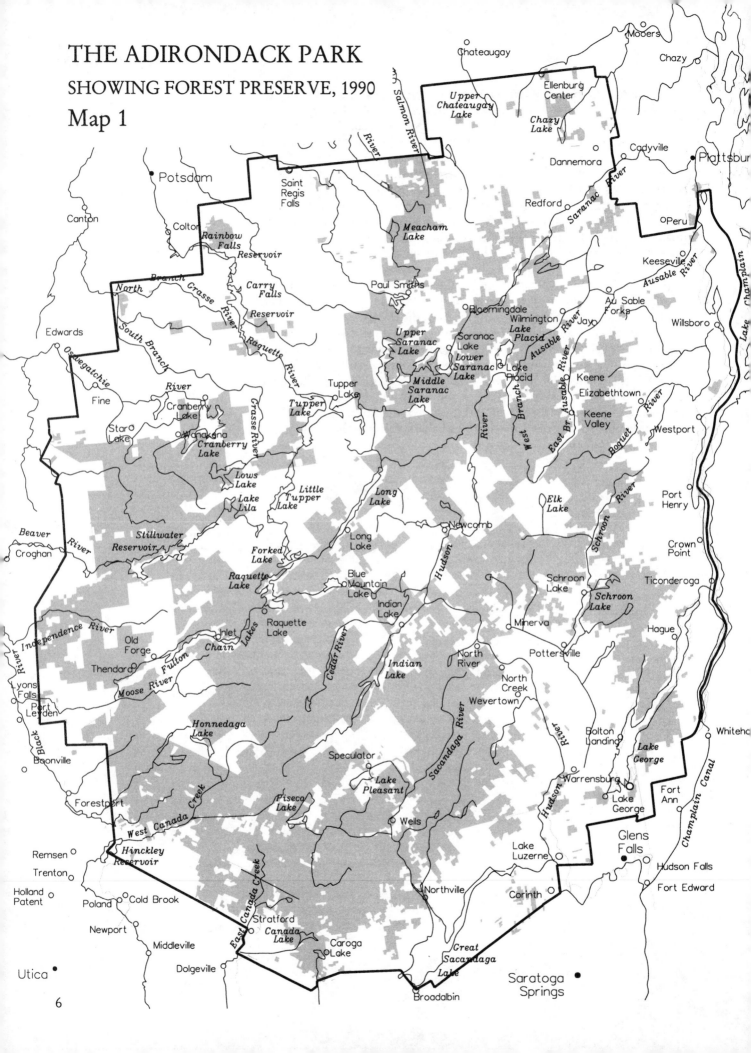

# THE ADIRONDACK PARK
## SHOWING FOREST PRESERVE, 1990
## Map 1

# II

# The Primeval Forest

I began my search for the great forest by trying to discover what was the primeval forest and what scientists mean by old-growth forest. This search took me back to the geological record.

As seen from far above, from a satellite perhaps, the dome that is the Adirondack region appears as a gently-wrinkled mass with rows of faults and mountains trending in a northeast-southwest direction. The ridges of mountains diminish in the west and rise in the northeast to the cluster known as the High Peaks. The rocks and the soils that cover them--albeit thinly over much of the area--are one of the most important factors determining the kinds of trees that populate today's forests.

The rocks that form the mountains are very old; they were formed 1,050 to 1,200 million years ago in the Grenville era when sedimentary rocks were buried and folded and metamorphosed--altered by heat and pressure. Intrusions of anorthosite followed, then a long period of uplift and erosion. In more recent times, the region has been scraped repeatedly and polished by advancing glaciers to accentuate the faults, sculpt the mountain ranges, and fill some of the lowlands, creating the landscape we know.

The bedrock that gives form to today's landscape ranges from the erosion resistant anorthosite of High Peaks to granitic soils in the central region, with scattered outcrops of Grenville marbles and other metamorphosed sediments. For the most part, the weathering of Adirondack bedrock produces acidic soils; lime-rich, basic soils occur, but are rare. The hard, coarse crystalline bedrock admits no drainage of water into the rocks; there are no aquifers within the Adirondack region. All of the average forty inches of rain that falls flows laterally away from the domed Adirondack region. The configuration of mountains causes rain to fall more heavily on the western slopes (weather patterns come basically from the west), leaving the eastern slopes in the rain-shadow significantly dryer. Places in the Champlain Valley receive half the rainfall of some southwestern regions.[1] But, in spite of the differences in rainfall, precipitation occurs uniformly throughout the year; the region's climate is moist and ideal for forest growth. In sum, the basic rock form of the dome determines the topography of the region, the varied amounts of rainfall, and the way water flows from the dome; and all this has implications for the forest.

As seen from the height of an airplane, the rock dome appears cloaked in summer with a mantle of green, embroidered in a tufted pattern of various hues that are anything but random. This forest mantle owes its different shades less to the bedrock than to the soils that support the forest. The green of flat lowlands is so dark it appears almost black; the bright greens speckled with dark tufts creep up the hillsides and slopes to the highest and most exposed ridges and the mountain tops where dark tones of green tinted with brown and black again dominate. The dark green of the lowlands fills flat valleys and the borders of meandering streams and rivers, indicating wetland areas that cover less than fifteen percent of the mantle's mosaic. The dark green of the high mountains covers even less. Blotches of dark that dot the lower slopes of the bright greens gradually give way to almost solid patches of the brightest green on the mid slopes of the dominant rolling hill country. Overall, bright green is the mantle's prevailing shade.

What the pattern of greens denotes will emerge as the principal explanation for the way man moved into the forest. The different kinds of forests represented by the varied shades were a more important factor in the movement of loggers into the Park than was the relative accessibility of the different forest patches. But, this observation is putting us ahead in the forest chronicle.

Before returning to the question of what the different forest greens represent, it is important to understand why the variations occur, and to do that, we have to look closely at the soils that determine where different kinds of forest can grow.

Soils range from the thin glacial tills of the mountains to deeper mineral soils in the central Adirondacks, which have promoted today's mixed hardwood stands. Sand flats and dry lake beds dot the region and dominate the far-western Adirondacks. Glacial depressions shaped some wetlands creating stagnant areas that today support only bogs or stands of cedar and spruce. The profile from flatland to mountain shown in figure 1 breaks into distinct elevational regions.

In their retreat, glaciers deposited the rocks and soils scoured from the mountain tops. Very quickly, geologically speaking, rains washed any mineral soil and rocks from the highest mountain tops and ridgelines, depositing them in depths that increased as the elevation and slopes decreased. Because of the severe climate and the absence of mineral soils, the highest mountain peaks, swept clean of mineral soils, support only mosses and lichens and plants of the northern tundra.

*Figure 1 is not drawn to scale; mixed woods and hardwoods dominate the forest today. The hardwood stands had a greater proportion of softwoods before they were logged.*
Source: E. H. Ketchledge, Ph.D.

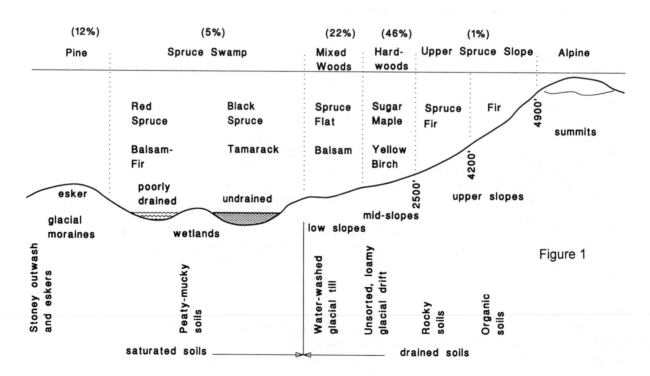

Distribution of Adirondack forest site-types
with respect to elevation, soils and drainage

Below the realm of bare rock and Alpine plants, down to 4,000 feet elevation in the high country, as low as 3,500 feet on lower mountains where there is at most thin layer of mineral soils, the accumulated mineral soils support balsam fir and mountain paper birch.

Down to about 2,500 feet in elevation, fine soils were washed away, leaving coarse mineral soils that are always wet because of the movement of water over bedrock. This realm of moderate fertility supports red spruce as well as balsam fir, with occasional yellow birch. The red spruce and balsam give the upper slopes their dark and somber tones.

In the vast mid-slope region that dominates the rolling hills of the southern and central Adirondacks, glacial debris ranges from fine clays to coarse mineral soils with stones, rocks, and boulders. Then as now, these layers are the richest soils, unsorted, well-drained, and capable of retaining the nutrients leached from the organic soils that gradually accumulated on them. This is the bright green province of our richest hardwood slopes. This is the region where maples, yellow birch, and beech dominate.

Lower down, on the more level terrain of the northwestern Adirondacks, in the water-washed soils where most fine soils and clays capable of holding minerals were flushed away, softwoods prevail. In this region of saturated soils, elevation of only a few feet above the water table allows red spruce to thrive, sometimes in almost pure stands--the spruce flats that proved so enticing to the lumbermen. Where the soils are undrained or stagnant, as in bogs, black spruce and tamarack are found; where some drainage exists, red spruce and fir dominate. Here sharp zones of soils are strongly acidic and support conifers, which in turn are perpetuated because the acidic litter they produce adds to the soil's acidity. Hardwoods, except occasional red maples, do poorly.

Where the deeper mineral soils accumulated, in lower slopes with good sub-surface drainage, on moist lake-shores and in deep ravines, dark greens of spruce, balsam, and hemlock intersperse the hardwoods. This mottled region of mixed-woods depends on water-washed till and the strong leaching of nutrients that produces well-defined layers of soil. Hardwoods mix with hemlock and red spruce; spruce flats spread out on the fairly-well-drained lowlands.

Winding through the lowlands are sinuous ridges and hummocks, eskers and moraines deposited by glacial rivers and ice that sorted the outwash and glacial till. Here pines reign among other conifers.[2]

Understanding the soils explains the broad placement of different forest types throughout the Adirondack region: the spruce-fir forests of the highlands, the vast hardwood stands of the rolling hills of the southern and southwestern region, the spruce flats of the wetter northern and northwestern region, the pine and hemlock stands of the dryer eastern slopes. Climate is determined by temperature: rain or snowfall that vary from north to south, from east to west; and elevation and location, which limit the short, 135-day growing season to 90 days. Climate, topography, and soils determine the precise kinds of forest stands that comprise the Adirondacks as well as their arrival after the last ice age.

Species advance in
Adirondack lowlands
after glacial retreat

| Climate | Years Before Present | Low Elevation |
|---|---|---|
| Gradual warming | 13,000 | tundra<br>white spruce |
| | 12,000 | open spruce woodland |
| | 11,000 | |
| Early Holocene | 10,500 | spruce in rapid decline |
| | 10,000 | poplar, tamarack, fir, ash, ironwood, elm, and basswood expand |
| | 9,000 | paper birch, white pine expand |
| | 8,000 | sugar maple, hemlock, beech increase<br>oak, basswood, elm, red maple |
| Warm and dry | 7,000 | pine, hemlock abundant<br>pine decreases |
| | 6,000 | hemlock dominant in forests with hardwoods |
| Hypsothermal maximum warming | 5,000 | hemlock begins abrupt decline<br>striped maple expands |
| Gradual cooling | 4,000 | paper birch, sugar maple, and especially yellow birch expand |
| | 3,000 | hemlock increases, but not to previous levels<br>hardwood dominant forests established |
| Cool and wet | 2,000 | red spruce expands from north to south |
| | 1,000 | decrease in hemlock, sugar maple and beech |
| | Present | spruce, northern hardwood with some pine and hemlock |

Figure 2

The forest ecosystems of the eastern United States, having been pushed south by the glaciers, gave birth to the forests that advanced into the Adirondack region following the glacier's last retreat. All of the elements that today determine the location of forest stands, determined the spread of forests from the south into the region. Climate changes dictated the larger thrust of forest advance and because climate since the last glacial retreat was not a gradual warming, the transition to modern forest was not an orderly advance of species.

The thirteen thousand years since the last glacial retreat have been a dynamic time. By looking at the pollen and plant materials trapped in mud in the depths of several Adirondack lakes, a picture of the transition to today's forest emerges.[3]

For a thousand years after ice disappeared from the tops of our tallest mountains, the lichens, mosses, flowering plants, and low-growing woody shrubs--a tundra-like vegetation--gradually covered the Adirondack region. For fifteen hundred years, spruce from lower elevations crept up the mountain slopes, covering them in open woodlands. For the next thousand years, green alders invaded the spruce woodlands. The ability of alders to fix nitrogen in the soil may have given rise to the next generation of forest--the pioneers we know today. Spruce, balsam fir, paper birch, tamarack, and aspen appeared.

White pine appeared around nine thousand years ago and very shortly large tracts of pines were found in the lowlands, probably exceeding the number but not the size of the giants that greeted the Swedish botanist, Peter Kalm, in the mid-eighteenth century. He marveled at the near 200-foot specimens he saw from the Hudson River above Albany.

In the next two thousand years, sugar maple and beech spread across the region, creating mixed forests of conifers and hardwoods. Hemlock appeared about 7,400 years ago, probably at first as low-growing forms that tolerated colder, exposed sites. Yellow birch worked into the region about 6,000 years ago.

These slow-growing, shade-tolerant trees--hemlock, sugar maple, beech and yellow birch--became dominant because of their ability to shade out spruce, fir, paper birch, and pine and thus limit their regeneration. It was warmer 6,000 years ago than now, and hemlocks grew further up the mountain slopes than they do today. This preponderance of hemlock in the warmest period since the last ice age is in stark contrast with the forest of today. However, a decline (caused by an unknown force--climate, disease, insects?) affected the hemlock stands and, over a period of a thousand years, they were gradually replaced by yellow birch and beech.

In the period of gradual cooling that was evident 4,000 years ago, yellow birch expanded its range. Then by 2,500 years before the present, stands of red spruce began to move into the region from north to south, the advance paralleling a change to wetter and cooler climate that prevails today.

It was not until the past 2,000 years that the pattern of alpine summits surmounting mixed stands of spruce and fir on the upper slopes was established, creating summit cover as it exists today. At the same time the lower elevation pattern of spruce flats, stands of hardwoods mixed with spruce and interspersed with hemlock and pine, and pockets of black spruce and cedar settled into their preferred niches. But these lower elevation stands were not--are not--static; the proportion of beech and maple was increasing even as white man appeared to begin the dramatic changes in the forest that have occurred over the past few hundred years.

However, the spread of tree cover northward following the retreating glacier was an even less orderly march than would have been orchestrated by climate changes. Both hardwoods and softwoods had to compete for their niche. The sixty-odd species engaged in a competition that goes on today in response to changing conditions. The role of soils and topography intertwined with climate to create various micro-environments that dictated the successors in the advance, just as they dictate today's dominant species. Several species may be suited to a site: a slight change in weather patterns may favor one species; periodic extremes of weather disturb another species; the opening created by a dying tree offers an opportunity for still another kind of tree.

A forest seems almost a static thing, slow-growing, stately and serene, almost immutable, but that image is not true. Forests change--were still changing when white man first arrived in the region--and they have continued to change in response to everything that happens to them.

Take any part of the great northern forest of New York, examine it, measure and assess it, core the trees to determine their ages, and record the variety of species, their relative ages and sizes. On the one hand, it is not possible to know it because it is a dynamic, growing, changing organism. Paradoxically, the natural changes occur so slowly that measuring them over such long periods has proven difficult. We can see the forest as it exists in the present, but predicting its future, especially when it is subjected to influences from outside its natural state, is almost impossible. Revealing the history of even a small patch of forest's past is almost as difficult.

Botanists looked at seemingly stable stands, noted that some appear to perpetuate themselves, and dubbed them the climax forests. But every patch is different. While broad sub-regions do perpetuate themselves, natural forces continue to change the environment, favoring one species or another. Add to this the unnatural forces inflicted on the forest in the past two centuries and the dynamics of even a small stand become more difficult to discern. The competition that impelled the advance of tree species in determined ways was so complex as to appear haphazard. That competition continues to determine elements in the forest mosaic today. Hardwoods can out-compete softwoods in rich soils; softwoods are the winners in poorer soils.

Species advance in the Adirondack high country after glacial retreat

| Climate | Years Before Present | High Elevation |
|---|---|---|
| Gradual warming | 13,000 | last glacial retreat |
| | 12,000 | tundra |
| | | spruce |
| | 11,000 | boreal woodland |
| Early Holocene | | juniper, willow |
| | 10,500 | alder, tamarack, spruce decline |
| | 10,000 | alder decline |
| | 9,000 | |
| | 8,000 | increase in birch |
| Warm and dry | | expansion of pine, sugar maple, hemlock, and beech |
| | 7,000 | |
| | 6,000 | expansion of hemlock to higher elevation than at present |
| Hypsothermal maximum warming | 5,000 | hemlock decline increase in striped maple |
| Gradual cooling | 4,000 | |
| | | expansion of yellow birch |
| | 3,000 | |
| Cool and wet | 2,000 | as spruce expands, fir increases and hemlock, beech, and maple decrease |
| | 1,000 | |
| | | spruce, fir, birch zone established |
| | Present | disappearance of hemlock, pine, and yellow birch at high elevation |

Figure 3

## Adirondack forest types
## and their habitats

**Spruce** is a climax type on granitic, acid soils.

**Spruce-fir** is a climax type at elevations of 3,400 to 4,000 feet on slopes with little soil.

**Red spruce and yellow birch** is a climax type on lower slopes and benches with acidic till and moist alluvial soils.

**Red spruce, sugar or hard maple, and beech** with spruce constituting 20% of the stand occupies niches from 1,500 to 2,500 feet.

**Paper birch, red spruce, and balsam** is a disturbed-stand type found at elevation 2,400 to 4,200 feet.

**Northern white cedar** is a stable forest type in swampy areas with limestone soils.

**Red pine** is an uncommon type in the Adirondacks; the species cannot tolerate shade, hence usually develops as a mono-culture after disturbances.

**White pine** stands develop after disturbances on dry, mineral soils. On some desirable sites it is self-perpetuating.

**White pine and hemlock** is a combination of the two long-lived species in which the hemlock gradually become dominant.

**Eastern hemlock** is a climax forest often found in pure stands with relatively little understory.

**White pine, northern red oak, and red maple** is a type that sometimes includes white ash; it is a transitional type between northern forests and those of the southern Appalachians.

**Hemlock and yellow birch** is considered a sub-climax type because the two species do not regenerate in the dense shade they create.

**Sugar maple** occupies the richest soils, in pure pockets or mixed with smaller quantities of ash, beech, birch, and maple.

**Sugar maple, yellow birch and beech** is a climax type of rich soils whose only instability results from the beech die-back.

**Black cherry and maple** is a transitional type that over time will give way to hemlock and maple.

**Beech and sugar maple** is a climax type of rich soils.

**Red or soft maple** is a disturbance type where the species occurs with many other species in wet, poorly drained sites.

Figure 4

Source: F. H. Eyre: *Forest Cover Types of the United States and Canada*

Even among hardwoods there are dominant species depending on micro-environments. Similarly among softwoods, variations exist. Hemlocks rule on the cool, more moist northern slopes and mix well with hardwoods even on fairly rich sites. Cedars prefer the northern, cooler, lime-based wetlands. Pines thrive on the dryer, well-drained ridges of the eastern Adirondacks as well as on the glacier outwash plains of the western Adirondacks. Spruce has a split lifestyle; it enjoys several locations: the high country, the spruce flats of the lowlands, as well as the shelter of lower hardwood stands.

The seeming immutability of gently shifting forests is reassuring. We can see something living that man has not significantly altered. The search for old forests is a part of our search for untrammeled nature. Inevitably we ask what is a mature forest, an old forest, or a natural forest, or in the vernacular of just a few decades ago, what is a virgin forest? Virgin was used to describe forests that were untouched by direct acts by man, cutting, burning, and so on.

Certainly we can find large tracts that are relatively uncut, and here the absoluteness of the word "virgin" makes the word unusable. So, dendrologists advanced the term "old-growth" to describe such relatively untouched forests. They even gave it scientific stature and a precise definition that can be tested in all forests.[4]

If the forests of the Adirondacks were uniform, of one type, it might be easy to ferret out some old growth stands, but the forests are of many types, as in many different organisms with different growth patterns. The earlier division of the forest into broad types reflecting different soils and elevations is just one way of describing the forest. Every place hosts a forest type that is as different as the sites and circumstances that produce them. The list at the side[5] is only one of many lists that attempt to classify forest types and, as long as the list is, its types weave together to produce even more sub-categories. Carried to extremes, the great northern forest appears a patchwork of uncountable types, each differing in composition, size of individual trees, and density of tree cover.

The combinations of species that out-compete other trees are sometimes called climax forests, the winners when nature alone determines the conditions of the struggle. Every natural site has a slightly different meld of environmental factors and blend of competitors that yield a different climax forest, by which is meant a form of old-growth, steady-state forest in natural balance with the environment, adjusting slowly to nature's swift or subtle changes.

While the scientist can differentiate the various types in their maturity, their attributes and histories are not so recognizable. Each growth pattern has a different look. Stands of mature spruce and balsam fir forests on the upper slopes are twisted, gnarled, and stunted--the "fish hooks and bayonets"[6] that defied the first surveyors. A few stands of hemlock and pine match the image of old-growth forest conjuring comparison with western evergreens. The windswept maples, beech, and ash on the top of a hillside may never reach great stature, while in a protected cove on the flanks of the same hill, the very same mix of trees can attain awesome height and girth. Only rarely are there stands of tall maples whose trunks and limbs invoke the soaring image of a Gothic cathedral. Often the magnitude of aged, giant spruce and hemlocks is obvious from the length of their fallen trunks as they lie moss-covered and disintegrating on the forest floor, while in the gap left by their demise vigorous, younger spruce and hemlocks compete to reach maturity.

Of primary concern is the question whether the term "old-growth" applies to all types of forest? How does it apply to forests where man's influence was felt, but only in a minor way? Are there stands whose recovery is such that they meet the criteria of old-growth today?

It would be wonderful if we could examine the forests as they were, then sum up the things man has done to them, and compute the results. But the ever-changing, constantly growing forest does not lend itself to such a linear model. We have to consider how each event has changed the forest, how its components interacted and competed and how they have responded. We need to determine what has been shaded out and what has been sheltered and protected. We need to know all this as we try to understand what the forest is like today.

This task is much simpler with respect to parts of the Forest Preserve, the public lands of the Adirondacks. The historical record shows that some areas have been untouched for well over a century and that what happened to them before they became part of the Forest Preserve was so minor that the effect was little more than what nature would have wrought. Even virgin forests, those completely untouched by man, of which there are scattered patches in the Adirondacks, would not look today as they did when white man first appeared, for the evolutionary forces started by the glacier's last retreat were incomplete at that time. Furthermore, natural forces--windstorms, tornados, and hurricanes--seem to have been perversely severe on some of the virgin stands.

The ability of a protected forest to recover from what was done to it over a hundred and fifty years ago is remarkable. If man altered a stand severely, the forest mimics the phases of recovery since the last ice age. The pioneering species are just those that pioneered after the last ice age. If man had a very slight affect on the forest, the differences between old-growth and virgin stands are almost imperceptible. Given no changes in climate (apparently an unlikely assumption at present), forest recovery should be complete no matter the past--the only variable would be the length of time needed for that to occur.

In order to compare what we see today with what white man saw when he first gazed on the great northern forests of New York, we need to know what those forests were like. In 1614, when the first settlements were being constructed in Albany and Manhattan, the entire State was forest covered. With the exception of a few small clearings around Indian settlements, New York's forests stretched in "a silent, unbroken wilderness where stood a primeval forest, which, in grandeur and undeveloped wealth, was unsurpassed in all the region of the Atlantic coast."[7] For nearly 200 years, Adirondack forests remained in the same state, untouched by the woodsman's axe.

Early settlers and visitors prized white pine and their descriptions of the forest are in terms of that noble giant, although pine probably never constituted more than three percent of the forest.[8] Despite the small role pine played in the forest, accounts of pine stands dominated the reports of early observers for their perceptions were subjective--shaped by those things they wanted to see. White pine, whose tall, straight trunks made the best masts for sailing vessels, were the subject of most early reports. Dr. John Torrey, in his 1843 "Flora of New York," called attention to the stands of pine on the headwaters of the Hudson and the rivers which empty into the St. Lawrence and Lake Ontario. André Michaux noted that the shores of Lake Champlain "appeared to be most abundantly peopled with this species." Warren County was noted for the "splendid pines with which the great Brant Lake Tract abounded."[9] Pines were abundant on the shores of Lake Champlain in 1801 and remained abundant as late as 1843 along the headwaters of the Hudson, the Salmon, the Black, and the other rivers that flowed north to the St. Lawrence. Stands of virgin pines lasted until nearly the end of the century near Cranberry Lake. Some remain today further south in the Five Ponds Wilderness Area.

The pines were the first to go, and then the lumberman saw mostly spruce--the next most desirable lumber. The lumberman harvested spruce along the region's rivers and streams and quickly exhausted those supplies. In turning to interior regions for spruce, loggers inspired descriptions of those virgin stands. In reading them, I not only learned about the role of that species in the harvest of the forest, I began to understand how old-growth stands might look.

High mountains and steep slopes protected some stands until the logger's axe could no longer be denied. Railroads, pulp mills, and new hardwood-consuming factories made it possible to harvest more and more of the forests. The changes wrought by natural causes are still occurring, but they pale to insignificance in the context of the man-made events of the past two centuries.

# III

## A Guide to the Park's Tracts, Patents and Purchases

An arcane scheme of geometric shapes, each identified with a number and an obscure name, constitutes the legal map of the Adirondack region. A convenient source of this information is the Department of Environmental Conservation's Adirondack Map, whose origins are discussed later in the context of the map's role in early attempts to protect the forests.

The identifying scheme has been used since the late eighteenth century to define areas within the great northern forest.[1] Despite its apparent complexity, the scheme is the best way to describe different areas and using it is analogous to finding your way with street names and numbers, and ultimately just as simple. Becoming familiar with the tracts and patents shown on map 2 reinforces the picture of how the Park was logged, first in the east and south, then in the interior. It also confirms the location of the best preserved areas.

In order to make the scheme more accessible, the named parts are introduced here with anecdotes from their history as mnemonic devices for quickly learning them.

Starting with the time that ownership of land was granted by England or permission was given to negotiate with the native Indians for the land, parts of the north country have been known by the names of those who first owned the land. The word **patent** or sometimes **purchase** applies to land that was sold or given directly to one individual or group. The word **tract** was applied to large areas of land that were subdivided and sold in pieces to various individuals. Most of the large purchases were further divided into townships, which often have little relation to today's towns. Townships were either numbered or named or both. Patents and townships were further divided into rectangular, triangular, or oblique lots, and each lot was given a number. Thus, by identifying the tract or patent, the name or number of the township, and the lot number, any part of the region can be located.

Originally, two square lots of 640 acres each were specially allotted within each township. These were not to be sold, but were to be reserved for income--one for Gospels and Schools for the residents of the township, the other for Literature for residents of the State. Gospel, School and Literature Lots were drawn only in the townships of one purchase, Totten and Crossfield.

Three great purchases cover most of the Adirondack region, while many smaller, subsidiary tracts and patents are found in its eastern and southern regions--the areas first settled. Because they were logged early and became State land at an early date, some of the smaller patents are very important for the story of Adirondack forests.

*In order to understand what happened historically to different parts of the Adirondack forest, a good map is essential for locating forest tracts, comprehending their history, and determining their owners.*

## Totten and Crossfield Purchase (1771)

The first great purchase was made in 1771 by Joseph Totten and Stephen Crossfield, acting for Edward and Ebenezer Jessup. From the Indians, they bought 1,150,000 acres, the heart of the future Adirondack Park, for three cents an acre. At first, forty townships, each of about 25,000 acres--a square six miles on a side, were surveyed. Later more townships were added making fifty in all, but no further divisions were made, hence the map of today is as it was in 1771. However, the two stages in the numbering resulted in a confusing and non-consecutive arrangement, as the map shows. The purchase is unusual in that the boundaries of the township are skewed--running approximately northeast-southwest and southeast-northwest.

Because of the crudeness of early surveys, some townships overlap; others have gores between them--tracts needed to identify areas where townships failed to meet. When their existence was discovered, these areas were later claimed by the State. Some of the townships were given to colonialists, but most of the purchase reverted to State ownership after the Revolutionary War. The State sold the townships to various patentees over the next two decades, although the State continued to own some townships as late as 1855. Parts of the Totten and Crossfield Purchase were the last regions of the Adirondacks to be explored.

## Macomb's Purchase (1791)

Alexander Macomb's purchase was even larger; in 1792 he bought 3,934,899 acres for eight cents an acre, but because of financial reverses he had to sell most of it to others almost immediately. His purchase stretched from the northwestern Adirondacks to the St. Lawrence River. It was divided into Great Tracts, with Great Tract One covering Franklin County, which immediately went to Daniel McCormick, and Great Tracts Two and Three lying in St. Lawrence County. Their township lines are regular-north-south, east-west lines. From this purchase were taken several tracts, most notable John Brown's Tract with its eight townships covering 210,000 acres and Watson's Triangles; the East Triangle in Herkimer County being joined to the west in Lewis County by a narrow strip of land. The 61,433 acres of this tract were divided on his death among the forty cousins of James Talcott Watson.

## Old Military Tract (1781)

The Old Military Tract with 665,000 acres in the northeastern Adirondacks lies in Clinton, Franklin, and Essex counties. According to a State law of 1781, the land was to be given as bounty to army recruits. The tract was surveyed in 1786 into townships ten miles on a side, but no part was ever awarded to recruits and the tract was sold in pieces by the Land Commission.

Similarly, the Refugee Tract of Clinton County was divided into lots to be given to Canadian sympathizers who had to leave their homes.

## Nobleboro and Arthurboro Patents (1787)

Nobleboro Patent with 40,000 acres lying in the southwest corner of the Park in Herkimer County, and Arthurboro Patent with 47,360 acres in adjacent Hamilton County, were sold in 1787 to Arthur Noble who was trying to build a settlement in the wilds. His efforts were a failure from the start so that almost all sign of his saw and grist mills had disappeared by 1811. Nobleboro Patent was allotted into small, narrow strips to accommodate the settlers who never arrived. Arthurboro Patent was settled after 1833 and it was divided into several tracts: Bethune, Maxwell and Tefft, all of which have remnants of the great forest.

## Moose River Tract (1820)

Between western Macomb and Totten and Crossfield Purchase lies the wedge-shaped Moose River Tract with its 207,360 acres. A southeastern part of it was sold to Anson Blake in 1847; much of it later went to the Adirondack League Club, but the bulk of the tract was only sold to the State late in the nineteenth century and part of the southeastern tip contains old growth forests.

## Oxbow Tract (1811)

East of Arthurboro Patent lies the Oxbow Tract, which was established after the Revolutionary War by the State. Its 70,000 acres are divided into 304 lots The lower portion of the tract was surveyed in 1829 by Duncan McMartin, Jr.

## Benson Tract (1795)

This truncated equilateral triangle with 61,920 acres lies between Bergen's Purchase (1785) on the east, and the Lawrence Patent (1792); its base rests on the north line of Glen, Bleecker and Lansing Patent (1793). It was named for Egbert Benson and was surveyed by Lawrence Vrooman. Benson was settled for farming and lumbering beginning in the early 1800s. Then, in 1860, the southeastern three-quarters became the Town of Benson, set aside from the Town of Hope from which it was effectively isolated by the Sacandaga River. In the process, the new town acquired a rectangular north portion of Mayfield in Fulton County: Hamilton County thus acquired a jog in its southern boundary.

## Lawrence Patent (1791)

With only 35,560 acres, the Lawrence Tract was granted in 1791 to Jonathan Lawrence who complained that he had not received all the land he expected and said he would have paid less if he had known that a portion to the west (probably the Caldwell and Sickles/VanAngle

Tracts) was not included. Fully a quarter of the tract, perhaps more, plus the gore that separates it from the Oxbow Patent to the north, contain old growth, with patches that probably never were logged.

## Jerseyfield Patent (1770)

Covering the very southwestern corner of the Park in Herkimer and Fulton counties, this patent was purchased in 1770 by Henry Glen in 1770.

## Chases Patent (1792) and

## Glen, Bleecker and Lansing Patent (1794)

Chases Patent, a small (12,000 acre) tract in Fulton County has some lovely and accessible old forests. In 1793 the legislature granted it to a sea captain, William Chase, in exchange for a bridge he had built across the Hoosick River.

He had wanted the area around this skewed rectangle, an 89,297-acre tract, which was acquired in 1793 by Cornelius Glen, Barent Bleecker, and Abraham Lansing after they nearly doubled the money they had offered for the tract. As a result, Chases Patent lies twisted in the regular lines of Glen, Bleecker and Lansing Patent, a most peculiar arrangement.

## Palmer's Purchase (1772)

Because it lies in the southern foothills of the Adirondack region, Palmer's Purchase was also logged early and parts of it qualify as old growth forest. Encompassing about 135,000 acres, it was purchased in 1772 from Mohawk Indians by Thomas Palmer and others, among them Dirck Lefferts, for whom a tract within the patent is named. It was surveyed by Lawrence Vrooman in 1788 and divided into four great lots: The State, Middle, Rear, and River lots.

A number of smaller tracts are mentioned in this book. They lie along the eastern edge of the original Blue Line and are variously named the Iron Ore Tract (1810), Brant Lake Tract (1803), Paradox Tract (1807), Hoffman Patent (1795), and West of Road Patent (1810). They generally do not have old growth forests, but parts of them are important to the forest story because they illustrate some of the questionable practices that occurred in the State's acquisition of forest land.

# ADIRONDACK TRACTS, PATENTS, PURCHASES AND TOWNSHIPS

Showing the principal divisions
in the area included
in the original
Blue Line

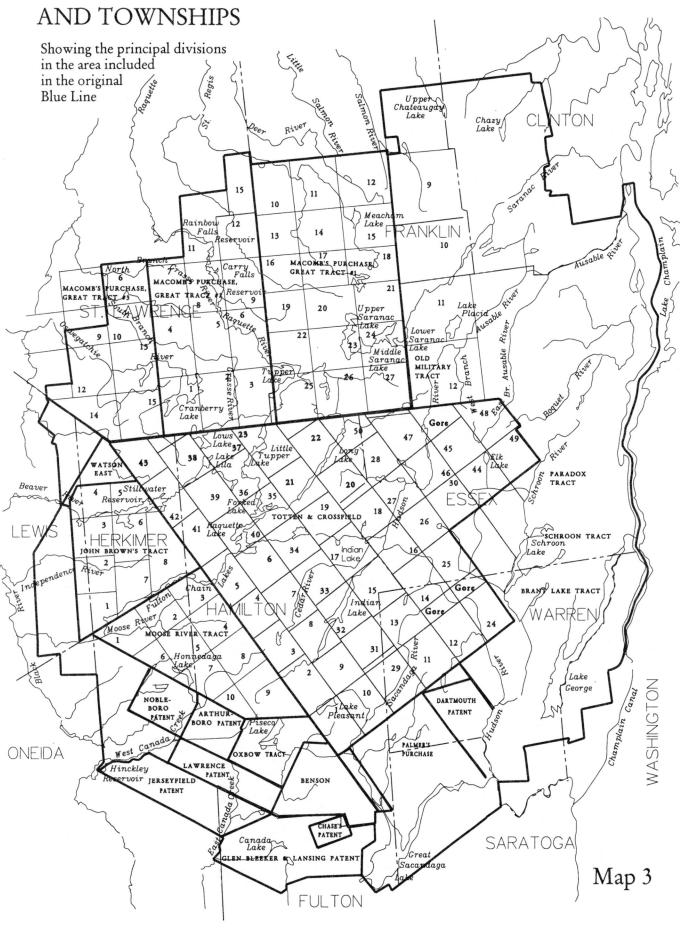

Map 3

# IV

# The Adirondacks in the First
# Half of the Nineteenth Century

The story of Adirondack forests in the first half of the nineteenth century is basically that of clearcutting patches of forest to create pastures and tillable land for farms. Industrially, it focuses on pine and hardwoods, but it is essentially the story of agriculture. Gleanings from the 1835, 1845, and 1855 New York State Census records present a sketchy picture of Adirondack life in the early part of the nineteenth century, but they do provide some quantitative information that is missing from most early histories.

Before 1800, only a few families pioneered in what is now the Adirondack region. They settled in the lowlands, along the Hudson River and Lake Champlain. A few ventured toward the heart of the mountains, again only along river valleys: the Saranac, the Ausable, the Sacandaga rivers and the West Canada Creek. From 1810 to 1820, waves of immigrants from New England tried farming a bit farther toward the interior, at slightly higher elevations. The State made it easy to acquire land, selling it at a few cents an acre, and farmers were tempted. But the initial influx of farmers was short-lived; most moved on to the Ohio Valley, the Middle West, and the region around the Great Lakes--a process hastened by the completion of the Erie Canal in 1825.

Those farmers who remained, and those who joined them in very slowly growing numbers, cleared the land, cutting and burning trees for potash. They set up small sawmills to saw wood for their homes and barns; a few began to export logs or lumber, mostly pine. Farmers raised sheep and some cattle and planted oats and potatoes; many farmers quickly became discouraged. The interior Adirondacks is not a farming region because the growing season is too short. Except for the dairies and apple orchards of the Champlain Valley and the northeastern potato fields, there is little farming within the Blue Line today, and virtually no commercial farming above 1200 feet in elevation.

Farming communities supported the early industrial centers created by iron making and tanning. These communities were usually found also in the flatland of the northeastern Adirondacks and in the lowlands along river valleys.

Adirondack roads--the early dirt tracks and the finished plank roads--all followed the river valleys. Farms sprang up along many roadsides. To the traveler, farms appeared to be ubiquitous. Thomas Cole painted views of Schroon [now Hoffman] Mountain from a sheep field that is today covered with forest. Sheep roamed the Town of Hope along the Stony Creek. The Plains of Abraham near Lake Placid were farmed. Fields in North Elba were cleared. Northern Warren County towns became small trading centers supported by the local agricultural establishments.

*Adirondack land cleared for farming, circa 1884*
Allen & Rowell, Sargent Committee
Report, presentation copy

So, how much of the Adirondack region was cleared for farming? Figures as high as fifty percent have been mentioned, but only the Town of Fort Ann had that much cleared land in 1835. The highest percentages showing the proportion of cleared or "improved" land occurred in Warren, Essex, and Clinton (which included Franklin) counties. The clearing was almost all in the eastern and northeastern region of the Park, and even there the amount of clearing was remarkably small.

Of Clinton County's 103,110 cleared acres, 60 percent was in two well-settled towns, Peru and Plattsburgh; over 32 percent was in the northern Champlain Valley agricultural region; and only 7.5 percent or 7,800 was in the rest of the region now encompassed by the Adirondack Park. Essex County's 114,488-cleared acres were also concentrated in Champlain Valley towns. The county's western towns had only a fifth of that total. Lewis County towns that are east of the Black River Valley had only 7,800 cleared acres. Warren County had 71,409 cleared acres, with 28 percent of those acres in Queensbury, around the burgeoning settlement of Glens Falls. The rest of the cleared acreage was relatively evenly spread around the county's rural towns. In all, less than 5 percent of the area within the future Park was cleared for farming in 1835, a figure that rose to 9 percent in 1855.[1]

Figures 1 - 3 compare the maximum cleared acreages in 1845 and 1875 for three different types of towns: those in Warren County that were among the earliest to be settled; those where farming and iron making brought large numbers of settlers; and those in the interior of the Adirondacks. The figures show that the cleared acreage in the first two categories of towns was many times greater than that in the wilderness towns.

## How the Forest Was Cleared

The figures for cleared acreage tell how much was farmland, but not how the forest was cleared. A farmer clearing land could make potash from the trees he felled, a sure and first cash crop. "A careful farmer could usually pay for the clearing of his land from the sale of potash."[2] The earliest Adirondack settlers brought this first industry to the mountains and valleys. In the process of clearing land, softwood trees were cut to use for buildings, and later sawn and shipped, creating the region's second industry, logging and lumbering. Later, hardwoods were turned into charcoal to be used in the making of iron, the Adirondacks' third industry.

## Potash

The potash industry was unique in that it involved a one-time use of the forest and almost every farm at one time qualified as an ashery, for this was the only cash crop available in those early years for the settler. Further, the settler had to clear his land to farm and harvesting softwood logs for his home and hardwood logs to be burned for valuable ash were the only way a pioneer could survive during the first few years of struggling to tame the wilderness.

To make potash, the farmer first burned the trees he had cleared from his land, carefully saving the ashes, which were leached with water to produce lye. The lye was boiled down in a large iron pot, then the residue was dried by evaporation, to yield potash, often called black salts because of its dark color. Thirty cords of wood would yield about a ton of ashes and a ton of ashes produced only a sixth of a ton of potash. Its worth, from sixty to eighty dollars a ton, seems small in light of the wood consumed and the labor to produce it; but it was large given the value of land, usually only a fraction of a dollar an acre.

Potash was used in "making glass and soap, in dyeing, and as a fertilizer,"[3] in making explosives and some matches, and in scouring wool. Potash was burned at high temperature to produce pearl ash (pure potassium carbonate), whose function was equivalent to today's use of bicarbonate of soda. Pearl ash brought $200 to $300 a ton in Montreal, and in 1805 over 1,000 tons of ash was shipped from just one port on Lake Ontario, Sackets Harbor.[4]

Potash from the eastern Adirondacks was shipped down Lake Champlain and Lake Ontario and on to Montreal for shipment to England. Potash making peaked in the early 1800s along Lake Champlain and the rivers flowing into it, but did not peak until two decades later in the west in areas adjacent to the Black River.

While shipping lumber from anywhere in the north country except the shores of Lake Champlain was difficult, "potash was one of the few farm commodities that could be transported fairly easily and cheaply."[5]

The 1820 Census shows no potash production in Saratoga County--much of its flatlands had been cleared for agriculture even before the Revolutionary War. The county did, however, produce over 5.5 million board feet of lumber. Lewis and Jefferson counties, on the other hand, shipped no lumber, but consumed 48,700 and 88,380 cords of wood respectively in the production of potash. Saratoga County's

## Potash Production in 1820

In terms of cords of wood burned

| | |
|---|---:|
| Saratoga | none |
| Lewis | 12,400 |
| Essex | 19,800 |
| Clinton | 10,200 |
| Warren | 510 |

The only other northern Adirondack County reporting ash production was Jefferson, with a production 50% greater than the combined total of the counties that touch the Adirondack region.

Source: 1820 Census

Figure 5

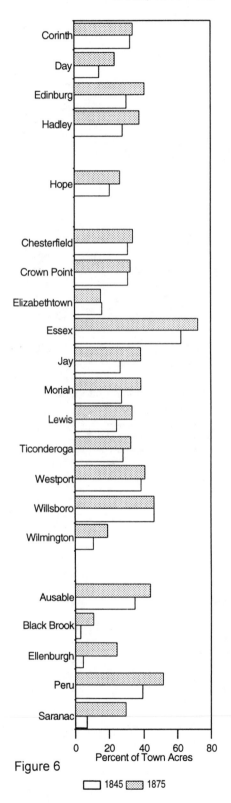

Cleared acreage in typical
farming or iron manufacturing
towns, 1845-1875

Corinth

Day

Edinburg

Hadley

Hope

Chesterfield

Crown Point

Elizabethtown

Essex

Jay

Moriah

Lewis

Ticonderoga

Westport

Willsboro

Wilmington

Ausable

Black Brook

Ellenburgh

Peru

Saranac

0    20    40    60    80
Percent of Town Acres

Figure 6

☐ 1845    ▨ 1875

farmland had been cleared and clearing for farmland in Jefferson and Lewis counties was just beginning. Herkimer County towns that lie within or near the present Park boundary produced as much potash as all of Clinton and Essex counties combined. In both Clinton and Essex counties, slightly more wood was cut for lumber than for potash. Hardwoods were already becoming valuable for charcoal to make iron.

Throughout the region, potash was made only in lowlands near settlements. Cleared farms in the interior mountainous region were never numerous; they existed mostly in conjunction with the later sawmills, tanneries or forges.

Translating the figures for all but Jefferson County shows that at most 18,000 acres were being cleared a year for both lumber and potash--this in a region that exceeds the present six million acres of the Park.

(Although it was a one-time crop for a farmer, the making of potash did pick up again early in this century. As hardwood logging increased after 1900, lumbermen found they could add to their income by shipping pearl ash. Through the years of World War I, Emporium Lumber Co. shipped a carload of this by-product every few months.)

## Sawmills

The number of early sawmills in the Adirondack region--at least one in every settlement--is quite astounding. However the number pales to insignificance when we understand that the sawmills were mostly very simple saws, set up by a local farmer to serve himself and his neighbors. For most mills, lumbering could go on as long as there was a nearby source of pine as well as the need for more houses. Local mills, which basically served the settlers, were quickly erected; and when the timber around them was exhausted, they were easily moved to a new location.

Technology, or lack of it, hampered the earliest days of the lumber industry in the Adirondacks and certainly limited the amount of lumber sawn. The first mills, improvements on the manual vertical pit saws, were up and down saws powered by a waterwheel. Waterpower proved so plentiful in most of northern New York that mills remained waterpowered late in the nineteenth century, while steam was used elsewhere at an earlier date.[6]

The first waterpowered mills, however, were exceedingly slow. It was "said that you could roll on a hardwood log--go in to breakfast and come out about the time the board was ready to drop from the saw."[7] These earliest recorded mills were at Wing's Falls (now Glens Falls), 1765; Nobleboro, where there was a short-lived mill about 1790; Black River near Port Leyden, 1797; and Castorland, also on the Black River, 1798. All of these early mills and most of those in the first part of the nineteenth century were essential parts of land clearing operations. The sawmill was "only an auxiliary device to help in the land clearing operation and to provide necessary material for houses, farms, furniture,"[8] and only peripherally for export downriver.

The tremendous number of mills present in 1820 reflects mostly their small size and the small area they served because of the constraints of transportation, which was either by water or oxen. The slow-moving oxen were perfect complements to the slow-producing mills.

Logs were hauled directly to mills where stirrups in a frame or "gate" held them against a single upright or up-and-down saw, powered by an overshot water wheel. Gradually more saws were added to a single jointly-powered array. From this evolved the early gang saws, where several upright saws were arranged in parallel together. Mills with gang saws could produce a commercially important amount of lumber and variations using gang saws were used until the end of the century.

## Logging and the Early Shipment of Lumber

Lack of transportation also hampered the early development of lumbering in the region. Rivers were the only means of transporting logs over any distance in the early nineteenth century. Except adjacent to the shores of Lake Champlain and the flat water of the Hudson River south of Glens Falls, the product of early sawmills was generally consumed locally.

The most sought-after logs were pine. Pine logs would float and they were easy to saw and plane. This meant that initially only pine trees were harvested; they were quickly stripped from accessible areas and either logs or lumber sent to mills in Albany or north to the St. Lawrence Valley. Logs with sufficient diameter and length to make the longest spars were exported to England, but the stories of pine being shipped north to Montreal to serve as masts for the British navy do not indicate how much pine was harvested.[9]

The pines were cut from the lowlands adjacent to the Hudson River below Glens Falls, from the shores of Lake Champlain, and then from the lower reaches of the rivers flowing into the lake. Rafts of hewn pine were also shipped down the lake for export to Canada. The year 1830 was said to be the peak of this shipment.

Hudson River loggers created huge rafts of solid logs or sawn timbers that could be maneuvered down the river, first to New York and later to Albany. Albany grew gradually to become one of the two most important lumber ports in the country (Chicago was the other), a role it achieved in the second half of the century, a development that will be discussed in a later chapter.

Rafts were formed by crisscrossing courses of thirty or more layers of inch thick planks, sixteen feet long. The courses were secured by poles, "grub stakes" cut from saplings. Chains of up to five of these rafts were connected to form a "five-platform piece."[10] Larger rafts were made by securing three of these five platform pieces side-by-side, so that a raft could be constructed that was over 48 feet wide, and 160 feet long, and could contain up to 180,000 board feet of lumber. The rafts barely rose above the surface of the water. Rafters used long oars to keep the raft in the river channel and the current did the rest, although Hudson River barges were at the mercy of tides and winds.

The 1820 Census reported that Essex and Clinton counties harvested some 69,600 pine logs, not a great number when compared with later harvests. The small amount of pine logs harvested reflects the fact that each tree was felled by axe and logs were hauled to water by teams of oxen. Further, Warren County was producing little more than a tenth that total, indicating the county's pine had already been cut.

## Pine Logs Sawn in 1820

| | |
|---|---|
| Saratoga | 27,700 |
| Essex | 28,500 |
| Clinton | 38,100 |
| Warren | *7,600 |

* Warren County's production is given in board feet. That can be translated to standards, but not to the pine logs quoted for the other three counties.

All other counties in the north country had insignificant production.

Source: 1820 Census

Figure 7

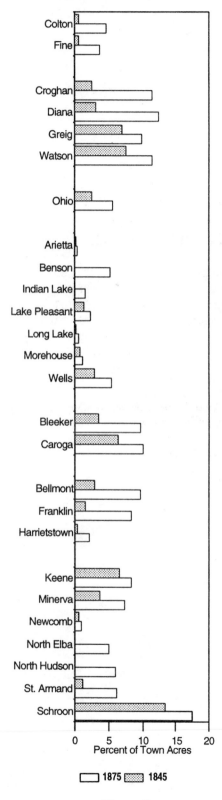

Cleared acreage in typical
forested towns, 1845-1875

Percent of Town Acres

☐ 1875   ▨ 1845

Figure 8

More than 4,440 acres of pine would have been cut over to produce the 1820 harvest,[11] but just how much more is a matter of speculation. If pines constituted no more than three percent of the original forest (and many believe that figure is high), as many as 148,000 acres could have been culled for their pines in a year. Since pines tended to grow in pure or relatively dense stands, often near water, fewer acres would probably have produced that harvest. No matter, the amount of pine taken in 1820 certainly gives credence to the claims that the pine accessible to the Champlain Valley and the lower Hudson River had been taken before 1830.

Just how much timber was cut in the Adirondack counties of Essex, Jefferson, Clinton, Saratoga and Warren in 1820? (The question is limited to those counties because Franklin was still part of Clinton County: Fulton and Hamilton counties were still part of Montgomery County.) Translating the census information to cords indicates that these counties produced only about 24,500 cords of pine sawlogs.

At the same time, those five counties were producing 12,700 cords of hardwoods to make the charcoal needed for blacksmithing and for producing iron. Harvest of hardwoods for charcoal emerges as the greatest industrial use of forests and the most destructive in the northeastern Adirondacks in the second half of the century, but even during the first half, its effects were great.

In Essex and Clinton counties, the value of the iron produced in 1820, $58,000, escalated rapidly to over $400,000 in 1835. Assuming inflation was not a factor, this translates into an increase of upwards of 90,000 cords of hardwood for charcoal. Add to this the product of the asheries, and a substantial harvest of hardwoods was occurring. All this was clearcutting and the impact on the forest was much greater than anything done by the lumberman.

Although most emerging communities around the border of the Adirondacks had blacksmiths who used charcoal, the amount of such charcoal use pales in comparison to that consumed in Essex and Clinton counties where bar iron was produced and where nails, wheels, and iron implements were manufactured. The production of iron in those counties continued to increase beyond mid-century. Its impact on the forest is discussed in the next chapter.

## Floating Logs to Mills

Experience with neither tide nor wind prepared lumbermen for the obstacles encountered when loggers reached upriver from the Hudson's quiet waters to the forests around that river's rocky and turbulent headwater streams. This period dates from the second decade of the nineteenth century, when the accessible pine (that from the Glens Falls region and south along the Hudson River or along Lake Champlain) had been harvested and loggers had to contend with the river's rapids and falls. Logging in the mountainous core of the Adirondacks settled early on into a pattern that was indigenous to the area. The mountainous region of northern New York contained almost no rivers that were wide and flat enough for rafts. According to Col. William F. Fox, historian and Superintendent of Forests for the State from 1895 to 1906, writing in a report to the Forest, Fish and Game Commission, two Adirondack lumbermen introduced a new method of bringing logs to mills, one that was suitable for the Adirondacks' wild and broken rivers. According to Col. Fox, the problems created by the steep, rocky, and fast-tumbling rivers were solved by two brothers from Brant Lake, Norman and Alanson Fox,[12] who were William's father and uncle. In 1813, the brothers began to float individual logs from the Brant Lake Tract down the Schroon River and into the Hudson River to mills near Glens Falls. (A Warren County history credits Abraham Wing, builder of Glens Falls' first sawmill with inventing river driving. Whatever its origin, river driving reached its apex on the Hudson in 1872, on western rivers in the next decade; its story, too, is thus part of the next chapter.

## Early Milling Centers

Clusters of gang mills sprang up along the lower reaches of the region's wild rivers at the most suitable sites for waterpower, particularly those adjacent to canals or railroads that could facilitate the shipment of sawn lumber. These mills began to attract logs floated from great distances upstream. Although the mills increased in size by adding more gangs in a gate and building more gates, milling technology changed very slowly throughout the rest of the century. The mills could handle ever-increasing numbers of logs because of the numbers of gang saws and because they ran night and day, except when closed by low water.

The first gang mill was built at Fort Edward in the early 1840s and before 1848 there were gang mills at Glens Falls and Sandy Hill, all sawing logs that had been floated down the Hudson River and its tributaries. The lower reaches of other rivers also had gang mills. The Hinckley and Ballou Mill was built in 1848 at a site known as Gang Mills on the West Canada Creek. The first gang mill on the Raquette River (1851) was well downriver away from the Adirondack plateau at Norwood.[13]

Gradually larger mills were built around the choicest waterpower sites. Floating logs downriver was the only way of transporting them to the mills. Softwoods float, hardwoods do not. From 1830 on, with the accessible pine gone, loggers turned to spruce, which not only could be floated to downstream mills, it was almost as desirable for construction as pine. By mid-century, spruce was the most sought-after wood, and that species dominated Adirondack logging for the next century.

## Regulating the Shipment of Logs on Rivers

In order to regulate the passage of logs on rivers and streams, the Legislature passed a series of acts, which fall into several broad categories. The acts indicate changes in the use of the rivers throughout the nineteenth century and the dates of the acts show the advance of the logging industry as it encircled the Park and reached into its heartland via the rivers.

The earliest law governing northern rivers applied to the Hudson River; an act of 1804 was designed to prevent theft of rafts of logs. Early acts declared a number of rivers public highways for the

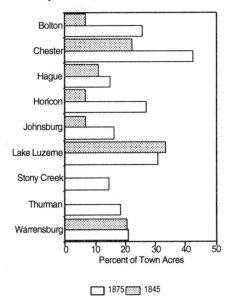

Cleared acreage in Warren County towns, 1845-1875

Figure 9

transport of logs via rafts or boats: the lower Salmon River in 1806, the lower Schroon River in 1806, the lower reaches of the Racket [sic] and St. Regis rivers in 1810, the lower Oswegatchie in 1816, the northern Schroon in 1819, the lower Black in 1821, and the lower Grasse in 1824. These acts were generally written to ensure that channels were kept open so rafts could pass. The prevention of obstructions on the East and West Stoney Creeks, tributaries of the Sacandaga River, was the object of an 1823 act, which did not mention the shipment of logs.

The practice of floating individual logs to mills was so quickly and universally adopted by loggers throughout the Adirondacks that it became the signature means of transporting logs. Within a decade and a half, the State passed laws to regulate the movement of logs on the region's rivers. The first such series of acts focused on the Hudson River and its tributaries. After 1825, all logs floated on the Hudson River and its branches were required to have identifying marks, which had to be registered by the Town Clerk of Queensbury. Already that town had become the principal destination of logs shipped down the Hudson . Marks were also required after 1825 on the Ausable River. An Act of 1830 regulated the building of booms on the Schroon.

With the exception of the Hudson River and its tributaries, all of the portions of rivers declared navigable before mid-century were outside the present Park. Many of those rivers, such as the Raquette, St. Regis, Oswegatchie, and Black, rose in and flowed through the Park, but their Park segments did not become river highways until well after mid-century. The laws regulating later phases of river driving are discussed in the next chapter on the second half of the nineteenth century, where the sequence of their passage demonstrates the pattern of the expansion of logging into the Adirondacks.

\*          \*          \*

The rate of growth of farmland in Clinton and Essex counties slowed between 1820 and 1835; the amount of ash produced in 1835 was less than one-tenth that of 1820. Farming mainly supplied the growing industrial communities, those that were beginning to produce iron, tan leather, and saw lumber for export. The farmer's hay and oats fed the local loggers' horses and oxen, but only apples and potatoes were exported from the region.

Sawmill production increased in those counties by less than fifty percent in the interval between 1820 and 1835, and even slowed to two-thirds the 1820 level by 1845. Iron manufacturing was becoming preeminent in those counties where the pine was gone.

Logging of spruce, which had begun in Warren County in 1813, focused the lumberman's attention on the Hudson River and its tributaries and the high forests that were the headwaters of the Hudson watershed. By mid-century, the region's shift from agriculture to logging was complete.

# V

## The Adirondacks From 1850 to 1890: Forests as Industry

The story of Adirondack forests after 1850 has two major components: their use by tourists and by industry. Both are significant, though in vastly different ways, for their preservation.

Populations in the Adirondack interior towns grew through the nineteenth century, peaking between 1880 and 1890. Logging, tanning, and iron making brought most of the people to the region in the second half of the century. Although there were enough farmers to support the industrial communities, agriculture was no longer the prime reason for cutting the forest. Nor was it the foremost reason for settling the region, in spite of the fact that appraisals of Adirondack tracts, made to help the State determine their value before sale to settlers and lumbermen, occasionally used the viability of the land for farming as the principal criterion of their worth throughout the entire period.

The amount of cleared or improved land increased in most towns until 1875, but the rate of increase after 1855 slowed appreciably, as shown in figures 6, 8, and 9. Farms were ubiquitous, but they were arranged along every road, where their clearings and fires made them visible to those who later worked to alert the public to the destruction of the forest.

The cover map was produced in 1884[1] to show the conditions of forests in the Adirondack region. Prepared originally for the Sargent Commission, which will be discussed later, the map was later reprinted to show the proposed boundaries of the Park as well as the original Blue Line. The huge swath of white in the eastern and northeastern Adirondacks depicts the area that had been cleared for agriculture and to produce charcoal and hemlock bark tannin. The white areas are larger than the figures for improved land from the State Census of 1875 would indicate, because most farms were not entirely cleared and improved. Each farmer usually retained woodlots, often the larger part of his acreage, from which he cut firewood and earned extra income by harvesting hop poles, cutting barrel staves from oak, and making shingles from pine, cedar, and spruce.

Two shades of green cover the heart of the Adirondack region. The dark green (the green of spruce) is land that had not been logged before 1884, even for softwoods; it was virgin land. This land not only contained uncut stands of spruce, it also had important stands of pine. Typical of the stands of pine on the interior were those along the shores of Round Lake, upstream from Tupper Lake, where a forester described seeing "great groves and belts of white pine with straight and clean shafts towering high above all other trees."[2] The grey-green is land that had been cut for softwoods only, land where logging was

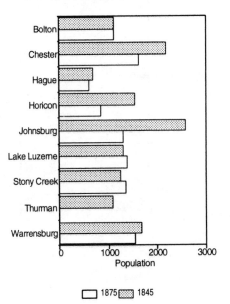

Populations In Warren County towns, 1845-1875

Figure 10

scarcely visible. The choice of shades of green reflects the similarity of the two forest areas, for logging before 1890 was so benign it changed the forest only moderately. It was still possible to depict 3.6 million acres of the great northern forest in shades of green because that forest was largely intact. The cleared acreage within this heartland amounted to a scant 100,000 acres.

Statistics published in 1888[3] indicate that nearly 2 million acres were virgin and little of the proposed Adirondack Park had been cleared. While some timbered lands lay outside the proposed Park boundary, probably as much as 1.5 million acres had been cleared, but not for lumber. To understand why the lumberman made such a slight impact on the forest, the reader will have to understand logging practices, the floating of logs to mills, the Big Boom, and especially why spruce was king.

Before exploring how the forests were changed by the lumber industry between 1850 and 1890, we first survey the way the tanning industry changed the forest, then look at the way forests in the northeastern Adirondacks were clearcut to produce charcoal for the iron industry. That clearcutting and the modest increases in farming in towns on the periphery of the Adirondacks that supported the tanning industry account for the amount of cleared land shown in the State Census of 1865 and 1875. It also explains why the Sargent Commission map shows so much land in white.

# Hemlock Bark Tanning

During the years from 1850 to 1890, hemlock trees were cut for their bark, which was stripped from the felled trees, carried to huge tanneries built on the edge of the wilderness, ground and leached to provide tannin to turn cowhides, shipped to the Adirondacks from Central and South America, into shoe leather.[4] Several important conclusions stand out concerning the effects of that industry on Adirondack forests.

First, almost all the tanneries were within a day's drive by horse and wagon from rail lines or canals, even though the tanneries and their settlements were carved from the wilderness. All were built on the periphery of the future Adirondack Park. Those on the western side of the Park were quite close to the Black River. Because of the configuration of rivers and roads in Warren County, tanneries there were built well west of the current Park boundary, but still at the eastern edge of what was then considered the great northern forest.

Second, the communities spawned by the tanneries became centers of commerce with farming communities surrounding them. The tanning industry induced more people to settle in the wilderness and accounted for the building of more towns than logging ever did, mostly because of the transient nature of the logging industry. Tanning required huge complexes and large capital investments. From 1850 to 1880 the industry accounted for more clearing of land than did logging, because of the amount of forest cut to supply bark as well as to create the farms needed to support the settlements.

There were some fifty odd large tanneries in the north country and seventy or so fairly small ones. The largest commanded 75,000 acres of land. It is not easy to estimate how much forest was cleared for

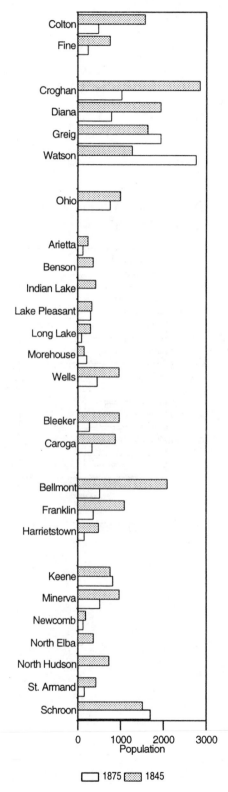

Populations in typical forested towns, 1845-1875

Population

□ 1875  ▨ 1845

Figure 11

hemlock bark. Hemlock constitutes about 15 percent of the forest, but in some parts of Warren County and southern Essex County, it was found in pure stands. The largest tanneries needed as much as 6,000 cords of bark, cut from 1,000 acres each year. The average large tannery exhausted the hemlock in a ten-mile radius over a twenty-year period, the average life span of most tanneries.

Conservatively, a million acres, perhaps as much as a million and a half acres, were cut over for hemlock bark. Most of the bark was taken from the areas shown as white on the 1885 map; in the southeastern Adirondacks, bark was taken from areas shown in the lighter green. Locally accessible supplies of bark were exhausted from those areas, and the depletion was most pronounced in Warren County. Nevertheless, when the industry left the region in the early 1890s, somewhere between a third and a half of the original hemlock stands remained untouched; the industry never reached into the heart of the great northern forest. Tanning ceased in the Adirondacks because the industry was consolidated in the southern tier of New York and in midwestern states. Up until 1926, the Adirondacks continued to ship some of the remaining hemlock bark to these relocated tanneries.

*Bark piled in long sheds, waiting to be used at the Jerden Falls Tannery*

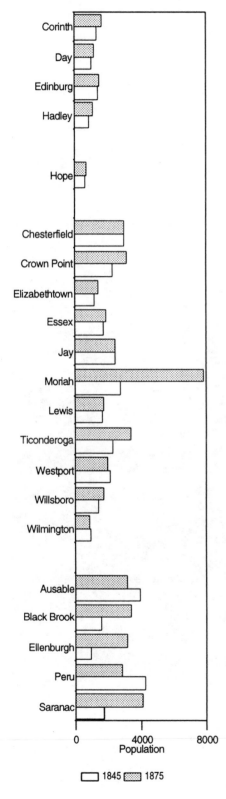

Populations in typical farming
and iron manufacturing towns,
1845-1875

1845 ☐   1875 ▨

Figure 12

# Iron and Charcoal

Iron was the second industry (assuming potash was first) to reach the north country, although the first forge dates back to 1760, almost as early as the first fields cleared for agriculture. The making of iron was the dominant industry throughout the middle and late nineteenth century, although in later years it was no longer dependent on Adirondack forests. Iron was the only industry that brought greater revenues to the region than did hemlock-bark tanning. It was not until the end of the century that iron production declined and was replaced in economic importance by logging.

After the 1823 opening of the Champlain Canal, ore from mines in Essex, Clinton, and Franklin counties could be shipped to metropolitan regions. Iron making developed rapidly after 1835 and was the dominant economic activity in the northeastern Adirondacks by 1850. Because of the difficulty of shipping iron from the interior of the Adirondacks, the development of mines and iron manufactures away from the Champlain Valley had to await the mid-century and later expansion of the railroads. Similarly, iron production in the western Adirondacks, particularly in St. Lawrence County did not expand until the arrival of rails. The manufacturing of iron peaked in the decade of the 1870s and early 1880s, then gradually declined.

The manufacturing of iron becomes a critical factor in the story of the Adirondack forests because no matter what process was used to produce iron, charcoal was essential. Charcoal can be produced from almost any species of hardwood trees. Even small trunks and limbs could be used, so that the northern forests, which were at least sixty percent hardwoods, were severely cut. And, of course, in the process of cutting hardwoods, the best of the softwood logs were also taken to nearby mills to be sawn for local construction. As a result, in charcoal-producing regions, the forest was actually clearcut.

Charcoal is made by burning the wood in an oxygen-deficient environment. Originally, wood was piled in great beehive stacks and covered with dirt to seal out the air. As the level of production rose, iron mines in the Adirondacks began to use beehives made of brick as the ovens in which to convert wood to charcoal.

## The Processs of Making Iron

Iron ore was processed either in a blast furnace or in a forge and both processes required vast amounts of fuel. Iron ore was first separated by various means, typically by roasting the ore on piles of wood, then stamped to further loosen the ore, and finally separated by water. While other separation means were tried, most did heat the ore, thus using more of the region's wood.

In a blast furnace, iron ore is heated to a liquid state. The furnace depends on tall stacks or chimneys, whose draft creates a sufficiently hot fire to bring the ore to a liquid state where liquid iron and liquid slag can separate. Blast furnaces initially used only charcoal, superheated by burning the charcoal and iron together with limestone or marble.

Before the Civil War there were only a few furnaces in northern New York, all fairly small with primitive water-powered blowing tubes. The furnaces were set in seclusion on a large tract of rural timberland. The most famous blast furnaces were built by the Adirondack Iron and Steel Company[6], which operated two furnaces at Tahawus from 1830 to 1855. Innovations at the Tahawus works may have actually employed technologies usually associated with the emerging use of coke.

In a bloomery forge, iron is heated with charcoal in hearth fires that use bellows to enhance the flow of air. The mixture is stirred with a long rod to separate the slag from the carbon-rich iron, which rises to form a sticky ball called the bloom--an elliptical mass weighing about 300 pounds. After the bloom is removed from the fire and cooled, it is hammered to force out the carbon.[7] Usually the hammers were water-powered, but only charcoal was used to fuel the forge fires.

The cottage-industry aspects of iron forging made the process well-suited to the region. It was a crude process that survived because of the abundance of wood for charcoal near the mines, the richness of the local ores, the fact the process did not require huge investments, and the part-time nature of the work, which was possible because the forges were easily fired and just as easily shut down. Manufacturing sites were enlarged by adding to the number of forge fires.

The two processes are very different, but both initially depended on charcoal. Early on, both kinds of iron operations were quite small, although the Adirondacks' produced a remarkably large proportion of the country's iron. Before the Civil War, the Adirondack-Champlain region was one of the ten principal iron producing regions of the country, accounting for ten percent of the country's iron.[8] The Adirondack region was unique in the United States in that so much of its iron was produced by forge; by 1880, the Adirondacks accounted for eighty-four percent of country's iron made in bloomery forges using charcoal.

As transportation by rail and barge improved, and as available hardwood supplies dwindled, coke gradually replaced charcoal in furnaces. Proximity to railroads or canals not only meant that coal or coke could be imported to replace charcoal in blast furnaces, but that forges could be replaced by furnaces.

In the years before 1890 when the production of iron using charcoal began to phase out, iron making had a tremendous impact on Adirondack forests. Every ton of iron required from 350 to 500[9] bushels of charcoal. Two-and-a-quarter cords of hardwood could produce 100 bushels of charcoal. In 1864, the Adirondack region produced over 28,000 tons of iron consuming over 6.5 million bushels of charcoal,[10] and the largest Adirondack charcoal forges had yet to be built.

*Figures 6 through 12 show that the average population and cleared acreage in typical forested towns was a small fraction of those totals in farming and iron manufacturing towns.*

## Adirondack-Champlain Furnaces before 1867

The Sisco Furnace in Westport was built in 1847, but it began to use coke produced from anthracite coal in 1853. The Port Henry furnace began to use coal a year later[11] A sharp rise in the cost of charcoal (a direct result of the depletion of the accessible hardwood forests) was partly responsible for the conversion to coke, which was complete throughout the region by 1900.

In 1867 there were only three blast furnaces in the Adirondacks that used charcoal, although there were several others just outside the present Park boundary: The Fletcherville Furnace at Witherbee was built in 1864 with an annual capacity of 3,300 tons. In 1845, the Crown Point Iron Company built a furnace at Hammondville, near Irondale. A second furnace, built later, brought Hammondville's annual production to 3,900 tons. Myers Steel and Iron Company began building a furnace in Clifton Township, west of Cranberry Lake, in 1867. It appears to have started as a charcoal furnace and was probably located at the site of one of the mines (possibly Jayville) later built by the Benson Family. The family's successor operation, the Magnetic Iron Ore Company at Benson Mines, was not built until the railroad arrived in 1889 when its furnace was fueled by coke.[12]

Those just outside the Park included several furnaces in Jefferson County; these were sufficiently distant from the Adirondacks that they probably used little Adirondack charcoal. The Port Leyden Iron Company, which opened in 1864-5 with a large capacity, 5,000 tons, functioned for a few years only

Of those dependent on Adirondack forests, Fletcherville Furnace consumed 164,860 bushels of charcoal produced in ten rectangular, closed kilns at the furnace site from wood from the company's nearby woodlands. Charcoal was made in kilns located four to six miles from the Crown Point Iron Company's furnace where there was an abundance of wood on the company's own extensive tract of land. Myers Steel and Iron Company had 23,000 acres of timberland available for charcoal.

The region's largest charcoal furnace was built at Standish in 1885. See details in the discussion of Chateaugay Iron Company below.

*Charcoal kilns and stacks of hardwoods cut for charcoal, near the Chateaugay Railroad*
S. R. Stoddard, 1880s

*Courtesy Adirondack Museum*

## North Country Forges

Forges were ubiquitous. Between 1845 and 1860 forges were located along the Saranac, Salmon, Ausable, Boquet, and Schroon rivers, with the greatest production coming from the Ausable Valley. Forges produced considerably more iron than north country furnaces, which, for example, accounted for as little as 7 percent of the region's iron in 1850.[13]

By 1864, the thirty north country forges with their 132 fires[14] consumed 6,658,000 bushels of charcoal annually. This figure rose after 1867 as several forges were just getting under way. The J. and J. Rogers Company's several sites, Upper and Lower Black Brook, the Sable Iron Works, and the Jay Forge consumed 1,550,000 bushels. The company owned 80,000 acres and had 52 charcoal kilns--17 in the Black Brook area, 6 at Taylor Pond, 4 at Mud Pond, 3 at Silver Lake, 3 at Military Pond, 7 at Wilmington, 4 at Jay, 2 at Keene, and 6 more under construction.[15] They were said to leave the country bare, cutting at the rate of 1,000 acres a year. J. and J. Rogers Company' iron production peaked around 1880 when the company needed 4.5 million bushels of charcoal, produced from 40,000 cords of wood.

The pace of charcoal consumption quickened with the opening of the Chateaugay Ore and Iron Company, which owned upwards of 100,000 acres and was cutting from 2,100 to 2,400 acres a year to fill its 126 kilns. That company was organized in 1873 from forges at Clayburg, Saranac and Russia, but after 1881 concentrated on its ore resources on Lyon Mountain. There, at the outlet of Lower Chateaugay Lake, the company built a large Catalan forge (essentially a bloomery forge), said to be the largest bloomery in the United States.[16] The company built a modern furnace at nearby Standish in 1885 using charcoal as fuel.[17] It was not until 1903 when the Delaware and Hudson Railroad took over the Chateaugay Ore and Iron Company, that the narrow-gauge railroad was converted so it could bring coal to the site. Thus, it was not until then that the last of the north country's charcoal furnaces was converted to coke.

Chateaugay's earliest charcoal kilns were open pits, but gradually beehive pits were built around Chateaugay Lake. The extension of the railroad to Lake Placid sparked the building of large-capacity kilns along the tracks near Loon Lake. The company's holdings grew to 100,000 acres, and it was estimated that a million and a half cords of hardwoods were consumed by the company's forges[18] between 1873 and 1903, when the last forge was abandoned and the furnace was converted to coke.

## Iron's Effect on the Forest

In 1864, 33,600 tons of bloomery iron were produced in the north country, while only 8,950 tons came from furnaces. In 1880, 37,633 tons of bloomery iron was produced in the north country; in 1882, the peak year of bloomery production, 48,000 tons was produced.[19] Charcoal alone fueled the production of bloomery iron, which remained at a high enough level to consume upwards of seven million bushels of charcoal a year for the thirty-year period of greatest production. To cut upwards of 160,000 cords of hardwoods a year meant that as much as 7,000 acres a year were cleared. To fuel the century's manufacturing of charcoal iron, it is estimated that between 200,000 and 250,000 acres of Adirondack-Champlain forest land were cleared.

The amount of clearing for charcoal is greater than the amount of and rate of clearing for hardwood logging in the northwestern Adirondacks in the first half of the twentieth century. The harvest of hardwood logs is limited and tame compared with the pervasive deforestation of this earlier cutting for charcoal. The two largest producers of charcoal iron, J. and J. Rogers Company and Chateaugay Ore and Iron Company, both later harvested softwoods on their forest lands. See appendix. Both were in areas where the visual impact of charcoal making was infinitely greater because the lands to be logged bordered railroads that carried passengers as well as logs and iron.

Beech, birch, and maple, the best trees for charcoal, constituted as much as sixty percent of the forest cover. Charcoal production not only exhausted that portion of the region's standing forests, it altered the forest's ability to reproduce itself. Such heavy logging exposed the

Map 4
ADIRONDACK
FORGES AND FURNACES
Forges and furnaces were built near
iron mines and water sources
throughout the northeastern
Adirondacks.

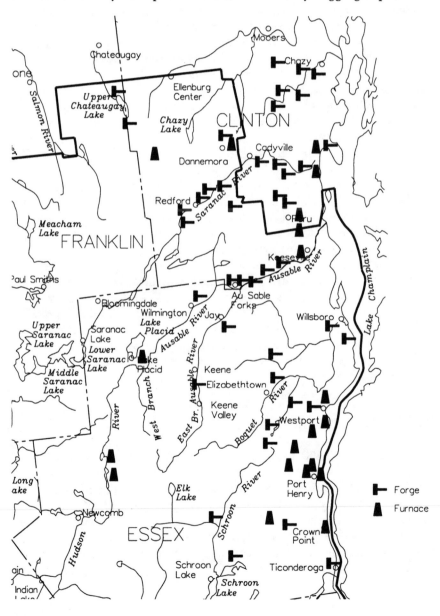

soil to direct sunlight, so the soil was dried out. This in turn changed the ability of the soil to retain water, and left the land prone to fire. Such harvest disruption of the forest's ability to protect water sources was a prime motivation for forest preservation in the 1870s and 1880s.

Is it any wonder that travelers to the region were struck by the devastation along the rail lines and the travel corridors through the northeastern Adirondacks? Is it any wonder that those who protested the cutting of any timber latched on to the horrors of the hardwood logging for charcoal to promote their call for forest protection? This destruction provided a strong visual image, one as powerful as Stoddard's picture of drowned lands, which is discussed in the next chapter. The image of clearcut charcoal lands was used extensively by writers who equated the destruction of forests for charcoal with logging for lumber.

A traveler in 1891 described the scene in an article in *Forest and Stream*. As part of a trip to circumnavigate the Adirondacks, the writer journeyed on the Chateaugay Railroad, anticipating the "grand old Adirondacks" as viewed from the narrow-gauge road. Instead, the trip gave him "... blues from the start. For miles and miles we went through and by acres of stump-covered rocks, covered with an inch or so of soil; millions of boulders, piles of iron ore, and worst of all, flock after flock of beehive-like structures, surrounded by thousands of cords of timber to be transformed to charcoal. It was a dismal ride; and the clearings of years ago as we neared Paul Smith's were like jewels in an ugly setting. If Dante had met me that day and asked my opinion as to a good model for his road to the inferno, I think I should have recommended a trip over the Chateaugay."[20]

In contrast, another traveler that same year indicated that not everything was horrible; in fact he reported a most delightful drive along Lake Road, leading to the Ausable Lakes. "Part of the forest along this road was cut clear twenty-five years ago by charcoal burners." The land was subsequently completely reforested, with little to indicate to the "casual observer that it differed from the original forest on the surrounding lands."[21] Similarly, along the road west from Keene there were reports of large areas "which have been cleared by charcoal burners, but which are rapidly recovering their growth. Beyond and west of Cascade Lake (Long Pond) are some abandoned charcoal kilns, and here everything was cut but now the land is covered with extensive second growth."[22]

The lands which supplied wood for charcoal as well as agricultural lands were left out of the Adirondack Park as it was originally proposed. It is interesting that, in the northeastern Adirondacks, these lands were sufficiently denuded of forest cover before 1892 so that they were not even considered for Park land, but the destruction of their forests continued well into this century. The extent of cutting on lands belonging to both J. and J. Rogers Company and the Chateaugay Ore and Iron Company later extended well into lands considered virgin on the 1884 Sargent Commission map. A clearcut is an ugly thing, but the only clearcutting done in the Adirondacks before 1892 was for charcoal and agriculture. And as will be shown, none of what the lumberman did before 1892 and relatively little of what they did after that date can be considered a clearcut. Destructive clearcutting is a modern-day phenomenon and a product of current market demands.[23]

# The Era of Logging

## Spruce, the Merchantable Lumber

With the depletion of accessible pine during the 1830s, spruce became the principal lumber harvested in the Adirondacks. When the lumberman spoke of *merchantable timber*, he meant only spruce; nothing else had its market value. The absolute reign of spruce began to weaken after 1890, and a slow decline in its dominance began. However, as late as 1950 when hardwood use for paper production was introduced, spruce was still the major component of merchantable timber in the Adirondacks.

Spruce, as noted earlier, occupies special and disparate niches in the landscape--the tops of mountains and ridgelines and wet places in the lowlands. Spruce grows best on hilly sites at low (up to 2000-foot) elevation, but also thrives in low, moist valleys and shorelines free of standing water.

Spruce trees are typically smaller than pine or hemlock or such hardwoods as maple and yellow birch. Mature specimens attain an average height of 80 feet with an average diameter of 18 inches; the largest spruce can be 105 feet tall and 36 inches in diameter.

Spruce, the essence of the merchantable forest, has different habits of growing in different areas. "In crowded forests, the spruce forms a long, clear, full bole, and a rather compact short, and blunted crown, attaining a height of 100 feet and a diameter of 34 inches. These dimensions are rare. ... On low, swampy ground spruce has a long crown, and is comparatively short. The average length of crown for all situations and soils is about 40 feet, and the average clear length from 25 to 30 feet. The average length of merchantable log was found to be about 46 feet."[24] Spruce is a long-lived tree, with hardy specimens reaching 350 years, a few 400 years.[25]

Spruce was desirable because as a softwood it was easy to plane, with medium strength and a straight, close grain. Its main advantage for the lumberman, however, was that it would float, and in the era before railroads, the State's navigable rivers offered the only practical avenues of transportation. River driving, navigable waters, and dams are discussed later.

Loggers, still using nothing more than the single-bitted axe, at first took no trees smaller than twelve inches (rarely ten inches) in diameter. The first cut in the Adirondacks not only took the largest spruce, but only those accessible to water, where it was easy to cut haul roads or skid roads to relatively dense stands of spruce. Sometimes a second cut took scattered and somewhat smaller trees after an interval of fifteen to twenty years. The trees were cut to the Adirondack standard thirteen-foot length (actually 13' 4", a peculiar choice of length which Col. Fox and others attributed to the logger's desire to minimize damage from river driving and ensure a 13' cut at the mill).[26] Spruce logs were driven to mills downstream on almost all the region's rivers.[27] Principally used for house building and other construction before 1890, spruce became important for paper making after that date and trees for pulp as small as five inches in diameter were taken. Spruce for pulp was harvested during a third cut, at least twenty-five years after the first, and cut into four-foot lengths to be floated downriver to paper mills, but that story belongs to a later chapter.

When the lumberman spoke of spruce, he meant red spruce, *Picea rubens*. Before the end of the nineteenth century, foresters did not recognize the difference between red and black spruce and lumped what we now know are two species under the name black spruce. In the Adirondacks black spruce grows in boggy soils and in a few instances on mountain tops in limited amounts. Black and white spruce are the dominant species of spruce to the north in Canada, but neither is commercially important in the Adirondacks.

Col. Fox, Superintendent of State Forests from 1895 to 1906, was an authority on spruce. From his treatise on Adirondack spruce, to countless articles on the health of spruce forests and the best ways to log them, Adirondack forestry literature dealt almost exclusively with spruce until well into the twentieth century.

Lumbermen had two basic rules of measuring the size of logs and evaluating how much wood they contained. In the Adirondacks, they often dispensed with such well-known methods as the Doyle and Scribner rules, which use arithmetic calculations based on length and diameter to yield the number of board feet in a log. Instead they used a measurement that was indigenous to the area. A log, 13 feet long and 19 inches in diameter at the smaller end, was considered by Hudson River lumbermen to be a **standard** or **market**, and all logs were measured by their relation to the market.[28] Converting each log to a multiple or fraction of a market made it possible to assess the amount of wood by means of a simple count. Adirondack lumbermen estimated that five markets equaled one thousand board feet of lumber. "The idea of buying and selling logs by count, using some fixed size as a standard unit, originated with Norman Fox, the pioneer lumberman of Warren County"[29] and the grandfather of Col. Fox. This method of dealing with logs in multiples would seem simple, except for the need to compute every log's relationship to a market and the fact that loggers in the far northern Adirondacks adopted a Saranac standard that was 22 inches in diameter. Loggers in the western Adirondacks sawed to 12, 14 or 16-foot lengths, most often using the Doyle rule, and all later adopted the 4-foot length for pulpwood. The Doyle rule gradually superseded the standard as measurement on the Hudson watershed.

The growth of spruce in the Adirondacks is, as noted, highly variable, with the geology, soils, slopes, and elevations all contributing to that variability. As the lumbermen observed, "it was found in ridges, streaks and places."[30] Fox stated that spruce made up an average of ten to fifteen percent of the Adirondack forest. Some localities reported densities of forty percent. Lumbermen learned that spruce grew in nearly pure stands in wet areas--the spruce swamps. Spruce are found interspersed with hardwoods on slopes at lower elevations. In such places where the soil is particularly rich and hardwoods are dominant, the proportion of spruce decreases so that on the richest sites there may be no spruce at all. Spruce mix with balsam fir on the highest slopes, but here individual trees are much smaller than on the lower slopes or in the spruce swamps.

Lumbermen evaluated Adirondack land by the density of spruce stands and their proximity to water. But in some places, hardwoods are so dominant that lumbermen despaired of finding spruce. Knowing the amount of spruce on a tract was vitally important, but not as essential as predicting how much regrowth would be available for a second or third cut. Foresters learned to evaluate the regrowth that could be expected in the different terrains. Much later, in the 1920s, when most of the lowland spruce had been harvested and the loggers advanced to the higher elevation stands of the High Peaks, loggers harvested both the spruce and balsam fir that grew there and lumped the two species together, as both were suitable for pulp.

Later scientific foresters learned that the regeneration of young spruce occurred only under the cool shade of other trees. There the spindly specimens struggled to reach the light in the upper canopy for upwards of a hundred years, achieving a trunk that was only a few inches (as little as three inches) in diameter in that time. During the next hundred years, upon reaching above the canopy, spruce matured almost to their maximum height and girth, and in their last hundred years, their senescence, they grew, but more slowly as they often gradually developed a rotten core. This information was not available at the time of the greatest harvest of Adirondack spruce. Lumbermen learned through experience that spruce would not reseed on the sunny and hot sites left after the forest had been heavily cut. Spruce were shown to be extremely variable of size and age. A 22-inch diameter spruce could range in age from 107 to 345 years!

## Spruce Stand Profiles

Scientific studies of spruce by Fox and others yielded corroborating evidence that associated the age of a tree with the number of rings in a cross-section of the stump. In the years after 1890, when the supply of spruce sawlogs was nearing exhaustion, many surveys of forest stands were made in which spruce trees on virgin stands were measured and their ages determined. These studies are detailed pictures of the type of virgin stands encountered by loggers in the late 1800s and the correlations between girth and age are equally applicable to today's remaining virgin stands.

It is appropriate to quote several studies that give first-hand accounts of spruce stands at this point, even though the context for and authors of those studies belong in later discussions.

The forester Gifford Pinchot noted the four types of spruce stands: swamp lands, spruce flats, hardwood lands, and spruce slopes. At Nehasane[31] he estimated that the swamp lands constituted 22 percent of the forest, spruce flats 10 percent, hardwood lands 42 percent, and spruce slopes, 26 percent. Spruce made up nearly 43 percent of all species present.[32]

At Whitney Park as well as at Nehasane, it was observed that

in general, on the hardwood land in Nehasane, the Spruce forms about 30 percent of the trees over 10 inches in diameter. The measurements from which this was taken include only those trees which were apparently sound. If the gnarled and unsound trees were included the proportion would be larger.

In the Whitney Preserve the hardwood forest contains a somewhat smaller proportion of Spruce than in Nehasane Park. The reason for this is that the land is less broken and irregular and there are a large number of long, low rides with moderate slopes on which the hardwoods thrive exceedingly well. On account of the great reproductive power and tolerance of the hardwoods, they are able to

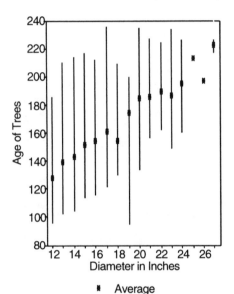

Comparison between age and diameter of red spruce trees

Average

Figure 13
Taken from 1,000-specimen plot in virgin tract at Nehasane Park in 1899, showing minimum, maximum and average age for each diameter.

Source: Fox, The Adirondack Black Spruce

occupy ground which is favorable to their growth often to the exclusion of other species. The insect pest, which occurred about 15 years ago, ... seems to have killed a large number of Spruce in the hardwood forest. The consequence is that in many places the Spruce has nearly all died out and the forest is composed almost exclusively of hardwoods. A number of sample acres were measured off in such places, and it was found that frequently there were no more than one or two Spruce trees per acre over 10 inches in diameter.

Wherever the land is considerably broken, as in Nehasane Park, there is generally a large proportion of Spruce and Yellow Birch, while Hard Maple and Beech are confined to the moderate northern slopes and bases of the ridges and to the high benches.[33]

On spruce slopes with steep, thin stony soil, where beech and hard maple do not thrive, the dominant spruce (almost fifty percent of the stand) grew tall and clear, but usually in smaller diameter than on hardwood land. "On Spruce slopes the danger from windfall is very great, and in consequence the forest is frequently comparatively young, the old trees having been blown down."[34]

In contrast to the reports of stands with such a large proportion of spruce, the 1884 State Engineer and Surveyor reported, "It is estimated by practical experts in the lumber business that the primitive virgin forests, in the best lumber districts of the Adirondack Region, have an average of one full grown tree to every square rod, or say about 160 trees per acre; and that, of this product, only about ten percent, or say sixteen trees to the acre is what is termed soft merchantable timber, such as pine, spruce and hemlock."[35]

The Sixth Annual Report (1900) of the Forest, Fish and Game Commission contains a description of the forest cover in Township 40, Totten and Crossfield, the lands surrounding Raquette Lake. The description was based on an actual timber-cruise of portions of the tract by professionals.

The tract was part of the Forest Preserve--lands on which no timber could ever be cut, according to New York State's Constitution. State foresters were advocating a change in the constitution to permit harvesting. Successive Commission reports bemoaned the fact that at the current rate of harvest, the northern forests would be totally depleted of lumber, by which it meant only the merchantable spruce. The study was made with federal funds at the request of the State Commission. It was carried out by two federal foresters recommended by Gifford Pinchot. Implicit in the design of the study was the desire to show the timber potential of the tract and thus bolster arguments for changing the State constitution.

The study recommended that a similar study be made of townships 5, 6, and 41 where there was also much Forest Preserve land and some private, but previously unharvested tracts.

The 1900 report noted that Township 40 was mostly virgin timber, heavy stands of mature spruce as well as mature pines and balsam and that there had been almost no damage by fire. From the profiles given in figures 14 and 15, it is easy to see why foresters coveted those stands!

In Township 5, spruce had been cut along the route of the Uncas Railroad, but the rest was untouched and contained a significant

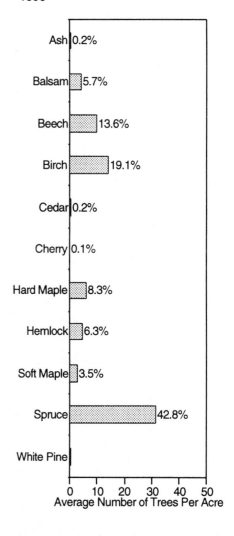

Distribution of tree species in virgin tract at Nehasane Park, 1899

**Figure 14**
This sample covering 1046 acres shows an especially high percentage of spruce.
Source: Graves, *Practical Forestry in the Adirondacks*

proportion of softwoods. Fires had burned less than five percent of the township, areas on Black Bear Mountain and in the Red River Valley.

The southwestern corner of Township 6 had been logged about 1870, when Township 7 was logged, but most of the township was covered with important stands of spruce. There had been almost no fires.

How typical were such township profiles? They were paradigms of northwestern Adirondack forests. But these descriptions cannot be extrapolated to apply to virgin forests encountered by the first loggers in other locations. Lumbermen claimed that lower Hudson watershed forests yielded at most fifteen percent spruce, often less. Most of Benson Tract, and parts of Oxbow, Nobleboro, and Arthurboro patents, and southern townships in the Moose River Tract yielded so little spruce that their owners abandoned them shortly after they were logged. However, today, one hundred and twenty years later, those tracts display the bright greens of hardwoods with distinct scatterings of spruce stands. Aerial views reveal a greater preponderance of lowland spruce stands in the southern portion of the Park than in the northern areas where they once were so prevalent, but where logging continued.

## Variations within Spruce Stands

The profiles showing age and diameter distributions were found to be even more variable than could explained by the differences in growing conditions. Foresters and observers from Franklin Hough to Verplanck Colvin to Gifford Pinchot noted occasional widespread decline caused by unexplained natural phenomenon. Perhaps because of its merchantable value, early observers were more apt to note any changes to spruce stands, and that may explain in part why the record for spruce is more complete than that for other species. Certainly, when foresters came on the scene, their studies were directed primarily to spruce. It is ironic, however, that the one species most affected by diseases and insects and changes in climate over the past century or so was also the most sought after.

## Diseases and Declines

Spruce declines have been noted in 1840-1844, 1845-1859, 1871-1880, 1933, 1937-1938, 1947-1950, and in recent years. Extremes of high temperatures in August and lows in December over the past 170 years correlate to these periods of spruce decline.[36] Since five of the eight driest growing seasons between 1832 and 1901 occurred between 1873 and 1881, there also appears to be a correlation between drought and spruce decline.[37]

First-hand accounts of these declines abound, and the decline of the 1870s was apparently the most severe. It was estimated that "one-third to one-half of the fully grown spruce timber" had been killed in the Adirondacks.[38] The First Report of the Forest Commission for 1885 contains descriptions of spruce mortality. In his 1895 treatise on spruce, Col. Fox observed that "about twenty-five years ago the black [red] spruce throughout the great forest of northern New York began

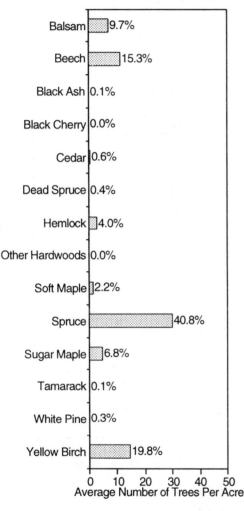

Distribution of tree species in
virgin tract in
Township 41, T & C., 1902

| Species | Percent |
|---|---|
| Balsam | 9.7% |
| Beech | 15.3% |
| Black Ash | 0.1% |
| Black Cherry | 0.0% |
| Cedar | 0.6% |
| Dead Spruce | 0.4% |
| Hemlock | 4.0% |
| Other Hardwoods | 0.0% |
| Soft Maple | 2.2% |
| Spruce | 40.8% |
| Sugar Maple | 6.8% |
| Tamarack | 0.1% |
| White Pine | 0.3% |
| Yellow Birch | 19.8% |

0  10  20  30  40  50
Average Number of Trees Per Acre

Figure 15
Sample covered 929-acre tract near
Raquette Lake.
Source: Forest, Fish and Game Commission

to show signs of blight, the first appearance of which was noticed in 1868. During the next ten years this blight spread through most of the forest, only a few localities remaining untouched."[39]

Colvin, in his survey for 1872, observed the forest on a day's march through the woods, near the Cedar River. Almost all the majestic spruce timber was either fallen and decaying or standing dead, so penetrated with dry rot and decay as to be crumbling to pieces. The same timber, only a few years since, was apparently sound and valuable."[40]

Die-back of red spruce and widespread devastation of the species in northern New York was also described in an 1877 forestry report.[41]

Franklin B. Hough, in a Report Upon Forestry, 1880-1881, quoted a writer from Colton in St. Lawrence County: "After getting about forty miles up the river we began to come into a region where a large part of the spruce was dead and at least half of it had lost its value. From such inquiries as could be made we learned that large portions of this timber were destroyed, including the best qualities and trees of the largest size. These injuries had been going on about ten years, and were still in progress. The yield of these timber lands was about 6,000 standards of 19-inch logs to the square mile."[42]

Another correspondent noted that dying spruce timber was limited to the trees growing in wet ground. In the Adirondack wilderness Hough observed that "extensive tracts of dead spruce line the borders of lakes and rivers where the casualty can be ascribed to a change of level in the waters from some obstruction in their outlet."

A report of the decline of spruce in this era is recorded in the Sargent Commission Hearings.[43] "The worm killing the spruce" was said to have decimated a 10,000-acre stand on the St. Lawrence.

The Second Report of the Forest Preserve Board described spruce stands near Follensby Pond that had never been logged. The fact that the largest spruce observed did not exceed 24 inches in diameter and that there were very few of these was attributed to a spruce blight, "which thirty years ago wrought great devastation in these woods, and which killed the largest or mature trees, the smaller ones being exempt."[44]

The earliest foresters, who came on the scene in the late 1800s, observed that spruce responded poorly to the droughts and high temperatures that became more prevalent as the nineteenth century waned. The historical and scientific record for spruce is as rich as it is because spruce was *the* merchantable tree for over a century. High elevation spruce continues to be the laboratory specimen for much of today's research into the effects of air-borne pollutants, even though spruce is no longer the only merchantable species. Today we know that spruce are exceptionally sensitive to heat and drought, and excesses of either weaken the trees making them susceptible to disease or modern stresses such as acid rain.

## Beaver

Anyone who walks Adirondack forests is aware of the work of beaver in recycling the forest. Beavers were heavily trapped in the Adirondacks throughout the eighteenth century and virtually extirpated from the region by 1840.[45] Despite their shrinking numbers, beaver continued to be a powerful force in forest. Building their dams on small, flowing streams, beaver-flooded areas most suitable for spruce. Balsam were often the first trees to repopulate these areas, but spruce followed and remained dominant, until beaver flooded the meadows again. In killing spruce through flooding and providing sites for their resurgence, beaver have played a significant role in creating uniform age spruce stands.

## Windfall

Nature's destructive winds, whether from local thunderstorms, tornadoes, or hurricanes have also changed the profile of spruce stands. Most windfalls are characterized by paths of destruction that wiped out all the trees, not just the spruce. Local windfalls, however, are often most severe on mature spruce because they are shallow-rooted and emerge unprotected above the canopy. From the great windfalls of the early 1800s to the local "cyclones" as tornadoes were called by early travelers who observed their damage, the effects of wind have always been of concern to the lumberman.

Windfalls, whether caused by hurricanes, tornadoes, violent thunderstorms and their accompanying winds, or isolated instances of windthrow of old or dead trees, are responsible for more extensive forest recycling than diseases and the work of beaver.

An 1815 hurricane probably leveled the knoll near Wells known as Pine Orchard, allowing pine to become established. Today the pines are interspersed with maturing spruce and hemlock.

Duncan McMartin, Jr. described an "ancient windfall" in his notes for the 1829 survey of the southern portion of Oxbow Patent. The path of the windfall was across the southern ridge of the western flanks of North Branch Mountain, just to the east of the West Branch of the Sacandaga River.[46]

The tornado that left the longest recorded path of destruction occurred in 1845.[47] The route of the "Great Windfall" route stretched from near Cranberry Lake slightly north of east through Windfall and on, skipping slightly, but touching down at several points all the way past Lake Champlain to Vermont. Years later, in 1864, the windfall was described as a "broad savannah, bare of trees and covered with wild grasses." Although parts of the windfall were later cultivated, most of the swath quickly grew back so that by 1893 it contained the largest (18" diameters were common) and healthiest stand of poplar in the Park.

This windfall is commemorated by two Windfall ponds and two Windfall brooks. It appears first on Stoddard's *Map of the Adirondack Wilderness, 1874*. Today you can have a dinner at the Windfall Restaurant, which is near the west end of the windfall, and across the road from the Windfall Club building.

Verplanck Colvin mentions this tornado as well as a parallel one, about fifteen miles to the north that started well outside the Park and went through the towns of Fowler and Edwards, then left a broad swath of destruction across the middle branches of the Grasse River. This one, ascribed to the same 1845 storm that spawned the tornado of the Great Windfall, stretched from Antwerp northeast to Kellogg Corners, across the West Branch of the Oswegatchie near Fullerville, across the Oswegatchie south of Edwards, across the South Branch of the DeGrasse River and on to Baldface Mountain. Baldface, known as Bald Hill to Colvin, was described by the surveyor as having "been swept clear of forest ... like a swath of grain, in a long narrow band, for a distance of over seven miles. ... This was what is known as the little windfall."[48]

In 1888 a tornado left a path of destruction 60 rods wide in Township 34 near Blue Mountain Lake. The results of the same tornado may have been observed by a traveler whose notes are recorded in the Forest Commission report for 1891. He wrote that, on the stretch of road between Indian Lake Village and the Cedar River, he encountered the "desolate track of a cyclone which swept over there on the 12th of July, 1888, and which nearly struck a passing stage coach. This cyclone did not cut a wide swath but its path was marked by evidence of a terrible restless force. It not only uprooted trees, but its rotary motion twisted the trunks of many large trees in two, wrenching off the entire crowns and limbs, and leaving the torn and broken trunks standing solid by the ground."[49] In 1891, a fire started on the dry, dead timber burned not only the area mangled by the tornado, but spread to nearby forests.

In 1898, Graves noted that the "danger from windfall on spruce flats is considerable, and young second growth is very common. It is in such circumstances that spruce comes up almost pure. This is well illustrated in Nehasane Park, where on the north side of the railroad, about two miles below Nehasane Station, there is a considerable stretch of dense second growth spruce which has come up after a windfall."[50] He observed also that the danger from windfall on spruce slopes was very great.

A storm in May of 1916, also in the vicinity of Nehasane, uprooted or broke about five percent of the timber over a large area. Observers claimed it did more damage than any other storm in memory. The greatest wind damage in modern times came from the Blowdown of 1950, see chapter VII. That blowdown and major tornado paths are shown on map 11.

Such storms are typical of the known windfalls that have changed Adirondack spruce forests over the centuries, but what of the many undocumented windfalls? There are whole hillsides where huge trunks lie pointing in one direction, usually northeast. One such windfall is north of Abner Creek, not far from the North Branch of the West Stony Creek. Another is near an old road to Tenant Creek Falls. The Windfall area north of Wells (and due south of Griffin) traces to an eponymous event of the early nineteenth century. An undated event undoubtedly was responsible for the naming of a hill southeast of Big Alderbed.

Windfalls are so common and so ordinary that it seems statistically impossible for a stand to remain untouched for more than a few centuries. Windfall is as natural an event as can befall a forest. Certainly it alters the way a forest appears, undoubtedly taking many of the more mature trees, and occasionally all the spruce that emerge above the canopy of hardwoods.

Isolated windfalls, which take down the old or dying tree or already dead snag, recycle the forest in a more modest way. The existing forest continues to grow with little change in its constituents.

### Fire

Nature's other destructive force, fire, played a very minor role in the Adirondacks before 1890. Fires were rare in the region before 1890, and those that occurred were mostly near settled areas where sparks escaped from fires set by farmers to clear land. Hunters and sportsmen were also an important cause of fires, but the total acreage burned was insignificant compared to fires after 1890, which will be discussed in the chapter on logging after 1890. No extensive stands of virgin forest were burned before 1890, except those being cleared. There are no records of fires caused by activities at logging camps; the lumberman and the loggers were very careful to protect their assets.

Even removing the spruce from a stand did not make it more subject to fires, for the tops quickly rotted down to become part of the duff and soil. Few stands were so rich in spruce that lumberman left large clearcut patches. The smaller openings were quickly shaded out by the hardwood growth and the rich humus of the forest floor could continue to function as a sponge.

## Lumbermen

Hindsight, the accumulation of wisdom from lumbermen and foresters over the decades, has given us a clear picture of what spruce stands were like in 1850. The lumberman venturing into the wilds in 1850 had a much more limited perception. He saw the forest only in relation to the waterways that could carry logs to downstream mills. He did not have the benefit of Colvin's Adirondack Survey--that was not started until two decades later. He had only sketch maps of the Adirondacks showing roads and waterbodies, and few patent, township and lot lines until the 1890s.[51] Few roads took him into the wilderness. For all practical purposes, the lumberman who wished to expand into a business that could export significant amounts of sawn wood from the Adirondack region was tied to two locations: either to the Hudson River and its tributaries, with the mill sites at Glens Falls and the canals and flat waters of the Hudson, which could carry lumber south to Albany and New York; or to the West Canada Creek and the cluster of mills near Forestport, which could ship southern Adirondack lumber directly to the Erie Canal.

Very quickly after 1850, there surfaced a group of entrepreneurial lumbermen who could take advantage of the river routes to the wild lands. But how did they obtain those vast forested tracts?

From the beginning, the State of New York was interested in selling its northern lands--in harnessing the wilderness and making it productive. Land was almost given away. In the eighteenth century, huge tracts were sold for small sums--three cents an acre for the million plus acres of Totten and Crossfield Purchase, eight cents an acre for the nearly four million acres of the Macomb Tract.

The State tried to give land in the northern Adirondacks to Revolutionary War veterans. In 1820, Duncan McMartin, Jr. surveyed the south part of Oxbow Patent and estimated that the timber on it made the land worth from $.10 to $.50 an acre. The State sold land at every opportunity and the price rose so gradually that by the 1870s, the State was still selling virgin timberland for about $.70 an acre.

For two decades after 1850, when logging in the Adirondacks focused on the Hudson River drainage, lumbermen acquired huge tracts in that watershed. Among the lumbermen who early on purchased timberland was one Lemon Thomson, who was born in 1822, read law in Albany, and started a lumber dealership there around 1855. His marriage to a banker's daughter apparently enabled him to buy considerable land in partnership with his father-in-law. Before his death in 1898, he had established himself as one of the more prominent lumbermen with a mill along the Hudson River north of Saratoga and tracts of timberland in the Hudson watershed as well as in the western Adirondacks. By 1867, L. Thomson and Co. expanded to include mills at Glens Falls, south of Fort Miller at a site later renamed Thomson, and Ottawa Canada.[52] Eventually the company expanded into the western Adirondacks as well.

Family connections in the Albany area had tremendous financial implications. A strong parallel exists between what was happening in the tannery industry's financial district, known as the Swamp, in New York City, where wealth and political power grew out of financing the expansion of the hemlock bark tanning industry and what was happening in Albany. Men with wealth and connections increased their financial and political base by acquiring mills and Adirondack timber tracts. Lemon's father-in-law was Augustus Sherman who owned several large tracts. Sherman, Thomson, and William Weed jointly owned several tracts, including part of what became Santanoni Preserve and land in Palmer's Purchase. William Weed's father, Thurlow, was perhaps the most powerful political figure in Albany, running the Republican Party or its predecessor the Whigs from the 1840s to the 1880s. William Weed became the State printer. John A. Dix, later New York State governor from 1911 to 1913, became Lemon Thomson's partner in the Thomson and Dix Lumber Company and the Moose River Lumber Company in the late 1880s and through the 1890s.

Lumbering interests were also clustered in the Glens Falls area where a local lumberman, J. W. Finch, bought most of Township 15, Totten and Crossfield, on the Indian River, so he could float logs to his mill. Jones Ordway and James Morgan, who later formed Morgan Lumber Company, the precursor of International Paper Company, owned large tracts, of which the best documented is Ordway's Township 34, which includes Blue Mountain Lake. The early concentration of lumbermen in the Glens Falls area included such names as McEchron, Sherman, Richards, Underwood, Tefft, and Russell. They built sawmills and bought tracts in the Adirondacks.

Gradually the land ownership concentrated into a fairly small group that included all of these men. Not only did they purchase land outright, but they acquired land at tax sales. The story of tax sales at the end of this chapter discusses how lumbermen themselves became delinquent in the payment of taxes, escalating the number of tax sales.

## How Much Spruce Was Logged and Shipped?

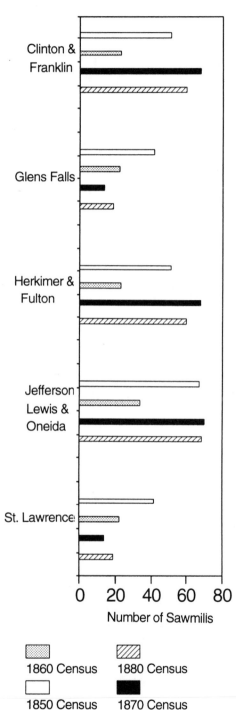

Number of sawmills by region,
1850 - 1880

Clinton &
Franklin

Glens Falls

Herkimer &
Fulton

Jefferson
Lewis &
Oneida

St. Lawrence

0   20   40   60   80
Number of Sawmills

1860 Census    1880 Census
1850 Census    1870 Census

Figure 16

Source: Census of Manufactures

Albany's location on the Hudson River at the tidewater end of the Erie and Champlain Canals allowed the city to grow into a principal East Coast port. Along a mile-long stretch of waterfront between the Erie Canal and the Hudson River developed one of the United State's two largest ports for the shipment of lumber (the other was Chicago). Over forty lumber firms and dealers had slips, built on land owned by the Van Rensselaers and rented from them at eighteen percent of the slips' construction cost per year. Underscoring rise of Albany's importance as a lumber market is the fact that the family earned $7,000 a year renting these slips in the 1830s, $80,000 a year in 1877. The port handled over 400 million board feet of lumber in 1871, employing 1,500 workers who received $600,000 in wages.[53]

The vast majority of the pine harvested in the north country in the first half of the century was sent via the Champlain Canal to Albany. By 1850, with the depletion of Adirondack sources, pine shipped to Albany was imported from Canada via the Champlain Canal and from Michigan via the Erie Canal.[54] New York imported eleven percent of the lumber shipped on the State's canals in 1840, but by 1850, the percentage of imported lumber rose to thirty-four percent, to forty-six percent in 1860, and to sixty percent in 1870. Additional timber was shipped on the State's railroads, but that, too, was mostly from outside the State. Lumbermen turned to out-of-state sources about the same time they turned to the Adirondack region, which, for all the logs cut, never came close to supplying the State's lumber needs.

Mills at Glens Falls began to saw coarser grades of lumber, spruce and hemlock when pine became unavailable, well before 1850. The emergence of Glens Falls as a lumbering center started slowly, however, for even by 1850, only 132,500 logs (mostly spruce) were sawn into lumber and shipped down river to Albany. This amount was not even twice the amount of pine sawn or shipped from Essex and Clinton counties in 1820 when that region was the chief producer of pine. It represented only a small fraction of what was shipped two decades later.

Glens Falls' region lumber constituted only 8.5 percent of the lumber sent to Albany dealers in 1850. While lumber sawn in Glens Falls increased dramatically in the next two decades, so did the amount of lumber arriving at Albany's dealers from other sources. The amount of lumber milled in Glens Falls rose to 21 percent of the total sent to Albany in 1870. At the peak of Glens Falls lumber production, around 1872, Hudson River lumber constituted 33 percent of that shipped to Albany from in-state sources.

The accompanying chart was produced from the United States Census of Manufactures in the years 1850, 1860, 1870, and 1880 and from Forest Commission figures for 1890 for all lumber operations in towns that are within or overlap the present Adirondack region. The increase in the production of spruce lumber over the second half of the century was dominated by Glens Falls area, which milled almost as much as the combined production of all the other Adirondack watersheds through 1870, when that region began to lose its preeminent position.

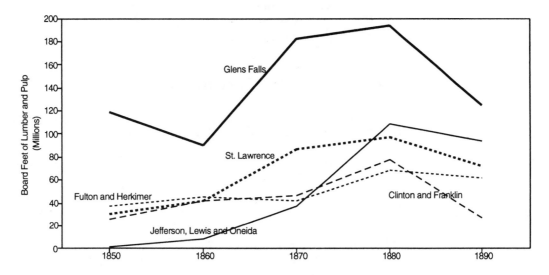

Lumber and Pulp production by region -- 1850 - 1890

Figure 17

The Adirondack timber harvest grew slowly between 1850 and 1860, then doubled by 1870. The 1880 harvest was triple that of 1860.[55] The accompanying charts, from which Jefferson County is omitted, show St. Lawrence County as contributing hardly enough to account for local growth in 1850; in fact, through 1870, St. Lawrence County produced very little lumber. Large scale milling did not commence there until 1880. The production from Franklin and Clinton counties grew slowly through the period. Lewis and Oneida counties' production paralleled this slow growth for the first three decades, but jumped significantly after 1880. Overall, however, spruce lumber production throughout the entire region increased through 1880, when it began to decline.

## Sawmills after Mid-century

Milling centers expanded in the same locations where the first sawmills had been built, at sites where waterpower and transportation to markets were available. Sawmills in the Black River Valley and the lower reaches of the Raquette River expanded into milling centers, but nowhere was the growth of milling so explosive as it was on the Hudson River near Glens Falls. This location had the benefit of canals and railroads to take lumber to markets in Albany and New York City. It also had the advantage of a vast network of waterways that funnelled from the heart of the mountain to Glens Falls via the river whose watershed is the largest in the Adirondacks (Map 5).

Although mills increased in capacity, they were just larger versions of the early gang mills. Mills added more gates at each source of water power as well as more gangs in each gate. The most notable change in milling technology was the introduction of circular saws, but these were employed only in connection with steam mills. Steam-powered mills were built only along streams that experienced shortages of waterpower. With the exception of the Black River, most Adirondack streams provided enough water that steam mills were not needed. Other than quantity, the only difference between the mills after 1850 and those before was that the later ones sawed mostly spruce, with a scattering of hemlock and pine.

# Dams and Navigation

The increasing volume of lumber production at downstream mills was only possible because of the highways created by the region's rivers.

Just before 1850, the importance of Adirondack rivers for floating logs to mills became obvious. After 1846, a second series of laws was passed declaring a number of rivers to be public highways. One of the first (1846) applied to the Saranac River, its two main branches and the connecting lakes and specified that those waterways were a public highway for "floating of timber, logs and lumber, and other proper public uses." All subsequent laws specified that the public highway was for "floating of logs and timber" only without mention of other purposes.

More important than the acts declaring the rivers to be public highways were those acts that permitted improvements. The improvements ranged from clearing channels (by dynamiting rock obstructions) to constructing dams, piers, and booms. The first river so designated was again the Hudson, whose upper reaches, including the Schroon and Sacandaga, were to have clear rafting channels. The act, similar to many later acts, appointed commissioners to carry out the improvements and specified the amounts the commissioners were to be paid. This act concluded that "The several tributaries of the Hudson river improved under this act shall be free and navigable for purposes of navigation, and rafting of logs and timber."[56]

The second river to be targeted for improvements was the Raquette[57]. New laws and appropriations in 1850 for clearing rafting channels and construction of booms, piers, and dams were applied to that river and its tributaries, specifically the river as far as the foot of Raquette Lake, Big and Little Tupper lakes and the Cold or Clear River. In this act as in all later legislation, dams were to be provided with aprons, thirty feet wide on the Raquette, "in the middle of the current of the river, of a proper slope, for the passage of logs and timber."[58] Further legislation in the 1850s concerned improvements for and regulation of the passage of logs. A series of acts starting in 1869 expanded the construction of dams for "navigation of the Racket River and of the hydraulic power thereon."[59]

The untapped virgin pine on the Bog River watershed beckoned around 1860 when four small dams were built between Winding River Falls and Bog River Falls, but there is no indication that spruce were taken then. The thousand-foot drop between Tupper Lake and Potsdam and the many rough rapids made driving logs from Tupper to Potsdam very difficult. The Raquette was not a river easily run for the big logs harvested before 1890, hence the need for more and larger dams. Despite the size of the St. Lawrence watershed, see Map 5, which included lands drained by the Raquette, its forest production was

## Laws Regulating

## Adirondack Rivers

1850 Racquette River to the foot of Raquette Lake.

1851 Moose River (both branches, but the south branch in Herkimer and Lewis counties only).

1851 Chateaugay River.

1851 Two branches of the Schroon.

1851 Minerva Creek and Trout Brook.

1853 Black and Beaver rivers.

1854 Salmon, Oswegatchie, and Grass rivers, West Canada Creek, and the lower West Branch of the St. Regis River.

1857 Grass and Great Chazy rivers.

1860 East and the remainder of the West Branch of the St. Regis rivers.

1865 The Branch, or West Branch of the Schroon.

1867 Deer River and two more tributaries of the Schroon, Mill and Trout brooks.

1869 The Sacandaga and all its branches.

1870 Platt Brook.

1872 Cold Brook and Otter Creek.

1878 The branches of the Oswegatchie.

Figure 18

considerably smaller than that of the forests of the Hudson River watershed.

The Saranac River was covered by legislation similar to that covering the Racket in 1851, as was Piseco Outlet. The Piseco Outlet dam was typical of the early headwater dams that could release large amounts of water to flood logs from downstream locations. Although logs were later floated from the Piseco area, at first the dam was used to control the flow on the West Branch of the Sacandaga.

The Black and Ausable rivers were slated for improvements in 1853. A tributary of the Saranac, the Salmon River and its tributaries, and Trout Brook (a tributary of the Schroon) were added in 1854. The 1854 legislation calling for improvements on the Grass River was expanded in later years to cover all of that rivers' three branches. Improvements on the Oswegatchie River were called for by 1854 legislation and expanded in 1865 to cover navigation on that river. The Beaver River was designated for improvements in 1864, the Great Chazy in 1868, and the Sacandaga in 1869.

The use of dams followed a tradition that lasted until the last river drive in 1950. Logs were often hauled to the banks of streams or rivers and piled on banking grounds or loaded on skidways so they could be quickly released. Flood dams were closed in late winter, just before snow melt, then opened to create a surge into which the logs were pushed. On smaller streams, flood dams were built in the fall and when the winter arrived, the gates were closed to hold water and snow. The logs were piled directly on the ice and when the spring thaws came, torrents of water, chunks of ice, and piles logs began the downstream journey.

In addition to authorizing the construction of larger dams, the improvements for rivers and streams ranged from building flood dams to straightening and clearing channels. Rock walls were constructed downstream from the site of many smaller dams to keep the logs within the confines of twisting streams. These walls are often more visible today than the remains of the flood dams. The convolutions of Adirondack streams were surmountable difficulties. Lumberman William McEchron said that the "crookedness of the river should not prevent successful driving;" and that he knows because he was the "owner of the Kunjermuk [sic] a stream that winds twenty miles in going a distance of five" where he had many successful drives.[60]

Locations of the larger dams are recorded on the 1885 Sargent Commission map, but records of the many smaller dams are harder to assemble. Flood dams, those not necessarily designed to launch logs, were smaller dams, whose flows were needed to insure that a larger stream below had sufficient water to carry logs. Most flood dams were placed across small side streams, freshets that dwindled to a trickle in summer. The dams created additional reservoirs and flooded at most a few acres--rarely as much as thirty or more acres. Sometimes the area behind the dams was a small, natural pond, which was enlarged to create the necessary water flow. Sometimes only open meadows formed behind the dams. Most often trees were cut from the area to be flooded. Unless logs were to be piled on the ice, a practice that became much more common later on in the western Adirondacks, the dams were not closed until the spring melt began and the flows from several freshets were released in sequence to create sufficient flow on the stream being driven.

Not all of the smaller dams were flood dams. Some of the streams dammed were so small and steep that it seems impossible they could have ever floated market logs, yet they did. Some, in fact, were so small that the flood of water they created was so slight it could move the harvested logs only a short distance. Hence, a series of dams was built and, sometimes, through the coordinated flooding of such a series, logs could make their way to the major rivers such as the Hudson, Schroon, and Sacandaga. On especially small streams, the flood waters had to be released in successive years, moving logs downstream in stages that might take several years.

Much of the information about which streams were used to float logs and which were used to supply water to other river drives is lost in history. What is known is that some very small streams were used tofloat logs because there is much evidence of river drives that took two or more seasons to complete.[61] To transport logs from the headwaters of the Hudson to Glens Falls required a drive of sixty to one hundred days. The Hudson's tributaries reached so far into the mountains that for years, the lumbermen planned drives of at least two years. It was a rare year when flow from the spring melt was sufficient to drive logs for more than sixty days. It was not until the 1920s and the floating of four-foot pulp logs that the drives regularly brought logs down in one year.

*Flood dam on Rock River*

These relatively benign dams did little more to change the forest than a family of beaver might do. These small logging dams were tucked in deep forest, far from public view. Today, more than a few such sites are regularly flooded by beaver, whose dams create the water to produce meadow and recovering forest in an ever-changing cycle. Logging dams did not destroy trees. McEchron and lumberman Erastus Darling both later claimed that water held about standing timber for a month in the spring does not injure it, especially if not held too long in warm weather after leaf-out.[62] Col. Fox agreed: "It is commonly believed that the lumbermen with their flooding dams are responsible for the killing of live timber and the destruction of the forest scenery. But, in nearly every instance, the dead timber in the flowed lands of the Adirondacks is the result of some dam or reservoir which was built in the interest of State canals, local steamboat lines, or the manufactories on the lower waters. The lumbermen had little or nothing to do with them."[63]

Typical of the many dams were those built on tributaries of the West Branch of the Sacandaga River before 1890. There were dams at Whitman Flow, Jockeybush Lake, and Clockmill Pond. Many of the flood dams were on tracts that were logged and sold to the State, or relinquished to the State for non-payment of taxes before 1892. Such dams were built at North Branch Reservoir and Jimmy Creek, and both these tributaries of the West Branch of the Sacandaga River have walls to deflect the logs into the channel. There were early flood dams on Silver Lake Outlet and Rock Lake Outlet in the same watershed, which also contained one of the most remote dams ever built--Hell Devil Dam on the headwaters of Nine Mile Creek. From it logs were brought down from the top of Three Ponds Mountain to the Sacandaga from this tiny body of water high on a mountain in the heart of the Silver Lake Wilderness. The impoundment's name undoubtedly reflects the horrors of construction in such inaccessible wilds. Logic would dictate that this tiny dam, a few feet high, less than twenty feet long, should have been a reservoir for other log drives, but the site once had a logging camp that actually sent spruce down to the West Branch of the Sacandaga.

River driving on the Moose River above its confluence with the Black began in the 1860s. Because the Black River has a comparatively small watershed, shipment of logs on its tributaries and production of lumber in its mills was always much smaller than that of the Hudson River. Gould Lumber Company built flood dams to sequence the flow from a series of small lakes in what is now the Ha-de-ron-dah Wilderness to drive logs to the Moose. Wooden sluiceways were built through rocky channels on Drunkards Creek, Pine Creek, and the Independence River. The lower Beaver River and other Black River tributaries were also highways for logs.

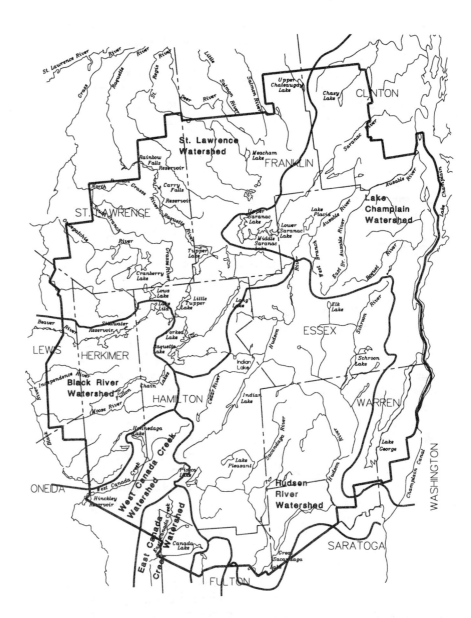

Map 5

ADIRONDACK
WATERSHEDS

Dams on the Beaver and the Black rivers were built for canal purposes and became a source of conflict with lumbermen. The Beaver River dam flooded timberland belonging to Mary Lyon Fisher in 1886, requiring the State to pay her damages.

There were rivers that were not used to float logs in this era because they had not been improved. The upper West Canada Creek above Nobleboro was not improved for the shipment of logs until after 1890. The headwaters of the East Canada Creek were not used for the shipment of logs, but only for power for mills in the lower reaches of the creek. These creeks had the smallest watersheds in the Park. Flood dams continued to be built into the twentieth century, upriver on the South Branch of the Moose and its tributaries, and in the High Peaks where one of the highest elevation dams was built at Lost Pond around 1912. These later dams saw the floating of much smaller logs than in the era from 1850 to 1890.

## The Big Dam Fiasco

In 1850 a small dam was built across the Raquette at Setting Pole Rapids, at the outlet of Raquette Pond, upstream from Piercefield Flow. The dam that creates the present enlarged Tupper Lake is at the same site. In 1870, in an effort to control the flow of logs through the river's rapids and falls, Potsdam lumbermen joined forces to erect a dam with a sufficiently large reservoir to provide water in summer and permit the floating of logs in spring. As part of the 1869 legislation authorizing the dam or dams on the river were two requirements. One specified that the consent of owners of two-thirds of the value of water power on the river had to agree to the construction. The other called for a survey and map to be made of the "river and the lakes and ponds connected therewith and the lands adjacent thereto which will be overflowed or liable to be overflowed." The fact that there were no surveys of the area (Verplanck Colvin was just beginning his Adirondack survey) figures largely in the problems created by the dam.

The dam constructed at Setting Pole Rapids as a result of this legislation was no small affair. It was much larger than any other dam constructed in this era to improve the transporting of logs. At 300 feet in length, it required 200 acres to supply enough large trees for the 12 by 14 inch hand-hewn square logs that created the dam. This was filled with 38,000 cubic feet of stone. All this construction was done by man and horse; no mechanized equipment was available.

The dam raised the level of Raquette Pond by ten feet and flooded the Raquette River for thirty miles upstream. The result was killed timber on the flood plain and shallows along a thirty-mile stretch of river, a very obvious scarring of the countryside.

This Raquette River Dam was highly visible and the flooding it caused attracted photographer Seneca Ray Stoddard. The trees above the dam were only partially harvested, leaving miles of twisted stumps. Everyone could see it and it became a cause célèbre--a rallying point for those who protested the evils of the loggers. While the dam was completed in 1871, laws of 1872, 1873, 1874, and 1877 repeatedly amended the act of 1869 to continue to require that the maps and surveys be completed within one year from their enactment. That no one had surveyed and predicted the extent of the flooding underscored dissatisfaction with the dam.

Flooding, however, was only one of the dam's problems. It gave way the year after it was built, and was repaired in 1872. It was gradually lowered and, in 1885, cut away to open farm meadows on the now-cleared flats. Finally, the dam was dynamited; the lowering of the dam was carried out by local people who protested the flooding. Land on which parts of the future Tupper Lake Village and the entire area around Faust, Tupper's lower village region, were built, was once under water. (The current dam was built in 1930.)

The dam had been built to bring export logs north to the St. Lawrence, but the river never carried a significant amount of logs, as the regional chart shows. Despite dissatisfaction with the dam, the improved river flow did spark enlarged lumbering operations downstream, operations that were sufficiently reckless with the river that legislation was needed in 1885 and 1886 to ban the "depositing of debris of saw-mills and other manufactures of wood" into the Raquette.

*Drowned lands near
Tupper Lake,
S. R. Stoddard*

    This dam and Stoddard's pictures of the flooded area were the rallying point for creation of the Forest Preserve. The dam helped move logs downstream for little more than a decade. Ultimately it became more important for the logging it halted than for the logs whose passage it aided.

    Many things changed after the watershed year of 1890, but not river driving. Although the practice gradually decreased, it continued for sixty more years; and the building of new flood dams for the shipment of logs continued for the first half of those years, particularly along the Moose River. The last drive on the Moose was in 1948, on the Hudson in 1950.

## Logging Camps

As quickly as log driving was accepted, a complementary method of logging was adopted. This method or protocol was well established by 1850 and remained basic to the region's logging practices until after World War II. Trucks and tractors may have supplemented the horses that were essential to early operations, but they did not completely supplant horses until the 1960s.

Logging camps were constructed in the wilds and their location and construction were according to a pattern that varied only with the size of the operation and the camp to be constructed. Even the size and number of workers was somewhat restricted by the limits of men and horses.

At first camps were restricted to tracts adjacent to navigable tributaries of the Hudson and the Black rivers. Within a mile or so from these streams, loggers felled the largest spruce and horses dragged chains of logs to the streambanks, where they were piled ready to be pushed into the spring runoff. After the trees closest to major streams were gone, some time before 1870, woodsmen headed deeper into the wilderness to set up remote camps.

Placing a logging camp was a skill that balanced the terrain and its watercourses with the size of the tract to be logged. A properly placed camp had to be near good drinking water and be capable of

*Hauling six sleds of logs*

Courtesy Adirondack Museum

serving as a base for at least three years, while at the same time every part of the cutting had to be within an hour's walk from the base.[64]

In the fall of the year, a small crew would build log shanties that would serve as bunkhouse, a cookhouse attached to a dining space, horse barns, a blacksmith shop, and a small office. Typically, a camp served forty men, though some were larger and more elaborate. (Later camps, those built after 1890, and in particular those built by Finch, Pruyn and Co. typically had camps that supported fifty to sixty men.) After finishing the roofs in spring, loggers moved in and began chopping the spruce in nearby stands.

After felling the trees, the spruce logs of the standard 13-foot length were cut from the lower trunks of the felled trees, the clear portions without side branches. Logs were sometimes peeled as they were cut to enhance their ability to float. The necessity to peel logs meant that logging occurred only when the trees were growing, that is in late spring or early summer, when the bark could be more easily prised from the logs. Starting by May 15 was ideal. Swampers cut the brush to create skid trails and horses then skidded the logs to skids, which are raised stacks of logs that permitted easy loading on sleds when winter arrived.

The loggers' work fell into four distinct types in four different seasons: After the season for cutting trees, late summer and early fall were devoted to constructing the main haul roads and landings. The roads were cut out and soft wood boughs were placed in the wet places. The haul roads generally followed stream beds along the levelest course that permitted a gradual descent.

*Building a skidway, circa 1893*
C. H. Rison, Forest Commission

*Courtesy Adirondack Museum*

Late fall and winter were the time to ice the roads, keep them in repair, and haul all the cut logs to streams for floating. Logs were hauled from the skids on the iced roads via sleds with eight-foot-long runners with ten-foot bunks (platforms). Depending on the terrain and the roads, several sleds could be chained together for the haul. Then the logs were carefully placed on the ice of rivers or small dammed ponds or positioned in stacks so they could be quickly dropped pushed into larger rivers.

Spring break-up of the ice marked the beginning of the final and most exciting season in the lumberman's life--the log drive itself. Where the current is swift, logs could travel thirty miles from a landing downstream to a boom in half a day. Large areas of flat water required that logs be rafted down. After the main drive was completed, the fly drive began, with men from the most distant landings heading downstream to clean stray logs from banks where they had been lodged by high water. The crews joined forces as they traveled downstream, stopping at downstream landing camps on the way. "As soon as the men reach the main boom at the mill with the fly drive, they are paid off. After taking a few days to enjoy themselves and spend their money they start back for the cutting and peeling, which by that time will have just started. Thus the men go back to start a new year's work which is divided into four parts as a year into seasons."[65]

The only variation in this description in the decades from 1850 to 1890 occurred in the first two decades of that period. Then, most logs were skidded individually or pulled in chains to the shores of rivers and streams. Spruce was so plentiful and accessible that haul roads and sleds were not needed. They became more prevalent as the loggers went back a second time--to harvest the logs that were more scattered or more remote from waterways.

*Logger and his horse*

Courtesy Adirondack Museum

The one thing that stands out in all this time was the fact that the logger used only an axe to cut trees. He had peaveys for moving trees, but the logger with his horse did all the work with brute force and no mechanical aids. And, throughout this period, only the largest logs were harvested, those above ten or twelve inches in diameter. This was the era of sawlogs, lumber for building.

Throughout this period, some of the hemlock, which was cut for bark for tannin, was harvested and floated to mills; but most outlying stands of hemlock were ignored until after 1890, when they began to replace dwindling spruce supplies. As the logger ventured farther and farther into remote regions, new stands of pine became accessible, and pine was harvested. However, sawlog spruce remained the prime object of the logger's work.

## The Big Boom

Every downstream mill had an area where logs could be stored after the spring drive. Sometimes a backwater created a mill pond that could be isolated from the main flow, sometimes a boom--a chain of logs strung together like a huge necklace--held the logs for future sawing. The number of mills in the Glens Falls area and the fact that the Hudson River was the highway over which most of the logs were shipped created a huge problem even before 1850. Use of the Hudson was so important that the Hudson River Boom Association was formed in 1849 to build the Big Boom at Glens Falls. The association was a cooperative of regional lumbermen that not only regulated but carried out the floating and sorting of all logs that were sent down the Hudson and its tributaries. Each of the millions of logs that arrived at Glens Falls was stamped on the end with a mark identifying the company for which it was destined.

Because the logs floated to Glens Falls were long (13' 4") and cumbersome, they often created jams that had to be broken up, making river driving so dangerous, it created heroes of the drivers and an aura of romance about their exploits.

*River driving on the Hudson*

*Courtesy Adirondack Museum*

Market logs received at the Big Boom -- 1850 to 1890

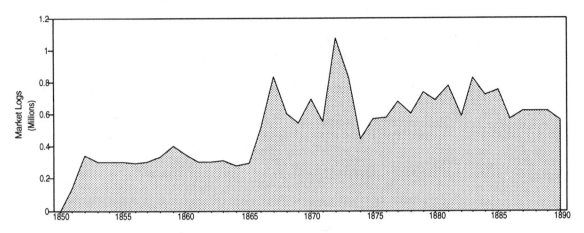

Figure 19

Records of the Boom Association show how Hudson River driving increased until 1872. The fact that both the increase and the decline in logs arriving at Glens Falls were not constant year to year is due to the changes in water levels. Tremendous variations from year to year meant that a large number of logs needed to be stored near each mill to provide a constant supply. The graph showing two-year averages smooths out the shipment levels.

One huge boom was constructed above Glens Falls to catch the logs and sort them. A series of smaller booms adjacent to downstream mills at Glens Falls, Sandy Hill, and Fort Edward facilitated the sorting of logs whose numbers grew to over a million markets in 1872. The awesome task of sorting that many logs was accomplished more easily than might be imagined.

> Below the large boom the river is boomed or divided, parallel with the current, into several different channels, each leading to a different mill or dock. The logs are taken past the first boom singly, and floating platforms are so constructed that the workmen can stand upon them and sort the logs directing them in any course they choose. For instance, all logs that are to go to Glens Falls are floated down the center channel, while those that go to the mills in the vicinity of the feeder dam are floated down the side channels to their respective mills. At the village of Glens Falls there is another boom, and the logs are again separated, those to go to Sandy Hill going down the center, as before. The same process is repeated at Sandy Hill and Fort Edward, until all the logs reach the respective mills of their owners.[66]

An agreement in 1862 described how the logs should be driven from Rist's Landing on the Hudson and from the outlet of Schroon Lake to the Big Boom, which was strung across the river between the Towns of Queensbury and Moreau. It called for sharing the expense of the drive in proportion to the number of logs and the distance they traveled. Payments were specified for all logs "put in the river, creeks, on the ice or banks to be rolled in in the usual manner."[67] Different scales of payment were attached to logs coming from different places: those that floated past the Indian Lake and Newcomb dams; those that came from North Creek, Mill or Factory Creek, and different points on the Sacandaga River such as above the mouth of Lake Pleasant Branch and from the Oxbow Tract below Piseco Dam; those coming from Stony Creek; those from the Schroon; and those from Trout Brook, Black Brook and the West Branch of Sturdevant Mill Creek.

Logs on each of these groups of streams were charged different proportions of the rates for two years depending on how many logs might require that long to reach the boom. Each company paid a fraction of the total cost per log the first-year the log was on the river, the rest the second year. The more remote the source of the log, the smaller the first year payment.

The streams mentioned indicate how even as early as 1862, logging was contemplated for most of the headwater regions of the Hudson; flood dams on all the Hudson's major tributaries were constructed beginning in 1862 (and the last was built in 1920).

## Glens Falls Lumbering

Fluctuations in the river level not only disrupted the shipment of logs, they subjected Glens Falls' waterpowered mills to periods of inactivity. "To rely upon the rain fall for keeping the river up to a sawing level has been found like 'building a house upon the sands.'"[68] Glens Falls' lumbermen could band together to harness the river as a highway, but the region looked to the State in 1877 to see that the Hudson's waters were evenly distributed throughout the year. In calling for protection for its watery lifeline, the lumbermen looked to the northern wilds to become a "great reservoir furnishing amply and with regularity the waters for mills"[69] and ship canals. They pointed to dams built on the Indian as a small-scale step in balancing nature.

MAJOR LUMBER MILLS ALONG THE HUDSON -- 1877

| Location | Firm | Number of Canal Boats | Number of Standard Logs Sawn Annually |
|---|---|---|---|
| At the Feeder Dam | Rugge, Sherman & Co. | 12 | est 100,000 |
| | Van Duesen & Freeman | 7 | est 100,000 |
| Glens Falls | Finch, Pruyn & Co. 2 mills | 15 | 200,000 |
| | Morgan Lumber Co. 4 mills | 15 | 150,000 |
| Sandy Hill | Richards & Green | 13 | 45,000 |
| | Kenyon & Baldwin | | 50,000 |
| | Eber Richards | | 125,000 |
| | Richards & Monty | * | 45,000 |
| Fort Edward | Bradley & Underwood | * | 75,000 |
| | Henry Tefft | * | 30,000 |
| | John A. Russell & Son | * | 50,000 |

Figure 20

* No canal boats listed. Fort Edward was located on the main line of the D & H Railroad, so canal boats may not have been as important. Some of the canal boats listed for Morgan Lumber Co. and Finch, Pruyn and Co. may also have been used to transport lime, whose production was fueled by the waste lumber from the mills.

The headwaters of the Hudson produced just as much flow as earlier--the amount of spruce and softwoods taken from the region did not alter the forest's ability to retain water. The lumbermen just wanted the river to give more water, more evenly, than was natural.

In 1877, there were eleven major lumber mills along the Hudson just below the Big Boom (figure 20).[70]

The history of Morgan Lumber Company is discussed in connection with its role in the formation of the conglomerate International Paper Company in the appendix. Reorganized in 1873 with six principals, all major lumbermen or lumber dealers, Morgan had four mills for sawing hemlock, spruce, and pine. The company kept two years supply of logs in bays adjacent to its mills along the Hudson River. Logs were transported from company lands from as far away as 75 miles, 100 miles by river.

Morgan's four mills had a total of 250 saws, including one mulay saw,[71] the only one of its kind in use at Glens Falls. A planing mill operated constantly to plane the lumber sawn at the four mills. The company also had two lumber yards in Albany.

## River Driving in the Western Adirondacks

The West Canada region was controlled by Gardner Hinckley 2nd and Theodore P. Ballou of Utica, who formed a partnership in 1848 to build a gang saw mill and a waterpowered planing mill at the dam site on the West Canada Creek. Originally called Gang Mills, the site was later renamed Hinckley. For half a century, the Hinckley Mill operated with largest capital investment of any mill in the western Adirondacks (see appendix).

River driving on the Black River began in 1859, although logging along some of its tributaries had begun as early as 1850 when Henry Wager bought 28,000 acres in Moose River Township 1 and began driving on Woodhull Creek. Lumber dams as well as flood control dams were built on many streams that fed into the Black; among the earliest of the lumber dams was one built by Anson Blake on Woodhull Creek at Chub Lake.[72] By 1867 there were eight or nine mills in the Forestport area, two on Bear Creek, three on Big Woodhull Creek, and two on Little Woodhull Creek. The dam at Forestport was constructed to allow diversion of Black River water to the Erie Canal and should have aided the region's lumber mills. However, all the water from the Forestport dam was needed by industries on the Black.

Lumbering in the Black River watershed differed from that in the Hudson River watershed in three different ways. The configuration of rivers, canals, and rails in the western Adirondack region determined a linear development along the Black, which contrasted with the Hudson River's focus on Glens Falls. The Black River Canal reached from Rome to High Falls (Lyons Falls) by 1855 and the railroad north from the Mohawk River opened as far as Lowville in 1867. With both the railroad and the canal in the Black River Valley, lumbering operations were built at many points along the entire length of river where there was thought to be sufficient waterpower. Particularly desirable sites were found near the confluence of the numerous creeks and rivers flowing into the Black. Instead of the clustering of mills that developed Glens Falls, mills on the Black River were strung out throughout the entire valley.

River driving on the Black differed from the Hudson in that parts of the river were so sluggish that booms had to be pulled across it so that winds would not blow the logs back upriver[73] Steam boats could carry the river drivers upriver to their jobs. Logs often got caught under the Black's numerous dams and were as difficult to dislodge as the Hudson's jams.

Sorting booms were located near the confluence of the Black and its many tributaries and along the Black, where traditionally crews sorted the long logs all night long. By 1890, the top drivers on the Black River were earning $2.50 a day for a work day that lasted from five a. m. to eight p. m.

The third and most important difference between the two regions can be traced to the fact that the Black River never did provide a constant supply of waterpower. A series of dams on the river and its tributaries, including the dams at North and South lakes, Big Woodhull Lake, and Stillwater Reservoir, were designed to control floods and provide water during the dry summer months. The ill-fated dam at North Lake gave way only two years after its construction, destroying three mills downstream on the Black River.

The Black River Canal was plagued from the start with low water levels. Lumbermen along the river's corridor were the first to use steam boilers to replace the river's unpredictable waterpower. The Erie Canal also suffered shortages of water, and even with the whole system of northern reservoirs and diversions, it was obvious from the beginning that having sufficient water would always plague the western waterways. Note especially that the water problems occurred well before the region drained by the river's eastern tributaries had been extensively logged. In 1888, the State Engineer and Surveyor reported:

> Most conclusively, that, from forty to fifty years ago, when the forests of the Adirondack Region were in their primitive state, they were much less reliable, as a source of water supply, than they have been during the past few years. ... The Hudson, Mohawk and Black with their numerous tributaries are the only ones that may be regarded as naturally available for purposes of increased water supply for the State canals, and ... the water of the Black River should not be regarded as naturally available in as much as their natural flow is into the St. Lawrence ... and the State has already diverted a large portion of these waters to the Erie Canal.[74]

The water shortage on the Black River proved to be a constant source of conflict between lumbermen and canal interests[75] "There still (1888) exists a great lack of water supply during the dry season along the valley of the Black River. ... Difficulties in policing discharges from the impoundments on the headwaters of the Black and its tributaries mean that lumbermen constantly used water surreptitiously "for the purpose of floating logs downstream."[76]

Among the other early mills on the Black was one run by the Shedd family whose gang mills date back to 1848 and James Merwin of Port Leyden who was the lumber tycoon in Port Leyden in the 1860s.

Gordias H. P. Gould, whose lumber and paper companies are chronicled in the appendix, began logging and river driving on the

Moose River and Pine and Otter creeks on land he obtained from the estate of Lyman R. Lyon. By 1879, Gould was driving some fourteen million board feet of spruce logs from those tributaries of the Black, eight million of them destined for his mill at Lyons Falls at the confluence of the Black and the Moose.[77]

There were numerous mills downstream at sites which later became pulp mills, as discussed in later chapters. Among them was Theodore B. Basselin of Croghan, an early lumber giant who also built and ran boats on the Black River Canal. Under contract to the State, Basselin built the State dam on the Beaver at Stillwater in 1886.[78] Taggarts Lumber Company was also located down river on the Black River.

## Logging for Lumber Wanes

By 1880, when the Glens Falls lumber production began to decline, so did that of Jefferson, Lewis, and Oneida counties; but the combined total of those three counties was only a little more than half that of Glens Falls district throughout. Lumber production from Herkimer and Fulton, the counties just north of the Mohawk, peaked around 1880 also, then fell dramatically. The amount of lumber produced in Franklin and Clinton counties was comparable to that of the Fulton and Herkimer, with the exception that production levels continued to rise slightly after 1880 in the north. Only St. Lawrence County, which produced almost insignificant levels of lumber through 1870, showed a real increase in the late 1870s.

The calculated levels of production are yet another confirmation of forest types depicted on the Sargent Commission map. The headwaters of the Hudson River were depicted as mostly the light, grey green, and they had been logged for softwoods only. The headwaters of the other rivers were largely dark green--the untapped lands. Much of this was in waters drained by the tributaries of the Black and rivers that flowed into the St. Lawrence. For all the logging in the western Adirondacks, logging had barely reached the Stillwater region upstream on the Beaver by 1893. Hence, logging history corroborates the 1885 Forest Commission report that the great northern forest contained nearly two million acres of virgin timber and 1.3 million acres from which only softwoods had been removed.

# After Most of the Sawlogs Were Taken

As production of sawlogs started to decline in the eastern Adirondacks, forest depletion sparked a peculiar phenomenon in the pattern of land ownership. In the decades just before 1870, most of the political entities of the Park were established--the county and town lines were drawn almost as they remain today. Taxes ranged from $.10 to $.30 an acre, amounts that did not seem particularly onerous to those who lived on and worked the land, who derived a yearly income from it, and who were residents of the towns. Local governments began to support roads and schools; they levied taxes on all landowners. Residents could work off the road taxes, which represented a significant part of local taxes. The lumbermen who harvested the spruce were almost all non-residents--in fact, most lived in Glens Falls, or Plattsburgh, or towns along the Black River. Their crops came but once in twenty years, a period that was long enough that to many it seemed foolish to pay taxes where there was no income, hence much land was abandoned for taxes. This did two things: the lumberman could obtain land others had abandoned and the land abandoned by the non-resident landowner-lumberman did not earn tax revenues for the local governments.

Several aspects of the tax situation have great import for the forest, so it seems appropriate here to back up and examine tax policies.

## Tax Sales: the Process

In 1808, the legislature enacted a law (Chapter 179) directing each county board of supervisors to levy property taxes and to send lists of delinquent taxes to the State Comptroller. The law also required the comptroller to sell all or part of the property of delinquent non-residents (anyone not residing in the town in question) to recover the amount of the tax plus interest. In effect the buyer obtained a tax lien on the property, which entitled him to obtain a deed for the property two years after the sale unless the property was redeemed during that time by the original owner, who only had to pay the back taxes and interest to do so.

From the beginning there were many problems for the potential buyer. Descriptions of the land on which taxes had not been paid were often inadequate and subsequent legislation tried to address this problem. Squatters could pay the back taxes and claim non-residents' land. The buyer bore the responsibility of notifying any squatters of their rights to redeem the land. (A law of 1820 required two such notices.) These problems made it difficult to obtain land through tax sales.

In 1850, the legislature (Chapter 298) transferred the function of selling and conveying land for unpaid taxes to the county treasurers. This function was returned to the comptroller in 1855 by a law (Chapter 427) that also abolished a portion of the requirement for notification of squatters.

Also in 1850, the legislature tried to guarantee the rights of tax sale purchasers (chapter 183) by declaring that the comptroller's deed was "presumptive evidence that the sale, and all proceedings prior thereto ... were regular." However, numerous court decisions continued to make tax sales vulnerable and practically unmarketable.

The most momentous aspect of the 1855 law was that it also permitted the State to "bid in" and purchase at comptroller's tax sales lots that were not sold to private individuals. From then on, the comptroller bid in on all unclaimed lands in Adirondack counties in the tax sale years of 1857, 1866, 1871, 1877, and 1881.

The process of bidding in was a peculiar one--the bids consisted of offers of the amount of land that the bidder would accept upon payment of the delinquent taxes. Hence the person who offered to take the smallest amount of the parcel was the winner.

As William H. Sanger of the comptroller's office explained at a legislative hearing in 1891, "The custom that usually prevailed at our tax sales is that when a bidder announced himself as an owner of land, it is a matter of courtesy not to run his land down, but to allow him to bid it in for the whole amount for which the land is offered for sale."[79] Often lumbermen could make arrangements with delinquent owners, to pay them and acquire the land.

Lands advertised for tax sales could be redeemed if the owner could demonstrate payment of taxes, occupancy of the land, or errors in the assessment or notification of tax sales. To do so the owner had to obtain a "letter patent" from the Land Office Commission (commonly called the Land Board), certifying his ownership of the land. The landowner had to prove ownership through deed and had to show that back taxes had indeed been paid.

Sanger said it was "State policy to encourage individuals to bid for tax sale land. ... No effort was made by the State to obtain this title to land through tax sales except to protect itself in the payment of taxes."[80] It seems that the comptroller had been forced to advance counties monies for delinquent non-resident taxes and then offer the land for sale. The State was buyer of last resort.

What is so striking about the years 1870 to 1890 is how much land was abandoned for back taxes. Up through 1890, more than half a million acres were abandoned and never claimed by anyone, forcing the State to pay taxes on them. The next chapter describes how the State protected that land, even before it was designated as Forest Preserve. By 1890 the availability of so much tax sale land had declined so much that lumbermen began bidding on almost all tax sale lands (in 1890, lumbermen bid in on a total of 390,000 acres.)

However, before 1890, it was the policy of the comptroller to get rid of land, which the State did not want, according to Col. Fox. "Anything like a fair showing in the matter of redemption or cancellation" and the State gave up the land. "The Land Office encouraged people to take back the land and pay taxes; the State's policy was to get all the money they could and collect taxes and not hold the land."[81]

So common were these tax sales over the decades that by 1900, with the exception of two townships, all of the land in the Adirondacks had been sold at some time for taxes.[82] This meant that in the years before 1890, lumbermen could obtain woodlands very cheaply, but also could and did lumber their tracts and then cease paying taxes on them. There was a lot of untouched forest to the north and no lumberman wanted to keep, care for, and bear the expense of taxes on land from which the accessible merchantable spruce had been removed. This situation promoted the practice of cutting and abandoning land, which gave obvious advantages to the lumbermen in the form of almost State-subsidized timberlands. Such benefits were great, but not nearly as great as those later reaped by a few who used clever but somewhat devious means to claim and log State land.

## The Effect of Logging on the Forest Before 1890

Nothing in the heart of the Adirondacks had been clearcut; in fact most tracts had not been cut at all. Because only spruce, hemlock and pine were logged, as late as 1885 no more than fifteen to thirty percent of the forest cover had been taken from little more than a third of the original Park. Less than that--virtually none at all--had been removed from the other half of what was considered then as the great northern forest. This uncut area was as large as a third of the present six million acre Park. The rest of the 25 million cords of spruce harvested before 1890[83] came from the white areas of the Sargent Commission map, the lands that were also stripped of hemlock for bark and hardwoods for charcoal as well as general forest cover for farms. Hence, during the entire forty-year period, each of the four million acres gave up only six cords of spruce and hemlock, a low enough amount to confirm the lumberman's minor impact.

Given that so much land really was uncut or cut only for spruce, it is unfortunate for future preservation efforts that such a relatively small amount of it became a part of the Forest Preserve in the next few decades. In fact, the rapacious harvesting of some of these lands will emerge as the hallmark of logging after 1890. The lands were not simply virgin or lightly logged, they were covered with the lowland forests that had the most spruce--they wore dark green mantle that cloaked the northwestern third of the Park.

On the other hand, even though the logger did take the larger spruce from the central and southern and parts of the southwestern region of the Park, he harvested only selectively throughout that forest. This was the bright green area of hardwoods where spruce was scarce. Here the logger sought out the pockets of spruce and built short tracks to them. Most often, these pockets were found along the rivers and streams so the logger merely felled the spruce within the valleys and moved on, never logging more than a few miles from waterways. Most of the early logging was done within a mile, rarely as far as six miles from them. The logger rarely bothered with the isolated giants--the spruce that could seed a future forest--they were too few and too far apart. It was not simply the presence of the marvelous river highway provided by the Hudson's waters that drew the logger farther and farther north to its headwaters. It was the fact that those headwaters had more spruce. On the other hand, it was not absence of good navigable water that kept the logger interested so briefly in the central and southwestern forests; it was the fact that there was not enough spruce to justify logging there. The logger would have needed roads or tracks for horses to reach the isolated pockets of spruce, and these were expensive to build. (This pattern of areas that were heavily logged and those that were not will be further delineated in later chapters where the reasons for that pattern are examined in the context of political events.)

Legislators struggled to understand what had happened to the forest that had been cut before 1890. Hearing after hearing in the next decade would elicit information confirming the ability of the forest to retain water and slowly release water even though the spruce had been removed. The remaining trees continued to provide a closed canopy protected from the drying rays of the sun. The State Engineer and Surveyor observed in 1884 that "The removal of this small percent of merchantable timber from the forests [ten percent] can produce no material effect either upon the rainfall, or the retention of snow upon, or moisture in the ground."[84]

Remarkably little had been done to the integrity of the forest, even to its ability to reproduce spruce. Just as the logging era was ending in the late 1880s, lumbermen were able to return to the areas from which spruce had first been removed--to the Hudson watershed lands they had abandoned for taxes during the previous two decades. More than a few possessed significant stands of spruce that had been judged too difficult to reach at an earlier time. Col. Fox testified that as late as 1890 there remained 45,000 acres of virgin timber in Minerva and other nearby towns in the Hudson headwater area.[85] Other tracts had been so lightly logged that they were ready to yield spruce sawlogs again, only by this time the lumberman no longer owned them or the virgin stands. Now he had to resort to stealing from State lands or move north to untapped tracts in the search for sawlogs. Alternatively, he could challenge the State's ownership of tax sale lands or he could get involved in the burgeoning paper industry and harvest ever smaller logs from whatever spruce lands he still owned.

Analyzing the way lumbermen harvested spruce and other conifers may absolve them of any charges of rapacious harvesting in the years before 1890, but it did not entirely clear their character, however. A fair number, or their agents, did resort to stealing timber from State land, which further tarnished their reputations. The public came to associate the misdeeds of that group with the perception of real forest destruction wreaked by charcoal makers and farmers. The perceived threats of increased harvesting due to encroaching railroads and pulpwood logging only fueled the erroneous view that the lumberman was a destructive force in the forest, one that had to be dealt with.

## Lumber Barons at the End of the Logging Era

Shifting ownership patterns concentrated ownership of almost all of the land in the Adirondacks into the hands of just a few people. The accompanying map details those holdings. The largest single landowner was William West Durant, either in his own name or through companies he controlled. His holdings accrued when he fell heir to the century's biggest land bonanza, by way of his family's railroad interests.

The 1848 law incorporating the Sackets Harbor and Saratoga Railroad allowed the owners, led by Dr. Thomas C. Durant, to purchase up to 250,000 acres in Hamilton and Herkimer counties for five cents an acre. Sales of these lands, whose value would increase with the coming of the railroad, were to generate the capital needed to build the railroad. These rights were liberalized by laws of 1850, 1862, and 1863, which also permitted the formation of the Adirondack

Company, still under the control of Dr. Durant, to complete the railroad, now named the Lake Ontario and Hudson River Railroad. Further, legislation allowed the company's lands to be increased to a million acres at the same low option price and it gave all of the lands an exemption from taxes until the year 1883.

Dr. Durant's railroad was completed from Saratoga as far as North Creek by 1870; and that year the line's terminus was shifted north to Ogdensburg rather than west to Sackets Harbor. In 1872, the company claimed ownership of 540,000 acres with options on another 100,000 acres.[86] In 1887, Dr. Durant's son, William West Durant, claimed the company owned over 650,000 acres in seven counties.[87] Papers recently uncovered prove that he or companies he controlled did, in fact, own over 670,000 acres, areas indicated on the accompanying map. Not all of it was acquired through the railroad options, however, for the Adirondack Company was an active bidder in tax sales throughout the 1870s and early 1880s and it appears that it acquired as much as 250,000 acres by this means.

Whatever the actual size of the Adirondack Company's lands, it is clear that they comprised almost a third of the virgin timber in the Adirondacks in the years just prior to the creation of the Forest Preserve, more land than the State was able to place in the Forest Preserve at its creation 1885.

Map 6
PROPERTIES OWNED
WHOLLY OR IN PART BY
WILLIAM WEST DURANT
CIRCA 1887

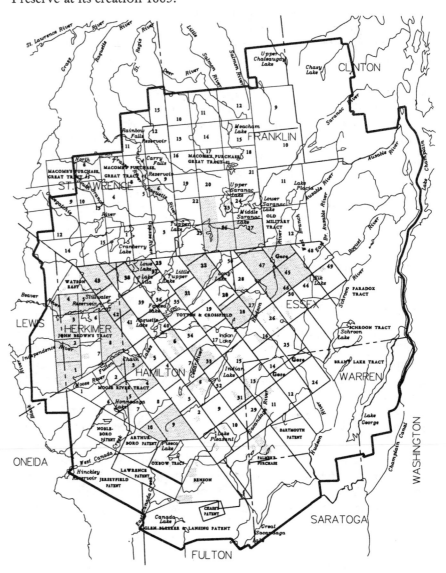

The State claimed most of Township 40 Totten & Crossfield for taxes in 1871 and after, and would not permit private individuals to bid on the land at the tax sale of 1877. (How it did this with Durant's exemption is not clear.) Courts later sanctioned the State's ownership of the bulk of the tract, but not that of much of the shores of Raquette Lake, which is surrounded by the tract.

That the bulk of Adirondack Company's land was exempt from taxes could only have put additional pressures on Adirondack towns and counties at a time when so much of the accessible land was being abandoned by its owners for non-payment of taxes. How much pressure this put on the State to reacquire tax-delinquent lands is subject to speculation. The fact that most of the lands were in areas that were still wilderness may have minimized the impact.

The Adirondack Company still held 317,318 acres in 1891[88]. Together with the 55,347 acres owned by Durant himself and the 19,435 acres of Township 40, over 390,000 acres can still be traced back to the Adirondack Company at that time. Much of this land was sold in the 1890s, some to men like Dr. William Seward Webb to create large estates and some to the State. Some additional 48,000 acres were sold to the Adirondack Timber and Mineral Company, of which 35,000 acres was later sold to Santa Clara Lumber Company.

In 1890, at the end of the era of the lumbermen, only a few giants of the industry controlled the bulk of the region's virgin tracts as well as much of those that had been logged only lightly for softwoods. Lumber companies or the men associated with them held most of the timber tracts. Finch, Pruyn and Company owned 135,137 acres.[89] Morgan Lumber Company had 69,213 acres. That company later became part of International Paper Company. Other companies or individuals held large tracts that later became part International Paper Company. They included McEchron, Moynehan, and Underwood, who together owned 18,000 acres; Underwood and Marsh with 17,555 acres; Palmer Falls Paper and Pulp Company with 19,720 acres; and Patrick Moynehan with 4,000 acres. Underwood was part owner in another 7,500 acres that may also have become part of International Paper Company. Patrick Moynehan later lumbered Whitney Park and sold land that became the part of two private parks: Santanoni and Huntington Preserve. William McEchron had been a lumberman based in Glens Falls from 1852 on, with lumber (later pulp) mills at Glens Falls, Norwood in St. Lawrence County, and Three Rivers in Quebec.

The Anson Blake Estate owned 77,406 acres, which that lumberman had amassed in the western Adirondacks--much of this would shortly become part of the Adirondack League Club.

Several Tracts had already been claimed for private clubs: Adirondack Mountain Reserve, 23,000 acres; the Adirondack Forest Preserve Association (North Woods Club) 4,583 acres; Wilmurt Lake Club, 1,800 acres; Morehouse Lake Club, 1,600 acres; Mountain Home Club, 350 acres; Kildare Club, 3,213; Upper Saranac Lake Association, 6,770 acres; Hamilton Park Company, 23,981 acres, which with S. A. Whitney's 5,067 acres became the nucleus of Whitney Park; and G. A. Brandreth's park, 24,192 acres.

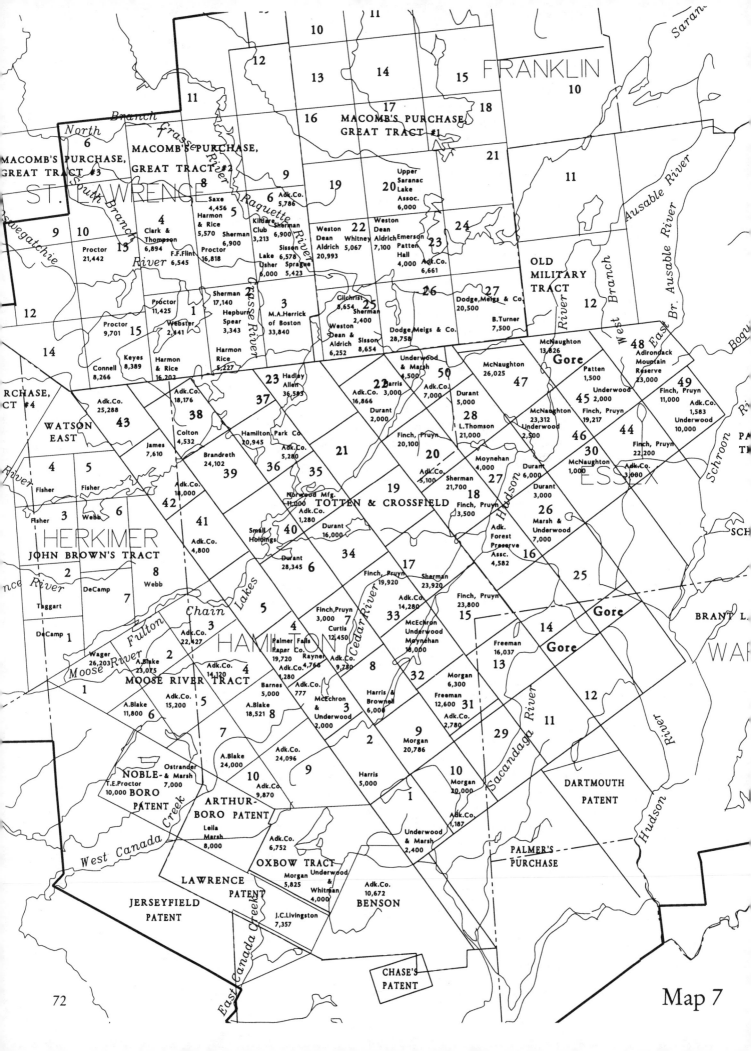

Map 7

The two-pronged impact of such private holdings on the forest, discussed in the next chapter, increased dramatically after 1890. Lumber interests would be replaced by private preserves as the owners of many large tracts. Owners of private preserves would attempt to manage the timber on their holdings in ways few lumbermen did.

James MacNaughton controlled 66,165 acres which had been part of the MacIntyre Iron Company, under an arrangement that permitted the tract to be leased to the Tahawus Club. Much of this land or its stumpage was later sold to Finch, Pruyn and Company

Other lumbermen controlled large blocks of land which were within the Blue Line of the proposed Park. By 1883, Lemon Thomson had acquired 21,000 acres, most of Township 28 that later became Huntington Preserve. H. L. & D. W. Sherman owned 45,620 acres; Norwood Manufacturing Company, 17,412 acres; Henry Barnes, 5,000; Haron & Rice, 31,176; A. Sherman Lumber Company, 27,580; Weston, Dean & Aldrich, 34,287; Benton Turner, 7,500; George W. Sisson, 15,232; and M. A. Herrick, 33,840 acres. Thomas E. Proctor, a magnate in the tannery industry owned 69,387 acres of timberland, which was incorporated in 1893 into the United States Leather Company, of which Proctor was the first president.

The complex web of two interconnecting circles of men and lumber companies ties many of these landowners together and to land speculators, who were just becoming a force in the region. The speculators owned much of the remaining timberland: George N. Ostrander and Lelia Marsh, the widow of his partner, P. J. Marsh, owned 17,400 acres; William Harris owned 8,000; and Henry Patton, a lumberman based in Albany, owned 21,836 acres. In the next two decades, as the next chapter shows, these speculators would spark the escalating rise in the cost of land and impede the State's land preservation. It is truly amazing how the vultures appeared on the scene well before the State began to acquire land. Their unscrupulous claims on land abandoned for taxes would open up huge tracts, much of it owned by the State, to a second harvest of spruce.

G. H. P. Gould, Theodore B. Basselin, Santa Clara Lumber Company and others controlled large tracts outside the proposed Blue Line in the western part of the Adirondacks as well as tracts within the Park boundary. The next chapter will examine their relationships to the land speculators.

Scattered throughout the proposed Park and outside the Blue Line were numerous small parcels, but in 1890, the non-resident holders of large tracts were already in control of most of the Park's timber resources.

Map 7, opposite page

OWNERSHIP OF LARGE
TRACTS OF PRIVATE LAND
CIRCA 1890

## A New King is Crowned

Logging and the lumber industry had enabled the Adirondack population to grow to a peak that was not reached again for almost a hundred years. Thirty thousand workers were employed in the region's lumber industry in 1890,[90] but this figure would shortly decline.

Franklin B. Hough, statistician of forestry who is introduced in chapter VII, noted the decline in forest production throughout the northeast in the 1870s and he worried that all of the country's virgin forests would similarly disappear. The decline in production in the

Adirondacks in the 1880s was quite real and the supply of accessible sawlogs was almost gone by the end of the 1880s. But the forest was not gone. The king--merchantable spruce in large dimension, sawlog form--had been deposed. Its puny sibling, the small diameter, four-foot spruce log to be ground for pulp was about to take the throne. Crowning pulpwood king, however, would require inconceivably large investments.

Certainly the number of logs floated down the major rivers before 1890 is staggering and the amount of lumber sawn made many individuals rich. The men who owned the mills and land and made fortunes from them were well-placed to invest in the machines that mark the next era of Adirondack forest harvest. And, while taking spruce, hemlock and pine sawlogs from the forest left it little changed, further logging and the harvest of pulp led to fundamental changes in the Adirondack forest.

# VI

# The Revolution circa 1892

The conjunction of events that occurred around 1892 marks a revolution in the history of the Adirondack forest. The events break into two sequences, both of which culminated around the year 1892. The political events that lead to the preservation of parts of the Adirondack forest make up one sequence of events. Its milestones are the State's early acquisition of land, the problems of clearing title to State land and of limiting trespass on it, the establishment of the Forest Preserve, the 1892 creation of the Adirondack Park, the Amendment--Article XIV[1]--that gave constitutional protection to the Forest Preserve, and the State program to purchase land for the Forest Preserve. This sequence began accidentally around 1870, and the fact that it began at all was to have a profound effect on the State's attempts to protect its northern forest.

The second sequence deals with the revolution in the forest industry. Five major elements of that revolution became critically important to the future of the forest on both public and private lands around 1892. The first railroad to penetrate and traverse the Adirondack wilderness was completed and was soon followed by others, which were built to permit logging over much wider areas. The use of wood in the production of pulp and paper meant that smaller dimension softwoods began to be harvested. Loggers returned to land from which spruce sawlogs had been removed to take virtually all the remaining spruce, including all the mature trees capable producing seeds as well as all the pulp logs as small as five or six inches in diameter. Factories designed to mill hardwoods were built as rail transportation was developed to take their products to markets. Large private preserves were established, and this combined with the increase in size of the Forest Preserve, caused the price of timberland to rise. Although most technological advances in timber harvest occurred later, the introduction of the crosscut saw in 1891 marked the beginning of significant changes in the way logging affected the forest.

The two sequences of events are intricately intertwined. The increasing loss of forest cover fueled the preservation movement, while at the same time the growing shortage of timberland encouraged lumbermen to try and thwart that movement. As a result, loggers were cutting more and more timber from smaller and smaller tracts of forest at the same time the State was acquiring more and more land to preserve.

The greatest harvest, measured in the number of trees cut by lumbermen occurred in the decades between 1890 and 1910. The view that greeted the traveler along the railroad corridors and major stage routes after 1890 was often one of devastation, but not always. While there was little or no forest remaining along the Keene-Keene Valley road, the region to the south owned by the State was dense wilderness.

Legislative Milestones

1872 Law creating the Commission of State Parks.

1873 Report of the Commissioner of State Parks, calling for the protection of the forest from "wanton destruction."

1876 Law prohibiting the sale of Lake George shores and islands.

1883 Appropriation to provide funds to clear titles to lands on which the State was paying taxes.

1884 Creation of a Commission to investigate forest preservation, headed by Charles S. Sargent.

1885 Report of the Sargent Commission on the health of forest lands with recommendations to acquire additional Adirondack land and to pass laws regulating public land by establishing a forest preserve and by fixing punishment for its destruction.

1885 Creation of a Forest Commission and establishment of the Forest Preserve in which the State lands in eleven Adirondack counties "...*shall be forever kept as wild forest lands. They shall not be sold, nor shall they be leased or taken by any person or corporation, public or private.*"

1892 Establishment of the Adirondack Park and its Blue Line boundary, within which State land purchases would be concentrated.

1894 Final passage of the constitutional amendment Article 7, Section 7 (later called Article XIV) *"The lands of the State, now owned or hereafter acquired, constituting the forest preserve as now fixed by law, shall be forever kept as wild forest lands. They shall not be leased, sold or exchanged, or be taken by any corporation, public or private, nor shall the timber thereon be sold, removed or destroyed."*

Figure 21

In 1891 a traveler reported that from "Cedar River to Blue Mountain Lake the road runs for ten miles through an unbroken forest, which, to the unpracticed eye, shows no diminution of primeval beauty. Though the lumbermen cut off years ago the merchantable spruce and pine, they took so few trees to the acre that little trace remains of their operations, especially as the smaller evergreens that were left are fast taking the place of those which were cut."[2]

By 1910, the problems that had plagued the State's efforts to protect its forest had largely been solved, while the lumberman had to face the prospect that the forest available to harvest had almost disappeared. A million and a half acres had been protected, almost half of which was heavily forested in 1890. By 1910, much of the lumber industry had moved west out of New York and the pulp and paper industry had to import logs to supplement what could be harvested in the Adirondacks. The traveler in 1910 would be pleased with the forest views, but the lumberman would not.

The complexity of tracing the two disparate sequences works against intertwining their descriptions, but separating them minimizes their synergism. For clarity, they will be separated, with political events dealt with first. This makes sense given the simplicity of the chain of developments affecting the forest products industry. The changes brought about in the period from 1890 to 1910 were so great that they resulted in a widespread harvest of such intensity that the supply of spruce, the merchantable timber, was exhausted. Anticipating this result makes political events of the era all the more dramatic.

# The Preservation of the Adirondack Forest

## The State Begins to Reacquire Land

"The area of the Forest Preserve consisted of scattered tracts, and the acquisition of these tracts was governed by accident instead of design."[3] Thus, the Forest Preserve Board in its first report in 1898 recognized the serendipitous beginnings of the State's reacquisition of Adirondack land. The Forest Preserve was not formally established by the legislature until 1885, but its birth was a decade and a half earlier. Given that the acquisition of those lands by the State was an accident, it was certainly a fortuitous one.

Although the legislature did not designate State lands in the Adirondacks as Forest Preserve until 1885 or vote funds to purchase Adirondack lands until 1890[4], the State began actively reacquiring land there in 1871. What happened in the twenty years between 1870 and 1890 is not merely the story of the origins of the Forest Preserve, it is an explanation of why the State was able to preserve so much valuable forest land--tracts that today resemble the great forest of an earlier time.

By 1870 the period of selling land to tame and develop the wilderness was drawing to a close. The legislation and constitutional amendments that underlie protection of our forests were enacted between 1885 to 1895, but the protection of land that began more than a decade earlier occurred independently of preservation efforts. The political history of the Park is well known.[5] This chapter explores the effects of the political acts on the forest, and it is more concerned with the untold account of the State's early and accidental protection of

Adirondack forests. It also focuses on the men who influenced that protection, for good or ill, rather than the preservation milestones and their origins.

Legislative acts and the impassioned pleas of such men as Franklin B. Hough, Charles S. Sargent, and Verplanck Colvin fail to account for the reasons why the amount of land in the public domain grew from 17,000 to well over 500,000 acres in the fifteen years after 1870. Tax sales explain the increase of State lands, but it is necessary to examine the underlying reasons why there were so many tax sales and why the State was able to acquire so much land as a result of these sales.

In 1871, when the State began paying taxes to local government on those tracts lumbermen had abandoned, the State discovered that it could not sell a great many of them because no one wanted them. As permitted by law, the State began claiming ownership of those tracts through tax titles. Such claiming of land for the State occurred a year before Verplanck Colvin called for the establishment of an Adirondack Park (1872), two years before the First (and only) Report of the Commission of State Parks. That commission merely recommended that "the wild lands now owned and held by the State be retained until"[6] the question of creating an Adirondack Park should be settled, but that recommendation was not acted upon at that time. Franklin B. Hough, the principal author of the 1873 report, later assigned the failure of the State to implement the commission's recommendations to the fact that the exhaustion of forests seemed too remote to take action,[7] and in reality that remoteness was real. The failure also stemmed from the fact that the commission undercut its own arguments by commenting that "the wild lands of this region are, intrinsically, of very little value."[8] However strong the arguments, nothing was done by the legislature for ten years, until the enactment of the 1883 law forbidding further sale of State-owned lands. By then, the State owned a significant and growing amount of unwanted land.

The report of the Commission of State Parks summed up the actions of lumbermen by stating that: Forest lands "are generally purchased, held and valued solely for the timber growing on them. As soon as the pine, spruce and hemlock trees have been taken off, the lands are often abandoned and revert to the State for unpaid taxes. The common and wasteful method among lumbermen, therefore, is to cut all the available timber from a given section once. This enables them to escape further taxes on that piece by abandoning and throwing back the same upon the State."[9] Taxes ranged from four to fifteen cents per acre per year and, for land that was worth less than $1.50 an acre, taxes could easily double the cost of the land long before it could be logged a second time.

Because much of the land in the southern and eastern Adirondacks accessible to the Hudson River and its tributaries had been logged for softwoods before 1870, it was considered worthless. (By today's standards, these forests were far from worthless.) Lumbermen had not only harvested all the large spruce that could be reached easily, they were discovering richer and more accessible virgin stands elsewhere. Lumbermen also stopped paying taxes on many unlogged tracts because their forests possessed such a small amount of spruce that logging operations were not justified.

The practice of defaulting on taxes was so severe and became so entrenched that a lumberman could acquire land from the State for back taxes, cut the merchantable timber on it, and abandon it by never paying taxes on it. This essentially amounted to a policy by which the State subsidized the lumbermen.

Economic upheavals, particularly the depression of 1873, which made money tight, explain in part the extraordinary amount of land on which taxes were defaulted. It could also have been the dictates of the marketplace that so much land was considered worthless, inducing the owners to stop paying taxes on it. Or it may have been simply that the logger saw unlimited opportunities elsewhere--and the more quickly he abandoned those that had been cut, the more quickly he could begin to cut elsewhere. It made no business sense to hold unproductive land for several decades and pay taxes on it.

In addition, the growth of Adirondack towns may have inadvertently caused so much land to become available for tax sale. The towns, in their pursuit of non-resident landowners as a source of tax revenues, may have unwittingly forced the State to claim the land by increasing local taxes beyond the ability of the land to produce revenue. The fledgling Adirondack towns had increased taxes through the Civil War years of the 1860s, voting bounties and expenses, with, according to Lemon Thomson, deleterious results for the lumbermen.

> I know of one town which is located within what is proposed as the Adirondack Park, which voted a tax for a single year of thirty-three percent on its whole valuation and that was not a small valuation. I knew of a large tract of non-resident land in that town which was valued on the assessment-roll for double the highest price that it ever had, or could be sold for. ... Whenever there was a call made for more troops the people came forward in all this region, and voted the most liberal bounties. They were willing that the bounty-jumper should be most richly paid if he would only put down the rebellion. They were willing to pour out their money like water, especially as the owners of non-resident lands had the most of it to pay. Even those who were drafted to fill up the army, but paid their money instead of serving upon the tented field, had their money refunded to them, and the amount made a tax upon the town. Some of these towns, with but few inhabitants, have an easy way to raise large sums of money--they assess the non-resident lands, return them to the State comptroller's office and get their money.[10]

Lemon Thomson was a lumberman and one of the most articulate spokesmen against proposals for establishing a forest preserve. He based his complaints about taxes on personal experiences as a non-resident owner of large tracts of Adirondack timberland.

> Not unfrequently the lands of non-residents are put on the assessment rolls at excessive valuation. I have known the valuation raised, where the lands were entirely unproductive and unchanged, three hundred percent in a single year. I know of towns in this region where the inhabitants have gone on and settled the most desirable lands, cleared and improved them, built houses and barns, factories and villages, and when the assessors came to make their valuation for the purpose of taxation, the mountains and deserts of the non-resident lands were valued more per acre than the inhabited and improved parts of the town. ... This tax [road-district tax] amounts usually to

three percent annually on the whole valuation. The residents can satisfy their tax by working on the highway, or paying a dollar for each day's work; but when returned to the comptroller's office the non-resident has to pay one dollar and fifty cents for each day's work assessed. All the taxes against non-resident lands, including town, county and State, road districts and school district taxes, are returned annually to the comptroller's office and the State treasurer is drawn on for the amount. The comptroller adds ten percent annual interest, and charges for advertising and sale. The charges frequently amount to more than the original taxes. ... I have known a good many cases of ambitious, active, energetic men, doing a good business and desiring to secure timbered land for future use, who have bought up large townships and tracts of non-resident lands; but the taxes were allowed to so increase and multiply that the profits of a good business would not pay these taxes, and such men have been compelled to succumb, give up their business, and go to the wall and allow their lands to be sold for taxes against them.[11]

The comptroller advanced money for delinquent taxes to the counties, then offered those lands for sale. If not redeemed within two years, "indefeasible title" to the land passed to the new owner, that is whoever claimed it by paying back taxes and interest. In many cases the State, which paid the taxes if no one else claimed it, became the new owner. These tax titles did not have the strength of underlying deeds; challenges to the State's titles and efforts to make them truly indefeasible became a major theme in the State's early acquisition of land. This problem is discussed later in the chapter.

The State was only required to "bid in" at tax sales when there were no other bidders and it was State policy to encourage individuals to bid for tax sale lands. It was the custom at tax sales that "when a bidder announced himself as an owner of land, it is a matter of courtesy not to run his land down [award the land to the bidder who would accept the smallest acreage for the payment of back taxes], but to allow him to bid it in for the whole amount for which the land is offered for sale. ... No effort was made for the State to obtain this title to land thru tax sales, except so far as to protect itself in the payment of taxes."[12] This strange policy meant that if the State had to pay taxes on delinquent land it did, reluctantly, but when it did, it claimed the land and continued to pay taxes on it to the local communities and, further, defended its ownership of the land.

The State simply could not sell the land fast enough throughout the 1870s and early 1880s. The taxes were so high no one wanted the land from which the mature spruce had been removed. Lumbermen testifying in 1884 before the Sargent Commission noted that land sold to individuals by the State was quickly reassessed by the towns for more than what the State had sold it.[13] It heard evidence that non-residents paid more taxes than residents. The State was urged to establish a policy of lowering the taxes on land while the timber was regrowing, thus encouraging "the care of the land, to make foresters of all [the lumbermen]."[14]

For these reasons, the State acquired much land in the tax sale years, 1871, 1877, and 1881. The 1877 sale, which alone added more than half of the lands acquired by the State in tax sales before 1885, was also as large as it was because of the diligence of the comptroller, who "went back for forty years, and took up the taxes rejected by his predecessors, and added them with their ten percent yearly interest to the non-resident lands."[15] These lands, especially those acquired before 1885, will be shown to constitute the largest core of old growth forest not only in the northeast but in the eastern United States.

There was no legislation mandating that the branches of government preserve this land, but the State, as will be shown, adopted many policies that enhanced its claim to those lands. Perhaps men like Hough and Colvin were able to influence government agencies, but that too makes it an accident that this is how forest preservation in New York began.

It is even possible that the unplanned aspect of the State's suddenly owning so much land may have made it easier for those like Colvin, who were calling for the preservation of the forests. Perhaps the legislature finally awoke to the bonanza created by the lands, for which the State was able to claim title because of unpaid taxes. If this awakening occurred then, it may have prompted the 1883 appropriation to clear title to those lands where ownership was split or disputed.

No matter whether these speculations are proved or not, it is certain that if, in the decade in which the State was acquiring these initial tax lands, the period before sales of State lands were prohibited and before the establishment of the Forest Preserve, the State had not received the bonanza, we would have had to wait a lot longer before we could celebrate the majestic nature of so much of today's Forest Preserve. Advances in the forest industry in the next few decades would have made such a thing impossible for many more years. The changes in harvesting timber that were in place by 1892 made the rapid depletion of the remaining merchantable spruce stands inevitable. Further, the changes were so great that if the State had not acquired so much land before the end of the century, the rising cost of land, explored at the end of this chapter, would have made it impossible to do later on.

## Tax Sales

All of the land, except a small percentage obtained by mortgage default, which the State acquired in the two decades between 1871 and 1890, was acquired through tax sales.[16] To determine how much land was acquired this way is not an easy task, for State records for the different intervals are contradictory. Some of the acreage on which the State paid taxes in one year was later reclaimed or challenged, so it disappears from following years' accountings. Until this century, the State had only a vague idea of how much land it held at any given time. The 1873 Commission of State Parks estimated that the State held nearly 40,000 acres, more than 17,000 acres earlier assumed. The Sargent Commission report believed that the State had 750,000 acres in 1884. The Forest Commission in 1885 tallied over 800,000 acres of State land in the Adirondacks, while one modern report gives 680,000 acres as the amount of land that was designated as Forest Preserve in 1885.[17]

Reported figures for tax sales that make up the above totals are questionable because it was not known how much tax sale land was

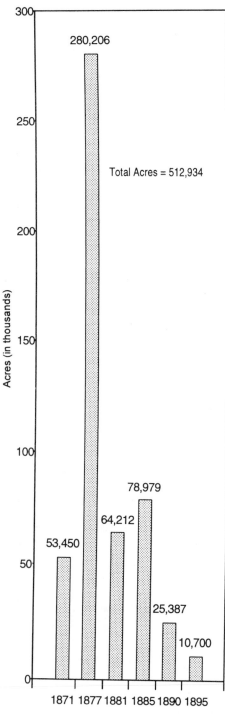

Land acquired through tax sales and held continuously by the State

Total Acres = 512,934

Acres (in thousands)

Years of tax sales

Figure 22

Source: See text

later redeemed. Figures quoted for a given year vary greatly depending on whether or not redemptions are included. Some land was reclaimed by individuals who retained it, but this amount, too, is not known and is assumed to be quite small because it is made up of mostly small, inhabited plots. However, ownership of a considerable amount of land claimed by the State or acquired by the State through tax sales was later challenged because of flaws in the tax titles. In addition, many of the larger tracts that were redeemed by lumbermen were for the most part abandoned again for taxes, and the State bid on them a second time, usually after 1883 when by law they could no longer be sold to individuals. The abandoning for taxes of recently purchased or redeemed land immediately after it had been cut over was such a widespread abuse that it figured prominently in calls for the establishment of a forest preserve.

When individuals challenged the State's claim to land that the State had bid in, the State was often forced to purchase the underlying titles to that land in order to defend its tax titles. To make sense of the conflicting information, the author compiled acquisition data by working backwards from the *List of Lands in the Forest Preserve,* published in 1920.[18] By taking out of the tax sale totals any acreage that was later redeemed and reacquired by the State, it was possible to establish the amount of acreage that had been continuously owned by the State. That analysis not only reveals what happened in the half century between 1870 and 1920, but it confirms the continuous ownership of half a million acres acquired before 1885.

The amount of land the State thought it owned and later had to purchase totalled 172,246 acres. (This figure includes the tax sale acreage shown in figure 23 plus nearly 17,000 acres that State obtained at tax sales between 1843 and 1867.) Because that reacquisition occurred after 1890, when the cost of land was rising sharply, the State often found it could purchase the disputed claims by allowing them to be logged again, thus reducing their value to something the State could afford. In order to clear title to this land, the State had to agree to timber reservations that permitted the removal of merchantable timber of a certain minimum dimension within a specified period of time after transfer to the State. It will be shown later, however, that even some of this land was not logged within that time, so, in fact, was never logged.

In addition, the State owned 23,562 acres in 1871, which was never again sold. This included 14,372 acres of original lands, exclusive of water, always owned by the State; 4,054 acres of mortgage foreclosures, and 5,136 acres acquired in the tax sale years of 1853 and 1866 that was never resold. Adding the total to the 610,950 acres acquired by the State through tax sales in the years 1871 through 1885 yields 634,512 acres, the size of the Forest Preserve when it was established in 1885. That land falls into three categories: land that had been cut over for softwoods and abandoned; land that was so far from river navigation or so lacking in spruce that it was not worth harvesting; or tracts that the State acquired through tax sales, where titles were imperfect, so they were later purchased by the State.

Deducting the amount of land that was later repurchased from that held by the State in 1885 gives 500,409 acres as the total of uncontested public lands at the creation of the Forest Preserve. This half million acres put in the Forest Preserve in 1885 was never cut again, except where it was subject to trespass (the significance of the

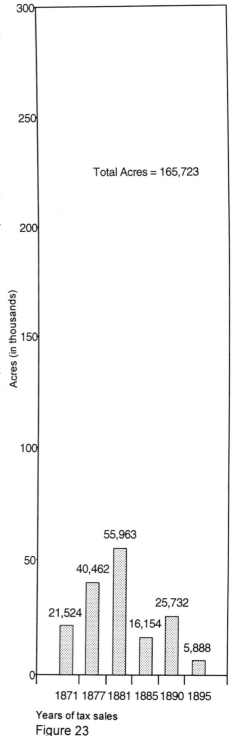

Land acquired through tax sales and later repurchased by the State

Total Acres = 165,723

Acres (in thousands)

21,524   40,462   55,963   16,154   25,732   5,888

1871 1877 1881 1885 1890 1895

Years of tax sales

Figure 23

theft by trespass is analyzed later) or where harvest of dead and downed trees was permitted after the 1950 blowdown.

Adding to the 1885 Forest Preserve acreage the known virgin tracts acquired in the two decades, specifically the Webb lands, yields over 560,000 acres, a good deal of which was never logged again. These tracts are the nucleus of today's great forest.

Included in the 1877 tax sales were parts of the present-day McKenzie Mountain and Sentinel Range wilderness areas, land south and east of Ampersand, and a tract in the High Peaks on and to the west of Mounts Street and Nye, which Colvin described as wilderness "covered with dense forest."[19] Parcels far from the Hudson River on the slopes of Vanderwhacker, and the northern parts of the Hoffman Notch Wilderness also became State land at this time. Except for the Totten and Crossfield Townships 5 and 40, the remaining tracts were scattered about the southern and western Adirondacks. Few were in the heavily logged eastern Hudson River corridor where most of the settlements were. Many were, as would be expected, in the more remote southern parts of the Hudson River watershed, in the western reaches of the Sacandaga River watershed, and in the northern drainage of the East and West Canada creeks. The headwater areas of those two creeks were still "relatively little cut" as late as 1899.[20]

Many parcels were in the cores of tracts far from navigable streams. The interior of Nobleboro Patent in southern Herkimer County was far from both the Black River and the West Canada Creek. The interior of the Benson Tract, which had been spottily logged for softwoods, was almost totally abandoned for taxes by 1885. Parts of southwestern Hamilton County distant from the West Canada Creek were likewise abandoned; this included land in Lawrence Patent that Colvin described as "covered with superb timber"[21] in 1883. It also included part of the no-man's land south and southwest of Piseco in remote corners of the East Canada Creek watershed. Tracts west of Indian Lake and far from the Jessup became State land at this time, including valuable spruce lands near Lewey Lake and the Blue Ridge. These were part of Hamilton County where Colvin noted "the State owns vast tracts of forest, more, in fact, than in any other county. Within the limits of this county are upwards of 1,000,000 acres of dense woods, much of it primeval wilderness, and of this area the State now owns 252,072 acres, This land is so wild and inaccessible as to be secure from the plunderers."[22] Colvin was particularly concerned with State-owned lots in Palmer's Purchase in southern Hamilton County where the land was covered with valuable timber. He observed that such lands, nearest the settlements or logging operations, were the most subject to theft. In order to protect them, he focused his surveying work and boundary marking on these lots, which were not far from Warren and Saratoga counties.

Colvin described the beauty of some of the tracts the State had acquired in tax sales, but was concerned that "few have any idea of the actual value of the State's possession or the exact location of State lands." He noted especially some northern tracts that did not become part of the Forest Preserve at that time: "the whole region between Duane in Franklin County and the hills toward Cranberry Lake in St. Lawrence County (with the exception of the vast marshes which extend over an area of thousands of acres from Mt. Azure toward St. Regis) is covered with one vast forest of valuable timber."[23] A dense forest of majestic white pine extended eastward from the Upper St. Regis Lake. State-owned lands in the northern Adirondacks were also covered with dense forests, in places like the high mountains to the south of Lake Placid and the valuable spruce and cedar on the slopes east of Marcy. He saw much valuable pine timber on State lands in Township 18 of Great Tract No. 1 of Macomb's Purchase. In St. Lawrence County, in the places where there had been little if any plundering of timber on State lands he found "unusually large and thrifty spruce."[24]

Colvin's knowledgeable observations and the reports of State agents were the basis for the Sargent Commission Map drawn in 1884, on which the dark green truly represented the uncut portions of the Forest Preserve. The map was indeed a fair representation of the Great Forest. The future Forest Commission continued to use the map, unchanged, through the next decade during which the boundaries of the Adirondack Park were drawn. Even though the forest was altered in that decade, the changes affected primarily the private land and not those owned by the State.

## Managing Tax Sale Land

Until 1883, State acquisitions and sales of land in the Adirondacks were handled by the Land Office. Although the State bid in on unclaimed tracts, it was really interested in selling land until that date. Before 1884, Land Office records consist of manuscript ledgers with notes of transactions, most of which are sales to individuals, where much of land had been acquired in the earlier tax sales. Some are applications for "letters patent" for tracts of Adirondack land, that is exclusive rights to property on which the State had paid taxes in sales of 1853 and 1861.[25] (Those who bought or recovered such tax sale land were said to obtain letters patent to reflect the fact that the State held tax title to those lands, not the underlying title.) The earliest records deal with lots in Oxbow and Benson tracts, where letters patent were given or lots were sold to lumberman Theodore Ballou, and other individuals. In 1866, the State sold land in Benson Tract to Ballou for $.70 an acre and land east of Wells in 1867 to William P. McEchron and another lumberman, for the same price. The Land Office refused to sell land at less than that price, but did accept partial payment for some large tracts with the rest guaranteed by bond, though cash payment was required for most lots. J. and J. Rogers Company obtained lots in the north country for payment of back taxes. A good proportion of the land that was bid in by the State in 1853 through 1861 was sold again in the years 1866 to 1883. (Only a few lots totalling just over 5,000 acres remained in State hands.)

Among the more unusual stories to emerge from Land Office records also concerns lumberman Lemon Thomson. His dealings not only illustrate practices of the day, they help pinpoint when land to the northwest of Vanderwhacker Mountain was logged. Most of that land was bid in for taxes by the State in the 1877 sale, presumably shortly after its spruce had been harvested. Thomson's application to acquire one nearby lot in 1871 had been rejected by the State, indicating he was just beginning logging in the area at that time. He reapplied for the one lot in 1877, after the timber on it had been cut.[26] The Land Office noted that the "property belongs to the State and the lumber has been cut. Thomson wants title to land to protect him in ownership of the timber. This is at least unusual, ordinarily the timber is stolen." The lot was assessed at $130 in 1875. Thomson paid $160 in back taxes, which "covers interest, etc. due the State and yields $.50 [an acre] in addition."[27] Even though he paid for the timber, Thomson was certainly cutting and running, for not only did he pay no taxes on the adjacent land, which the State obtained in 1877, but he did not pay further taxes on this 160-acre lot, which the State obtained in the tax sale of 1885.

This one entry not only illustrates that the tract was logged between 1871 and 1877, it also implies that although the Land Office was selling land with timber on it for $.70 an acre, individuals were willing to pay $1.00 an acre. Even the State had to pay about $1.00 an acre to bid on land for back taxes in 1880.[28] Assessments and the value of land were beginning to rise!

Thomson also obtained a large tract northwest of Harrisburg in western Warren County in 1871, land which the State reacquired for back taxes in 1890. The Adirondack Lumber Company was actively buying land southeast of Vanderwhacker in 1871. That year McEchron, Morgan, Underwood, and Ordway (future incorporators of International Paper Company) were obtaining tax sale land in Oxbow Patent.

Such information confirms the dates when logging reached land accessible to various tributaries of the Hudson such as the Boreas and the West Branch of the Sacandaga, and it also documents how many other lumbermen took advantage of the practice of cutting and running. Ironically, in an address before the Albany Institute in 1884, Thomson castigated the State for encouraging this practice.[29]

That the State could not sell so much land after the 1877 and 1881 tax sales is perplexing. Lumbermen were bidding only on the most desirable tracts. But all this would change rapidly. Later studies indicate that a forest from which only mature spruce had been removed would double the volume of standing spruce in twenty years or so.[30] The land logged in the early 1870s was ready to be harvested again by 1890, but by then the State, not the lumberman, owned it.

## Protecting Tax Sale Land

What was even more fortuitous for the Forest Preserve than the State's policy of acquiring land by bidding in at tax sales was the way the State proceeded to protect it. After the tax sale of 1881, the comptroller's office hired agents from Adirondack counties to assist the office in tax sales.[31] They were hired with funds from a legislative appropriation of several thousand dollars annually. Agents had to check parcels of land to determine if there were actually residents living on them--often there were--and serve those residents with notice of tax sale. Without the notice, residents could overturn tax sales as many frequently did.

Agents were also given the task of assessing land, with the assumption that the State might still sell it. One, George Leavitt of Chestertown, was very conservative in his appraisals. He judged land to be more valuable if it had any potential for farming. Timberland, no matter how much spruce was on it, was thought to be valuable only if it was close to navigable streams, so much good timberland was appraised at only $1.50 an acre because it was difficult to harvest. One lot, the Tefft Tract, notable for its virgin stand of spruce and hemlock, was judged to be worth only $1.25 an acre because it was not accessible to the upper branch of the East Canada Creek; in fact the "timber is not really accessible to any market yet."[32] He noted that a tract just to the north, which was covered with good spruce, was possibly more valuable because of the proposed railroad that might go south of Piseco. He appraised a few tracts at $2.00 or $2.50 an acre and was admonished by the comptroller to keep his findings secret. Leavitt wrote the comptroller that "I mind what you say in regard to divulging appraisal on lands to parties" who may purchase the land.[33]

However, the most important task assigned to the agents was to discover and pursue the perpetrators of trespasses (stealing of timber) on State land. Trespass was also occurring quite frequently on private land,[34] and it was becoming a source of conflict between Adirondackers and the owners of newly-established private preserves. Natives, who had been able to use the forest as they wished, both for timber and for game, were reluctant to change their ways. Trespass on State land, especially on the earliest logged tracts adjacent to the Hudson River, became extremely serious. Natives and local residents stole timber, but the many of the largest thefts in that region were accomplished with the knowledge of non-resident lumbermen.

It is significant that the State began investigating trespasses as early as 1881, and equally significant that with the exception of several accessible areas there were few thefts throughout the Adirondacks before 1884. Leavitt noted that one trespass in Benson, lot 220 quite close to the Sacandaga River, was a "bare faced steal." He had caught Stephen Griffin 2nd in a trespass on Totten and Crossfield Township 14 that occurred during the years 1877-1880. Leavitt wrote the comptroller that Griffin "has promised to pay about fifty times the stipulated price of the land. I have been dunning and teasing Griffing [*sic*] to pay a certain sum which he always promises to pay in a month or two."[35] He did pay up and in 1884 Griffin himself became an agent for the State. His tenure lasted only a year and during that time he found most instances of trespass were "mistakes," although he nevertheless prosecuted a share of the trespasses he investigated.

A major problem in dealing with timber thefts was the fact that the boundaries of State land were poorly marked or not marked at all. Verplanck Colvin's survey was supposed to correct the old and obliterated lines, but his testimony on problems in Jerseyfield Patent shows that more than surveys were needed: "When a man desires to get timber from State lands he will send some one ahead to cut every blazed tree on the lines, then cut them up and remove them to some distance, and so remove all evidence of lines. After this is done he will send men to cut logs on some piece near State land, telling them to cut only to the blazed trees, but there are none."[36]

Hundreds of letters to the comptroller give overwhelming proof that many of the early agents, unlike Griffin, were serious about their roles as protectors of State land. For instance Leavitt became involved in a possible trespass by one R. B. Poole of Stratford on virgin spruce lots, some of which have never been logged to this day. Leavitt and Surveyor John B. Koetteritz managed to protect most of those lots.

Koetteritz, a German immigrant who trained as a civil engineer and surveyor, came to the Dolgeville area to work for Alfred Dolge, owner of a piano factory and large tracts of land (see Jerseyfield in the appendix) that supplied the wood for the pianos.[37] In 1882, Koetteritz became an agent for the Comptroller.[38] His letters to the comptroller not only describe the problems he and other agents faced, they show how dedicated most agents were in protecting State land.

In 1883, Koetteritz found many trespasses in the area east of Oregon, a mill site on the East Canada Creek just south of the Hamilton County line. He wrote the comptroller that "I have hired one man for a few days to get more information as I could obtain, being too well known." With a Mr. Bronk of Lasselsville, he

made a raid on both sides of the East Canada Creek [where] at present there are three sounding board factories, Dolgeville, Devereaux [Stratford], and Oregon, which buy for high price all of the fiddlestuff [the first log cut from the choicest spruce trees]. $25-30 per 1000 feet is a strong inducement to every man in that poor country and this without regard to private or State property they steal wherever they can find such lumber, leaving the rest of the trees in the woods, taking only the lowest 13 feet.

We will see how the woods in this section have been spoiled. The sudden rise in the price of the above mentioned lumber from $15-18 per thousand caused even the inhabitants of far off counties to immigrate for the season to get out some fiddlestuff.

There is no part of the great woods where so much timber is stolen as on the SW border from the West Canada Creek to the Canada Lakes in Fulton Co.

During the last spring and summer I was able to keep off the thieves entirely by making weekly or semi-weekly rounds over my territory but since snow they commence to steal on every lot.[39]

An agent's lot was not an easy one, as Koetteritz described in his letter of January 27, 1884 to the Comptroller.

I like to mention here that I intended not to hire out as a watchman or informer when applying for the agency--but failing to get reliable parties I had to perform part of such duties. Why I failed to get reliable men for informers I will try to tell. Stealing of timber is not considered a crime in a country like here where everybody is more or less connected with the lumber or bark market. Five-sixths of the population make their living by piling, cutting, drawing or sawing wood, bark and timber. The lumber or bark has to be sold and those parties who buy it will generally take well care not to preach morals to the sellers, being too much interested to get their good for which is always demand. I have had chance enough to learn how lumbering is done and how very few men here around have a clean record--and these few are afraid of the rest. I know the name of two reliable men whose houses were burned down within the last 4 years because they had given some information. Other men have been threatened--others again are town politicians who do not dare to arouse the public sentiment against themselves. There are a few left who offer only too readily their services and information but <u>they</u> will make just as soon false reports or notify the thief at the same time or use the time during which the attention of the agent is thus called away to steal on some other lot. I speak here in particular of that section indicated in my letter of January 1st. Near the West Canada Creek and further up I found not so much difficulty to obtain good men and good reports. But you cannot expect that a State agent will gain so much confidence in such a short time that those very few reliable men will be of some service to him--there is too much on stake for them. After they know sure that he will not give them away and not make any use of their names, then they will do as their conscience tells them to. You will please consider one more point--a point of which I was not fully aware when applying for this position. For some reason or the other a State Agent is considered a doubtful character, a man who makes his living by the misfortunes of others, a man always meddling with other people's business and a man always ready for a bribe. People expressed their wondering why I accepted such a place. Gentlemen from Brooklyn and Albany will hardly understand this reasoning-but take the settlers like here on the outskirts of the North woods-generations have made their living by lumbering where ever they pleased to and most prominent men in town, the very pillars of the church have a rather queer view about stealing timber. The idea of having a State Park established will find very few disciples among them. Such people, as a matter of course consider the agent who tries to protect the forest and to stop the depredations, as an infringer on their rights.

They understand that a man might take care of private lands, but to look after State lands-lands belonging to "nobody," as they reason, that is interfering with other peoples business. These are the principal reasons why I spent more time going over the State lands in my district and I believe that I have saved at least that amount of timber to the State. I do not pretend to say expressly in my report here under, but I am sure I checked it considerably.

Referring to the first point of your letter of January 11th, I would say: As early as November 1882--before I had any connections with your office--I heard that R. B. Poole was again cutting timber on State land, a story which was told all over and told by his own men and neighbors, some of these being well acquainted with the lines. I did not know to that time that his trespasses amounted to much and though it was gossip of the backwoods. About the middle of January 1883, G. I. Kibbe of this place, who owns an interest in lot 45 Lawrence (Poole buying the timber only) came to me with the report that Poole's jobbers worked across the North line of 45 and were cutting on State land on Tefft Tract and on lots in Oxbow Tract [virgin forests]. He offered to give me further information and I sent him out there with the order to follow Poole's teams and to see where they were drawing logs from. G. I. Kibbe returned after one week (he got delayed at Powley's by snow storm and blocked

*John B. Koetteritz
circa 1885*

Courtesy John A. Koetteritz

up road) and reported the same as his first information.

As G. I. Kibbe is well acquainted with that locality I relied on his statement and came to your office and made my report. Early in February I received from another source the communication that Poole got some how wind of the matter and drew off his logs as fast as he could. I sent G. I. Kibbe out there and he informed me that that report was true and I urged in one of my letters to your office the speedy investigation of this matter.

I did not want my name mentioned more than necessary as people would have thought that Mr. Alfred Dolge was the originator of this affair while I undertook it solely in the interest of the State. Mr. Leavitt did not make his appearance and I learned that Poole was drawing off the last piles from the other side of the Lawrence line. I thought it would be advisable to look up the trespasses before all traces were extinguished and I went up to the Shanty on 45 and to Powley's--pretending some other business--not making an official investigation. I followed the Northline of Lawrence Patent and ascertained that Poole had been cutting over on Morehouse and Oxbow Tracts to quite an extent. Early in March Messrs Leavitt and Rhodes came to Dolgeville. I gave them all the desired information and Mr. Leavitt engaged me to run these lines for him in May--the snow not permitting then a thorough investigation. I did not hear anything from Mr. Leavitt till about May when he and Messrs Francisco and Rhodes came to Dolgeville. Then Mr. Leavitt told me that there was not any doubt about Poole's trespassing and that he was going to make him pay heavily for it. That was the last what I heard about it officially till I received your letter. I was told that Poole has been cutting "only one tree" over the line. I heard from private persons that the matter has been settled i.e. Poole had to pay $100 for the damages done. While on State land Survey in August I boarded with my party for one week at Oregon, where Mr. Poole lives; then I heard that the surveyors had decided in favor of Mr. Poole.

From his letter of March 19, 1884:

All of the logs of 88 stolen by W. H. Lyons have been sawed by Bingham and Pierce at Bunktown Mill--the lumber has been partly bought by them for A. Dolge-partly sold by Lyons to A. Dolge. If we could make one of these piano concerns pay--Lyons cannot pay--it will help wonderfully. I would like to get access to the mill books-how could I manage that. State land in 88 being in Fulton Co I mention a tale which is rumored around, that the State has no right to hold any land in that county for taxes unpaid, before I think 1874. Before that year the board of supervisors of Fulton Co. has made mistakes in regard to the taxes, which make it impossible for anyone-State or private owner--to hold land on tax titles. I heard this story last from D. Helterline, supervisor of Stratford who told me that George Leavitt of Salisbury Centre Herk Co N. Y. and Thos. Bradley of Newkirks Mill Fulton Co N. Y. were well posted about the matter.

From his letter of January 31, 1886 to Hon. Thomas E. Benedict, Deputy-Comptroller:

Stealing on State and private lands has been going on in the towns of Mayfield, Bleecker, Caroga, Stratford, Salisbury, Ohio, Russia, Forestport and in the southerly parts of Wilmurt, Morehouse and Arietta since long years. Since about 10 years the trespassing has become completely organized in some towns and a large part of the population makes its entire, though scanty living by stealing timber. I will not be far out of the way if I place the number of families, whose main income during the year derives from stealing at 325 to 350, i.e. for all the towns mentioned above. The strongest and best organized colonies are Bunktown near Devereaux (about 25 families) and Bullhill near Gray (nearly 40 families). All of these make their living by trespassing on wild lands. A great deal of timber is stolen by the Morehouse people, but they are vary shy and careful and they would stop entirely if they were properly watched.

About 10 years ago sounding board lumber came in good demand and everybody, who had two old plugs, a log board or sleighs, went to getting out fiddlestuff, i.e. wherever they found a nice spruce tree, they cut out one 13 feet long and left the rest to decay. Sounding board lumber brought then a fair price and kept rising in value till about one year ago. It gave the thieves at first a very fine profit, but soon the business was overdone, the purchasers became very particular about the quality and the thieves had to work for less than a living. Three sounding board factories spring up and each one of these bought whatever lumber or logs they could get. Agents of the leading piano makers bought up all the lumber they could get. All of these purchasers know that they were buying stolen goods and they helped and encouraged the thieves. After small parties were so successful, the larger concerns the sawmiller and manufacturers tried their hands in it and stole like the rest. At that time the title of the State began to be questioned and as soon as it was generally known a rush on the State lands followed. In Salisbury and Stratford, where the majority of the people is interested-directly by teaming, chopping and sawing or indirectly by trade, furnishing of teams, lending of money and the purchase of the stolen goods, the depredations had grown to an alarming extent and it required constant watchfulness to keep the thieves from the State lands.

Near Morehouseville, on Bullhill near Gray and in some parts of Russia and Wilmurt the shinglemakers steal every year good many thousands of the best spruce trees. Near Forestport spikes are cut and a large part of them stolen.

Where no fiddlestuff and shingle butts can be had, common timber and lumber is manufactured, hop poles cut, stovewood stolen, railroad ties burned or sawed.

Lately hardwood, especially Maple & Birch, has become more valued and hundreds of logs are carried every day to Devereaux and Dolgeville.

*The largest part of the stolen timber comes from private lands*, but the State land has to furnish a goodly share. It is under the present circumstances almost impossible to stop the stealing and hard enough to check it. The strong combination of the interested parties makes it up hill work for the agents. The lawless people sees a hero in the trespasser and sneaks and spies in the agents. It is absolutely necessary that you make an example of one case at least-then it will stop. The State's title is all right now and it would be well to try one good case.

There ought to be more stringent laws in regard to trespass on any wild land, whether State or private-the present laws are entirely inadequate. The purchaser of stolen timber ought to be liable. There are a number of mills in this section which do no other sawing but of stolen timber and are patronized only by thieves. Here we want no protection from fires, there is hardly any burnt land in the towns referred to but the strictest enforcement of the laws regarding trespasses. The lawful lumbering has been almost crowded out by the competition of the thieves. The agents, private and State are threatened and molested, every accommodation, like boarding, putting of horse in barn etc, refused. During this winter my wife received five threatening letters from different quarters, telling her that I never would return alive if I dared to come in the woods again and offering for my transfer to another world a variety of routes viz: by hanging, shooting and by putting me in a hollow tree. --

Imagine Koetteritz's chagrin when the comptroller repeatedly questioned his expenses, challenging bills that were not covered by the amount of fines Koetteritz was able to levy. Koetteritz complained that he had to pay for a hired horse from his own pocket, that he had "caught severe rheumatism by sleeping in an open shanty," and that the comptroller did not understand how long it took to survey a piece of land to determine the State's ownership. Such complaints are reminiscent of the similar injustices suffered by Verplanck Colvin all during the many years he worked to complete the Adirondack Survey.

Koetteritz's efforts were even thwarted by other officials: "Regarding a man cutting on 67 [a lot east of Oregon]-heard a story many times ... He is one of those wretches who made a scanty living by stealing logs and being too lazy to keep at any steady work he and his family have been several times a charge of the county. I have learned that one Supervisor in Fulton Co. prevailed with Mr. Bronks never to proceed against him & others caught stealing as they better might reap benefit from the State as to be a charge to the town or county."[40]

Koetteritz wrote many letters detailing thefts in areas south of the line adopted as the original southern border of the Park. Some of these tracts and lots he so carefully protected were later sold, then recovered by the State when the Park boundary was expanded. His fear of reprisal was real and shared by other agents, one of whom wrote the comptroller advising the State to settle on "fair terms. If the State attempted to slaughter these men, it would be the worst thing the State could do to preserve the land." He intimated that the trespassers "would retaliate by firing [sic] State land."[41]

Despite the hard work and his complaints, in 1885 Koetteritz applied for and received a position as a State Forester under the newly created Forest Commission. Many of the policies of the new commission, such as levying fines on the purchasers of stolen logs as well as on the thieves, may have resulted from his suggestions. He continued to work for the commission through 1892, and served also as a surveyor for the State during that time.

In 1890 the Forest Commission noted that it had been hampered since its creation by the lack of an adequate map of its domain. The commission felt that neither the Sargent Commission Map nor the map drawn by B. C. Butler in 1879 were adequate, despite the fact the latter did show patent and township lines. Their biggest failing was that neither showed existing State lands and their relation to geographical features in a way that would be useful both to the commission and to the public. The commission asked Koetteritz to produce the desired map; he began by compiling an exhaustive list of all earlier Adirondack maps and surveys.[42] The proposed map should show correctly the various townships of the Great Forest with all the allotments and must reconcile conflicting maps and overlapping patents.[43] By 1893, Koetteritz had completed such a map although the earliest version to show State lands was not published until 1895. Not only did it show patents, tracts, townships, and lots but it also showed lakes, streams, roads, railroads, and settlements. Most important of all, it showed the Forest Preserve lots, colored in pink, a color whose hues have survived to show State land on all succeeding maps produced by the State at intervals up to the present. The original map was not without faults, however. Certain geographical details of the map were found to be in error, in particular the location of some of the High Peaks. John B. Burnham, the prominent conservationist, wrote a letter to the editor of *Forest and Stream* in 1898 asking why the Colvin's survey material with its unquestioned accuracy had not been put to better use.[44]

This question leads to an unsolved mystery concerning just how much of Colvin's work was used by Koetteritz and why the Forest Commission considered Colvin's maps to be inadequate. At least one of the maps done under Colvin, the northeast quadrant completed in 1880 under the direction of H. K Averill, Jr., survives in State archives. It is a beautiful rendering of geographical features, lot lines, and signal stations. It would have been a simple matter to transfer to it information on the lots owned by the State. Colvin wrote extensively about his frustration with the State's failure to fund his activities, and his frustration led him to withhold some maps and survey material from the State. Presumably, by 1893, the Averill map and other quadrants were available to Koetteritz, but were they? Or, were they among the materials stored at Colvin's home, only part of which survived to be placed in State archives? Colvin's relation to the Forest Commission is not really clear.

Verplanck Colvin (1847-1920) and John B. Koetteritz (1853-1928) were contemporaries. With Colvin's topographical survey and Koetteritz's map, the State was finally in a position to protect its lands. The parallels and differences between the careers of the two men who did so much for the State reflect their dedication and their characters. Both suffered from lack of State funds and support. Colvin suffered in public and wrote extensively on his version of his own accomplishments. Koetteritz complained in personal letters to the comptroller, but never protested publicly. After he was hired by the Forest Commission, he worked diligently and so quietly that today his name is known only to a few. The State had expected Colvin to prepare a map based on his survey, something he never did. Koetteritz succeeded where Colvin failed; he did so without the fanfare that might have etched his mark in history.

## The Mid-1880s

Verplanck Colvin noted in his 1883 report that the sentiment of the people of the State ran against further land sales. Chapter 13 of the Laws of 1883 prohibited the State from selling any State lands in ten Adirondack counties; this act has been described as the "first recognition shown by the legislature of the need for overall control" of the Adirondacks.[45] A second act of that year, Chapter 470, gave the comptroller funds to purchase lands in which the State was part owner, should those lands be sold as a result of a court judgment. Although very limited in scope, this was the first appropriation for the purchase of lands by the State.

For all the later complaints by the legislature that the State was dealing improperly with Adirondack land, the first printed Land Office proceedings, which covered the year 1884, indicate that the Land Office responded quickly to the laws of 1883. The minutes show[46] that a request to purchase State land near Raquette Lake was referred to the Attorney General who reported "that, in his opinion, Chapters 13 and 470 of the Laws of 1883 take away from the Board any power to dispose of any lands in said county by either sale or exchange."[47] As a result, the Land Office rejected many applications for letters patent for claims in the Adirondack counties.

During 1884, the Land Office also ordered eviction of squatters on State land in those counties, and generally sought to defend the State's claim to lands acquired for tax sales in previous years. Refunds were granted purchasers of land only in cases where owners showed clearly that taxes had been paid and letters patent were issued only when owners could clearly show that taxes had actually been paid on land later bid in by the State. The following years display the same pattern, and there were remarkably few applications for State land, though in 1889, refunds with interest were granted a few individuals who purchased State land where taxes had been "illegally levied."

The Sargent Commission issued its report in 1885 calling for protection of the State's forests and berating the State for selling land and then taking it back after it had been logged and the taxes not paid. From that report came the legislation of 1885, Chapter 283, establishing the Forest Preserve, those lands that "shall be forever kept as wild forest lands."

In visits to the region, members of the Sargent Commission had traveled the eastern edge where the most extensive clearing for agriculture had been done. They rode the railway through lands in Clinton County from which all trees had been removed for charcoal and observed how fire had further denuded those cut-over lands. They saw the destruction caused by a flood dam on the Raquette River near Tupper Lake. They extrapolated their observations to the rest of the Park fearing that without some action, the prosperity of the region, whose "future lies in the Adirondack forests, ... will disappear forever." For all the destruction they observed, the commission reported that "the lumbermen, however, have inflicted little direct damage upon the Adirondack forests."[48]

The lumberman's failure to pay taxes inspired the claim that the first years after the establishment of the Forest Preserve was a period of "free lumbering." Lemon Thomson disagreed in his speech before the

Albany Institute, in which he pointed out that the State had only recently acquired its Adirondack lands.[49]

> The *Albany Evening Journal*, and others of the same kidney, who depend upon their imagination for their facts, boldly charge that the "lumber interests have resisted the Adirondack reservation because it is likely to deprive them of the lands on which they have trespassed for years, and from which they have earned a profit at the expense of the State." The real truth is that twenty years ago the State owned no lands in the Adirondack region. The seven hundred and fifty thousand acres of which the friends of the great park now so frequently boast as belonging to the State, is made up entirely of lands seized by the State officers, and wrenched by oppression and unjust laws from the citizens of the State without paying the real owners one dollar for their lands.[50]

The legislation creating the Forest Preserve also provided for a Forest Commission to oversee the Forest Preserve. The political climate at the creation of the Forest Commission almost doomed it from the start. Its first chairman, Townsend Cox, a resident of the Hudson Valley, was primarily concerned with the Catskills. He proved to be a weak leader, overpowered by the other two members: Sherman W. Knevals, a businessman from New York City with little knowledge of the Adirondacks, and Theodore B. Basselin, a very successful lumberman from the Black River Valley. As later assembly hearings[51] demonstrated, the latter tried to use his commissioner's position on the Forest Commission to further his own interests. His appointment was equivalent to the proverbial placing of a fox as guard to a henhouse.

No statute regulated the relationship between the comptroller's office and the Forest Commission in the matter of tax sales, but the commission went on record as opposing all redemptions or cancellations of comptroller's tax sales.[52]

Despite having Basselin, a lumberman, as commissioner, the Forest Commission was initially as diligent in protecting State lands from trespass as the comptroller's office had been. A ledger survives[53] with the records of all reported trespasses after 1885. It is reassuring testimony to the diligence with which State foresters continued to pursue the trespassers.

As earlier, only a few of the trespasses involved a large number of trees or substantial acreage and the vast majority of these appears to have been the result of loggers exceeding the time allotted to harvest timber reservations on land the State owned or where the State was seeking to clear titles. Every one of these transgressions resulted in sizable fines, which were assessed directly by state foresters. In 1885 and 1886, the only significant thefts were perpetrated by or for lumbermen: D. W. Sherman, Faxon and Knapp, and Thomas Powers as an agent for Kenyon and Baldwin Lumber Company These thefts occurred in Totten and Crossfield Township 26 surrounding the Boreas River.[54]

Many small trespasses brought appropriate fines as well, which were either paid to the forester or challenged in the courts. There were several challenges to the fines levied by John B. Koetteritz, whose district was close enough to civilization to continue to attract many timber thieves. This territory had "numerous small saw mills on [the East and West Canada Creeks] and their tributaries where stolen

### 1888 Classification of the Great Northern Forest

| Acres | |
|---|---|
| 104,123: | Improved, cleared for agriculture. |
| 855: | Wild meadow. |
| 67,886: | Water. |
| 31,121: | Waste--rocky, barren or sterile, incapable of raising forest. |
| 27,274: | Burnt since 1886. |
| 77,027: | Denuded or stripped of timber before 1886, not yet occupied by new trees. |
| 1,348,587: | Lumbered, soft timber removed. |
| 1,932,130: | Forest, virgin, unharmed and untouched. |
| 3,588,803: | Total. |

Source: Forest Commission Report

Figure 24

timber is sawn and sent to ready markets in Gloversville, St. Johnsville, Dolgeville, Utica, and Little Falls." In 1888, Forester Jacob H. Houck, covering the same area, found fifty-seven fiddlebutts in the yard of Charles and Harry Powley, for whom the lovely road south of Piseco is named. They had taken the trees from lot 33 on the way to Big Alderbed where Houck found the fallen trees, minus their fiddlebutts.

The forester in Long Lake settlement reported that its residents "are mostly a poor class who own little or no land of any character and have despoiled the timber lands of the State to supply their families with firewood or to obtain the necessary timber for dwellings and out buildings." Given the small population, these people were not the source of wholesale trespass. "There are however a few cases of trespass where valuable pine for shingles and boats and spruce and hemlock for lumber have been stolen, the logs having been sawn at one of the two small mills near the village and the shingles shipped to Newcomb or Minerva."[55] Pine was so rare in the heart of the Adirondacks it was called "Hamilton County wheat," and tempted residents to go miles to steal a tree.[56]

Not only were the loggers fined, but also the companies which purchased the stolen timber were often penalized. Morgan Lumber Company was fined for timber taken from what is now the Silver Lake Wilderness; Finch, Pruyn and Company was fined for a number of illegal purchases of timber taken from State land in the eastern Adirondacks.

When fines were challenged, agents were forced to take the cases to local courts, where they were usually, but not always upheld[57] Equally assuring as the commission's pursuit of timber thieves is the fact that most trespasses continued to be relatively small, the vast majority for fewer than a hundred logs. A survey of the lots where trespass occurred shows they generally happened on cut-over land, land close to roads, and land in the lower Hudson drainage. Interior or difficult-to-reach tracts were almost never logged illegally.

One of the largest timber thefts--30,000 logs--occurred in the Town of Minerva in 1885 and 1886. It was typical of the trespasses on previously logged lands like those along the Boreas and Minerva Creek and confirmed reports that there was a considerable amount of timber along streams in the lower Hudson watershed, which was ready for a second cut. There were, as well, virgin stands that had been left "way back," but that now proved accessible.[58]

One especially notorious thief in the northern Adirondacks surfaced in this period. Called one of "the most troublesome depredator of State lands in the northern Adirondacks,"[59] Benton Turner stole a lot of lumber from State land in 1886 and 1887 and after every charge of trespass, he sought to redeem the land in question. In 1887, Turner bought a tract from the land speculators, Ostrander and Marsh, who claimed afterwards that they had title to the land. Chairman Cox charged that they had obtained the title through "fraud, collusion, or carelessness."[60] In reality they did not have title, and although there were no taxes outstanding, the State claimed the land. Turner was brazen enough to try, without success, to get the legislature to pass a bill authorizing the State to sell him the land at far less than its worth.[61]

In addition to providing funds for Colvin's topographical survey and for the Forest Commission, the only other appropriations relating to the Forest Preserve in this period were for the payment of taxes on that land to local governments as authorized by the legislature of 1886, an appropriation which did little to stop the criticism of the Forest Commission. Newspapers and periodicals of the day were as vehement on the subject of the abuses of State forests as they had been before the establishment of the Forest Preserve. In fact that criticism became increasingly vocal in the next two decades, during which time the commission was reorganized and renamed several times in attempts to make it more responsive to continuing abuses of the forest. Allegations of improprieties on the part of the commissioners were the principal reasons for later investigations.[62]

The Hadley Act of 1887 authorized exchange of separate or detached parcels of land in Forest Preserve counties. Twenty-five thousand dollars was appropriated for the purchase of land at $1.50 an acre, and several tracts were offered, including 1,100 acres made up of several small lots owned by P. J. Marsh.[63] The Forest Commission refused all but one proposed exchange on the grounds that the boundary of the proposed Adirondack Park had not been fixed. The one exchange they authorized turned out to benefit interests traced to Commissioner Basselin, although he later protested that his fellow commissioners did not like the bill and "decided not to carry it out."[64] The proposed exchange that the commission chose to consider would have gained the State part of 36,399 acres scattered throughout the southern Adirondacks in exchange for 13,556 acres of State land that Everton Lumber Company wanted. The land offered by Everton included isolated, and generally never logged, Gospel, School and Literature lots acquired by Adirondack Company or by the railroad at five cents an acre in 1856.

Basselin had to defend his actions in relation to the placing of the Blue Line that circumscribed the Adirondack Park; the choice of the western boundary was thought to benefit him directly.[65] He later denied connections to the interlocking land and lumber companies that had purchased land at tax sales and conspired to keep valuable land from the State, sell worthless land to the State, or exchange tracts with the State to their benefit.[66] Testimony in the 1891 Assembly Hearings points to many such land deals that were detrimental to State interests. The Hearings also uncovered connections between Basselin and many companies in the western and northern Adirondacks, including Everton Lumber Company The full extent of Commissioner Basselin's involvement is shown in figure 25.

Basselin was not the only member of the commission whose actions were questioned. Chairman Cox was ridiculed for the way the other two commissioners held meetings without consulting him. Daniel Lynch, one of the commission's agents who had been fired, tried to get his job back by threatening to reveal details of what he thought were Cox's misdeeds; he wrote the chairman that he was "collecting material for a series of sketches of the Adirondacks to illustrate the present methods of preserving the forests."[67] The commissioners took very seriously Lynch's claims that he could reveal their improprieties in order to coerce them into rehiring him, but they did not rehire him.

# CONNECTIONS BETWEEN ADIRONDACK LUMBER COMPANIES CIRCA 1890

Figure 25

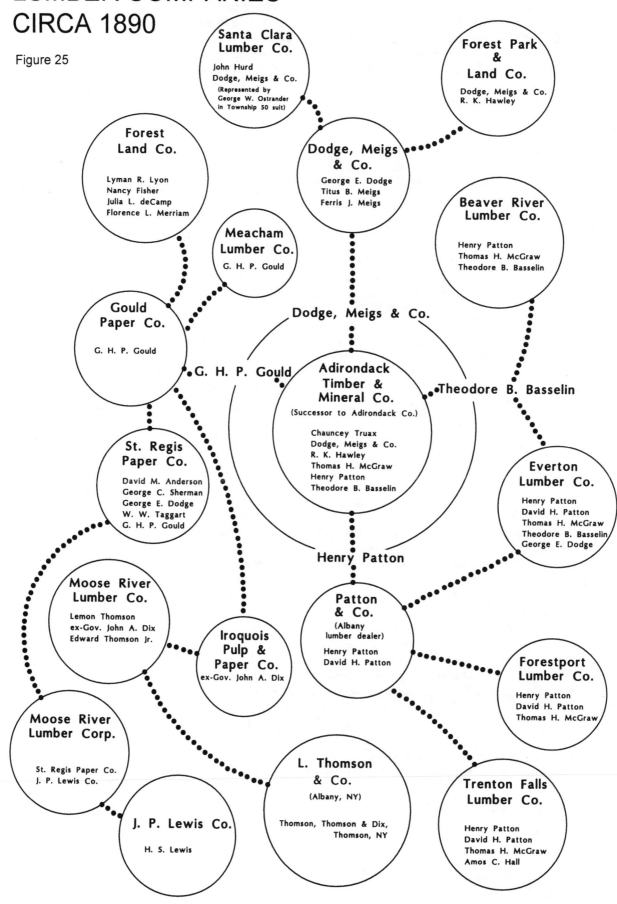

# Land Purchases in the 1890s

By 1890, it was obvious that the State could no longer rely on tax sales to increase the size of the Forest Preserve. Of the 390,000 acres offered at the 1890 tax sale, the State bid in on only a few acres, less than 3,000 new acres.[68] (The State did bid in, essentially paying taxes on other land, which the State had previously claimed but where the State's title was not yet cleared.) At the time, the comptroller's office still did the actual bidding for lands at tax sale; the Forest Commission had nothing to do with tax sales.

Lumbermen were eager to bid on previously logged tracts on which others had defaulted. Elbert Crandall bid for 150,000 acres at this sale; Henry Patton bid for 18,000 acres; Finch, Pruyn and Company, Morgan Lumber Company, George F. Underwood, and George W. Ostrander also bid on tax sale land. The State had real competition for land, even before the 1890 legislation, which authorized a paltry $25,000 for land acquisition.

In 1891, the Land Office authorized the first purchases of land for the Forest Preserve at $1.50 an acre, the value assigned land from which the merchantable timber had been removed. The Assembly Committee on Public Lands and Forestry examined the appraisals of land offered to the State. Well-timbered land far from water courses was valued at only $1.50 an acre, but accessible virgin land was appraised at $4.50 an acre. Exercising Chapter 37 of the Laws of 1890, the board authorized purchase of scattered tracts throughout the Park. From this fund, 27,273 acres were purchased in 1891, 27,445 in 1892, 9,068 in 1893, and 9,140 in 1894. It is likely that the appropriation was augmented by monies received from the sale of State land, although application of funds derived from the sale of land toward Adirondack purchases was not authorized by legislation until 1892. In any event, the size of acquisitions subsequent to 1890 exceeded what could have been expected from the $25,000 appropriation.

At the same time, the Forest Preserve was still increasing through tax sales. Despite the fact that others bid in for 390,000 acres and despite the fact that the State bid for only 3,000 acres not claimed previously,[69] the tax sale of 1890 resulted in State acquisition that year of 51,119 acres, 407 acres more in 1891, as well as an additional 25,732 acres, which the State later had to purchase in order to clear challenged titles.

A law (Chapter 217) passed in the year 1891 included a potential boon for lumbermen and land speculators. It permitted anyone, not just the purchaser, to petition the comptroller for cancellation of any tax sale. Governor Roswell P. Flower was instrumental in repealing this condition which benefited no more than a half-dozen individuals who had filed the 300 requests for cancellation that followed the passage of the law. He argued that "the law was not in the interest of wronged or innocent owners--they had then and have now their means of redress--but in the interest of land and timber speculators, who by acquiring some remote interest in the lands sold and by proving some technical defect or oversight in the original assessment of taxes or in the tax sale might be able to cancel the sale and for a mere song get possession of lands long held by the State without dispute over title.[70]

## The Creation of the Park

Establishing the Adirondack Park in 1892[71] had little immediate effect on protection mandated to State land. The law was intended to consolidate State holdings within the Park's new Blue Line boundary by focusing future purchases there; it also permitted sale of lands outside the Park. The commission had debated the location of the boundary, considering several alternatives. The candidate lines and the Blue Line adopted in 1892 were all shown on the Sargent Commission map, but the map had not been updated since it was drawn. Its depiction of virgin forests on private lands had certainly become outdated by 1892, although as Colvin noted, many tracts remained uncut. In 1896 he noted the existence of original hemlock, spruce and pine in the vicinity of Big Brook and Grampus Pond. A tract, whose ownership was disputed and later logged, the Gore between Totten and Crossfield and Macomb purchases in the vicinity of Preston Ponds, was "covered with a magnificent primitive forest of most valuable timber."[72] But how much of the forest on State land shown as dark green had been compromised? Colvin found State land southeast of Long Lake covered with hardwood forest and good spruce timber; the mountains south of Gore also contained large timber as did the areas southeast of Indian Lake village. The map would have to be revised mostly in the river corridors, but there State land parcels had been colored in lighter green already.

A second 1892 law authorized that funds from the sale of State lands should be used to purchase lands within the Blue Line. In 1892, there were a few sales of land outside the Park. Tracts, presumably virgin, with merchantable timber, in Franklin County brought the State $3.00 to $3.50 an acre. Most other lots were sold for that amount, including tracts south of Giant Mountain, indicating they, too, might not have been logged. Several lots in Franklin County brought over $6.00 an acre. Among the many sales made the following year was that of a $5.00-an-acre tract south of Debar Mountain that contained virgin timber.

These lands outside the Blue Line, which were sold after 1893, had for the most part been acquired through earlier tax sales, and some of them make up a portion of the 172,000 acres that the State later repurchased. Tracts in the southern Adirondacks were also offered for sale, but the few scattered lots were so isolated they were not purchased.

The growing shortage of timberland, evident at the time of the Park's creation, in part due to the locking up of the Forest Preserve, promoted a climate of greed and sparked an upward spiral in the cost of land. The rise in the cost of land occurred despite the depression of 1893. It continued almost until World War I, all through the time the country went through a series of minor depressions that resulted in little inflationary pressure on the nation's economy as a whole.

The upward trend in land values brought about a new round of threats to public lands immediately after 1892. Thefts from State land persisted and more and more titles were challenged, but even more ominous were efforts to open up the Forest Preserve to lumbermen.

Proposals to permit cutting on State land loomed as the greatest threat to the Forest Preserve from the time of its creation almost to the present. The most serious of these, one that nearly resulted in the sale of timber from State land, occurred the year after the Park was established. The legislature passed a bill (Chapter 332) permitting sale of spruce greater than twelve inches in diameter from State land. Even though the uproar in the press was unprecedented, the Forest Commission voted to proceed with the sale of timber. Fortunately, an opinion from the Attorney General declared that applications for the sale of lumber had to be approved by the Land Office and that the Forest Commission could not act alone.[73] The Forest Commission assented to forty-one applications (each of which differed only in the amount of timber to be cut, the locations, and the price to be paid the State, which averaged thirty cents per log). The Land Office appears to have taken the high road in this matter for it forwarded resolutions authorizing the sales to the State Engineer and Surveyor[74], who noted that the Forest Commission's recommendation that sales proceed and the Governor's "emphatic approval [of such sales] as the most practical means of attaining the end sought, viz.: The acquisition of more forest land by the State, which has the formal approval of the American Forestry Association,[75] ... and which is joyfully approved by some of our citizens whose business interests will unquestionably be enhanced by putting it into effect, and whose same interests, they say, will be alarmingly hurt by contrary action."[76]

Fortunately, the State Engineer and Surveyor responded according to his own judgement, finding that the trees covered by the proposed contracts should not be removed.

> The standing spruce ... should not be removed from the forests owned by the State. ... The State now owns within the Forest Preserve 555,000 acres. Most of it is virgin forest. A glance at the map of the Preserve shows the State's holdings scattered the length and breadth of it. Maintain these tracts in their natural wildness and they will continue to exert a potent influence on the water supply of our canal system. The forty-one contracts cover 80,000 acres, nearly all the watershed feeding the streams that supply the canals. It will not pay these contractors to cut over a tract showing less than a dozen standard spruce trees, and beyond a doubt from ridge after ridge within these acres will be cut forty or more trees of legal size. After being lumbered these ridges will show a mass of prostrate tree tops and limbs strong enough to bear up under the burden of next winter's snow, and after a season's exposure, they are in just fit condition to burn and fire may reach them from many sources. Once burned over and that tract has lost its value forever as a water conserver."[77]

Furthermore, the State Engineer determined that the conditions of cutting were not sufficient to protect the forest and that the State was not being offered as much money as sales from private owners had brought. Additionally, the fact that the lumberman did not have to pay the State anything until after three years meant that "The State really [was] furnishing so much capital for the lumberman's stock of 250,000,000 feet to be cut from these 80,000 acres of State Land."[78]

The Land Office heard further arguments against the contracts from the American Forestry Association, one of whose members, the lumberman Morton S. Parmalee, was also opposed to the sales. He cited the fact that "the expected revenue from sale of timber will be largely used up in the added cost of protecting what is left from fire and timber thieves." He noted the extremely slow growth of spruce, the loss of "the integrity of the forest," and most surprisingly, the potential damage that would be done by lumbermen who did not own the land they logged. He was concerned for the wilderness itself and said:

> You can't slaughter your forest and preserve it. Once gone, it is easier to rebuild a cathedral than to replace those trees. A State that spends twenty millions in one granite pile, that builds on every side monuments of man's thoughtfulness for his fellow man, does not need to demand a "revenue" from the forests that holds the safety of its rivers, the health and happiness of its people; a forest which up to now has cost it practically nothing.[79]

The Land Office voted to refer the matter to the Senate and did not approve any of the proposed sales of timber, in spite of the Governor's claim in 1894 that timber had been sold from 17,468 acres.[80] The delay until 1894 allowed the passage of Article VII of the Constitution, which took the question of logging the Forest Preserve out of the hands of the legislature. And, as a result of the Land Office's delay in approving the contracts, no contracts for timber sales were consummated.

However, even the constitutional amendment was not the end of proposals to cut timber on the Forest Preserve. A later chapter describes continuing threats, but one in particular bears previewing for it came from the very commission that was designated protector of that land. In 1901, the Forest, Fish and Game Commission obtained federal funds and the services of two foresters trained by Gifford Pinchot, an advocate of scientific forestry. Their surveys of the virgin spruce stands[81] on Totten and Crossfield Township 40, expanded the next year to Townships 5, 6, and 41 went to great lengths to demonstrate the economic value of cutting those tracts. Concealed in those 1901 and 1902 studies was the justification for harvesting timber on those State-owned tracts, making the reports the most egregious of many such proposals espoused by the Forest, Fish and Game Commission.

The passage of the Forest Preserve amendment to the constitution and its signing on January 1, 1895 should have absolutely stopped government proposals to sell timber from State lands within the existing Blue Line. As the story unfolds, it will be shown that lumbermen and land speculators, with some help from members of the various commissions, devised other methods of obtaining that timber. In fact, flagrant violations of the public trust in following years contrast sharply with the earlier zeal with which the laws were extended to the protection of State lands, even in the absence of the constitutional amendment.

## Land Acquisition Accelerates

In 1894, a sub-committee of the Forest Commission reported on the escalating cost of land, noting how it had quadrupled in the previous decade. In responding to the need for vast sums to acquire land, far in excess of anything the legislature had appropriated, the sub-committee recommended the annual sale of a million dollars in bonds for each of the next four years.

### Commission Chronology

**1872 Commission of State Parks**

**1874 Land Office**

Circa 1884: seven commissioners including Lt. Governor, Speaker of Assembly, Secretary of State, Comptroller, Treasurer, Attorney General, and State Engineer and Surveyor.

**1885 Forest Commission**

1885-1893: three commissioners.
1894-1895: five commissioners.

**1895 Fisheries, Game and Forest Comm.**

1895-1900: five commissioners; William F. Fox, Supt. of Forests.

**1897-1900 Forest Preserve Board**

1897-1899: three commissioners, Woodruff, Lt. Gov.; Babcock, Comm. of F,G and F Comm., and Adams, State Engineer and Surveyor.
1900: Woodruff, Babcock, and Bond.

**1900-1910 Forest, Fish and Game Comm.**

1900: five commissioners; Fox, Supt. of Forests.
1901-1902: three commissioners, Woodruff, Dewitt C. Middleton, Babcock; Fox, Supt. of Forests.
1903: two commissioners, Middleton and Lawrence.
1904-1906: Commissioner Whipple; Fox, Supt. of Forests.
1907-1908: Commissioner Whipple; Clifford R. Pettis, Supt. of Forests.
1909-1910: three commissioners: Pettis, Supt. of Forests.

**1910-1914 Conservation Department**

Three commissioners.

Figure 26

In 1895, the legislature appropriated $600,000 for the purchase of lands belonging to Dr. William Seward Webb. The Land Office in conjunction with a Forest Commission sub-committee spent much of 1895 dealing with that purchase. Some of Webb's lands had been flooded by the building of the dam on the Beaver River, which created Stillwater Reservoir and was designed to regulate the flow of water in the Black River. Webb sued for compensation for the flooded lands. He also claimed that his virgin lands north of the reservoir, an enormous tract of 66,000 acres, had become inaccessible to the railroad and thus impossible to log.

To settle the suit and acquire the land, the legislature appropriated a sum which is not mentioned in the appropriation, but which totalled $600,000.[82] The most important part of the purchase was the area north of the reservoir, but the State did gain other virgin lands. The transaction included were parts or all of Totten and Crossfield townships 38, 42, and 43 and the triangle north of 38 and John Brown's Tract Township 8 as well as land in John Brown's Tract from which only softwoods had been taken. On completing the State purchase, the newly appointed Forest Preserve Board (see below) observed that the land north of the Beaver "is a primitive forest in which no cutting has been done or on which no timber rights were reserved." The board was proud that the purchase included settlement of Webb's $184,000 law suit.[83]

This purchase, which escalated the cost of virgin timberland to $7.00 an acre, gave the State the largest tract of virgin timber ever placed in the Forest Preserve.

# Trouble in the Forest

## Renewed Threats from Trespass

A legislative committee held a series of hearings in 1895 at various locations in northern New York to "investigate the depredations of timber upon State lands." The hearings had elicited information on many trespasses according to the committee's report to the full assembly in early 1896. That record indicates that the greatest number of trespasses still occurred in the eastern Adirondacks, in areas near settlements, and on tracts that had been cut over or cleared earlier in the century. Few of those who testified at the hearings were willing witnesses. One forester said, "They are all neighbors and they all want to trespass some if they can get a chance, and, as a rule, they won't squeal on each other."[84] The majority (72) of the 122 trespasses reported occurred in Essex County, with 23 in Hamilton and 21 in Warren County. Several of the largest thefts were committed by or for Moynehan and other well-known lumbermen and for some of the larger lumber companies, including Morgan Lumber Company.[85]

The Committee reported that few among those questioned knew the exact location or bounds of the State lands in any township because "many lots have been burned over, and the old blazed marks on the lines have thereby obliterated." Most of the thefts were common knowledge locally; "trespasses are not made where discovery would be difficult."[86] Colvin confirmed this in his 1895 report, noting that the rivers continued to make it easy to steal from State land. This was especially bad in the areas where the Indian, Cedar, and Boreas rivers meet the Hudson.[87] The committee observed that established fines had proved no deterrent to thefts: most were settled for less than the value of the timber. (Timber on the ground where cut was worth between $.10 and .30 a standard or market, spruce piled at the river was worth from 1.10 to 1.40, hemlock from .90 to 1.10 a market in 1891.) One of the Forest Commission's first decisions had been to raise fines to .75 to 1.25, whereas the comptroller had been settling for from .05 to .25 a market. The Committee concluded that a measure to impose a fine of twenty-five dollars for each tree cut on Forest Preserve land was not the solution to the problem,[88] so it decided that those who transported or aided in the cutting of timber should also be charged with a misdemeanor.

Loggers kept cutting after the expiration of the time permitted for land sold with timber reservations and this accounted for most of the major trespasses investigated. Few, very few of the trespasses, involved large tracts of land or large amounts of timber. The commission's severest critic, Charles S. Sargent, writing in *Garden and Forest*, even admitted that no more than 35,000 acres were involved. Despite that admission, the magazine continued to exaggerate the problems of theft in an attempt to sway opinion. The magazine charged that there would soon be "no timber left on state lands, at least on the small and isolated parcels of such lands."[89] In fact, while almost all of the thefts occurred on just such isolated patches, the bulk of the timber stolen was spruce and not all of the forest cover as the magazine implied.

Lumberman Patrick Moynehan was already earning a reputation as a "persistent trespasser on State lands."[90] He was responsible for many of the largest thefts, including 7,000 markets in Johnsburgh, 5,000 markets near Vanderwhacker Mountain, and 4,000 from land adjacent to the north end of Long Lake. With few exceptions, the larger thefts occurred where the State had to grant timber reservations in order to clear title to disputed land and the lumbermen exceeded the time limits imposed by the reservations.

Still, during this time of greatest theft, the five years after 1889, no more than seven percent of State land was affected. The 1895 Assembly hearings appear to have been very effective, because by 1898,[91] trespass had all but been eradicated. This only meant that lumbermen began to employ a subtle and ultimately more insidious means of obtaining timber from State lands than overt theft.

## More Cancellations of Tax Sales

An act of the legislature in 1885 helped perfect titles to land acquired at tax sales by declaring that the comptroller's deeds for tax sale lands in Forest Preserve counties, were conclusive evidence of the regularity of the process. That law also shortened the time in which individuals could seek cancellations of tax sales.[92] Despite this act, there were still loop-holes that permitted land to be reclaimed and there continued to be challenges to the State's titles.

After 1895 timberland was becoming so valuable and the price of timber was so great that a few very clever lawyers and land speculators, either independently or working for lumber companies, began researching the titles to land claimed by the State as a result of tax sales. By diligently studying the records in county tax offices as well as in the State comptroller's office, they uncovered many problems with the tax sales. Upon discovering any flaw with a tax sale, these individuals bought presumed title to the questioned lots or made arrangements with the original owner, who had defaulted on taxes, to act on their behalf. Then they claimed the land from the State, which all too often could not prove clear title. Over the years the State was faced with claims on over 172,000 acres it thought were Forest Preserve. Purchases of 112,000 acres by the State between 1895 and 1901 were for land the State had acquired at earlier tax sales, land the State believed it owned.

Many of these purchases were at inflated prices. More than a few tracts had such valuable timber on them that the State had to allow it to be harvested to reduce the price of the land to something the State could afford. The problem with these timber reservations granted near the turn of the century is that they were granted at the time the demand for pulp was escalating, encouraging the lumbermen to make smaller dimension cuts. Reservations permitting the cutting of spruce down to ten inches were common, and reservations down to eight inches occurred in later years,[93] but there is evidence that these reservations were not respected and that considerably smaller timber (down to five inches in diameter) was actually taken.

Obviously none of this would have happened had there not been flaws in the tax titles, but most of them seem so trivial that they make the speculators' research appear to be unscrupulous. More often than not, the titles were clouded, not because of what the State had done, but because of minor problems created by local assessors and local governments. The faults involved errors in the dates of documents or in descriptions of the land. Given the small populations in the towns, the problems of often casual record keeping, and the part-time jobs of local officials, it is easy to see that mistakes were made. Nevertheless, these seemingly trivial errors did create huge obstacles to the State's efforts to preserve its forests.

The legal quagmire provided a bonanza for lawyers. With timberland becoming scarce and a second crop available, speculators looked to State lands, not to steal timber, but to claim them. As Commissioner Basselin later testified, it was the "general opinion prevailing that any bright lawyer could beat the State Title."[94]

Through the late 1890s and into the first years of the new century, numerous suits of ejectment were filed to show that the State did not have clear titles. Among those filing were George N. Ostrander, Lelia Marsh, Patrick Hanley, Smith M. Weed, and Martin V. B. Turner. The latter's son, Benton Turner, took one such suit all the way to the United States Supreme Court, using the argument that the oath of the assessors to the assessment order was taken on August 10 and not the third Tuesday of August as proscribed by law. This minor act occurred some thirty years before and was Turner's reason for challenging the State! He had harvested timber on land in Township 24, Macomb Great Tract 1, in Harrietstown on a tract the State had acquired through the tax sale of 1877 and the State sued to recover the costs of the lumber illegally harvested. Turner's suit claimed the State's tax deed was invalid because such irregularities (as the questioned times of oath-taking) were jurisdictional and that the State's act permitting tax sales was unconstitutional.

The Supreme Court ruled in favor of the State; New York's attorney general reported that "it is believed that the decisions in this case will quiet the title to State lands in the Forest Preserve, and, it is hoped, will prevent further litigation." The statute thus upheld as constitutional, declared that "deeds from the Comptroller of lands in the Forest Preserve, sold for non-payment of taxes, shall, after having been recorded for two years, ... be conclusive evidence that there was no irregularity in the assignment of taxes."[95] Speculators and lumbermen continued to find flaws in titles and they challenged the State's tax titles, but the State's ownership of most of the Forest Preserve was safe.

# Political Turmoil

## The Forest Preserve Board

The Forest Preserve Board existed for four years, from 1897 through 1900. (Irregularities by its members accounted for the board's short existence.) It functioned like the Land Office, taking over all of that office's activities in Forest Preserve counties, in particular, all acquisitions of land for the Adirondack Forest Preserve. It published the minutes of its proceedings annually. The Forest Preserve Board had similarly placed but fewer members than the Land Office: Lieutenant Governor Timothy L. Woodruff; Commissioner of the Fisheries, Game and Forest Commission, Charles H. Babcock; and State Engineer and Surveyor Campbell W. Adams.

In addition to completing the Webb sale and acquiring the Adgate Tract from the Adirondack League Club, the Forest Preserve Board, in 1896 and 1897, purchased over 17,000 acres from lumberman William P. McEchron for $1.50 an acre. Part of this tract in Hamilton and Warren counties had been logged, but only for softwoods: hemlock for the Griffin Tannery and spruce, which was floated down the Sacandaga River. Its hardwood cover remained intact and its softwood forests were not greatly disturbed[96] so that today, less than a hundred years later, its second-growth hemlock stands are among of the finest in the Adirondacks. Surveys made at the time of purchase indicated that "on some of the hills, or mountains so-called, where it was impractical to lumber, there is quite a growth of spruce left."[97] Much of these tracts that the State picked up for the going rate--$1.50 an acre--appeared covered "in dense forest and indicate that within a few years they will again be interspersed with large-sized evergreens, ... that is to say, with a good, fair proportion of spruce and hemlock."[98]

In a preamble to its 1897 report, the board observed that "the area of the Forest Preserve consisted of scattered lots, more or less isolated and detached, some of them being many miles from the main forest." The board believed its missions were to consolidate the State's holdings and deal with the problems of existing holdings diminished by redemptions and cancellations of tax sales. In this regard, the board remarked that "cases are rare in which title of the State to a desirable tract is acknowledged," and that "the bogus title burrows farther out of sight the longer it is let alone."[99]

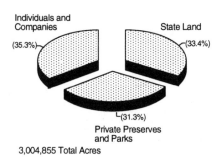

Adirondack Park land ownership, 1897

Individuals and Companies (35.3%)

State Land (33.4%)

(31.3%)

Private Preserves and Parks

3,004,855 Total Acres

Figure 27

The legislation creating the board also gave it new latitude in acquiring land. The board could enter and take possession of any land, estimate its value, offer reservations which permitted timber cutting if no agreements on value could be reached. However, no payments for land were to be made before timber reservations had been consummated. Most important of all, the legislature passed a series of appropriations for land acquisition, which brought much land to the State: $1,000,000 in 1897, $500,000 in 1898, $350,000 in 1899, and $200,000 in 1900. With 69,969 acres acquired in 1896, 178,194 in 1897, 139,483 in 1898, 58,404 in 1899, 84,624 in 1900 added to acreage obtained through tax sales in those years, the Adirondack Forest Preserve grew to over 1,200,000 acres. The average price paid per acre in 1900 was $3.60.[100] The State acquired additional lands with a $200,000 appropriation in 1904, $350,000 in 1906, $500,000 in 1907, and $200,000 in 1909. By 1909, the Adirondack Forest Preserve had grown to almost a million and a half acres.

A storm of criticism of astronomical proportions accompanied acquisitions in this interval. Certainly greed and questionable practices were rampant and will be discussed for they did affect the Forest Preserve; but they should also be viewed from a modern perspective: Even accounting for the inflation that followed each of this century's wars, the amount of money spent seems small in light of what was accomplished. By 1909, the State had obtained almost 1.5 million acres through tax sales and appropriations of 3.89 million dollars. It took four and a half times that much money to obtain less than a million acres in the 1919-60 interval.

Also, in light of later criticism, it is important to note that the Forest Preserve board began by establishing real criteria for valuing land. The price of land from which spruce had been removed was fixed at $1.50 an acre, but the price of virgin land continued to vary according to the quantity of merchantable timber (spruce) which a tract would yield, and the proximity of the tract to streams or roads.

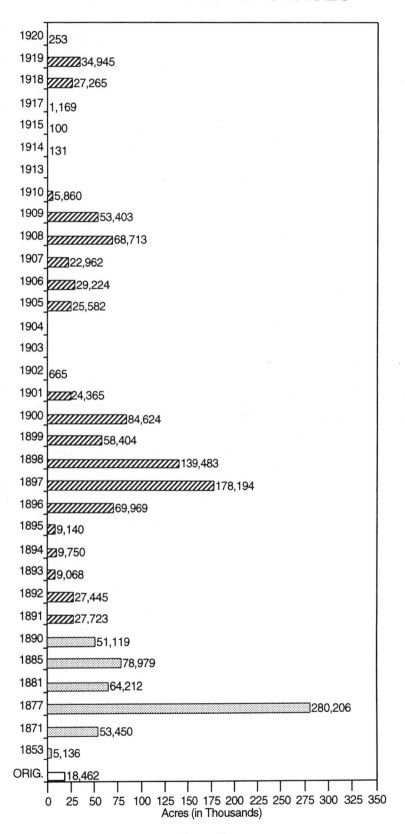

## LAND ACQUIRED THROUGH TAX SALES AND PURCHASES

☐ Original   ▨ Purchases   ▦ Tax Sales

1920  253
1919  34,945
1918  27,265
1917  1,169
1915  100
1914  131
1913
1910  5,860
1909  53,403
1908  68,713
1907  22,962
1906  29,224
1905  25,582
1904
1903
1902  665
1901  24,365
1900  84,624
1899  58,404
1898  139,483
1897  178,194
1896  69,969
1895  9,140
1894  9,750
1893  9,068
1892  27,445
1891  27,723
1890  51,119
1885  78,979
1881  64,212
1877  280,206
1871  53,450
1853  5,136
ORIG.  18,462

0  25  50  75  100  125  150  175  200  225  250  275  300  325  350
Acres (in Thousands)

Figure 28

105

The board decided it would pay no more than $7 per acre for virgin land, the price having been determined by the sale of timber on Webb's Township 8 in John Brown's Tract.[101] In effect, land was worth little more (in this case only $1.) than the timber growing on it. Since on average the cutting of spruce meant "only the removal of fifteen to twenty percent of the standing timber, all of these lumbered tracts were still under good forest cover... On many of these tracts of lumbered lands, the hemlock was left standing because there was no tannery near enough to enable the operators to utilize the bark." The board differentiated two other categories of land, that bordering lakes and that called primitive or virgin where only pine had been removed and the original growth of spruce remained untouched. The former class reflected the emerging appreciation of land for recreation and was valued at $2.35 to $2.75 an acre.

The board concluded that prices could only be determined by examining the land, which meant "a careful counting of the trees." Actual inspections by State agents described forest conditions; today these assessments provide valuable historical information on those stands. The board boasted that it bought several tracts as well or better timbered than Township 8 for $7 per acre, including land and lakes.

Also considered were tracts from which large spruce had been removed twenty years earlier. The board set their price higher than for cut-over lands, but lower than for virgin lands. The board noted that lumbermen had taken "only the largest trees, and further, that there had been a thrifty increase of timber growth in the meantime on the trees that were left, the tract was ready for what the lumbermen call a second cut."[102]

Exercising its ability to trade timber reservations for title, the board was able to make significant acquisitions which greatly maximized its limited funds. Lands involved were in the southwestern corner of Hamilton County and the tract that encompassed the Cedar Lakes and Whitney and Pillsbury lakes.

The board's first transactions (1897) indicate strict adherence to its pricing guidelines. In fact, the price of some purchases indicates the tracts were virgin or heavily timbered and ready to be logged again, and where this occurred that information will be used in the last chapter along with data from early tax sales to identify portions of the great forest. Between 1897 and 1901, the State acquired approximately 185,000 acres that had never been logged, another 60,000 acres that had merchantable stands of spruce.[103]

In 1901, Edward A. Bond, as the new State Engineer and Surveyor, joined the Forest Preserve Board. The report for that year noted the recent rise in land values because of the "prosperous condition of the lumber and pulpwood market. [Because of this] the amount of money necessary to acquire the rest of the Adirondack Park is so great, and the appropriation by the legislature so small, comparatively, that this board has given careful consideration to the suggestion that, where it may become necessary, these lands should be purchased, subject to the reservation of timber rights."[104] The steps taken by the board to correct the situation demonstrated its good intentions.

Under the provisions of chapter 135, Laws of 1898, the board is authorized to bring special proceedings "to set aside the cancellation of any sale of land for taxes, or to ascertain and determine the title to lands in the Forest Preserve claimed adversely to the State."

Prior to 1888, the State owned various large tracts of forest land, the title to which was subsequently cancelled, in accordance with applications filed in the office of the State Comptroller. The applicant, in each case, based his claim for a cancellation of State's title, on some alleged irregularity in the assessment of the taxes, for the payment of which the land was sold at public tax sale and bid in by the State. These irregularities were trivial and did not conduce in any way the legality of the assessment and validity of the tax title, because the Board of Supervisors, at their annual meeting, adjourned before their clerk had extended the figures on the tax roll, although the total valuation had been agreed upon. Others based their applications for cancellation on an assertion that the assessor had made his return on the second Tuesday in August, instead of the third. Some claimed an agricultural "occupancy," which, on investigation, often proved to be a trespass instead. Others claimed that the property was assessed erroneously as nonresident land, although on inquiry, the alleged resident generally proved to be some squatter or roving trapper.

One State title was cancelled because the applicant claimed that the lands were not properly advertised; another, because the county treasurer's certificate was not attached to return. For such or similar reasons, the State's title to over 100,000 acres of Adirondack forest was cancelled.

It seems proper to explain here that, in making these cancellations, the comptroller's office followed the custom hitherto observed in that department, and that they were made in accordance with the provisions of the general tax law, although in doing so more importance was attached to trivial technicalities than to the forestry interests of the State or the rights of the people at large.

The Forest Preserve Board, however, believed that there had been too liberal an interpretation of the tax law, and that the applications for cancellation had in many cases been improperly granted. Therefore, acting under the powers conferred by law, the board instituted proceedings in the courts to recover the lands thus lost, and to re-establish the State's title. Their efforts in this respect have been rewarded by the restoration to the people of 61,271 acres of forest, which had at one time passed out of the possession of the State; and it is expected that the area thus regained will be still further increased through the suits which are still pending.[105]

## The Moreland Commission

The actions of the Forest Preserve Board, however, did not always reflect its high-minded intentions to uphold the State's interests in land acquisition. In 1900, the board was replaced by the Forest, Fish and Game Commission and land acquisition was assigned to a Forest Purchasing Board. Several new pressures against land acquisition occurred between 1898 and 1905. These included numerous actions by private individuals who were able to profit at the State's expense and possible wrongdoings on the part of Forest Preserve Board members. In 1910, the State convened a Moreland Commission to investigate these questionable practices. (A Moreland Commission is a special State investigative commission, appointed by the governor. The one appointed in 1910 was charged specifically with investigating the Forest, Fish and Game Commission and the Forest Purchasing Board.)

The workings of the Land Office, the Forest Preserve Board, and the Fisheries, Game and Forest Commission, and the Forest, Fish and Game Commission were intertwined and equally subject to criticism. The Moreland Commission uncovered many abuses such as the overpayment for State land. These do not, in retrospect, seem so egregious because, during the first decade of this century when they occurred, the State was able to acquire some of the most treasured parts of the Forest Preserve.

Further, this all happened during the period of extraordinary change--the completion of the railroad through the Adirondacks and the building of rail lines to facilitate logging, the surge in the pulpwood market, the creation of the first significant markets for hardwoods since charcoal-making days, the increased demand for wood of all kinds, a shrinking forest resource, and the rise in the cost of buying land.

The various boards and commissions were caught between these six factors and their mandate to acquire more land. They also suffered from the improprieties of at least one of their members. Even the increases in appropriations for land acquisition compounded their problems because the availability of so much money not only sparked the rise in the cost of land but it attracted those who figured out ways to profit at the State's expense.

Adding to these problems faced by the boards and commissions were the fact that the land to be acquired was owned by two major sources--the private clubs with 700,000 acres and lumbermen with approximately the same amount. The clubs did not want to sell their land and because State funds were insufficient even if they had wanted to sell, the Forest Preserve Board and the Forest Commission felt it necessary to justify their inability to acquire any of the private preserves. They found the owners to be good stewards of the land (whether they were or not) and remained content to let their holdings remain as they were.

Lumbermen, however, were another matter. One series of sales to the State can be traced to William West Durant. In 1899, in an effort to avert bankruptcy, Durant sold 400,000 acres of land to a lumber syndicate, the Forest, Park and Land Company, whose members included George E. Dodge, Titus B. Meigs, and R. K. Hawley. Dodge, Meigs and Company and its successor, Santa Clara Lumber Company, proceeded to log the part of the purchase which included the Seward Range before it was sold to the State.

Some of the Durant land went to Adirondack Timber and Mineral Company,[106] which in turn sold much of it to the State in the next few years. In 1898, the company sold 33,575 acres to the State at $6.47 an acre. This price was high, but a justifiable one, because little timber had been taken from the tract, whose inaccessible interior was covered with virgin forest. The company also sold land to other lumbermen, particularly Moose River Tract Townships 3, 4, and 5 to G. H. P. Gould, who paid only $3.50 an acre for land most of which had never been cut.

Durant's Forest, Park and Land Company had offered the State 24,000 acres of virgin land, south of Raquette Lake but had held back tracts around the lakes known today as Sagamore and Kora. The company received $7.00 an acre for the remaining land plus $15,000 additional for frontage on Raquette Lake. Commissioner Woodruff (he served on both the Forest Preserve Board and on the Forest, Fish and Game Commission) bought 880 acres surrounding Lake Kora. While Vanderbilt's lavish Camp Sagamore might have justified the State's failure to purchase that property, there was only a small hunting cabin on Lake Kora, which was surrounded on three sides by State land. With the State acquisition of a tract on the west, Woodruff, who seems to have been the mastermind of the scheme, acquired a magnificent property, totally surrounded by Forest Preserve.

Other questionable but not illegal sales occurred in 1899. The State "resold" about 3,548 acres, virgin parcels mostly in Hamilton and Herkimer counties, that had either never been sold by the State or had been acquired at very early tax sales. These small lots were probably not logged before 1899, and their inaccessibility suggests that they were not logged in 1899, but that cannot be proven. All reverted to the State, the majority within the year for non-payment of taxes. However unlikely, it is possible that this was merely a gimmick by the State to clear titles.

Timber thefts continued in the period 1898-1905, sometimes with the help of men who were supposed to prevent them. Dewitt C. Middleton, a member of the Forest, Fish and Game Commission between 1901-1903, was charged with "practically selling" to the J. and J. Rogers Company and to Patrick Moynehan, the standing timber through which the 1903 forest fires had run. J. and J. Rogers Company was accused of being a "notorious trespasser" as well.[107] Commissioner James S. Whipple, who became the single head of the Forest, Fish and Game Commission in 1904, was censured for not prosecuting trespassers vigorously enough.[108] Both J. and J. Rogers Company and Patrick Moynehan were fined for large thefts. J. and J. Rogers' claimed it was only cutting burned timber in North Elba but agreed to pay a large fine when it turned out the timber was green. Moynehan, still "one of the most persistent trespassers on State land,"[109] took timber from State land in the vicinity of Big Brook.

Col. Fox, Superintendent of Forests for the Commission, was especially castigated for a large theft, in which Syphert and Harrig cut 24,350 trees in southern Hamilton County. Fox had not investigated the theft until prodded by Governor Hughes. Two State game protectors, Harvey Gaylord and Charles Klock, were indicted for extorting $7,750 from James Gallegher for permission to cut 2,000 cords of spruce in Nobleboro. The agents were convicted for stealing timber, but not for grand larceny as charged.. Gallegher was working for Syphert and Herrick and Hinckley Fibre Company, but none of the lumbermen were ever indicted. Although he was implicated, no charges were ever brought against Fox.[110]

All of these thefts seem trivial compared to the efforts of several land agents and speculators. These men continued to discover land where the State's titles were not perfect and in selling the titles to the State, they made extraordinary profits.

# THE OSTRANDERS' CONNECTIONS
# TO LAND SALES TO THE STATE

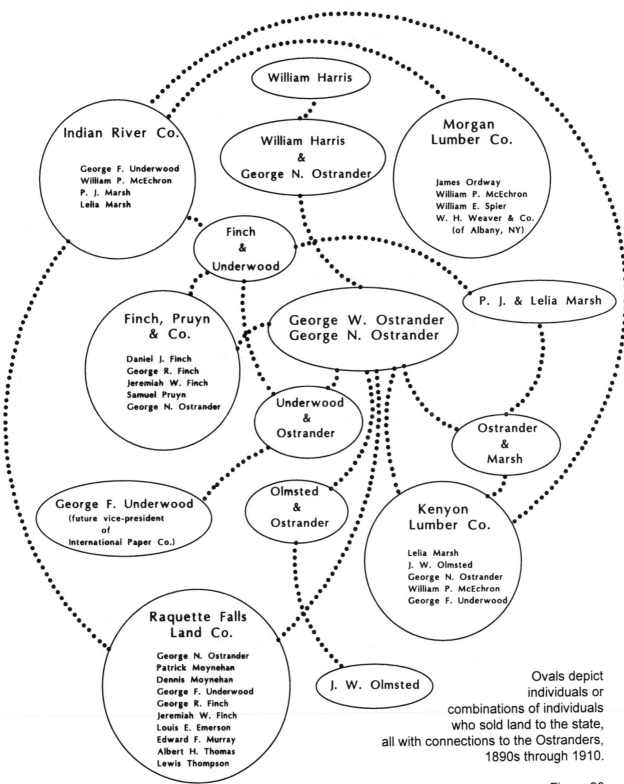

Ovals depict
individuals or
combinations of individuals
who sold land to the state,
all with connections to the Ostranders,
1890s through 1910.

Figure 29

The man most successful at this kind of profiteering was George N. Ostrander, who has already been mentioned in connection with several land exchanges. In fact, the one name common to the majority of transactions in this period was his. His father, George W., was a lawyer and land agent with an office in Albany, and in 1883, he was in partnership with P. J. Marsh. The son, also a lawyer and a land agent, joined the firm and later became woodlands manager for Finch, Pruyn and Company (it was said that he was like an adopted son to Samuel Pruyn). He also represented George F. Underwood, a vice president of International Paper Company, William Harris (see below), Lelia Marsh, the widow of his father's partner, and even, at times, the State. The complexity with which the interests of the lumber companies and land speculators were interwoven is baffling.

Ostrander became a master at ferreting out land where the State had lesser or questionable title, buying up the underlying titles, and challenging the State's ownership. He challenged numerous titles, either for others or for himself after he had acquired the land in question. He lost a few cases, but more often settlements resulted in the State's paying him for the land. In others, the State got title to the land, but only after its merchantable timber had been removed. Ostrander and Marsh both testified before the 1897 Special Assembly Committee. Marsh suggested that the legislature purchase all the old, original titles and stop litigation because, he claimed, even when the State was victorious, the litigation cost the State more than if it had "bought the titles in the first place."[111]

Summarizing the State's legal actions against various lumber and pulp interests, the Moreland Commission concluded that in many of the compromises where the State relinquished timber rights, "the papers and documentation upon which the settlement was based, if any such were ever in existence, cannot now be found."[112]

The commission uncovered evidence that "for himself and persons whom he represented, Mr. Ostrander has sold to the State more forestland during the administration of Commissioner Whipple than all other persons combined, and at a much greater average price, though of no greater value."[113]

The Raquette Falls Land Company (variously Raquette Falls Lumber Company) was incorporated in 1901 to conduct real estate and lumbering business. George N. Ostrander was the secretary; and in addition to Ostrander the original stockholders included Louis F. Emerson, Edward F. Murray, Patrick Moynehan, George F. Underwood, and George R. Finch. The company sold $332,000 worth of real estate, of which $246,000, nearly seventy-five percent, went to the State. It sold land in Watson's East Triangle that the State thought it had owned for years. It sold timber on State land to International Paper Company for $20,000, for which the State exacted a settlement of this amount plus additional acreage.[114]

The Moreland Commission heard testimony that Raquette Falls Lumber Company had tried to recover 1850 acres in various lots claimed by the State and threatened to take the timber from these lots. The State sought "actions of ejectment" but settled for the land minus the timber on nearly 2,000 acres.

Raquette Falls Lumber Company was involved in the sale of Townships 19 and 34, in the Blue Mountain Lake area, some 24,433 acres, which the company purchased in 1901 for $84,615. However,

Union Bag and Paper Company had bought the timber rights on the land for $26,250.[115] and these rights went with the Raquette Falls' sale to the State, a sale that brought the company $152,314.

George N. Ostrander was involved[116] in the sale of land to the State for $6.89 an acre, land which had been purchased from the MacIntyre Iron Company land for $2.50 an acre and was "mountainous and expensive to lumber."[117]

Among the most suspect transactions investigated by the Moreland Commission were those of William Harris, a member of the Assembly who lived in Northville. He owned some 1,700 acres of virgin land, most of it north of Lake Pleasant, which he offered to sell to the State. He claimed he was told by Colonel Fox to buy up cheap lots and mix them with the sale of his virgin lots so the State could afford them.[118] He claimed the virgin lands were worth $15.00 an acre, though he later sold other virgin lots at $5.00 an acre to International Paper Company. The Moreland Commission found no record of sales at even $10.00 an acre up to that point (1901). The result was that the State bought 9,500 acres from Harris--land that had been lumbered and was "worth only $1.50 an acre,"[119] in order to obtain 1,700 acres of virgin forest. The purchase price was $6.50 an acre for all the land, some $71,656. A sampling of Harris' scattered sales to the State indicates that he bought $12,600 worth of land and sold it within a few months for $40,724.

After the sale of all his land to the State in 1901, Harris began acquiring more land, 11,500 acres of which he sold quickly to the State, this time for a profit of $3.75 an acre, or $43,150.

Behind Harris' activities was the ubiquitous George N. Ostrander. Harris said at one point that he only paid Ostrander a fee of $1,000, but he admitted at the Moreland Commission hearings that he gave him one-half his profits on at least one of their joint transactions.

Harris, with Ostrander, sold another tract, said to have virgin timber, to the State for $7.25 an acre. Harris had paid only $5.00 for these lots in Moose River Tract Township 9, which he held only briefly.[120]

In 1904, Ostrander represented the Santa Clara Lumber Company at a trial concerning that company's claim to the 2,000-acre gore north of Township 50. The settlement required the State to grant a timber reservation down to eight inches in diameter for spruce.

Between 1905 and 1910, the State purchased 147,742 acres at $848,990. Of that, 100,831 acres was purchased from Ostrander for $639,461 or $6.43 an acre. Among these purchases was Ostrander's biggest known coup, which included lands that lie in the heart of the Pharaoh Lake Wilderness, one of the Park's most beautiful tracts. Because of the tract's mountains, myriad lakes, and pockets of beautiful forest, it might seem petty to complain about the additional cost to the State caused by Ostrander's interventions or the Forest Commission's failure to deal with the owners directly. Ostrander purchased a large tract east of Schroon Lake from the Pickard estate. He sold most of it almost immediately to the State for a profit of $70,000. He retained a thousand-foot strip of valuable waterfront along the east shore of Schroon Lake, which he did not offer to the State. He was later able to sell acreage in that long strip for far more than the average he had paid for the whole tract, adding substantially to the profits he realized from the sale to the State. Shortly after, the State acquired another chunk of the future Pharaoh Lake Wilderness from Raquette Falls Lumber Company, which had purchased the tract in 1903 for $2 an acre and sold it to the State in 1908 for $7.25 an acre. Ostrander did not benefit directly from this sale, but he was the secretary and a stockholder of that company.

Ostrander was connected to many more transactions. The chart, figure 29, which identifies many combinations and permutations of speculators, all of whom sold land to the State, shows that Ostrander was either a member of the board of companies selling land or a partner with individuals who sold between 400,000 and 500,000 acres of land to the State.[121]

Typical of Ostrander's behavior was his role in a lawsuit involving Nehasane Park. His activities behind the scenes were characterized as "steering and regulating" transactions. He stood "back of all this conveying, furnishing the money, directing and controlling matters."[122]

In a published summary of its findings, the Moreland Commission concluded that Ostrander's abstracts of title sent to the purchase board "either on behalf of himself or others whom he represented as an attorney, have ordinarily been approved with a speed not always justified, while those titles which were offered by other persons have in most instances remained [with the board] for more than one year, and in a large number of cases for more than two years before being disposed of."[123] Further, Ostrander's titles never showed previous money considerations attached to the tracts. The commission observed that if the board had this information, then it would have had proof of the profit made in sales to the State.

The Moreland Commission concluded that, "in a great majority of cases a price has been paid largely in excess of the market value of the land purchased. By far the greater portion of Adirondack lands purchased by the State changed hands at least once within five years preceding the transfer to the State." The value of Adirondack land had been rising in this interval, but the rise applies only to lands covered with softwood timbers and "the State has not been purchasing this class of land," only land covered with hardwood timber.[124] The commission discovered "little or no sales between individuals for land which has been lumbered for its softwood timber, except as such sales are made to persons who quickly sell the same to the State."[125]

Evidence that Commissioner Whipple had financial ties to Ostrander brought about Whipple's abrupt resignation from the Forest, Fish and Game Commission.[126] Claims that Ostrander could be tied to Superintendent Fox were never proven. However, the Moreland Commission's summary of its findings concluded that "If Commissioner Middleton, Commissioner Whipple, and Superintendent Fox had deliberately started out to assist Ostrander to purchase these lands [later sold to the State] at low figures, it is doubtful whether they could have pursued a course more likely to aid Ostrander than the one adopted."[127]

The commission also heard testimony justifying the State's acquisitions between 1897 and 1901: "The large acreage purchased by the State in the years 1897-1901 has already (1910) doubled in value." Much of the land purchased had not been lumbered and was a primeval forest. Land comparable to the State's $7 an acre purchase near Raquette Lake was already worth $35 an acre.

# VALUE OF AN ADIRONDACK ACRE

### Representative sales and appraisals (state purchases unless noted)

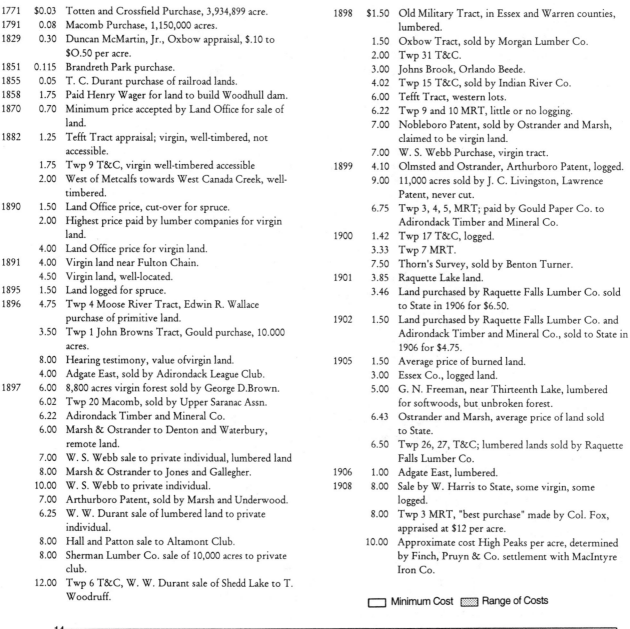

| | | |
|---|---|---|
| 1771 | $0.03 | Totten and Crossfield Purchase, 3,934,899 acre. |
| 1791 | 0.08 | Macomb Purchase, 1,150,000 acres. |
| 1829 | 0.30 | Duncan McMartin, Jr., Oxbow appraisal, $.10 to $0.50 per acre. |
| 1851 | 0.115 | Brandreth Park purchase. |
| 1855 | 0.05 | T. C. Durant purchase of railroad lands. |
| 1858 | 1.75 | Paid Henry Wager for land to build Woodhull dam. |
| 1870 | 0.70 | Minimum price accepted by Land Office for sale of land. |
| 1882 | 1.25 | Tefft Tract appraisal; virgin, well-timbered, not accessible. |
| | 1.75 | Twp 9 T&C, virgin well-timbered accessible |
| | 2.00 | West of Metcalfs towards West Canada Creek, well-timbered. |
| 1890 | 1.50 | Land Office price, cut-over for spruce. |
| | 2.00 | Highest price paid by lumber companies for virgin land. |
| | 4.00 | Land Office price for virgin land. |
| 1891 | 4.00 | Virgin land near Fulton Chain. |
| | 4.50 | Virgin land, well-located. |
| 1895 | 1.50 | Land logged for spruce. |
| 1896 | 4.75 | Twp 4 Moose River Tract, Edwin R. Wallace purchase of primitive land. |
| | 3.50 | Twp 1 John Browns Tract, Gould purchase, 10.000 acres. |
| | 8.00 | Hearing testimony, value of virgin land. |
| | 4.00 | Adgate East, sold by Adirondack League Club. |
| 1897 | 6.00 | 8,800 acres virgin forest sold by George D. Brown. |
| | 6.02 | Twp 20 Macomb, sold by Upper Saranac Assn. |
| | 6.22 | Adirondack Timber and Mineral Co. |
| | 6.00 | Marsh & Ostrander to Denton and Waterbury, remote land. |
| | 7.00 | W. S. Webb sale to private individual, lumbered land |
| | 8.00 | Marsh & Ostrander to Jones and Gallegher. |
| | 10.00 | W. S. Webb to private individual. |
| | 7.00 | Arthurboro Patent, sold by Marsh and Underwood. |
| | 6.25 | W. W. Durant sale of lumbered land to private individual. |
| | 8.00 | Hall and Patton sale to Altamont Club. |
| | 8.00 | Sherman Lumber Co. sale of 10,000 acres to private club. |
| | 12.00 | Twp 6 T&C, W. W. Durant sale of Shedd Lake to T. Woodruff. |

| | | |
|---|---|---|
| 1898 | $1.50 | Old Military Tract, in Essex and Warren counties, lumbered. |
| | 1.50 | Oxbow Tract, sold by Morgan Lumber Co. |
| | 2.00 | Twp 31 T&C. |
| | 3.00 | Johns Brook, Orlando Beede. |
| | 4.02 | Twp 15 T&C, sold by Indian River Co. |
| | 6.00 | Tefft Tract, western lots. |
| | 6.22 | Twp 9 and 10 MRT, little or no logging. |
| | 7.00 | Nobleboro Patent, sold by Ostrander and Marsh, claimed to be virgin land. |
| | 7.00 | W. S. Webb Purchase, virgin tract. |
| 1899 | 4.10 | Olmsted and Ostrander, Arthurboro Patent, logged. |
| | 9.00 | 11,000 acres sold by J. C. Livingston, Lawrence Patent, never cut. |
| | 6.75 | Twp 3, 4, 5, MRT; paid by Gould Paper Co. to Adirondack Timber and Mineral Co. |
| 1900 | 1.42 | Twp 17 T&C, logged. |
| | 3.33 | Twp 7 MRT. |
| | 7.50 | Thorn's Survey, sold by Benton Turner. |
| 1901 | 3.85 | Raquette Lake land. |
| | 3.46 | Land purchased by Raquette Falls Lumber Co. sold to State in 1906 for $6.50. |
| 1902 | 1.50 | Land purchased by Raquette Falls Lumber Co. and Adirondack Timber and Mineral Co., sold to State in 1906 for $4.75. |
| 1905 | 1.50 | Average price of burned land. |
| | 3.00 | Essex Co., logged land. |
| | 5.00 | G. N. Freeman, near Thirteenth Lake, lumbered for softwoods, but unbroken forest. |
| | 6.43 | Ostrander and Marsh, average price of land sold to State. |
| | 6.50 | Twp 26, 27, T&C; lumbered lands sold by Raquette Falls Lumber Co. |
| 1906 | 1.00 | Adgate East, lumbered. |
| 1908 | 8.00 | Sale by W. Harris to State, some virgin, some logged. |
| | 8.00 | Twp 3 MRT, "best purchase" made by Col. Fox, appraised at $12 per acre. |
| | 10.00 | Approximate cost High Peaks per acre, determined by Finch, Pruyn & Co. settlement with MacIntyre Iron Co. |

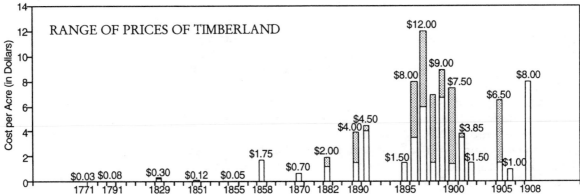

▢ Minimum Cost    ▨ Range of Costs

RANGE OF PRICES OF TIMBERLAND

Cost per Acre (in Dollars)

$0.03 $0.08  $0.30  $0.12  $0.05  $1.75  $0.70  $2.00  $4.00 $4.50  $1.50  $8.00  $12.00  $9.00 $7.50  $3.85  $1.50  $6.50  $1.00  $8.00

1771  1791  1829  1851  1855  1858  1870  1882  1890  1895  1900  1905  1908

Figure 30

The board had acted cautiously in its acquisitions because many owners of properties offered to the State had only the "marketable tax titles" to them. The Forest Preserve Board was wary of purchasing those tracts even though this type of title was recognized by the courts.

As for the State's granting of timber reservations, the commission was told that "it is doubtful whether the people would approve, at present, the action of the board if it were to buy virgin forest land and pay the price which the lumbermen and wood pulp companies are giving for that kind of property."[128]

Between 1898 and 1901, the State was able to buy large areas of hardwood lands for $1.50 an acre, but by 1910 prices had risen so that the State could no longer purchase even such logged land. As the last chapter will show, today much of the $1.50-an-acre land comprises scattered stands of magnificent spruce that meet the definition of old-growth forest.

In 1894, the Forest Commission had estimated that it would take something over 3.5 million dollars to buy the remaining 1.2 million acres within the Blue Line, excluding settlements and private preserves.[129] In 1897, an Assembly Committee observed that if it had had the funds, twenty million dollars, at the time cutover land or land with reservations was worth $1.50 an acre, the State could have acquired all of the land within the Blue Line.[130] In reality, the Forest Preserve Board was able to acquire 850,000 acres before 1910 for just over 3.7 million dollars.[131] The average cost of $4.42 per acre seems modest in light of the escalating price of land.

Advances in the cost of land in this period were partly caused by the State paying a price "largely in excess of the market value of the land purchased."[132] In almost all instances, land purchased by the State had changed hands at least once in the five years preceding its acquisition. Between 1905 and 1910, the Forest, Fish and Game Commission was forced to pay as much for logged land as it had for virgin tracts just a few years earlier.

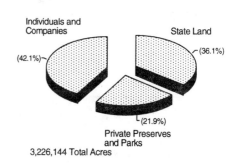

Adirondack Park land ownership, 1902

Individuals and Companies (42.1%)

State Land (36.1%)

Private Preserves and Parks (21.9%)

3,226,144 Total Acres

Figure 31

## Conclusion

The four decades after 1870 were turbulent yet almost miraculous times. From next to nothing, the lands of the State obtained in tax sales grew to a substantial total at the creation of the Forest Preserve. The first Forest Commission report for 1885, remarked that "with but little exception [the Adirondacks] is but unbroken wilderness." The State continued to acquire virgin tracts through the 1890s although many of them were inaccessible. Private sales of never-logged tracts continued into the 1900s.

Gradually the proportion of privately held wilderness tracts declined, while the proportion of State land in the Adirondacks increased. The tremendous growth of the Forest Preserve occurred at a time when lumbermen were virtually eliminating privately-owned virgin stands. Lumbermen turned to speculation, which indicates that there was more money in buying and selling land than in logging it. For all the shenanigans reported, the Park emerged with substantial tracts of State lands, remarkably consolidated into contiguous tracts given their origin. And for all the thefts of timber and cancellations of tax sales, which permitted a second or third logging for spruce, the acts that diminished the quality of State forest land were largely confined to the boundary of the Park and scarcely touched the more than half-million-acre nucleus of the Park. They were confined to the 172,000 acres the State had to purchase in order to clear title and to no more than 100,000 other acres of the land held in 1885. The later acquisitions of virgin and lightly logged tracts push the amount of great forest that was preserved almost in its original condition to well over half-million acres.[133]

It is amazing that so much of the State's public land should have been accumulated in a period of such great turmoil in the private sector. It is equally amazing that there were so many threats to the public land both from within and without government, and that these threats ultimately did not affect the integrity of the core of public lands. After 1890, the dichotomy between public and private lands became more and more pronounced. Timber on the already protected portions of the Forest Preserve was poised to grow so that all signs of past history would be obliterated in the next hundred years. And, as the next chapter shows, the private lands were about to be logged in a way that would require centuries before they would again resemble the great forest with which they were once covered.

Adirondack Park land classifications showing increase in lumbered lands between 1888 and 1902

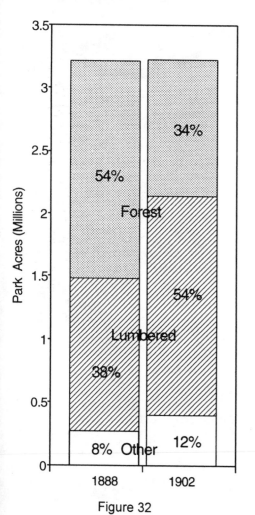

Figure 32

# VII

## After 1892:
## The Revolution in
## Private Lands

The revolution in the logging industry in the Adirondacks between 1885 and 1910 not only kept pace with but induced the growth of the Forest Preserve. In the period from 1890 and 1910, when the State made the greatest strides in preserving its northern forests, it will be shown that logging had its most significant impact on the forests.

By 1890, the Glens Falls area had begun to lose its dominance as a lumbering center over other regions of the north country; but other, more remarkable changes in Adirondack logging were beginning. The most dramatic was the explosive growth of the pulp and paper industry. Evidence for this lies in the tremendous rise in the harvest of pulp wood, which was virtually all spruce (in 1910, ten percent was hemlock and pine, less than ten percent was poplar). Complementing this rise in pulp wood cut was a decline in lumber produced from Adirondack spruce sawlogs. The peak year for shipping spruce sawlogs from the Adirondacks was 1882. The combined spruce sawlog and pulp production shows that the amount of spruce harvested in the Adirondacks nearly doubled between 1890 and 1905, when it peaked and began an abrupt decline. Hemlock sawlog production also rose in the interval, but also began to decline, supplanted by the more accessible stands in Pennsylvania.

By 1910, there were few softwood stands left on private timber tracts. The cut of over 19 million cords in two decades before 1910 represents a near doubling of the average rate of cut in the four decades between 1850 and 1890 and demonstrates how the lumberman's greatest harvest of the forest occurred after steps toward forest preservation had been established. Despite that harvest, only the merchantable timber was gone--the forest still survived.

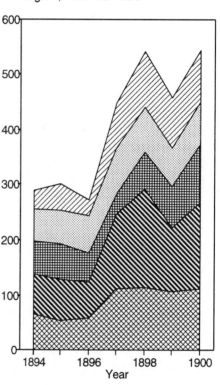

Lumber and pulp production by region, 1894 to 1900

Board Feet of Lumber and Pulp
(Millions)

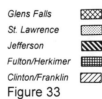

Glens Falls
St. Lawrence
Jefferson
Fulton/Herkimer
Clinton/Franklin

Figure 33

## Pulp and Paper

The shift to the use of wood from the region's forests to make pulp and paper completely altered the Adirondack logging industry. Until the later part of the nineteenth century, paper was made basically from rags with some vegetable matter and it was very expensive. In 1827, a paper mill at Saugerties was the first in New York State to use the revolutionary European machine--the Fourdrinier,[1] which produced continuous rolls of paper instead of individual sheets. Two years later, a Fourdrinier machine was produced in America, making mechanization in paper making an accomplished fact.

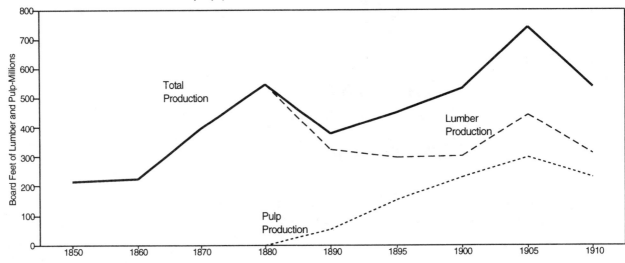

Figure 34

The most basic revolution in paper making could not happen until a new source of pulp was perfected. Europeans also led in this research to replace rags. In 1858 an English company patented a method of producing wood pulp for paper. That same year a patent was granted for a process for stone-grinding wood fiber into pulp.

## The Processes

The production of pulp from wood is the first of the two basic steps in which paper is made. To make **pulp**, wood is treated to separate its wood fibers. The first process, to do this was the grinding of wood to separate the fibers mechanically resulting in **groundwood pulp**. In the Adirondacks, grinding was used primarily for spruce and one ton of spruce pulp could be ground from one cord of wood.[2]

Shortly after the development of the groundwood process, chemical methods were invented to remove the lignin that binds wood fibers together. Chemicals permitted the use of different types of wood and in one later-developed process, chemical and mechanical means were combined. Although developed early on, chemicals were not used at all until after 1880, and not used extensively until much later.

The first chemical process to be introduced made **soda pulp** by cooking the wood in a solution of caustic soda (sodium hydroxide) to release the fibers.[3] Two cords of mixed poplar and conifers yielded only one ton of soda pulp.[4] **Sulfite pulp** substitutes one of several different sulfite solutions, of varying degrees of acidity, to produce almost pure cellulose fibers. By 1920, fully half of the pulp produced in New York employed a sulfite process. Typically, two cords of spruce, hemlock and balsam yielded one ton of sulfite pulp.[5] **Sulfate pulp** is made by cooking the wood in a solution of sodium hydroxide and sodium sulfide. This process was not introduced until 1883 and although it eventually made possible the use of a greater variety of woods, it was not used in New York until the early 1920s. Combining mechanical and chemical methods to make pulp from wood was not widely used in the Adirondacks until after 1950.

To make **paper** from pulp, a slurry of the pulp fibers is deposited in a thin sheet that is dried. The Fourdrinier machine was revolutionary because of its ability to deposit the pulp slurry continuously on rotating drums and to dry it quickly.

A paper mill was thus dependent on a large and steady supply of water to make the slurry of wood fibers, access to raw materials, and proximity to a means of shipping paper to market. These conditions were available in the southeastern corner of the Adirondacks.

South of the region, a paper company was established at Fort Miller (downriver from Fort Edward) in an old grist mill in 1865. Although it used rye straw in nearly equal proportion to rags, this mill, like all paper mills of the day, depended on the limited supply of rags.

The first factories to use the new groundwood process were established in Massachusetts in 1867 by two German brothers, Albrecht and Rudolf Pagenstecher. The company used a German process and German machines (the Keller-Voelter wood grinding machine) with a version of the Fourdrinier. The Massachusetts company made newsprint from poplar (aspen or popple) and, unexpectedly, the nearby supply of popple was quickly exhausted. One brother returned to Germany and discovered that there too the supply of popple had been exhausted, but that the Germans had figured out a way to use spruce.

It is ironic that the Adirondacks' only merchantable timber was identified as the next source of pulp for paper. Returning to the United States and searching about for spruce, the brothers were directed to Luzerne, at the confluence of the Hudson and Sacandaga Rivers, by Senator Warren Miller, who promoted the use of spruce for pulp. (Miller himself had a wood pulp mill as early as 1867 near Herkimer. However, this mill did not use the revolutionary Keller-Voelter machine initially.)

Because the shores of both the Hudson and Sacandaga rivers above their confluence were said to have abundant spruce, the brothers established the Hudson River Pulp and Paper Company, which began making paper from groundwood in 1869 near Luzerne and shortly after at Palmer Falls (now Corinth).[6] The Corinth mill was the oldest mill to be incorporated into the International Paper Company when it was formed in 1898.

## Adirondack Region Pulp and Paper Mills

Northern New York had four major areas that could support the new pulp and paper process and three of them were on the periphery of the Adirondacks: near the Hudson River and its tributaries, in the Champlain Valley, and along the Black River in the western Adirondacks. Many of the new pulp or paper mills were installed by companies that had already had sawmills in those areas and that owned large tracts of timberland. These companies were the only ones with the capital to build the new mills, which required extraordinarily expensive machines. Between 1890 and 1910, many new mills were built and older ones were converted to the use of wood pulp.

At the same time, reflecting the pattern of industrial consolidation that was occurring throughout the United States in all its industries, the mills in these three areas were merged into conglomerates to form the region's largest pulp and paper corporations. Some of these giants survive as the largest pulp and paper

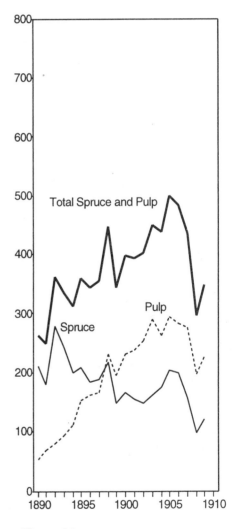

Production of spruce sawlogs and pulp, 1890 - 1910

Total Spruce and Pulp

Pulp

Spruce

Figure 35

manufacturers in America and they still retain mills in the Adirondacks.

Two pulp mills were built in Warrensburg, one by Adirondack Pulp Company (J. T. Outerson) in 1878, the second by the Schroon River Pulp Company the following year. In the 1880s, six others were built on the Hudson River between Glens Falls and Cohoes.

By 1890, there were eleven pulp and paper manufacturers in the Upper Hudson area: The early paper company at Fort Miller added a groundwood mill in 1891, becoming the Ground Wood Company, later Fort Miller Pulp and Paper Company. The Hudson River Water and Power Company at Mechanicville was expanded in 1885 by its new owners, the Duncan Paper Company, and this later became an important part of West Virginia Pulp and Paper Company. From 60 tons of paper a year in 1880, the region's production jumped to 110 tons a day by 1890, 40 of which were made by the Hudson River Pulp and Paper Company.

International Paper Company was established in part from the mills at Glens Falls, Fort Edward, and Palmer Falls. Finch, Pruyn and Company was incorporated in 1904 from the merger of three companies (the history of both companies is detailed in the appendix). By 1910, the mills along the Hudson River produced 700 tons of newsprint daily, almost seven times the total of two decades earlier.

Mills in the western Adirondacks were built along the Black River or near its confluence with the tributaries that flowed from the Adirondack foothills to the east. By 1890, there were ten pulp and paper companies in the western Adirondacks. The largest was at Watertown and the smallest (with an output of three tons a day) was the Lyonsdale Pulp and Paper Company. Watertown, on the Black River, became a center of paper making. In 1889, John M. Tilden formed the Tilden Paper Company and one of his backers was David Anderson, who a decade later would be one of the founders of St. Regis Paper Company. Anderson was also associated with Taggarts Paper Company, along with B. B. and W. W. Taggart and George C. Sherman.

Gould Paper Company made a modest amount of paper before 1900, the year that the production at its Lyonsdale plant trebled. The only mill in the Black River Valley larger than Gould's was the one built by International Paper Company at Watertown. The rest of the twenty mills along the Black River in 1900 were very small, including J. P. Lewis' Beaver Falls mill. St. Regis Paper Company was organized 1899 and built a huge mill at Deferiet. Theodore B. Basselin's Beaver River Pulp Company, near the confluence of the Beaver and the Black, was built in 1909, one of the last of the new pulp and paper mills to be formed. The production of nine mills in the western Adirondacks rose from 70 tons a day in 1890 to 548 tons in 1910.

As the production of iron in the northeastern Adirondacks declined or came to depend on coal (coke) rather than charcoal, pulp and paper companies were formed to continue the use of the forests. Col. A. Paine built a soda pulp plant near Willsboro on Lake Champlain in 1882; originally the Champlain Fibre Company, it became part of the New York-Pennsylvania Company, of which Peter S. Paine was president. The J. and J. Rogers Company, which originally produced iron, began making paper in 1894? J. and J. Roger's mill (1894) and International Paper Company's Cadyville mill

(1899) were the northeastern Adirondacks' two largest mills. There was a moderate sized mill in Plattsburgh but all the other paper mills in the northeast region were quite small.

The southern Adirondacks had only one mill, a very large one, owned by Hinckley Fibre Company in Herkimer County on the West Canada Creek. It alone produced almost five percent of Adirondack pulp in the late 1890s.

St. Lawrence County's largest paper mill, Piercefield Paper Company, was built in 1892. Dexter Sulfite opened a substantial pulp and paper mill at Dexter in 1900. In 1900, the county's seven other mills, including Newton Falls Paper Company, all had a considerably smaller capacity than Piercefield and Dexter.

A year after it was incorporated in 1898, International Paper Company had eight mills, which were among the largest in the regions and scattered throughout the Adirondacks. Collectively, they consumed 103,000 cords of pulp annually, while the entire north country region consumed 356,000 cords. From 1898 to 1905, two-thirds of the spruce harvest in all regions was pulpwood, and in the Hudson drainage, the harvest was mostly for pulpwood, see figure 35.

In 1896, the Fisheries, Game and Forest Commission[8] reported an annual cut of 110,000 acres, eighty percent of it spruce, of which over half was for pulp. That year saw a strong rise in price of spruce stumpage, with spruce pulpwood bringing more than sawlogs. Such small trees were being taken that the commission feared continued spruce harvest would lead to the extinction of the species.

By 1905, when the region's level of lumber production began its precipitous slide, the harvest of spruce for pulp was three-fourths as large as that for lumber. Pulpwood harvest, which was 90 percent spruce, also declined, but more slowly after 1905, because of the very real shortage of spruce. Enough new pulp and paper mills had been erected in the north country, so that by 1905, it had become obvious that the industry had overbuilt. Pulpwood was imported from Canada to New York's mills before 1900, and by 1910 more than half the pulpwood consumed in New York pulp and paper mills came from across the border.

The results of building all those paper mills in the 1890s were astounding. A newspaper that cost 14 cents in 1869 cost 2 cents in 1898. But the shortage of spruce pulp was growing so that the price of a cord rose from $2 a cord in the late 1890s to $3 a cord by 1904, to over $4 a cord by 1909, to nearly $5 a cord by 1919. The shortage must have been greatest in the western Adirondacks because as early as 1896, a cord of spruce pulpwood brought $6.50 delivered at a Black River mill, $10.00 if rossed or debarked.[9]

The price of pulp and hence that of paper rose gradually up to World War I, then jumped 350 percent during the war.[10] Pulp prices were said to be sky-high in 1920, just before the bust of 1921, which temporarily reduced them.

Even the price of hemlock sawlogs rose in the interval from 1897 to 1910, from $11 to $28 per thousand board feet.

In 1896, the commission had predicted that nearly two million remaining acres of primitive forest or unlumbered lands would be destroyed in twenty years. By 1910, part of that prophesy had been fulfilled--Adirondack spruce trees, even the smaller ones, were gone. Equally foreboding was the statement that "the woods would be wiped

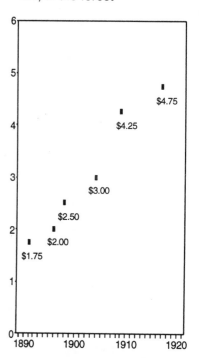

Average cost of a cord of wood cut, in the forest

The cost at mills varied greatly, depending on the distance from the mill and whether the pulp had been debarked. Rossed pulpwood at the mill could cost as much as $8.00 a cord around 1900.

Figure 36

out as a place of interest, of beauty, and of value."[11] That this did not occur was the result of political actions of the years between 1885 and 1895 and the fact that spruce never constituted more than a quarter of the forest, so that even the excesses of spruce harvest did not destroy the woods.

Paradoxically, the extreme spruce cutting by the pulp industry did effect a change in forest management. Forests could no longer be harvested and abandoned. The extraordinary capital investment required to build pulp and paper machines rooted the industry at fixed locations near forests.

> Little or nothing was done about forest management until the coming of the pulpwood industry. The sawmill outfits had cut out and got out; they either migrated or liquidated, but wood-converting plants could not pull up stakes and move on because they had large investments in site, power, water sources, buildings and specialized equipment. Wood supplies must be assured for a long operating life. A forest becomes the first essential to the capital structure of such an enterprise. It must be an immense forest, and it must be under management.[12]

## Foresters and Scientific Forestry

Adding to the unlikely coincidence of events that seem to converge around 1892 was the arrival of trained foresters and the infant science of forestry. Foresters tried to play a major role in the establishment of the Adirondack Park and the passage of Article XIV of the Constitution in order to ensure that forests would be managed, not preserved. Their attempts to influence the State to establish State forests where lumbering would continue were unsuccessful, partly because they were unable to provide a united front. Their continued disputes about what constituted scientific forestry confused the legislature and caused it to fail in its efforts to create and regulate such forests. This failure strengthened the preservationists' positions and led to the constitutional convention,[13] which gave the Forest Preserve one of the strongest legal protections possible.

The advice given landowners by foresters had little impact on the forests during the two decades after 1890, and in fact, until much later, its effect was relatively insignificant. Scientific forestry was ineffective at first for two basic reasons. In its infancy, it was groping for methods to manage forests. More importantly, the market place always took precedence over science. As a result, scientific forestry did not come of age in the Adirondacks until well into this century.

The need for a science of forestry was foreseen not by a forester, but by the philosopher George Perkins Marsh in 1864 in his seminal work, *Man and Nature*. He noted the presence of lumbermen and settlements in northern New York, but observed that "forest covers for the largest proportion of the surface." Marsh, however, saw a comparison between these forests with the ravages he had observed in European forests. His book called national attention to the "effects of clearing already perceptible in the comparatively unviolated region." He predicted that, as in Europe, the waters and climate would ultimately be affected. This connection between forest and water preservation inspired the Adirondack's first foresters.

Franklin B. Hough was not trained as a forester either, but he became the father of forestry in the United States. He began as an historian of four northern counties, Lewis, Jefferson, St. Lawrence, and Franklin and in 1865 supervised the State census. Traveling about the United States in the early 1870s, he became concerned about deforestation and was impressed by the discussions among Europeans about deforestation and its effects on climate and rainfall.

"In computing the statistics of distribution and amount of lumber produced as shown in the [New York] Census of 1855 and of 1865, I had noticed a great falling off of some regions indicating an exhaustion of supplies, and an increase in others, showing that new fields had been opened.[14] It did not take much reasoning to reach the inquiry: `How long will these supplies last, and what next?'"[15] Timber production decline in the northeast in the 1870s prompted Hough to speculate that all of the United States virgin forests would disappear.

Throughout his career, Hough, was concerned with the future of the forest. He and his followers believed that annual consumption must be balanced to ensure a supply for the future.

Hough followed the reports of European scientists, who equated forest harvest with rainfall declines and he drew a parallel between the situations in Europe and in the Adirondacks. He linked the future of agriculture, industry, and canals in the region to rainfall, which in turn he believed was dependent on the forests.

In 1872 he served on the commission of State Parks with Colvin and was responsible for most of the writing[16] of the commission's report, which stated: "the chief and very important influence which the forests exercise upon the rain-fall is their power to moderate storms and distribute the annual quantity of rain more equally throughout the year. ... The presence of great forests increases the amount of annual rain-fall."[17]

The United States Department of Agriculture established a Division of Forestry in 1874 at Hough's urging, and he became its first head (although he was not given the title of Chief). His varied interests and native talents, his broad background in history, statistics, botany, meteorology, and geology enabled him to formulate the basis for an American version of this new science, which had begun in Europe.

In 1885, after he had resigned his federal post, he proposed a law for a Forest Commission that would have permitted the selling of timber. He espoused a forest reserve, not preserve. This idea failed, but his influence shows in the commission's 1886 Report, which discussed the relationship between forests, drought, stream flow, and climate. Further, because of Hough's efforts, the commission was impressed by the science of forestry that was emerging in Europe.

The first record of a professionally-trained forester working in the Adirondacks preceded the establishment of the Forest Preserve. In 1881, Alfred Dolge, owner of a piano factory in Dolgeville south of the Adirondacks, hired a German forester to supervise his forest on the Jerseyfield Tract. Over the years, Dolge hired a succession of Germans, the first from the Forest Academy at Tharand, others "graduates of the best German forest academies." Dolge felt that "with the exception of Mr. George Vanderbilt's experiments near Ashville, the experiment of practical forestry has nowhere been so carefully made as in our forest during the last twenty-two years,"[18] that is since 1876, when Dolge himself started practicing forestry on the tract. He was convinced that "the forest is now worth far more than when I bought it."

Germans had practiced forestry for decades, and in the last two decades of the nineteenth century either exported foresters to America or trained Americans as scientific foresters.

Among those to immigrate to America was Bernhard E. Fernow, who in 1881 became the first chief of the Division of Forestry in the United States Department of Agriculture, a position he held until 1889, when he established the ill-fated Cornell experimental forest at Axton near Tupper Lake. See appendix. In 1890, Fernow prepared the country's first large-scale management plan for a private forest--for the Adirondack League Club.

Gifford Pinchot, who replaced Fernow at the Department of Agriculture, was the son of a wealthy New York merchant. He was influenced in college by reading George Perkins Marsh's *Man and Nature* and because there were no forestry schools in America, he went to Europe to complete his education, studying in France and Germany in 1889-90. His first commission to practice forestry was on the North Carolina estate belonging to George W. Vanderbilt. His success in creating a healthy forest from woodland that "never in its best days was very good [and was growing] steadily worse."[19] Vanderbilt recommended Pinchot to his brother-in-law, Dr. William Seward Webb, owner of the 40,000-acre Nehasane Park, and lands later flooded and isolated by Stillwater Reservoir.

Fernow and Pinchot had widely different personalities and equally diverse ideas on scientific forestry. Fernow favored stand management through improvements brought about by heavy cutting and reforestation; Pinchot relied on restrained harvests to preserve natural reproduction. Because the whole science of forestry in America was in an embryonic state, there were many different concepts of what constituted good practices. Most early theories later proved inadequate. Fernow and Pinchot represented the two most prominent points of view, but even these were subject to criticism.

Although he devised a market for hardwoods that would pay for their removal and enhance softwood growth, Fernow's Cornell experiment to demonstrate his theories was so poorly funded that he had to cut more timber than he had envisioned; in addition, the shortage of funds made his plans for reforestation impossible on the scale that was needed. Even the future recovery of the forest[20] did not demonstrate that Fernow's theories would have produced an economical sustained yield. Fernow's personality, that of a dogmatic utilitarian, may have had more to do with the lack of acceptance of his ideas than their scientific merit.

Pinchot's approach was less radical than Fernow's virtual clearcutting. Pinchot promoted a form of selective cutting--the harvest of merchantable timber of a certain minimum size. Even this did not ultimately provide for an economical sustained yield, which Pinchot admitted would probably would not be possible. Col. William F. Fox, Superintendent of State Forests, and a disciple of Pinchot, had little faith in Fernow's planted forests. He espoused the "selection" method of cutting for revenue, but he believed it could only achieve the desired results when confined to mature trees.[21]

Within the next few years it became obvious that cutting for pulp meant that cutting for revenue could not be confined to mature trees. Forestry would yield to the marketplace.

Henry S. Graves, a protege of Pinchot, followed him as Chief Forester of the United States. Graves conceived a management plan for the Whitney Park as well as for Nehasane. Published in 1899, it stated his objectives for the two tracts: "to obtain for the owner a large revenue from the timber, but at the same time to leave the forest in a condition to produce a second crop in a comparatively short time, and to reseed the openings made in lumbering with young growth of valuable species." However, in order to satisfy the goals of the owners for revenue as well as for future returns and "to secure favorable contracts for cutting the timber, a number of measures, usually considered a necessary part of forest management, must be given up." Not possible are "the maintenance of a sustained annual yield, the removal of dead and unsound trees, thinnings and improvement cuttings, and planting,"[22] all practices that are today and were even then considered essential elements of scientific forestry.

Between 1898 and 1909, Whitney Park (see appendix) was logged using Graves' recommendations, with spruce cut to a minimum of 10 inches.[23] The second cut, which began in 1934, after an interval of thirty-six years, was to harvest balsam fir, hemlock and hardwoods. Graves anticipated that spruce would yield a marginally smaller number of cords per acre of the size cut before, and that the tract would yield fifty percent more spruce if all trees five inches and up were harvested. In practice, even with the smaller diameter allowance, the second cut yielded no more than the first in total volume and considerably fewer spruce sawlogs. The foresters managing the operation concluded that the 1934 cut was profitable only because of the conservative cut of the turn of the century.[24]

Col. Fox adhered to Pinchot's philosophy, but saw how difficult it was to achieve its goals. In his monograph *The Adirondack Black Spruce* Fox noted that:

> In several instances the owners of spruce timber lands in northern New York have shown encouraging and commendable tendency to manage their property with reference to sustained productivity. Instead of taking all the merchantable timber available for immediate profit, they have restricted their cutting materially with the intention of securing further growth. ... Although this is a step in the right direction, and something of an improvement on previous methods, there is little in it worthy of the name of forestry. As an approach to scientific or even intelligent forestry methods it is a very slight advance indeed.[25]

Fox was aware that many tracts had been cut over on two or three occasions at intervals of about twenty-five years, but these cuts had not produced an improved yield. He attributed the fact that successive harvests were possible at all to the limited extent of the earlier cuts.

> In the first cutting only the larger and easily accessible trees were taken. Large trees were often left because it did not pay to cut roads to them, the roads being confined to the areas on which the timber grew

thickly. ... In the second cutting the roads were extended into these areas of scattered spruces ... and the large trees left at the first cutting were then taken with many others which had become large enough. The third cutting becomes feasible twenty-five years later by reason of increased market values, improved means of access, and the demand for pulpwood--the latter demand alone making it profitable in many instance to cut over an old tract where the sawing timber by itself would not yield enough to pay the expense of "lumbering it."[26]

Further, he concluded cutting for revenue rather than improvement "cannot secure the desired result--that of the perpetual maintenance of a merchantable species."

Pinchot theorized that perpetual harvest would be possible if only large trees were cut, but even this is questionable. Studies showed that successive cuts yielded reduced amounts of spruce, but these studies could not be continued because the private tracts were subject to pulpwood cuts that contravened all of the foresters' plans. Fox was skeptical of establishing a minimum diameter limit, feeling that it was necessary to have a century of experience in improvement cutting, seeding or planting.

A 1917 study blamed the inability of Pinchot and Graves to predict future yields on their failure to understand forest types. According to E. F. McCarthy, Professor of Forest Utilization at the College of Forestry at Syracuse, "hardwoods are inclined to dominate the forest after the cutting of softwoods to a diameter limit."[27] At Brandreth Park, it was observed that twenty years after cutting, "the hardwood crown has closed over the spruce trees remaining after the first cut so quickly as to have made their [the softwoods] recovery brief and to have added very little extra volume to even the larger diameter classes and almost none to the lower." McCarthy presented data to show that "the increase in the rate of growth after the first lumbering operation was not greatly in excess of what might be expected from the virgin stand untouched." He found a similar result at Whitney Park, where forest management had called for the cutting of both hardwoods and softwoods and was supposed to have secured a second cut for pulp. In the era when spruce reproduction was a paramount concern, McCarthy found that the methods recommended by earlier foresters all resulted in good hardwood sapling growth, the reverse of what they had wished to achieve.

Even if the plans put forth by foresters had been appropriate, it is clear that they were rarely followed. The Forest Commission's working plan for Township 40, see Chapter IX, which calls for circumventing the tenets of the forever wild clause, touts what was at the time considered proper forestry management. Implicit in the report is the fact that even though foresters knew what to do, very few were following the recommended techniques. The realization that the forests were not limitless had convinced lumbermen and owners of large tracts to look to scientific forestry for help; the appendix profiles of individual tracts is full of examples showing that the advice of foresters was generally ignored.

Fernow was at his most eloquent and persuasive in his 1891 forestry report for the Adirondack League Club. (See appendix) Fernow bravely predicted income from the club lands, modest expenditures for forest improvement, and "the certainty of having present expenditures returned in increased value," despite the fact that these results had never been achieved before. He claimed his theories of forest management could be achieved by clearing away unwanted species to regulate light, thus encouraging desirable species.

The lumberman places only a temporary value on his property, quickly gets out the most valuable timber, taking the cream and leaving the balance, like skimmed milk, in the woods, to rot, burn, deteriorate. If nature so wills it, and some cream was left in the first operation, he may return and repeat the skimming process once or twice, leaving at last an undesirable scrub growth or "bush."

The forester considers his property as a permanent investment, to produce revenue constantly and forever, in increasing rather than decreasing ratio. The factor of permanence is ever present in his methods.[28]

The results of early timber harvesting on the Adirondack League Club property did not bear Fernow out. His plan was impeded by unsupervised and uncontrolled loggers. Most loggers were distrusted even when they were under the direction of a forester, and their activities on the Adirondack League Club forests were not unique. When asked if he would favor scientific forestry, that is, the cutting of mature timber on State land, the manager of the Saranac Club replied that "you will have to have a man on the ground all the time to watch them or they will cut everything." Asked if that wasn't "a pretty tough criticism," he countered, "Well, I don't know any lumberman I would want to trust on a lot of mine."[29]

Foresters were just beginning to understand their science, and much remained to be learned about managing forests. Their efforts, however, were undone, not by what they failed to understand, but by their lack of influence on the owners of timber tracts, by the independence of loggers, and by the owner's inability to control loggers.

# Hardwoods

The harvest of hardwoods began slowly, rising from virtually nothing in the 1880s to almost six million board feet in 1890. In the next fifteen years, hardwood lumber production increased nearly sixteen-fold to almost 79 million board feet, an amount that was still less than twelve percent of the total Adirondack harvest of all species. The total hardwood cuts exceeded twenty percent of all timber harvested only once before 1910. The growth of hardwood production was directly attributable to the railroads that crossed the Adirondacks and to the many railroad spurs that made hardwood logging possible.

Col. Fox observed that before 1890 most hardwoods were logged only on the edge of wilderness, especially in Fulton and Herkimer counties where they were used for furniture. Hardwood logs were taken from the border of the southern Adirondacks to Mohawk Valley mills by horse-drawn sleighs that traveled upwards of thirty miles.[30] Cherry and white ash were harvested in the Beaver River area.

Tupper Lake became the only large center for hardwood milling in the heart of the Park. However, the real growth of hardwood

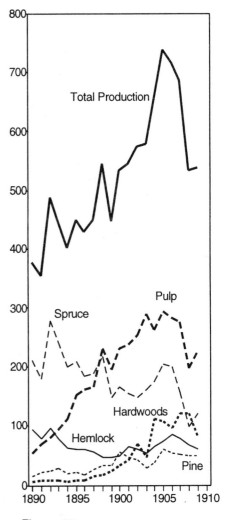

Total Adirondack production of sawlogs and pulp, by species, 1890 - 1910

Figure 37

production in the Tupper Lake area did not come until after 1910 and the arrival of Emporium Lumber Company.

The value of hardwoods, which had been virtually worthless, rose in this period, but remained way below that of spruce. The price of hardwoods doubled between 1900 and 1910 from $2 or $3 per thousand board feet to $5, but did not compare with the price of spruce which was still bringing $7 to $10 per thousand.[31]

Hardwood logging began on lands that had been cut over for softwoods, some of them more than once, so that hardwood crowns had closed in and inhibited the growth of softwoods, greatly reducing the amount of softwoods available for succeeding cuts. The increased hardwood logging, which resulted from the new mills and transportation, did little to change the fact that privately-owned Adirondack forests were becoming ever more dominantly hardwood stands.

# Railroads

Railroads brought about the first technological changes in the transportation of logs. There had been some logging by rail before 1892, but after that year, loggers were able to reach remote stands not accessible to rivers and streams. The growth of railroads was one of the factors in the shift of lumber production away from the Glens Falls area. See figure 33.

For all the railroad building in the north country, railroads had little effect on the forest products industry until 1885, but after that railroads became the catalyst for change in the industry. A glance at the map will show why railroads had such a minor effect before 1885--no lines penetrated the heart of the Park. A line approached from the north in the late 1880s, and it was not until 1892 that a railroad finally crossed the Park.

The absence of rails cannot be attributed to a lack of proposals to build them. From the 1830s on, the legislature chartered a number of lines, a few of which were incorporated. In some cases the incorporators even printed pamphlets soliciting investors. The stories of the phantom railroads are entertaining reading and they do represent the great movement of the day to tame the wilderness and settle it. But, the Adirondacks resisted settling.[32] With the exception of the New York Central Railroad, even the lines that were built around the perimeter of the Park, in the valleys of the Black and St. Lawrence rivers and of Lake Champlain, were not constructed until the middle of the nineteenth century.

The Northern New York Railroad (also known as the Ogdensburg and Lake Champlain Railroad) was proposed in 1844 and built between 1848 and 1850. Its route, in the far northern part of the State through agricultural lands in the St. Lawrence River Valley, outside the present boundary of the Park, would have had little effect on northern forests, had it not been for two north-south lines, constructed nearly four decades later, which crossed the Ogdensburg and Lake Champlain Railroad at Moira and Malone.

A line north from Plattsburgh was started in 1852, but it developed financial problems, and did not reach its destination, Montreal, until 1868. A line north to Plattsburgh from Whitehall also faced financial difficulties. Incorporated in 1866, it was not completed until 1875, when it and the line north of Plattsburgh were taken over by a branch of the Delaware and Hudson Company and the line between Whitehall and Plattsburgh was completed. This enabled the first train to run from Albany to Montreal in 1875, a remarkably late date for train service to traverse the western side of the Champlain Valley.[33]

In 1853, at the time these Champlain Valley routes were begun, the Sackets Harbor and Saratoga Railroad was chartered and two potential routes studied, both of which would have cut through the heart of the wilderness. The northern route was planned from the Hudson River to Raquette Lake and then west, following either the Beaver or the Moose rivers to the Black River Valley. The southern route would follow the Sacandaga Valley, turning west south of Piseco to the Black River Valley. The incorporators secured an option from the State to acquire a quarter of a million acres of Adirondack land at 5 cents an acre. The sale of this land, which would increase in value with the coming of the railroad, would finance its building. The cross-Adirondack line was never built, but the land option, as discussed in chapter VI, became a boon for logging interests.

After a series of financial problems and disputes that seem to be common to all the period's proposed railroads, a New York capitalist, Dr. Thomas C. Durant, invested in the venture, reorganizing it as the Adirondack Company. He determined the route would go from Saratoga to North Creek, then on to the north of Long Lake and down the valley of the Raquette River to Tupper Lake, then northwest along the Grasse to Ogdensburg. By 1871, the railroad was completed to North Creek, where it stopped until World War II, when it was extended north to the iron and titanium mine at Tahawus. Even the early arrival of the line at North Creek in 1871 had little effect on logging, because the railroad followed the Hudson River, whose corridor had been largely cleared for agriculture and where all the spruce that could be dragged to the river had been cut. Durant's railroad may have been the first to penetrate the Adirondack region, but it did not reach the wilderness.

The first north-south line to the west of the Adirondacks was the Rome and Watertown line, incorporated in 1848, and completed to Lake Ontario in 1852. The Utica and Black River Railroad was completed to Boonville in 1855, to Lowville in 1868, and extended to Lake Ontario as the Carthage, Watertown and Sackets Harbor line in 1870. The latter spurred industry in the Black River Valley and certainly led to Watertown and Lyons Falls becoming centers for the pulp and paper industry, but all shipment of logs to the numerous sawmills and later pulp mills built along the Black River were still floated down the Black and its tributaries to these mills.

One of the first lines built expressly for the lumber industry was began at the Black River Feeder Canal at Forestport. It had wooden rails and horses for locomotion and was called variously the Forestport, Grants Mills and Bellingertown or the Black River and Woodhull. Started in 1867, one branch swung north and east toward Little Woodhull Creek and Albert C. Grant's mill, another branch headed south of east toward Pine Creek. It apparently ceased operation after the Black River flood of April 21, 1869 caused by the washout of the dam on North Lake.

# ADIRONDACK RAIL LINES

to Montreal · to Montreal

St. Lawrence River · River · River · Little River · to Ottawa · to Montreal

Massena · Raquette River · St. Regis River · Salmon River · Chateaugay · Mooers · Chazy

Grass · Winthrop · Brushton · Malone · Ellenburg Center · CLINTON

Deer River · Salmon River · Cadyville · Plattsburgh

to Ogdensburg · Ogdensburg & Lake Champlain RR · Potsdam · Dannemora · Redford · Peru

Watertown & Potsdam RR · Canton · Colton · Saint Regis Falls · FRANKLIN · Chateaugay RR · Saranac River · Keeseville · Ausable River

to Watertown · North Branch Grasse River · Edwards · ST. LAWRENCE · Paul Smiths · Bloomingdale · Wilmington · Jay · Au Sable Forks · Willsboro

Oswegatchie · South Branch River · Adirondack & St. Lawrence RR · Saranac Lake · West Branch Ausable River · East Br. Ausable River · Keene · Elizabethtown · Boquet River · Westport

Fine · Raquette River · Tupper Lake · Lake Placid · Keene Valley

to Carthage · Carthage & Adirondack RR · Cranberry Lake · Star Lake · Wanakena · Grasse River · Port Henry

Beaver River · Croghan · Newcomb · ESSEX · Crown Point

Long Lake · Hudson River · Schroon River · Ticonderoga

LEWIS · HERKIMER · Blue Mountain Lake · Schroon Lake · Hague

Independence River · Raquette Lake · Cedar River · Minerva · Pottersville

Old Forge · Inlet · Fulton Chain Lakes · North River · WARREN

Thendara · Moose River · HAMILTON · North Creek · Bolton Landing · Whitehall

Lyons Falls · Black River · Wevertown · Delaware & Hudson RR · Hudson River · Warrensburg · Fort Ann

Port Leyden · Speculator · Sacandaga River · Lake George

Boonville · Champlain Canal · WASHINGTON

Forestport · West Canada Creek · Wells · Lake Luzerne · Glens Falls · Hudson Falls

ONEIDA · Northville · Corinth · Fort Edward

Remsen · Trenton · Cold Brook · Stratford · SARATOGA

Holland Patent · Black River · Poland · East Canada Creek · Caroga Lake · Saratoga Springs

Newport · Middleville · Dolgeville · Broadalbin · Map 8

to Rome & Syracuse · Utica · to Little Falls · FULTON · to Johnstown & Fonda · to Albany & Schenectady

to Herkimer

Lines in the northeastern Adirondacks served the iron industry and made possible the harvest of hardwoods for charcoal. The completion of the Delaware and Hudson Railroad paralleling the shore of Lake Champlain made it possible for coal to supplant charcoal for making iron. The hardwoods, and most softwoods, were rapidly being harvested from the northeastern Adirondacks. A spur from Plattsburgh southwest was constructed in stages beginning in 1868. It reached Arnold near the J. and J. Rogers' Palmer Iron Mine in 1878. It was not until 1894 that a spur of the railroad was extended to the J. and J. Rogers' pulp mill upriver from AuSable Forks. Because the line passed through regions that had been clearcut, it had little effect on the lumber industry.

Further north, a railroad was built in 1879 to the State prison at Dannemora from Plattsburgh. That same year it was extended to Ore Bed, near Chateaugay, taking the latter name for the line. The extension was primarily designed to serve mines near Lyon Mountain. While much of that route was not exactly virgin forest, further extensions of the line, which reached Saranac Lake in 1887, were through territory that had seen little logging. With the building of over a hundred kilns along its route, hardwoods were rapidly stripped from the entire route and along several of the line's spurs. The route of the Chateaugay became the quickest way to reach Saranac Lake from metropolitan areas on the east coast. It was the route used by all those who by 1890 were decrying railroad penetration into the wilderness.

"What is true of the desolation along this Chateaugay Railroad is true, and worse, if possible, along the other railroads which have penetrated the forest."[34] This narrow-gauge line, sometimes called the Plattsburg-Lake Placid Railroad, was acquired by the Delaware and Hudson Company about 1903.

About the same time that first railroad approached the heart of the Park from the east, a line was built started from the west. The Adirondack and Carthage was conceived in 1865 as an extension of the Rome, Watertown and Ogdensburg Railroad, but building did not begin until 1883. The line was completed as far as Jayville in 1886 and to Oswegatchie and Benson Mines in 1889.

Lines reached toward the southern Adirondacks from the New York Central's line in the Mohawk Valley. The Little Falls and Dolgeville was built in the 1870s, but it was not extended into the Park until this century. An extension of the Fonda, Johnstown and Gloversville Railroad reached Northville in 1872. Both lines served a multitude of other industries.

## Railroads Built for the Lumber Industry

The first railroad to reach into the Adirondacks that was built to serve the lumber industry, was John Hurd's Northern Adirondack line. In 1883 Hurd built the eleven-mile section stretching from Moira on the Ogdensburg and Lake Champlain (or Northern Railroad) south to St. Regis Falls, where he and his partners acquired a sawmill and 60,000 (variously stated as 75,000) acres of forest land that stretched to the south and southeast. See appendix. Hurd bought out his partners and continued his railroad venture "entirely alone."[35] The twenty-mile stretch from St. Regis Falls through Santa Clara and Brandon was

*Map 8, Adirondack Rail Lines,*
*on the opposite page*
*depicts schematically*
*the dense network*
*of logging railroads*
*and tram lines*
*in the northwestern Adirondacks.*

completed in 1886, the last fifteen miles through wilderness. By 1889, Hurd's railroad had reached Tupper Lake. Every stop on the line from Moira south became a logging and lumbering center.

An 1890 account in *The Boonville Herald*[36] informs that Hurd planned an extension of his railroad south to Utica, taking a route from Fourth Lake south between Bisby and Canachagala lakes, right through what is now the Adirondack League Club. This proposal was not a serious one, because it was made as Hurd's fortunes were fading, but it certainly interested local businessmen with the prediction that the line would carry twenty-five carloads a day with a quarter million board feet of lumber from the mill at Tupper Lake to Utica.

Hurd, that "overnight creator of mushroom mills and hamlets and reckless speculator in lumber lands," had "many other irons in the fire, all hastily and precariously financed, [and] soon found himself in trouble."[37] With his railroad in receivership, it was sold to a syndicate, becoming the Northern Adirondack Railroad. It was extended to Ottawa, renamed the New York and Ottawa Railroad, and sold to the New York Central Railroad, all by 1906.

Even with Hurd's line, in 1890 there was no railroad crossing the Adirondacks--just the threat that there might be one--and the conflict surrounding its threatened arrival filled the newspapers and periodicals around 1890.

## Dr. William Seward Webb

Dr. William Seward Webb did not become formally involved with the railroad which would finally cross the Park until 1891, but his genius for organization and experience with railroads enabled him to complete the railroad in a little over a year. This feat appears all the more remarkable in light of the problems he encountered.[38] The logistics of crossing streams and swamps and lakes were comparable to the plots surrounding the line itself.

Webb, the son-in-law of William H. Vanderbilt, began buying lands for his Nehasane Park and tried to interest the New York Central Railroad in building a railroad through his preserve and failing that, Webb decided to build the line himself. Opposition to the railroad was well-organized, led in part by Charles S. Sargent's *Garden and Forest*. "If the woods were crossed and recrossed with railroads, settlements would spring up at their intersection, the deer would be frightened from their ranges, the fish in the streams and lakes would be caught for city markets, and the wildness would be chased away with the game. The place would still have attractions, but it would no longer be a wilderness."[39] Webb promised to protect the forest, not permitting his line to carry any trees less than 12 inches in diameter.[40]

Webb built his line as a common carrier and passengers and tourists from metropolitan areas were his primary concern. From the start he planned to sell the line to the New York Central. However, opponents of the line saw the potential damage of its use as a logging railroad, and, as it turned out, the line benefitted the lumber industry as much as it did tourism. Not only were railroads thought to be capable of destroying the woods, the railroads did not have consistent benefits for the traveler. A tourist in 1891, writing in *Forest and Stream*, noted that "The hotels in the Adirondacks are no longer in the woods.

There are no woods where there are railroads a year old. We have stumps and dead trees in lieu of forest; hotels with electric lights and Chicago beef in lieu of hunters' camps and venison."[41] In spite of the opposition, Webb prevailed.

The location of the line was determined by two series of events. A line following the West Canada Creek was surveyed in 1836 but not built until 1880. The Herkimer, Newport and Poland Railroad, a narrow gauge line, reached Middleville in 1881, with plans to extend it further north.[42] In 1890, a group of investors secured control of the foundering line by paying half the value of its stock. The public was alerted to the possibility that the syndicate, a disparate mix of investors,[43] those seeking to preserve the region mingled with those seeking to exploit its timber resources, might extend the line to Jock's Lake (now Honnedaga). Dr. Webb acquired the line in 1890 as a southern anchor for his planned route.

A part of the northern route had its origins in Durant's railroad, which was reorganized in 1863, to include the rights to a million acres of Adirondack land free of taxes until 1883 and the option to extend his line to either the St. Lawrence or Lake Ontario.[44] Both Durant and Webb tried to gain permission to cross State land, Webb for his projected railroad, Durant as an extension of the line from North Creek. The State granted neither man a right-of-way across State lands. Durant was stymied but Webb bought 115,000 acres of private land for an alternative route. That brought Webb's line to Tupper Lake, and would have solved the problem of crossing State lands if he had then been able to use Hurd's railroad as a northern connector.

As Webb was negotiating to buy Hurd's line, Hurd sold it out from under him.

> That night, Mr. Paine, of the Pope-Paine Lumber Company, saw Hurd at his hotel and offered to raise his price fifty thousand dollars if he would grant an option on the road for a short time. Hurd agreed. The next morning, instead of signing the papers, he merely called to say that the deal was off. There was no angrier man that day than Dr. Webb. Later Paine came in and tried to sell his option at an advance in price. That did not improve the Doctor's temper. He told them both that he would parallel the Hurd Road within a year, and he kept his word.[45]

Webb decided to take his line north to Malone instead of Moira, but this again involved crossing State lands. Webb's solution was ingenious. Dr. Samuel B. Ward acquired title to a 30,000-acre tract north of Tupper Lake by successfully challenging the State's acquisition of the land through tax sale.[46] Ward sold a strip through the tract to Webb for his railroad.

Webb's line, the Adirondack and St. Lawrence or the Mohawk and Malone Railroad, was completed in late 1892 and leased to the New York Central Railroad in 1893, becoming the Adirondack Division of the New York Central. A spur from this line connected Lake Clear Junction[47] and Saranac Lake in 1892. Another spur to the east of Tupper Lake was built to accommodate Bernhard Fernow's forestry experiment at Axton. This one was so hastily constructed that the manager of the Tupper Lake Chemical Works wrote Fernow, "We are having considerable trouble in keeping the wood cars on the spur tracks leading on your property. Today there have been five cars off the track."[48]

In 1898, Dr. Webb entered into an agreement that called for the New York Central Railroad to operate the line and share profits or losses and in 1905, the New York Central Railroad purchased the entire outstanding capital stock of the Adirondack and St. Lawrence Railroad.

## Railroad Spurs Used to Harvest Logs

With the completion of both Webb's and Hurd's railroad, spurs like the legs on a centipede reached into virgin hardwood tracts and pushed logging operations farther and farther into the wilderness. Verplanck Colvin had noted the arrival of this phenomenon and its impact on the value of land as early as 1883. "The construction of narrow gauge railroads into the forest has been commenced and, timbered lands along the routes of such roads are held at an increased valuation."[49] In reality, most of the railroads built in the Adirondacks were standard gauge to accommodate the engines that lumber companies imported from other lines.

A spur built in 1886 from Hurd's line enabled the logging of land east of Everton, and logging along that line continued after the line was rebuilt by Brooklyn Cooperage Company about 1904, specifically to carry hardwoods to the Tupper mill. This was one of the first spur lines built for logging and it continued to operate under Brooklyn Cooperage until about 1920. Brooklyn Cooperage also built thirty miles of track in several branch spurs west from Meno after 1909; one spur reached all the way to Lake Ozonia. A second logging line in the St. Regis Falls vicinity served the Watson Page Lumber Company.

In 1924, a line was extended through the Bay Pond Tract to the West Branch of the St. Regis. Spurs from McDonald Station were used until 1937, though much of the area reached by the spur burned in 1934.

Around 1886, Kinsley Lumber Company built a line west from the New York Central Railroad through Tekene west to the south shore of Debar Pond. The sale of the lumber company to Baker Brothers, who had connections to the Delaware and Hudson, meant that this short line was rerouted and connected to the Chateaugay Branch.[50] Another short line connected the Delaware and Hudson Railroad at Onchiota with the Roak Sawmill at Roakdale between about 1887 and 1895.

Oval Wood Dish Company of Tupper Lake established logging headquarters at Kildare in 1916 and the next year began constructing a logging railroad to the southwestern corner of Township 19 in Franklin County, just short of Mount Matumbla. Shortly afterwards the company built a line north from Kildare toward St. Lawrence County, which remained in operation until 1926. The main tracks totalled thirty miles, a figure that was doubled by spurs, which were used only for a year or two, then picked up and moved; elsewhere.

In acquiring the Herkimer, Newport and Poland line, Webb also obtained a charter for a line east to Nobleboro along West Canada

Creek. Only the first short part of that line was completed as far as Hinckley (Gang Mills) to serve the huge sawmill there.

A group of businessmen built a spur to Old Forge where passengers could board steamers for travel up the Fulton Chain. Another line was constructed north of the Fulton Chain in 1899 by the Raquette Lake Railroad; it was designed to serve wealthy landowners, visitors to the resorts at Blue Mountain (via the Marion River Carry Railroad), and to carry timber cut by former Governor John A. Dix near Rondaxe Lake. Dix was a partner with Lemon Thomson and Edward Thomson Jr. in the Moose River Lumber Company which had a lumber mill at McKeever on the rail line. Not built, but proposed was an extension of the Raquette Lake Railroad to virgin timber on Township 40.

Webb's railroad was used to transport logs not only from his Nehasane Park, but it also opened many private tracts to logging, encouraging intensive harvest on an unparalleled scale. While Webb's, line carried passengers as well as logs and lumber, the spurs were designed only for the latter use. The first connecting routes, built solely for logging, were those constructed out from Horseshoe by A. A. Low. His Horseshoe Forestry Company Railway built three spurs from the New York Central Railroad in 1897 to harvest wood on his 40,000-acre tract and ship maple syrup and spring water. Logging stopped after the disastrous 1908 forest fire, and the spur ceased operating in 1911.

A five-mile spur was extended out from the New York Central Railroad's Partlow Station as the Partlow Railroad and it was used to haul logs between 1900 and 1905 on Webb's own lands.[51]

The railroad also made possible the logging of Brandreth Park, where in 1912 the Mac-a-Mac Lumbering Company built a branch to take logs and pulp wood from the 26,000-acre tract. The logging operation ceased in 1920, but the tracks were relaid in 1936 to Whitney Park. This line was extended into the Whitney lands and was used to haul hardwood logs until 1939.[52]

Even Paul Smith's Electric Railway, which connected his resort with the New York Central Railroad at Lake Clear Junction, was used to haul logs for a few years after 1905. Logs were dumped on the ice at a jackworks at Lower St. Regis Lake, from which they were floated to Paul Smith's sawmill.[53]

## Spurs from the Adirondack and Carthage

Spurs from the Adirondack and Carthage Railroad were extended south to previously untapped forests.

*Tram line*

*Courtesy Adirondack Museum*

The Post and Henderson Lumber Company opened a sawmill at Jayville in the early 1890s, and toward the end of the century the company opened a large sawmill at Benson Mines and shortly after one at Little River to the south. All were on the rail line and spurs from this main line gave Post and Henderson, Mecca, Rich, and other lumber companies access to untapped wilderness tracts.

Post and Henderson Lumber Company built a Pole Road, a railroad of sorts south from Jayville in 1898. In 1903, the Mecca Lumber Company built a sawmill at Little Mill, which the company renamed Kalurah. A logging railroad was constructed south from the mill to Scuttle Hole and Round Lake. Mecca exhausted the timber on its holdings and moved away in 1910. Around 1905, Post and Henderson built a logging line south from Benson Mines.

The Adirondack and Carthage extended its line from Aldrich to the Newton Falls Paper Company's pulp mill at Newton Falls before 1900. Newton Falls Paper Co. built a line south beyond Streeter Lake. Its eastern spur reached a jackworks and boom at Scanlons on the Middle Branch of the Oswegatchie. According to Michael Kudish, railroad historian, "Jackworks were places where railroad flat cars were loaded or unloaded into bodies of water such as rivers or lakes. Conveyor belts caught on to the logs and hauled them up or down the ramp."[54] Like railroads, jackworks were more common in the northwestern Adirondacks.

In 1908, the Higbie Lumber Company formed the Newton Falls and Northern Railroad, a seven-mile long logging railroad that extended north from Newton Falls to New Bridge. It remained in operation until 1919.[55]

All of the lumber companies that used the Adirondack and Carthage Railroad to bring logs to their mills quickly exhausted their resources, and none any faster than Rich Lumber Company

## Rich Lumber Company

Rich Lumber Company brought the expertise it had gained in using rails for logging in Pennsylvania to the north country after 1901, when the company acquired 16,000 acres south of Wanakena. By 1905, the company had built fifteen miles of railroad tracks to harvest the white pines and spruce of the Plains, a flat area bordered on the west by a wide arc of the Oswegatchie River. A huge sawmill was constructed by the company and a shoe last factory and a veneer mill were built nearby by other interests.

To connect the logging line with the Carthage and Adirondack Railway (which was now part of the New York Central Railroad), the company was able to obtain a charter for the Cranberry Lake Railroad in 1902 and the six miles of track from Benson Mines to Wanakena was laid the next year.

The railroad facilitated the harvest of one of the last stands of giant pine trees in the Park. Rich Lumber Company only cut sawlogs, and took almost no pulp wood. The company used Shay locomotives almost exclusively. Shays were geared engines of a unique design that had the power to pull heavier loads of logs than any ordinary engine could. Shays had "three vertical cylinders on the right side of the boiler and a horizontal drive shaft along the right had outside face of the wheels."[56] This type of engine, the Shay and two others, were capable of handling crooked track with grades up to 10 percent. Introduced to the Adirondacks in the 1880s, geared engines were used also by Brooklyn Cooperage, Higbie Lumber Co., and Mac-a-Mac, among others.

Rich Lumber Company's mill closed in 1912 and in the short seven-year interval, the company turned this magnificent wilderness stand into a "desolate area of logging slash and gaunt tree skeletons left by forest fires."[57] Some of its land was given to build the Ranger School at Wanakena, some went to the State University at Syracuse to be used as an experimental forest, and the bulk became Forest Preserve.

## Emporium Forestry Company and the Grasse River Railroad

The most complex network of rail tracks built for logging in the north country was the work of William L. Sykes and his three sons. Sykes' Emporium Lumber Company began purchasing land in the Adirondacks in 1905 and over the next thirty-eight years bought and logged 125,000 acres. Their first mill, 1911, was at Conifer, the site of a small mill built to saw logs harvested on International Paper Company's 35,000 acre tract.

To harvest Emporium's land, a first section of railroad was built from Childwold on the New York Central Railroad, west to the mill at Conifer in 1913, and on to Cranberry Lake, a distance of sixteen miles. This well-built line could handle the company's standard rod locomotives. The Grasse River Railroad was chartered as a common carrier from Cranberry Lake to Childwold shortly after 1915.

The company began buying land around Cranberry Lake, and in 1920 added large tracts which had been logged, sometimes twice, for softwoods by International Paper Company. A second sawmill was built on a pond just north of Cranberry Lake Village. Hardwood logs were floated down Cranberry Lake on rafts where steam-powered Barnhart loaders lifted them to cars of the Grasse River Railroad. The Cranberry Mill closed in 1927.

Tracks for a north tram line were laid to the north and west from the Grasse River line along the Middle Branch of the Grasse. Tram lines were used only for the logging; they were not permanent lines, and their tracks, sometimes built of wood, though in the Adirondacks almost always of steel. The tracks were laid down in such a way that they could be picked up and relocated as soon as an area had been logged. The roadbeds of tram lines were crudely built; they were not graded, no trestles were built, few banks were cut, and slab wood was often used to fill holes and depressions in the ground, with ties placed right on top of the slabs. The tram tracks etched wide sweeping curves into the wilds in order to avoid hills or sometimes climbed over them, using much steeper grades than regular lines. The Shay engines proved their worth here on the Grasse River Railroad.

Spurs, short tentacles, reached out for the main portion of the Grasse River Railroad to the company's tracts that stretched almost to Clare on the North Branch of the Grasse. The tracks and spurs of this tram line totalled forty miles in length.

After the depression, the company began selling its land, with the last major sale occurring in 1945 and the railroad ceased shortly after. Before its demise, the railroad had made possible the harvest of over 1.1 billion board feet of hardwoods.

## More Tram Lines

In addition to the spurs built to haul logs to mills, a handful of lines were built for that purpose alone. The first of the rail lines intended expressly for logging appears to have been the tram line built around 1871 in the area east of Chases Lake by Lewis, Crawford & Company The five-mile long line brought logs to the company's two lumber mills. The company was also one of the earliest manufacturers of tanning extract from hemlock bark.[58]

Two logging lines were built as extensions of the Adirondack and St. Lawrence Railroad. About 1913, a standard gauge logging line was pushed six miles east from McKeever to the foot of Woodhull Mountain to haul out hardwoods to supply the Moose River Lumber Company's mill. In 1916, International Paper Company built a spur from Woods Lake to Twitchell Creek. This three-mile long spur was used until 1926.

The Little Falls and Dolgeville line was extended north through Salisbury Center almost to Jerseyfield Lake by the Jerseyfield Lumber Company. This tram line was built in 1914 to bring hardwoods to a stave mill that was built in Salisbury by Brooklyn Cooperage Company of Tupper Lake. This line with several spurs carried logs from the Trammel Creek area until 1925 or 1926.[59] The Little Falls and Dolgeville Railroad kept the tract as far as Salisbury Center through 1946 and the railroad served to haul softwoods for West Virginia Pulp and Paper Company from the Jerseyfield Tract. (See appendix.)

The impact of railroads on Adirondack logging began not long before 1892; logging by rail diminished sharply after 1920 as the logging industry itself shrank. Railroads permitted operations that were so intense that some of them lasted less than a decade. The corridors rails opened to logging were not much wider than those accessible to rivers and streams, but spurs were easily built to enlarge their range.

Logging by rail proved to be very expensive and was used primarily where no floatable streams existed or where hardwoods were harvested. Testimony given during Webb's suit to recover damages from land flooded by Stillwater Reservoir claimed that lumbering by rail was at least three times as expensive as lumbering by water.[60] As part of the testimony, one lumberman noted that the bare cost of loading logs on cars was high; another said that railroads wiped out profits. The railroads charged a substantial rate for hauling logs, disproportionately more than they charged for transporting finished lumber products. As a result of the large initial investment to build a railroad and the operating costs, there was a tendency to clearcut all available timber[61] in order to make a profit.

Because of such excessive cutting, the predictions and warnings about the negative consequences of the railroads came to pass; and, to compound the problems, not only did they spark fires along their route, see below, but the lands, which had been heavily cut because the railroads traversed them, were the most apt to burn.

# Fires and Drought

Before 1890, fires had been small and scattered. The Sargent Committee heard testimony from lumbermen that, while fires were the biggest threat to the forest, they were not caused by lumbering operations. Fires were attributed to squatters, careless guides, and hunters, and burned only cutover land; it was thought that fires could be controlled by keeping settlers out.[62]

In the period between 1890 and 1910 however, fires, mostly caused by railroad locomotives, plagued landowners, seriously affecting timber tracts for the first time. Figure 39 gives the amount of acreage burned in this period. The statistics show three facts concerning fires: there were widespread fires in only two years, almost all of the land that burned except in those two years had been cut-over, and most of the tracts that burned, especially in the first bad fire year, burned again in subsequent fires.

A certain cause of the severity of the fires is a general drought. Recall that the Forest Preserve and its constitutional protection came about largely because of the desire to protect the watersheds, but the impact of logging on the Hudson watershed was light enough before 1890 that it is unlikely that it caused the drought. Furthermore, the drought appeared to weaken during the years of heaviest logging.

Droughts, however, were real. In 1898 Orlando Beede had to add an extra pipe to serve his hotel (the future site of the Ausable Club), even though, as he said, there had been no logging nearby.

Nineteenth-century Adirondack weather records are incomplete. It is impossible to take information from one part of the Park during a decade or so and combine it with subsequent information from another part of the Park because of the wide variations in rainfall throughout. In general, the southwestern Adirondacks receives almost twice the rainfall as the northeast. There are no cumulative statistics for any one Adirondack location before 1890, but there are many anecdotes to show that rainfall and levels of rivers and canals were down. Precipitation declined during the second half of the century.

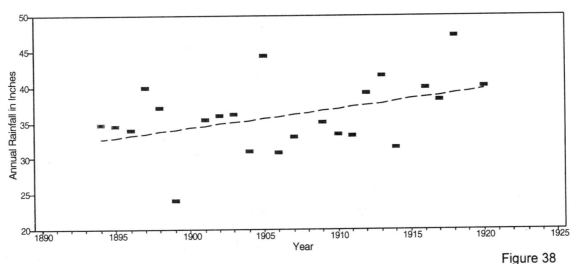

Average annual rainfall at Saranac Lake and Gabriels

Figure 38

139

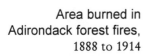

Area burned in
Adirondack forest fires,
1888 to 1914

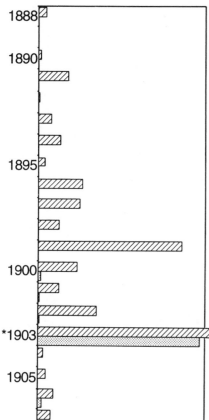

0        20        40        60
Acres Burned
(Thousands)

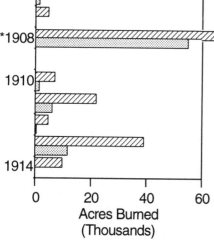

State        Private

Figure 39

However, after 1895 the average rainfall at Saranac Lake and Gabriels gradually increased, even though year to year amounts varied widely. (The reports from these localities are used because they provide a complete record after 1895 and because they represent conditions in northern Adirondack areas where fires were most severe.) These records indicate a gradual increase in rainfall during the period of heaviest logging in the Park as well as during the period of the greatest fires.[63]

Despite the fact there was a general drought throughout the region, it was less a factor in the fires than the peculiar pattern of rainfall during the two worst fire years.

Fires in the year 1903 resulted from a spring drought when "no rain, except slight local showers, fell in the Adirondack region from April fourth to June eleventh. The month of May was the driest in seventy-seven years, the driest since 1826. In Albany the rainfall was only fifteen one hundredths of an inch, and it was still less in northern New York. Combined with the lack of rain there was an unusually high temperature, the month of May showing an accumulated excess above the normal, ... and on June sixth and seventh it reached over ninety in the shade"[64] at Saranac Lake. The conditions were the worst possible. Not only was it hot and dry, but the heat came before leaf-out so that the soil was further exposed to drying. Fires were inevitable and over 464,000 acres burned.

In 1908, just the reverse occurred: the summer was dry and the worst drought conditions occurred after leaves had fallen so that both soil and fallen leaves were dry as tinder. Such a fall drought also makes fires inevitable, and over 308,000 acres burned.

The years 1899, 1910, 1911, and 1914 were relatively dry but only in 1899 and 1913 did the number of burned acres exceed 50,000, barely 12 percent of the amount burned in 1903. In every other year, with or without drought, considerably less acreage burned.

Other than exacerbating the fires, it is difficult to say how much the drought affected logging in this period. It did however, have a real effect on river driving. Records from the Big Boom in the 1890s and early 1900s indicate that it took three years to float logs to Glens Falls because of low water levels.[65]

## Fires Caused by Man

The one natural cause of fires--drought--would not have accounted for many fires if there had not been the three major man-made causes: the vast amount of land cleared for agriculture, sparks from the engines of trains, and the practice of leaving tops of logged trees uncut, so huge piles of tops and branches were exposed to sun and drying winds, which turned them into tinder. The fires along railroads were so severe that a private fire-fighting train was stationed at Nehasane Park.

The Forest Commission and successor agencies kept statistics on forest fires after 1889. Information about fires before that date is anecdotal, but indications are that there were relatively few fires, except those that escaped from tracts being burned to create farmland, although one large fire in Franklin County in 1874 may have burned partially logged timber lands.

Fires were the subject of much testimony from lumbermen at the Sargent Commission Hearings of 1884.[66] Lumbermen believed that fires were the worst threat to the forest. Lemon Thomson claimed that hunters were responsible for many fires, though clearing of land caused many. Finch[67] thought that squatters were the worst and he reported a loss of fifty thousand logs in the Big Brook area from a squatter-caused fire. Fishermen were also said to cause many fires. One of the worst, however, a large fire that raged over a thousand acres south of Griffin, was caused by a smudge built to keep flies from a horse.[68]

William McEchron testified that if fires are kept out and only big trees are logged, the forest will persist. "It is natural for forests and it is not natural for agriculture."[69] G. H. P. Gould testified that "my experience from the devastation of forest fires in lands I have attempted to hold have been such that I preferred to let them go back to the State."[70]

---

406,071 acres

The clustering of fires along the Adirondack Railroad is obvious from the 1903 fire map,[71] but there is also a pattern to the other fires. Most of them occurred on lands that had been heavily cut--on lands denuded for agriculture or charcoal production.

292,041 acres

Many areas, once burned, burned again because it takes so long for a forest to become mature enough to shade the soil and keep it moist. Even in the worst fire years, 1903, 1908, and 1913, the years when fires were caused primarily by railroads, the majority of the fires did not reach virgin timber, or stands from which only spruce had been removed, or tracts that were then a part of the Forest Preserve. The bulk of the forested lands that were burned were privately owned.

As a result of all the fires, the State built sixty-one fire towers throughout the north country. More importantly, the State banned wood- or coal-burning locomotives. It imposed a "top-lopping" law that required tops to be cut up so that branches rested close to damp earth and could not dry out. There they quickly rotted and almost never caused fires. What finally caused the reduction in fires to today's levels--the lifting of the drought or the regulations on railroads and logging or the fire towers? It seems possible that the towers were not really that important, even though they did give early warnings. The fact that their construction coincided with a period of diminishing fires may not be a causal relationship; it is possible that the regulations were sufficient. What is obvious is that towers are no longer needed today

## Causes of forest fires

|  | 1908 | 1912 | 1913 | 1914 |
|---|---|---|---|---|
| Lightning | 9 | 34 | 14 |  |
| Railroads | 89 | 93 | 78 | 14 |
| Hunters | 100 | 10 | 26 |  |
| Fishermen | 19 | 37 | 120 | 120 |
| Smokers |  | 59 |  | 224 |
| Campers |  | 32 |  |  |
| Burning Brush |  | 10 |  |  |
| Clearing land |  | 7 |  |  |
| Berry pickers |  | 7 |  |  |
| Bee hunters |  | 2 |  |  |
| Burning buildings |  | 5 |  |  |
| River drivers |  | 2 |  |  |
| Children |  | 4 |  |  |
| Carelessness |  | 10 |  |  |
| Incendiary |  | 20 |  |  |
| Unknown |  | 48 |  |  |

Source: various commission reports
Figure 40

*Fire train at Nehasane Park*

*Courtesy Adirondack Museum*

and even airplane surveillance is only necessary in periods of extreme drought. Now as then the only fires that occur are on land recently logged or previously burned.

Besides railroads, the biggest single cause of forest fires was the practice of setting fires to clear land for agriculture. As railroads decreased as a cause, careless smokers became an increasing menace, as were fishermen and campers. According to Forest Commission reports showing the cause of fires, fishermen were the worst. Among other causes of fires noted were "incendiaries" or willfulness [arson], bee hunters, and berry pickers. A significant proportion were unknown. Many fires were described in the annual commission reports:

1895--Of a 300-acre fire on Potter Hill, north of Old Forge, near railroad, the fire warden said "that hill has been burned over, or partly over, every year or two since I have lived in this town, and that is since 1865. But, the burned spot is not 50 acres larger than thirty years ago."

1899--In 1899 there were more fires than ever reported before. An exceptionally large one near Tupper Lake resulted in no loss of timber, in fact most did not destroy merchantable timber. Exceptions were a fire near Indian Lake and one on Black Bear Mountain above the Fulton Chain where the mountain appeared to be "smoking like a volcano."

1903--The worst fire year had the highest proportion of timbered lands burned. One fire in Totten and Crossfield Township 41, caused by a train on the Raquette Lake Railroad, burned virgin tracts that were already included in the Forest Preserve. This was an exception, for fires on Forest Preserve lands were limited. That year saw the fires that threatened the village of Tupper Lake and swept the Cornell Forestry School's lands at Axton, see appendix.

1908--Fires occurred on and off for four months during the Adirondacks' most severe period of drought. There were some 2,400 fires, the greatest number of any year, but they burned less timber and a smaller acreage than 1903 because of the State's greater vigilance.[72]

They differed from other years in the number of man-made fires; arson was widely suspected, although the railroads still accounted for many fires. The most severe fire raged along twelve miles of railroad tracks at Long Lake West (now Sabattis). Other fires were most severe in northwestern Warren County, west of Cranberry Lake, and in the Grass River watershed.

The High Peaks area was severely damaged in 1903 and 1913 by fires fueled by the logging debris from the mostly spruce and fir mountain stands. However, the extensive logging that continued on through 1924, with much slash at high elevations on such places as the slopes of Giant, produced no further fires.

# AREAS BURNED IN 1903 AND 1908 FIRES

## Map 9

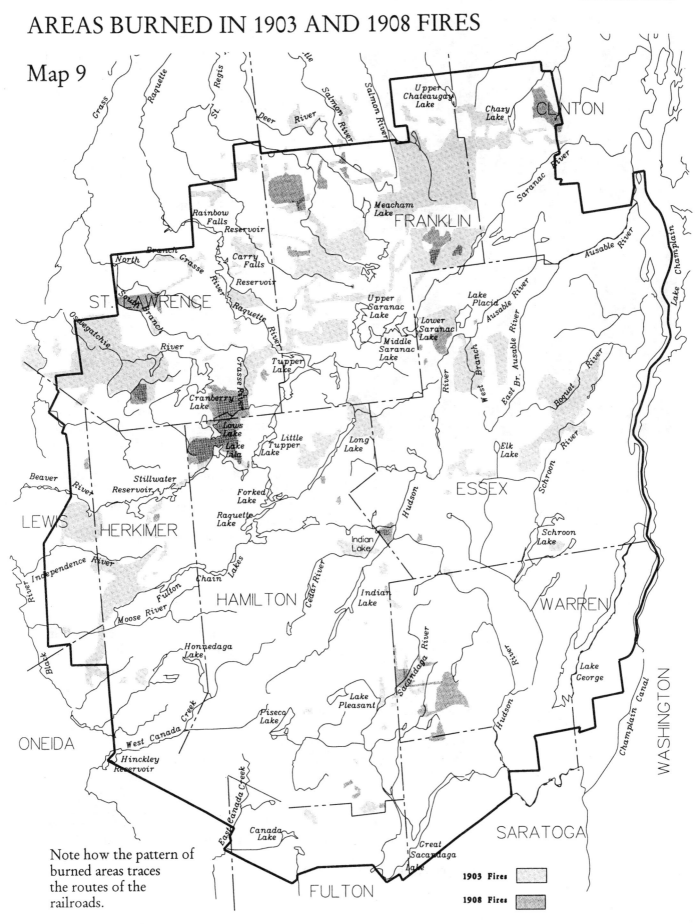

Note how the pattern of
burned areas traces
the routes of the
railroads.

1903 Fires

1908 Fires

*Courtesy Adirondack Museum*

*Sawing with a crosscut*

# Changes in Logging

Except for railroads and the introduction of the crosscut saw, technological improvements in the logging industry were minor during the period from 1890 to 1910; and the full effect of mechanization was not felt for several more decades.

The bucksaw, introduced in the 1860s, proved to be a quicker way to "buck" the limbs from felled trees and to saw logs to length. It is not certain just how quickly it reached the Adirondacks, but it was said that bucksaws were not used on Goulds early Moose River operations.[73]

The most important innovation was the 1891 introduction of the crosscut saw. As an sign of how the logging industry had moved to Michigan and Wisconsin before 1890, the crosscut was invented in Wisconsin and introduced to the Adirondacks in 1891. Thus the crosscut arrived in time to be considered a part of the convergence of change centered on 1892, but its influence grew slowly as loggers were reluctant to give up the axe. Patrick Ducey of Brandon, Franklin County, was said to be the first in the 1890s to saw, rather than chop, trees.[74]

The crosscut saw gave the woods a different look--stumps were lower than were normally cut by axe. Harvests were slightly greater as more of the tree could be harvested, except when trees were logged in deep snow. Logging with axe and the new crosscut saw was still dependent on the muscle of the individual logger and he was still dependent on his horse.

## Reaching Previously Inaccessible Stands

As important as the saw were emerging technologies that made it possible to harvest timber from more and more inaccessible locations under increasingly difficult conditions, such as high elevations. This trend becomes most evident in a later decade--between 1910 and 1920, when improved transportation and methods also made possible a greater intensity of harvest than ever before.

The earliest technological changes centered around ways of bringing logs to the edges of rivers and streams. In 1883, Verplanck Colvin reported that logging for the best spruce at elevations between 1,500 and 2,000 feet in areas that "hitherto were practically inaccessible; [and] are now found to be the only source of supply. By 'slide-ways' or 'dry sluices,' timber can be sent down to the valleys from nearly half a mile vertically above the sea." The new use of sluices observed by Colvin was adopted in many different areas--logs from Round Pond south of Shattuck Clearing were shunted to Long Lake, logs were dropped from the slopes of Whiteface to the Ausable River.

These innovations were in response to the demands of logging in previously untouched and inaccessible areas. The accessible lands had been logged and the logger was forced to find timber on steeper slopes and at higher elevations, places where logging's visible degradation of the land was more obvious.

Logging on the eastern slopes of the High Peaks had begun with charcoal making in the 1870s in the Town of Keene. The present Adirondack Mountain Reserve lands supplied kilns that stood near the present gate. Logging for pulp began in 1898 near Johns Brook in Keene Valley, where Orlando Beede found thirty standards on an acre, but he had to cut down to six-inch diameters to harvest this much. This virtual clearcut was not as significant as the earlier harvest for charcoal nor as complete as that caused by the fires of this era, but it did cause alarm.

In the 1890s, logging in Indian and Avalanche Pass and the rest of the headwaters of the Hudson were thought to "ruin the Hudson watershed beyond repair."[75] The men who bought the Adirondack Mountain Reserve land with the intention of protecting it, also bought land in adjacent valleys to help finance their investment.[76] In the 1890s, Finch, Pruyn and Company cut timber under contract to Adirondack Mountain Reserve in the stillwater area south of Panther Gorge.[77] "Clearcutting for pulp wood was done in the valleys of the North Fork of the Boquet River, Elk Lake's East and West Inlets, Johns Brook and the north-flowing Marcy Brook valley." The Beede brothers logged the north slopes of Wolf Jaws and Armstrong also under contract with Adirondack Mountain Reserve.[78] The pulp logs from these cuts were shipped to the J. and J. Rogers' mill at AuSable Forks.

*Log chute between Round Pond and Long Lake*

Courtesy Adirondack Museum

## The Western Adirondacks

The decade between 1890 and 1910 marks the emergence of the Western Adirondacks as the major supplier of pulp for paper. River driving on the Black River and its tributaries peaked in this period, in sharp contrast to the decline on the Hudson; moreover, it had some peculiar aspects not found on eastern Adirondack rivers.

River driving on the Hudson River was always free; on the branches of the Moose, where that river flowed through private lands, fees were established. Around 1890, G. H. P. Gould began to pay the Adirondack League Club tariffs for logs floated from the Moose River Plains; his payments amounted to about $5,000 to $6,000 annually.

Thomson and Company (Lemon Thomson, Edward Thomson, Jr., and ex-Gov. John A. Dix) acquired land from Dr. William Seward Webb with the expectation that the pulp wood could be floated to mills via the North Branch of the Moose. That branch flowed through 32,000 acres of John Brown's Tract in Townships 1 and 7, inherited by Julia Lyon deCamp and owned by her and her husband, W. S. deCamp. The deCamps objected to the Thomson Company's use of the river, claiming that the drives "injured her bridges, flooded her land, scared the fish, and otherwise infringed on her rights."[79] The ensuing legal battle continued for nearly a decade. In 1894, Thomson somehow got the legislature to pass a bill permitting his company to use the river. In 1899, the Court of Appeals held that legislation giving private individuals special rights in the use of specified waterways was unconstitutional and the deCamps were awarded damages. This decision held that no logs could "be floated down a stream without the consent of the owners of the riparian rights, which means that these owners can charge such tolls as they see fit for the use of the stream."[80]

*Skidway with huge stack of spruce sawlogs waiting to be hauled from the woods, H. M. Beach photo of Mac-a-Mac operation*

*Courtesy Adirondack Museum*

Most of the tributaries of the Black River had been dammed or redirected to supply the Black and Erie canals, as well as to provide water for downstream mills. There was constant conflict between lumbermen, who owned timberland in the river's watershed, mill owners, who were dependent on the water for power, and those who depended on canals for transportation. Water levels were unpredictable. Water was never adequate and the Black and the Erie canals suffered especially during drought years. The State Engineer and Surveyor noted that "lumbermen virtually empty the Black's reservoirs in order to provide water for spring drives. The interests of the State thus becomes secondary to that of lumbermen."[81]

In 1899, as shipment of logs on the Black was peaking, loggers began to cut deCamp's tracts in John Brown's Tract, Township 6, which included 6,000 acres of virgin timber. Land in Township 7, in the vicinity of Big Moose Lake and First and Second lakes, was also being cut. The most extensive lumber operations along a tributary of the Black were those of Dennis and Patrick Moynehan, who were harvesting forty million board feet of spruce a year at Nehasane and north along the railroad in Whitney Park.

*Large load of sawlogs coming
down a hillside*

*Adirondack Museum*

The drought of 1895 had left logs hung up on Woodhull Creek, but water was exceptionally low in the Black River in 1900 and 1901. In the spring of 1900, water dropped so fast that the upper tributaries of the Black were "lined with logs that have been started and left stranded. There was not enough water to supply pulp mills. All reservoirs were closed and all water from Forestport Feeder, which redirected the headwaters of the Black River, was diverted to the Erie."[82] Huge quantities of logs were destined for downstream mills; only the 140,000 cords floated down Otter Creek and the Independence River made it to sorting booms downstream on the Black River.

In 1901, fourteen million board feet of spruce including pulpwood were stranded. But that year marked the last large drive on the Black River, the supply of lumber "being nearly exhausted."[83] Denton and Waterbury were expected to cease operations on the Black River. Forestport Lumber Company had enough for one more year; others had little timber left.

# ADIRONDACK PRIVATE PARKS, CLUBS AND PRESERVES 1893 TO 1902

## Map 10

**Clubs**, their formation date when known and acreage in (1893) or [1902]

A Adirondack Club (later Tahawus Club), 1877 (96,000)
B Adirondack Mountain Reserve, 1887 (28,626)
C Adirondack League Club, 1890 (104,000)
D Altamont Club, (1894), [4,959]
E Caughnawaga Club, 1894 (8,835)
F Deer Lick Rapids Club, [7,500]
G Granshue Club, (1890), (8,752)
H Grasse River Outing Club, [5,520]
I Hollywood Club, 1890 (10,796)
J Lake Placid Club, [2,148]
K Massawepie Club, [1,720]
L Moose Pond Club, [800]
M Morehouse Lake Club, 1889 (1,662)
N North Woods Club, 1886 (4,583)
O Inlet Club Preserve, [6,700]
P Kushaqua Club (4,332)
Q Beaver River Club 1893, lease from Mary Lyon Fisher (6,200)
R Raquette Club 1889
S Stillwater Club Preserve, 20,000
T Saranac Club, 1889 (267)
U Upper Saranac Association, (27,030)
V Vilas Preserve, 1893 (36,195)
W Wilmurt Club, 1887 (1,655)
X Adirondack Forestry Assoc. (3,500)

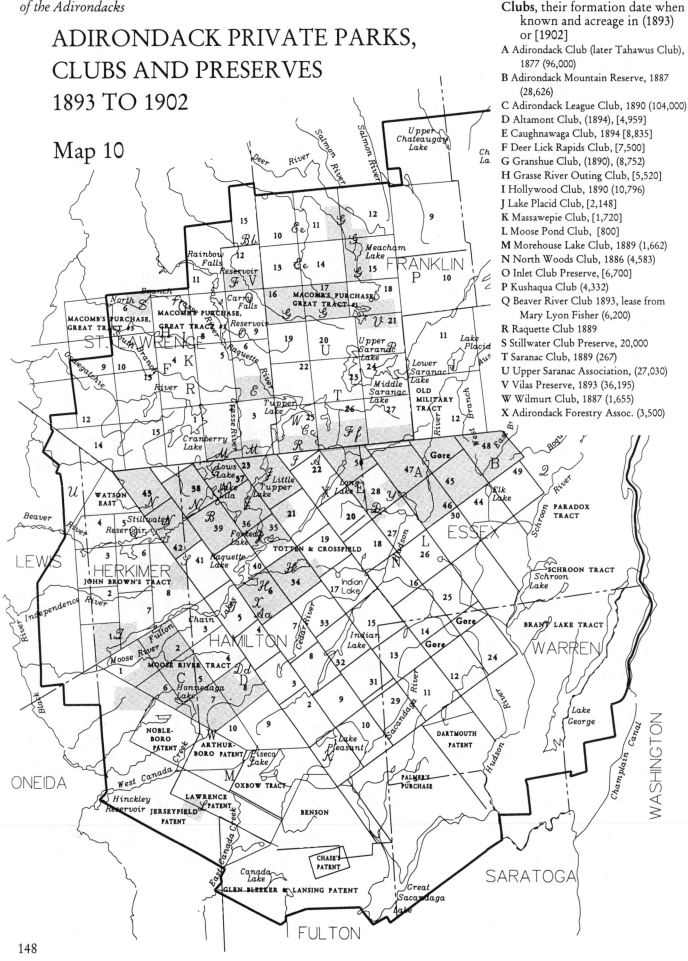

# Private Parks and Preserves

In 1876, 1877, and 1893, laws were enacted to protect private parks and grounds and encourage the propagation of fish and game. These laws allowed posting, enclosures, and penalties for trespass. A few individuals or families had established private parks before 1890, but the majority of them were established in the late 1880s and early 1890s. Similarly, the formation of most preserves, which were created by clubs formed to acquire or lease Adirondack land, occurred in the years after 1890.

In 1893, forty-five private preserves encompassed 941,000 acres. The Forest Commission observed:

> they were designed for fishing and hunting, for summer resorts, or for the revenues derived from the sale of such timber as may be cut without injury to existing forest conditions. The aims and objects of the various proprietors are wholly dependent on the preservation of their forests. ...Owing to the persistent refusal of the legislature to appropriate money for the purchase of Adirondack lands, the preservation of its forests, outside those owned by the State, is dependent largely on the existence of these private preserves.[84]

The private preserves had a great advantage over the State--their lands were in solid blocks, with a few over 100,000 acres. "The State has not 15,000 acres in any one parcel."[85]

In 1901, there were sixty private preserves with 791,000 acres, some of which were outside the Blue Line. The total acreage of these preserves had fallen because of sales to the State. The 1902 report for the previous year concluded that "it is not necessary that the State should purchase these private holdings in order that the tree growth may be protected, for the owners can be relied upon to preserve the forest conditions that are so essential to the enjoyment of their property. The acquisition of these high-priced lands may be safely deferred until the rest of the Adirondack Park has been purchased."[86]

Lumbermen not only had to compete for land with the State, they had to compete with those who wished to establish private preserves. Despite the fact that many parks and preserves were logged to finance their acquisition and improvement or enrich their owners, lumbermen reaped questionable profits from them. In the process of competing and negotiating for logging contracts, lumbermen often settled for returns that squeezed their profits. Often they resorted to exceeding contract conditions such as diameter limits to increase their profit potential. (See the appendix, particularly the description of the Adirondack League Club's experience as an example of this.) As a rule, lumbermen also had to pay more for what little timberland was available for sale. The three-way competition for land by the State, park and preserve owners, and lumbermen resulted in the price escalation depicted in figure 30. The Forest Commission, in acknowledging that the State was the inevitable loser because of restricted funds, rationalized its inability to compete for land by arguing that private preserves were accomplishing the task of forest preservation for them. This is in direct contradiction of the fact that at first many such preserves were unable to manage their forests for future harvests, let alone for forest preservation, any more effectively than

**Individual family preserves**, their formation dates when known and acreage (1893) or [1902]

*A* Anthony Ponds, Harper brothers, [7,221]

*B* Brandreth Park, Benjamin Brandreth heirs 1851 [27,298]

*C* Bog Lake Camp, Tatum and Converse, (5,618)

*D* Camp Arbutus, Archer Huntington, 1895 [1,699]

*E* Childwold Park, A. Child, H. G. Dorr, [13,090]

*F* Cutting Preserve, F. A. Cutting, (7,510)

*G* William G. Rockefeller's Preserves: DeBar Mountain Park [11,675], Everton [20,000], Rockefeller Preserve [52,335]

*H* Summer Park, W. W. Durant, (56,000)

*I* G Lake Preserve, Wright and Collins, (520)

*J* Hamilton Park, William C. Whitney (started as a club in 1887) [71,281]

*K* Hamilton Lake Preserve, J. A. Starin, [3,202]

*L* Jerseyfield Preserve, A. Dolge [29,000]

*M* Horseshoe Forestry Co., A. A. Low [27,431]

*N* Nehasane and Lake Reserves, Dr. W. Seward Webb 1890 (112,000)

*O* Kildare Club, Ehrich Brothers, (9,903)

*P* Knollwood Club, Louis Marshall, [450]

*Q* Putnam Preserve, H. A. Putnam (3,540)

*R* Litchfield Park, Edward H. Litchfield 1893 [12,427]

*S* Lloyd Triangle, Theodore Page, [3,600]

*T* Mohegan Lake Camp, J. Pierpont Morgan, 1893 [1,551]

*U* Forest Home, W. Humes (30,000 lease)

*V* Paul Smith's Reserve 1859 (18,700)

*W* Read and Strong Park, [7,375]

*X* Sagamore Park, Alfred G. Vanderbilt, 1897 [1,530]

*Y* Santanoni Park, Robert C. Pruyn (1892), 11,205

*Z* Wilderness Park, Julia Lyon deCamp's (1892 the date the lands were incorporated into a park, but the tract was inherited years before), 29,567

*Aa* Kamp Kill Kare, T. G. Woodruff 1897 [1030]

*Bb* Connell Preserve, D. C. Connell (8,266)

*Cc* King Park, F. A. King, (8,600)

*Dd* Hall and Patton Preserve, (5,000)

*Ee* Santa Clara Preserve, Dodge, Meigs & Co., 1892 (62,000)

*Ff* Ampersand Preserve, Dodge, Meigs & Co., 1892 (50,000)

**Key to Map 10**

lumbermen had been doing. With few exceptions, most notably the Adirondack Mountain Reserve, most private parks and preserves were ultimately logged. The cumulative experience of Whitney Park, Nehasane, and even the Adirondack League Club in its early years demonstrates the difficulties of husbanding the forest, as shown in the profiles in the appendix.

Purchases to establish private parks put even greater pressure on the cost of land that was most valuable to the public as Forest Preserve. Although these preserves encompassed large forested and often virgin tracts, they also contained some of the Adirondacks' most beautiful lakes. In 1896, Col. Fox, in testifying at a legislative hearing, was asked about the value of tracts with lakes. He indicated that lakes had previously had little value, and that, in fact, the lands which were available for private preserves had no definite value as recently as ten years before. Then, there were so few transactions that virgin land even with lakes could be "obtained at a nominal price; in fact, anyone could claim a large tract at tax sale." Superintendent Fox observed that the value of land was appreciating so rapidly that lands for a "private preserve in Herkimer County were sold for $10 an acre and the land has been lumbered clear of both saw timber and pulp.'[87]

*Logs from a private preserve,*
*Mac-a-Mac operation*
*at Brandreth,*
*H. M. Beach*

Courtesy Adirondack Museum

A SKIDWAY OF PINE MAC A MAC   BRANDRETH LAKE, N.Y.

Unquestionably, the acquisition of land for the Forest Preserve also affected lumbermen. At the 1891 Assembly Hearings on the future park, a lumberman was asked about the relationship between the value of land and the proposals to establish such a park where the State would be a probable purchaser of a large quantity of land. He replied that a "great many people had put a higher price upon their lands. Land that went for $.20 to $1.50 for taxes is now worth $5.00 an acre," if it has primitive timber stands.[88]

However, the escalation in the cost of an acre of land, as shown in figure 30, was even greater than might have been expected as a result of the work of speculators, as documented by the Moreland commission. There was a real shortage of timberland, this despite the fact that many tracts in the Hudson watershed, which had been logged two decades earlier, were available to be logged again for the smaller pulpwood as well as for significant amounts of timber that had matured to sawlog size by 1890. By 1910, land with merchantable timber, was becoming unavailable.

## The Adirondacks Loses National Rank

The total production of Adirondack forests, which still consisted almost exclusively of conifers, predominantly spruce, peaked sharply in 1905 and began to fall off, beginning an inexorable decline that continued almost to the present. The chart gives New York's rank, but because the Adirondack region was the State's principal source of softwoods, it mirrors the decline in the Adirondacks.

Until 1880, New York State had ranked near the top nationally; the decline that began in 1890 was caused by the dramatic rise in timber shipments from the mid-west; but after 1900, the sharp decline in New York's rank was directly the result of the decrease in Adirondack timber production.

The shortage of Adirondack timber is evident from the increasing amounts imported from Canada and the mid west. A subtler form of the evidence pointing to that shortage can be found in changes in the outlook of foresters and lumbermen. These changes are seen in various writings as that shortage was highlighted by reports and analyses, first in the Reports of the Forest, Fish and Game Commission, then in articles by foresters published in the *Journal of Forestry*, and also in studies made by the Empire State Forest Products Association. These reports attempted to determine the amount of timber needed in the State and, for the first time, to figure out how much timber was left in the State's forests. The conclusion that there was little merchantable timber left--that there was a real shortage--produced a plethora of new arguments, by both foresters and State officials, in favor of harvesting timber from State land.

Adirondack
Lumber Industry
National Standing

| Year | Rank |
|------|------|
| 1850 | 1 |
| 1860 | 2 |
| 1870 | 3 |
| 1880 | 4 |
| 1890 | 7 |
| 1900 | 17 |
| 1910 | 22 |

Figure 41

## A Picture of the Forest in 1910

What did the forest look like in 1910? Lumbermen looked at it and saw that the merchantable timber was almost gone, but was the forest gone? In 1888, the Forest, Fish and Game Commission had developed a plan for classifying land being considered for inclusion in the future Park. In the words of the Commission, *cleared* or improved land usually meant farmland; *meadow* referred to wild, unused meadows, which if pastured or mowed would be classed as cleared; *water* meant ponds and lakes, not streams; *waste* referred to rocky, barren land, incapable of supporting a forest; *burnt* meant land burned since 1886; *denuded* meant stripped of timber by fire before 1886 and not yet covered by new trees; *lumbered* meant that only softwoods had been removed; and *forest* meant virgin, unharvested and untouched.

The decline in forested land between 1888 and 1902, so evident in figure 32, continued. A 1913 summary is not comparable to the earlier statistics because it describes only land acquired by the State. Virgin or forested land amounted to a small fraction of the Forest Preserve but the bulk of State land had only been partially lumbered, with half the State land having heavy forest cover, a quarter of it having a medium forest cover. Except on tracts cleared decades earlier for charcoal and farms or burned in the fires of 1903 and 1908, the picture of private lands was comparable. Although the proportion of hardwoods had increased, private lands remained forested.

The years between 1850 and 1890 had seen a constant growth in the harvest of Adirondack forests, but logging between these years appears relatively benign when compared with the harvest in the interval between 1890 and 1910. It is ironic that during those two decades in which the State's preservation efforts came to fruition and so much of the Forest Preserve was assembled that there was a surge in logging. Instead of curbing the lumbermen, the 1890s saw loggers, impelled by their quest for pulp, become so rapacious in their harvest that merchantable timber supplies were noticeably exhausted by 1910.

*Adirondack Forest - 1910*

*The method of lumbering was that of culling the forest, so that at no time were large areas clearcut to burn over and become desolate wastes. Owing to water transportation, as much as to any other factor, which permitted the removal of logs without a heavy initial investment, this region has been spared the complete denudation seen in the Great Lakes states.* *

* *Sixteenth Annual Report of the Forest, Fish and Game Commission*

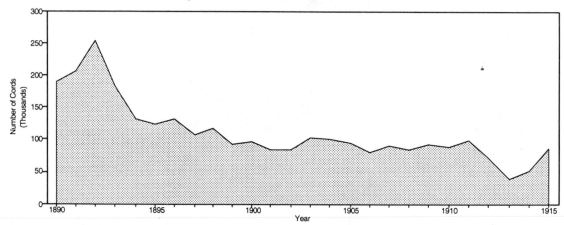

Market logs received at Big Boom -- 1890 - 1915

Figure 42

# VIII

## The Forest Products Industry From 1910 to the Present

This chapter paints a picture of events in private forests in the past eighty years with broad brush strokes. Giving the period the same detailed analysis as earlier eras is beyond the scope of this book. This survey focuses on technological changes in the industry and underscores the contrasts with earlier logging periods. The eighty-year span breaks into loosely defined periods and subjects. The period through the 1920s was marked by sharply declining supplies of merchantable timber and the corresponding scramble to harvest remaining stands from increasingly remote locations. The revolution in transportation, highlighted by the introduction of the Linn Tractor in 1918, culminated with the building of gravel-surfaced logging roads on which heavy trucks could haul loads of logs. The depression in the forest-related industries in the Adirondacks, which reflected both the national Depression of the 1930s and the dwindling supply of softwoods, was interrupted by increases in the use of hardwoods, by responses to World War II, and the boost in production provided by salvage after the 1950 blowdown. The introduction of methods that used hardwoods in the pulp and paper industry around 1960 changed the way Adirondack forests were logged. However, this new market for hardwoods still did not make forest management economical. Throughout the entire period, the forest became oversupplied with hardwoods and trees incapable of producing sawlogs, for which there were insufficient markets, and foresters began to play an increasingly important role in directing management of timberlands.

## Merchantable Timber Supplies Decline

There are no precise records of the extent of timber cover remaining on private lands around 1910, the year which marks the end of the period of heaviest logging, but the decline was inevitable and response to it took several different forms, of which the first was the establishment of the Empire State Forest Products Association (ESFPA). Lumbermen and those in the pulp and paper industry must have seen a crisis looming after the peak harvest year, 1905, for they joined to form ESFPA the following year. The organization's reports confirm that after 1914, Adirondack forests were being harvested at five times their rate of growth, a situation that did not bode well for the future of Adirondack logging. The reports used the term "Adirondack forests," when in fact, they still meant only merchantable timber, spruce, hemlock, and now, balsam.

Adirondack reforestation began with Fernow's experiments (see appendix) at Axton east of Tupper Lake in 1898. In 1905, Santa Clara Lumber Company established a nursery to reforest some of its lands

### ESFPA Survey of Members' Timberlands 1917

| | Acres |
|---|---|
| International Paper Co. | 170,734 |
| Finch, Pruyn and Co. | 137,817 |
| Chateaugay Iron Co. | 100,199 |
| Oval Wood Dish | 75,413 |
| Emporium Forestry Co. | 74,426 |
| MacIntyre Iron Co | 60,135 |
| Brooklyn Cooperage Co. | 56,452 |
| Nehasane Park Assn. | 42,000 |
| Piercefield Paper Co. | 40,618 |
| Jerseyfield Lumber Co. | 38,600 |
| Raquette River Paper Co. | 33,951 |
| Paul Smiths Hotel Co. | 33,000 |
| Champlain Realty Co. | 30,530 |
| R. W. Higbie Co. | 31,000 |
| Mac-a-Mac Corp. | 28,200 |
| Aldrich Paper Co. | 25,000 |
| Santa Clara Lumber Co. | 21,367 |
| Dexter Sulphite Co. | 19,496 |
| Lyon de Camp | 17,000 |
| Newton Falls Paper Co. | 16,000 |
| F. L. Merriam | 11,800 |
| A. Sherman Co. | 17,050 |
| F. A. Cutting | 9,000 |
| Five others | 13,204 |
| | |
| Total | 1,156,806 |

64% of total acreage was said by its owners to have merchantable timber.
Source: ESFPA papers at the Adirondack Museum.

Figure 43

north of Tupper Lake. Concerned about fire damage, the loss of timberland in general, and by the statewide abandonment of farmland in particular, the Forest, Fish and Game Commission began reforesting denuded areas of the Forest Preserve in 1902. Plantations of conifers were established on burned tracts in Franklin County near Lake Clear Junction, along the railroad from the junction to Saranac Lake Village, beside the highway between Paul Smiths and Meacham Lake, between Saranac Lake and Lake Placid, and near Ray Brook. Today, at these locations and at many other sites throughout the Park, majestic stands of native red and white pines and red spruce join exotic species such as Norway spruce and Scotch pine (the latter the only exotic to reproduce in the Adirondacks). It is easy to spot these stands with their straight row plantings and their even ages. The exotics were chosen not only because both pines and spruce were suffering blights but also for their rapid growth and disease resistance.

The first sales from State nurseries to private landowners were made in 1908; in 1909 one million trees were sold to individuals. Finch, Pruyn and Co. began large scale replanting in 1911. By 1920, seven large nurseries supplied almost fifteen million trees annually. Reforestation continued through the 1930s, carried out in that decade mostly by Federal Civilian Conservation Corps workers.

# High Peaks Logging

By the early 1900s, so much of the private land available to logging had been cut over more than once that lumbermen resorted to logging on increasingly inaccessible stands, where without new techniques, logging would have been difficult if not impossible. Lumbermen began to harvest the untapped stands on the steep slopes of the High Peaks area. At these high elevations, balsam fir intersperses with spruce and the two species were both logged for pulp. The high mountain region remained the major source of spruce and balsam logs through the 1920s as well as the locale for some of the Adirondack's wildest and most dangerous logging ventures. Santa Clara Lumber Company continued logging in the Seward Range until 1919. Finch, Pruyn and Company logged the headwaters of Cold River, the flanks of Santanoni Mountain, and to within a mile and a half of Lake Tear of the Clouds, the source of the Hudson high on the shoulder of Mount Marcy.

Even before 1915, Finch, Pruyn and Company accomplished amazing logging feats on MacIntyre Iron Company lands that extended up the slopes of Mount Colden and the MacIntyre Mountains. To conquer the near-vertical terrain, the company built a log chute on Colden above Avalanche Pass. Elsewhere, the company used cables as well as dry chutes to bring logs from the High Peaks in the 1920s, but they relied mostly on horses to bring logs down from the heights.

Mountain logging was at a peak in the Keene-Keene Valley area between 1919 and 1924. The notch between Green and Giant mountains was clearcut above the 3100-foot level.[1] A logging road followed Johns Brook to the foot of Big Slide Mountain and beyond, through land owned by J. and J. Rogers Company, which harvested the steep sides of Big Slide all the way to the cliffs. The road leading out through the valley was constructed without rises because horses could only move the great sled loads downhill or on the level.

Cables and brakes were first used in the country's northwestern forests as early as 1904 to bring logs down from the tops of tall, steep mountains. They were introduced to the Adirondacks by Santa Clara Lumber Company in the teens:

> The Company, in the later years, was logging on steep, rocky hillsides, and the roads were too steep to permit hauling by teams unaided by some mechanical device to prevent the loads, often weighing fifteen tons, from running away,-the horses being powerless in front of a load of logs to hold them on the hills. So the Company developed a brake. This was a modification of the Barringer Brake (grooved friction wheels around which many turns of a steel cable were wound, and operated by two hand levers). The cable was a double-ender,-one end attached to the load of logs, and the other end running free.
>
> It was interesting to see a green team in its first trip down these steep hills. At first, full of fright as the sled pitched over the top of the hill, they realized fully how powerless they were to hold back such weight on such a steep grade. Then, after the first few trips, they became conscious of the powerful brake, and the fact that they were safe. ... Actual measurement showed some of these hills to have a grade of over 40 degrees from horizontal. The log roads were made with steep hills, alternating with levels, and at every hill, a brake and cable.[2]

J. and J. Rogers Company also relied on horses, but used them to pull chains of "bobs" or small sleds carrying logs down from Giant, Green, and Hopkins mountains where logging continued until 1924.

> On steep draw roads, loaded sleds dragged 'bobs' of chained masses of logs behind the sled to slow them down. In certain steep sections, ropes snubbed around trees and occasionally cables were required to hold back a load. Most large lumber sleds were equipped with an iron brake which the driver could lever into action in extreme emergencies; but using a break was avoided if possible because it would wreck the road. In spite of all the devices to help them, horses had to be specially trained for lumbering operations. I have seen horses practically on their bellies with their legs straining forward to keep a load from over-riding them.[3]

Fires swept these recently logged lands and burned over into uncut stands. The fires of 1903 and 1913 swept the valleys of the North Fork of the Boquet and up the slopes of Giant and Rocky Peak Ridge[4] Salvage operations cut logs for J. and J. Rogers Company on Adirondack Mountain Reserve lands in the Boquet Valley and on Bear Den and Noonmark, as well as "on other privately owned lands that were burned on the sides of Rocky Peak Ridge, Round Mountain, Porter, Cascade and Pitchoff, and north of Hurricane."[5]

*J. and J. Rogers Company
flume on Spruce Hill, circa 1900*
F. A. VanSant, Forest, Fish and Game
Comm.

Much later, around 1947, Finch, Pruyn and Company employed a cable system more closely resembling those developed in the western United States. The crane, called the Wissen Skyline, consisted of a very long steel cable anchored in rock at the top of the mountain, then extended out from the top of a large tree to another tree at the bottom of the mountain. The company used the Wissen Skyline near Salmon Pond in its Blue Mountain Tract, where the cable was 3,400 feet long (as long as this seems, it was shorter than the mile-long cables used in the west). A carriage, connected by a smaller cable and powered by a thirty horsepower motor at the top of the mountain could carry a 3,000 pound loads of logs.[6]

Flumes, or chutes with water, were also to float logs to mills from steep slopes in the early 1900s. The best documented are those erected after 1910 by the J. and J. Rogers Company--a seven and a half mile long flume delivered pulp logs to the Ausable River and a three-mile slide carried logs down from the heights of Esther and Whiteface mountains. In the western Adirondacks, there was a three-mile slide at Benson Mines in St. Lawrence County capable of transporting sixty cords of pulpwood an hour.

# Mechanization Comes to the Woods

Santa Clara Lumber Company was among the first to use motorized equipment in Adirondack woods. As early as 1912, that company was driving lumberjacks from Tupper Lake to camps along the Cold River. The company devised "mountain buckboards," platforms built on the back of trucks each capable of carrying eight men into the woods.[7]

Around 1900, Alvin O. Lombard of Maine invented a steam-driven log-hauler, which equipped a steam engine with endless-belt, traction treads called Caterpillar treads. While steam engines had been around since the mid-eighteenth century, the salient feature of this invention was the treads, which became the subject of patent infringement litigation for a decade. The first record of such a machine being used in the Adirondacks dates to 1907 in Franklin County; photographs depict extensive use of a steam-powered log hauler in the Old Forge area in the teens. Steam-powered log haulers were used for many years and proved economical if used on long hauls. Their use continued even after the next innovation, which permitted the building of smaller and more versatile machines. Both Lombard and Linn invented gasoline-powered log haulers, the former dating to 1904.[8]

The story of the introduction of the Linn tractor in 1918 has become almost a legend. Logging operations in the Moose River Plains and around North Lake were being carried out by John B. Todd for Gould Paper Company. Pulp logs were sent down the Moose to the Iroquois Pulp and Paper Mill at McKeever (this mill was shortly taken over by Gould Paper Compan.) Gould had proposed moving logs from the region of Ice Cave Mountain and North Lake on the headwaters of the Black River to a jackworks on the Moose, in order to eliminate the drive on the Black and consolidate both river drives on the Moose. Linn tractors, propelled by treads in the rear and steered by sled-like runners in the front, were a tempting solution for such a long haul. In a demonstration, Todd was convinced the gasoline-powered vehicles could pull the loads of twenty teams. Despite the price tag, $6,000 per tractor, which proved an initial sticking point in their early acceptance,[9] Gould purchased three of them and they proved so effec-

*Linn Tractor hauling sleds with logs, Oval Wood Dish Co., Tupper Lake*

*Courtesy Adirondack Museum*

tive they were quickly acquired by loggers throughout the region in spite of their cost. A total of twenty-eight Linn tractors were used in the Moose River Plains alone.

In its 1921 Bulletin, the Empire State Forest Products Association explained to its members how to choose a tractor, how to select auxiliary equipment, how to employ competent drivers and mechanics, and how to adapt the tractors to field conditions. The economics were favorable--in summer, savings for timber transportation alone amounted to from $1.88 to $4.60 per thousand board feet, and winter savings were even greater. A 1920 report indicated that over one million board feet of hardwood had been hauled for ten and a half miles with tractors for $1.50 per thousand feet, as against a cost of $10.00 per thousand with horses.[10]

Stanley Sisson of the Raquette River Paper Company noted that his company had bought two caterpillar tractors in the fall of 1919, but they proved inappropriate for the job. The following year, the company began using Linn tractors with rebuilt log sleds and other better equipment. With six Linns, the company moved 15,000 cords in thirty-eight days. Hauling with teams, Sisson estimated, would have cost one third more.[11]

In winter tractors were employed to haul logs during the day and haul water to ice the roads at night. Tractors required the same iced roads for hauling sled loads of logs in winter as were needed for horse teams. On steep downgrades, a man had to be stationed to "guard" the tract, that is cover the ice with straw or cinders so the tractors would not slide and tip over.[12]

In the 1920s, George Sykes combined tractors with a dry flume to move logs over relatively level ground. He invented a portable slide made of three eight-foot boards attached so as to make a trough with tapered sides. Slots allowed the slides to be fitted together in chains of more than a hundred units through which a train of logs could be pulled long distances by a pair of horses or by tractors. Obviously, the uphill and level portions were kept well-greased.[13]

Even though the superior Linn tractors were available, Little Rapids Lumber Company used surplus World War I tanks to haul log sleds at Brandreth. Lombard tractors were used nearby for logging at Partlow. Linn tractors were still in use in 1940 on Gould's Moose River Tract lands. That year the first snowmobiles were used for Adirondack logging operations, again by Gould Paper Company![14]

The first truck roads built on a logging tract were those constructed on Everton and Meacham tracts around 1935. The first bulldozers employed to grade a logging road were employed at Jerseyfield in the 1940s.[15] After World War II, it was recognized that trucks could haul logs almost anywhere as long as there was a reasonable road. Networks of gravel-surfaced logging roads soon covered most logging tracts; the network built by Gould in the Moose River Plains has persisted for the thirty years in which that tract has been State land.

Self-loading trucks, that is trucks equipped with a hoist to lift logs, were introduced in Oregon and California in 1952 and they, too, quickly gained acceptance in the Adirondacks, where they had the greatest impact on small jobbers.[16] They permitted any number of loggers to enter the business and begin logging for contract. Where supervised by foresters on large company tracts, this did not prove a problem. On small private holdings where owners did not seek the services of foresters, this permitted the unethical or untrained logger to practice poor forestry. It is thought that the self-loading truck is one of the principal causes of "high-grading," that is harvesting only the best trees without regard to the future of a stand.

Small tractors proved their worth for skidding logs--transporting individual logs down narrow tracks in the woods to skidways from which they could be loaded on sleds or trucks. However, as late as 1954, properly trained horses were considered better for skidding logs than tractors.[17]

Innovations in logger's tools kept pace with changes in transporting logs. By 1910, the crosscut saw, introduced in 1891, was widely accepted. Just as the logger did not take up the crosscut immediately, he also resisted the introduction of the portable power saw, known as a chain saw. Many experimental models were brought into the woods around 1940, but all were heavy and cumbersome, with some requiring two men to operate. John E. Johnston pioneered their use on the Jerseyfield Tract in 1940.[18]

Not only were loggers slow to adopt the new machine, but they were also loath to give chain saws the degree of care they needed. "A good many chain saws purchased during the war are now lying unused in tool sheds. They were tried out with old-time falling crews of two or three men, uninterested or untrained in their use. The crews never learned the tricks of using it successfully. With a crew of this size it lay around half the time while the men were limbing and swamping with the axe."[19] As a result, after World War II there surfaced a lot of chain saws thoroughly rusted away.

*Two-man chain saw*

Courtesy John Stock and Adirondack Museum

Inevitably, the chain saw gained acceptance, but there are still those who believe the older generations of loggers with their axes accomplished just as much. In the 1950s, one two-man crew with a chain saw cut and stacked forty cords of wood in a week. Finch, Pruyn and Company has records of legendary individuals who could cut and pile ten full cords of four-foot length wood per day, six days a week, with a buck saw, a feat that would be difficult today for the average two-man crew with chain saws. A better comparison comes from statistics showing the combined efficiencies of both chain saw and improved transportation. Five hundred men were needed to cut 40,000 cords of pulp wood a year in the 1940s; today forty men can do the same.[20]

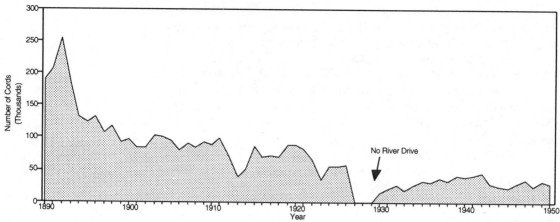

Sawlogs and pulp received at Big Boom, 1890 - 1950

Figure 44

Sources:

19th Century, Forest Commission Reports;

20th Century, Richard Nason

# River Driving Ends

While new methods were being used to harvest logs and transport them to mills, river driving persisted even as it declined. The South Branch of the Moose River was becoming the major highway for logs, thanks to Gould's operations in the Moose River Plains. Gould built a network of dams on the Indian and Red rivers and Sumner and Benedict creeks, tributaries of the Moose.

After World War I, four-foot pulp logs began to replace the standard thirteen foot logs in Hudson River drives, although the long logs were floated down the Hudson River until 1929. After that year, Finch, Pruyn and Co. was the only company still driving four-foot logs down the Hudson. All river driving on the Hudson ceased in 1950, the riverman replaced by truck drivers. Thirteen-foot logs were floated down the Moose to its junction with the Black during the 1930s and 1940s. Several companies continued drives on the Black, but river driving ceased on both western rivers in 1948. The biggest of the last drives occurred the year before when Gould Paper Company crews moved 50,000 cords to the pond at McKeever and on down to mill at Lyons Falls.

The volume of logs driven down Adirondack river drives is charted in figure 41. World War II's shortage of trucks and fuel undoubtedly prolonged the life of these dwindling drives, which were differed from earlier drives for several reasons. Some of them ended at jackworks where the logs were loaded on trucks for shipment. The last drive on the Jessup started in 1942, but instead of driving its logs down the Hudson, International Paper Company boomed them down Indian Lake from the mouth of the Jessup to a jackworks near Indian Lake dam. From there they were hauled by truck to the company's mill at Corinth. Between 1942 and 1948, 150,000 cords had been driven down the Jessup and the Indian.

THE LAST YEARS OF RIVER
DRIVING IN THE
ADIRONDACKS

Figure 45

| Year | Hudson Finch, Pruyn | Western Gould | St. Regis | Total Western | Total Adirondacks |
|------|------------|-------|-----------|---------------|-------------------|
| 1939 | 42,000 | 18,000 | | 18,000 | 60,000 |
| 1940 | 40,000 | 25,000 | | 25,000 | 65,000 |
| 1941 | 40,000 | 25,000 | | 25,000 | 65,000 |
| 1942 | 40,000 | 20,000 | | 20,000 | 60,000 |
| 1943 | 30,000 | 17,250 | | 17,250 | 47,250 |
| 1944 | 20,000 | 12,000 | 15,000 | 27,000 | 47,000 |
| 1945 | 20,000 | 12,000 | 25,000 | 37,000 | 57,000 |
| 1946 | 36,000 | 10,000 | 19,667 | 29,667 | 65,667 |
| 1947 | 28,000 | 50,000 | 19,000 | 69,000 | 97,000 |
| 1948 | 28,000 | | | | 28,000 |
| 1949 | 13,000 | | | | 13,000 |
| 1950 | 10,000 | | | | 10,000 |
| Totals | 202,000 | 121,250 | 78,667 | 199,917 | 401,917 |

*Pulp logs in a river*

Many of the later drives took place on small streams which could accommodate only smaller, four-foot pulp logs. The outlet of Knapp Reservoir (east of Stratford) might float logs, but the three streams that flow into it, the ones used in the Knappville logging operation, are all so small and sluggish it seems impossible that they ever had enough water for driving logs, even with the impoundments of the spring freshets that fed them. The 1940 drives on those tributaries of the East Canada Creek ended at a jackworks where logs were loaded on trucks for shipment to Black River mills. Jones Brook is a very small tributary of the West Canada Creek, but it too saw pulp wood drives. Dug Mountain stream is an even smaller tributary of the Jessup, and it too was used.

From the closing years of the river driving era come some of the most vivid first-hand accounts of the practice. In winter, pulp logs were dumped across frozen stillwaters on the rivers, creating "bridges," where they were left "until the weather warmed up enough to weaken or rot the ice and let the logs down into the tumbling current. As soon as the ice rots enough to let the logs through, the dam at the head of the river is opened and thousands of tons of water came rushing over the rocky bottom of the river."[21]

The Reverend Frank Reed, editor and founder of *Lumber Camp News*, reported that the Hudson usually had enough water to support a two-month-long main drive to Glens Falls, but drives on western Adirondack rivers were often hampered by low water. Gould Paper Company's drive on the South Branch of the Moose was interrupted in 1941 by low water and had to wait for rain to resume. Remsen Falls and the dam at McKeever were only two of the choke points on that drive where jams often occurred.

*Loading logs on a train,*
*Emporium Lumber Company*

# Hardwoods, Railroads, and Trucks

For all the advances in transportation and creation of new markets, it still was not practical to harvest most hardwoods throughout this era, even if that harvest would benefit the young spruce, which remained the premier marketable species. Not surprisingly, hardwoods had become dominant on most logged forest stands. A paper delivered to the Society of American Foresters in 1919 proved that logging methods used to that date increased the percentage of hardwoods.

> Logging to a diameter limit, while it leaves the woods clear, and comparatively free from fire risk after a decade, makes no progress toward future softwood production, or the disposal of the poor grades of hardwoods which are taking space and making no timber growth of value. Any heavy cutting of hardwoods will make a large amount of slash, increasing the fire risk until the crown cover has become dense enough to retain the moisture, and decay the slash. In the meantime a good growth of hardwood saplings will start on every area of this type if the woods are opened sufficiently, [producing] a stand of hardwood much superior to that found in the original forest.[22]

Finding a market for hardwoods was crucial, but the Tupper Lake area had the only significant hardwood market in the

Adirondacks up until hardwoods could be used for pulp. Here the initial increase in the harvest of hardwoods was completely dependent on railroads. Rails made it possible to ship logs to the new mills built near Tupper Lake, Brooklyn Cooperage Company, Tupper Lake Chemical Company, and Emporium Lumber Company (see appendix). Rails were equally important as a means of exporting lumber products from these mills.

Railroads also continued to be essential to the hardwood harvest north of Cranberry Lake through the 1930s. The effective use of railroads required the invention of all sorts of loading equipment. George Sykes of Emporium lumber led the industry in patents involving improvements of log-loading mechanisms for rails.

Even before the 1940s when the last logs were hauled by railroad, trucks had begun to supplant trains. Trucks were more cost effective for several reasons: railroads required a high initial investment for land, grading, and equipment, and expensive handling facilities; they were limited by steep grades and the need for heavy-duty bridges; and finally, railroads could not compete with government financing, which built and maintained public roads used by trucks for hauling logs.

In the late teens and early twenties, there were 150 lumber camps in the Adirondacks employing 7,000 men. The number of camps declined to twenty during the depths of the Depression in 1933 and rose again to 60 with 3,000 men in 1940.[23] The war brought shortages of everything--pulp, paper, wood, fuel, and especially the manpower to harvest logs, forcing several camps to contract with the federal government to use prisoners of war to maintain even this level. After World War II, trucks were so common loggers could drive daily to logging operations in the woods and lumber camps quickly became a thing of the past.

Shipping logs to mills by railroad became so expensive that clearcutting was necessary to make operations pay. When loggers employed railroads "everything of merchantable value is taken and all that is left is young growth, defectives, and a number of small and badly suppressed softwoods. Because it has not been found possible to utilize hardwood tops, these lands are left littered with great quantities of slash, which constitutes a fire menace and a partial hindrance to reproduction."[24] This was true of Kildare and the Cutting Tract, where "the tops in many cases stand up ladder-like, twenty feet above the ground."[25]

Not only did the use of railroads encourage clearcutting of hardwoods, but so did the development of hardwood specialties (floors and doors, for instance) and the rapid rise in hardwood stumpage values through the 1920s and into the 1930s. Often "uncontrolled and shortsighted overcutting of mature and immature timber" during the Depression resulted in partial and occasionally complete destruction of future stands.[26]

Still, throughout this period, spruce and other conifers continued to constitute most of the Adirondack harvest, and thus lumbermen experimented with a number of different ways to get rid of hardwoods. Throughout the 1950s, hardwoods were girdled (killed by cutting away a ring of bark) as a means of improving the softwood stands. Finch, Pruyn and Company(see appendix) girdled trees on 12,000 acres for this purpose between 1918 and 1960.

# The Blowdown of 1950

In light of the continuing shortage of spruce, it was unexpected that an act of nature could cause even a temporary glut. However, the most destructive storm of any type in recent years managed to do just that. Known as the big blowdown, it struck in November of 1950, and did the most damage in the western and central Adirondacks. This powerful northeaster affected 420,000 acres and was said to have caused a loss that ranged from a quarter of the trees to the entire forest cover. The loss was estimated at two million cords of softwood and forty million board feet of hardwood. The Cold River country between Seward and Santanoni experienced the greatest destruction, followed closely by the Moose River Plains, but private tracts such as 60,000-acre Whitney Park, parts of the Adirondack League Club property, or Finch, Pruyn's 183,000-acre holdings were also severely damaged.

The storm was particularly devastating to old-growth forests. The wind came from the east and northeast, while the mature trees had grown wind-firm in the direction of the more normal west winds. Because spruce had shallow roots making it prone to wind damage and because it towered above the canopy of hardwoods, this most prized species was stripped from most virgin stands as well as some from State land that had been logged a half century or more earlier.

The 1950 blowdown provoked a storm of political controversy that equaled the severity of the northeaster. Aerial surveys confirmed what observers on the ground could see. Although some hardwoods were affected, spruce was the focus of concern not only because it was the most heavily damaged, yet most desirable species, but because the fallen trees were so susceptible to fire. After the damage was assessed, the State sought to harvest the fallen timber on Forest Preserve lands, using the argument that the downed trees constituted a fire hazard. An Attorney General's opinion confirmed the State's constitutional right to do so despite the forever wild clause.

Hundreds of tracts were surveyed and offered to loggers who bid on the salvage. The clean-up operations prompt two observations: a great many of the tracts put up for bid were stands of old growth or virgin forest; and second, some of today's most spectacular woods--places where forty years later there is little evidence of blowdown--were earmarked for salvage. Other stands, like those in Totten and Crossfield Townships 5, 6, 40, 41, stretching to the northwest from the borders of the Sagamore Lake tract to the Pigeon Lake Wilderness west of Raquette Lake and east to the Blue Ridge Wilderness, were among the best documented of Adirondack virgin spruce forests, and there the damage was quite severe.

Unfortunately, no record has been found describing which bids were actually let, which makes it difficult to analyze the extent of the actual salvage. The Cold River area was large enough to justify a full-scale clean-up and gravel-surfaced truck roads were built. The decision to build roads was at the root of the controversy over the salvage of blowdown from the Forest Preserve. A few other public tracts were salvaged, including the area south of Raquette Lake; but many of the smaller sites were not, perhaps because they were too fragmented or isolated or perhaps because the bonds required were too large for most loggers. Whatever the reason, the Cold River clean-up was the most extensive and the principal one to be one documented.

## Salvage Operations in 1952

Finch, Pruyn and Co., 24,000 cords, Blue Mountain and Inlet area and State land.

Ward Lumber Co., 20,000 cords, the McKenzie Mountain Wilderness.

Fisher Forestry and Realty Co., Beaver River, Panther and Francis lakes, and Stillwater Reservoir areas.

International Paper Co., 8,000 cords, Speculator Tract and State lands near Raquette Lake and Inlet.

St. Regis Paper Co., from Martin Brook area, north of Pepperbox Wilderness area.

Whitney Industries, 10,000 cords from company tract.

U. S. Bobbin and Shuttle Co., 120,000 cords Cold River area, National Lead Tracts and the Forest Preserve.

C. J. Strife, 18,000 cords, near Raquette Lake and 1,500 cords, Forestport area.

Draper Corp., 6,000 cords, Litchfield Park.

Source: 1952 issues of *Lumber Camp News*

Figure 46

Salvage operations were also carried out on many private tracts, including Gould's lands in the Moose River Plains. Finch, Pruyn and Company's only harvest in 1952 was salvage spruce from company tracts near Tirrell Pond and Inlet and some from State land near Raquette Lake. Overall, the harvest on both public and private lands was so large it resulted in such a glut on the market between 1951 to 1955 that the price of spruce was temporarily depressed.

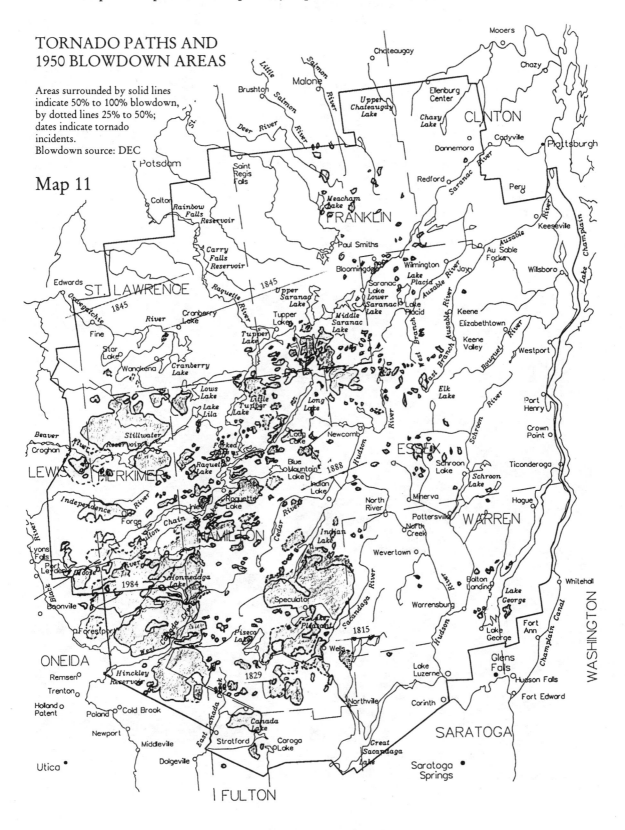

TORNADO PATHS AND
1950 BLOWDOWN AREAS

Areas surrounded by solid lines indicate 50% to 100% blowdown, by dotted lines 25% to 50%; dates indicate tornado incidents.
Blowdown source: DEC

Map 11

# The Pulp and Paper Industry after 1920

Shortages in pulp and increased demand for paper created a boom that resulted in a sharp increase in the price of pulpwood in 1920. Pulp wood was valued at $4.25 a cord on the Robert C. Pruyn Tract, Santanoni Preserve. Finch, Pruyn and Company consumed 20,000 cords on the average each year all through the 1920s, although it had to import spruce from its Canadian holdings between 1920 and 1928 to maintain that level without cutting its immature Adirondack stocks.

Changes in the pulp and paper industry included improvements in the way wood was debarked. Stripping the bark from logs to make them float was done manually until long after the 1895 invention of a rossing or debarking machine. Santa Clara Lumber Company pioneered the development of machines to produce rossed pulp wood.[27] In 1942, Moose River Lumber Company installed a huge debarking drum (capacity twenty cords of wood) at Nobleboro to bark the pulpwood driven down the West Canada Creek for shipment to St. Regis Lumber and J. P. Lewis companies.[28]

By contrast, there were few technological advances in pulp and paper making machinery. From 1915 to 1940, these machines evolved slowly with gradual improvements in the time it took to make paper and increases in the size and efficiency of paper making machinery.[29]

*Breaking a log jam and driving*
*logs on the Moose River*

*Courtesy Adirondack Museum*

After 1910, the mills of northern New York had expanded their capacity far beyond the supply available from the local forests. To supplement the shrinking spruce supply, mills began adding balsam and hemlock to spruce to make pulp. By the end of that decade, foresters were predicting Adirondack forests would fail to sustain the industry. New York pulp production was so great that the State led the nation in 1916. To maintain this level of production, already in 1919, nearly forty percent of the pulpwood consumed in New York State had to be imported, mostly from Canada. That year, A.B. Recknagel, consulting forester for Finch, Pruyn and Company and one of the leading forestry theorists in the first half of this century, declared that the supply of spruce, balsam, and hemlock on private lands in the Adirondacks would be exhausted in six and a half years, four if there were no further imports.[30] In 1928, the Society of American Foresters echoed this view with similar but slightly less pessimistic predictions. The problem was perceived to be so critical that one source concluded that Adirondack forests could not supply the region's mills even if pulp was harvested from the Forest Preserve.[31]

Throughout the 1930s, production of the region's mills declined, with a corresponding decrease in the rate of pulpwood consumption. The Depression was largely responsible for the decline, which can also be attributed to the fact that older paper mills were shut down and not replaced or modernized. However, the size of the pulpwood harvest from the State's forests decreased even more dramatically than the capacity of the State's mills. In 1937, New York imported forty-seven percent of its pulp from Canada and seventeen percent from other states.[32] In only twenty-three years, from 1916 to 1923, New York's rank in pulp consumed had fallen from first to seventh place nationally.[33]

New York's Department of Commerce attributed the decline in output of pulpwood to the "past failure of the timber-using industry to cut forests selectively so as to insure a new crop within a reasonable period of time and the locking up of 2,000,000 acres of potential timber-producing land in the Adirondacks in the Forest Preserve."[34]

To compensate, imports from Canada were increased in an effort to make New York's mills more efficient. Even so, production in the southern United States proved much more economical. For a time, Canada banned shipment of logs from provincial forests to the United States. New York's paper companies were able to import wood from Canada only if they owned timberland there. These two events forced the northern New York industry to change its mills to focus on specialty papers rather than newsprint. From 1925 to 1939, specialty paper production rose twenty-five percent.[35]

Paper production increased during the years of World War II, despite shortages of labor and fuel that made timber harvest difficult, while that of newsprint gradually declined, falling seventy-eight percent between 1925 and 1958.[36] During that time, Canada built many new newsprint mills; the United States removed tariffs on Canadian newsprint; and the southeastern United States began producing newsprint from fast-growing southern pine. Mills in eastern Canada and the southern United States became the dominant producers of newsprint on the east coast.

A change in paper making, second only in importance to the development of methods employing wood to make paper, occurred in the mid 1950s, when northern New York's paper companies developed the technologies to reformulate their processes to use hardwoods. In the 1940s and early 1950s, hardwood stumpage had almost no value. By 1960, mills that had been converted to take advantage of the new processes, were able to use significant amounts of hardwoods for pulp.[37] The increase in hardwood consumption meant a resurgence in regional dependence on northern New York supplies. Finch, Pruyn and Company began to use beech, of which there was an overabundance in Adirondack forests, and other hardwoods by 1957. International Paper Company's pulp mix was more than half hardwoods after 1960. By 1963, hardwoods constituted 60 percent of all pulpwood harvested in New York.[38] New York's mills today use anywhere from fifty and seventy-five percent hardwoods, all supplied by regional forests, and import softwoods to supplement the State's production of them.

It might be supposed that the new markets for hardwoods would encourage better forest management through the sale of culls, but when hardwoods were first used, the mills demanded only the best lumber, so the practice of high-grading continued.[39]

Paradoxically, even after the pulp and paper industry began to use hardwoods, the rate of hardwood forest recovery was so great that by 1980, the Adirondack region became "overstocked" with them.[40] Because the focus was no longer on spruce, harvest reports no longer indicated that the forest was being harvested at a rate greater than that of regrowth. The region still has an overabundance of hardwoods, although it cannot meet demands for the region's most valuable species--maple and yellow birch of veneer quality. The problem is that there are not many such high-quality trees in the north country.

*International Paper Company pulp mill at Piercefield, H. M. Beach, circa 1915*

Courtesy Adirondack Museum

# A New Generation of Foresters

In 1910, Finch, Pruyn and Co. was the first of the major pulp and paper companies to hire a forester. In 1911, after only a year with the company, Howard Churchill completed his working plan for the timberland, which Finch, Pruyn put to use immediately.

In 1915, Dean Baker of Syracuse University School of Forestry argued against a fixed diameter limit as the basis for a selection system of logging.[41] He proposed substituting the soundness of remaining trees and their predicted rate of growth as criteria for management.

By 1920, Adirondack forests had been seriously depleted, despite all the forester's earlier recommendations that might have prevented this. In 1922, a Syracuse University Forestry Professor H. C. Belyea argued that "while present methods of lumbering have not resulted in forest devastation they have resulted in forest deterioration both in species and amount and in soil deterioration."[42]

In 1934, A. B. Recknagel helped plan the second cut of smaller diameter softwoods at Whitney Park. While noting that the results of the second cut under regulated management would be "watched with great interest" by foresters, the plan predicted that the tract would be ready to harvest again in 1970. There was no confidence, however, that the 1970 yield would be as large as that obtained in the mid-1930s' cut. Economic forces once more prevailed and logging began again in the 1950s. A 1952 offer from Gould Paper Company to buy the spruce, balsam, hemlock and large hardwoods on the tract included the information that Whitney foresters anticipated a yield of eight cords per acre, but Gould's forester, Karl Kornmeyer noted that a more realistic figure would be six cords.[43] Both estimates are below the rate of harvest for spruce alone achieved in the harvest of the 1890s.

Recknagel produced a "Sample Working Plan for Adirondack Softwoods,"[44] the goal of which was to provide a periodic sustained yield of pulpwood. However, such restrictions as the cost of logging forced him to conclude that "management, then, is a compromise between the necessities of logging and what is the best forestry practice."[45] Thirty-four years later, Recknagel quoted Pinchot's remark that "Forestry is practiced everywhere in New York -- except in the woods" and added that "his remarks were directed primarily at the Forest Preserve but would have been equally applicable to the privately owned woodlands."[46] In reviewing the impact of a half century of scientific forestry in which he played a significant role, Recknagel noted that in the teens the membership of ESFPA had not looked favorably on private forest management. With the exception of Finch, Pruyn and Company, Fisher Forestry and Realty, Emporium Lumber Company, and Whitney Park, none practiced scientific forestry according to Recknagel. Today we know that little scientific forestry was practiced on the last three named tracts except as instituted in recent years at Whitney Park. Emporium Lumber Company so completely depleted its timberlands that it engaged in a desperate search for new tracts in the last few years before the company left the Adirondacks (see appendix).

In 1922, Theodore S. Woolsey, Jr.. writing in the *Journal of Forestry*, proposed legislation to control "forest devastation."[47] The legislation would have empowered the State to hold vacant land which was not being protected and managed with reasonable efficiency for the growth of timber and pulpwood and to have the State Forester oversee forestry on that land. Woolsey's proposal would have created an auxiliary class of State forest land. This too was a means of getting around the constitutional protection of the Forest Preserve and can be considered a harbinger of modern proposals that create a category of lands--easements--that permit forestry and assist the forest products industry. It might be concluded that easements are just another means of bypassing Article XIV, the only difference being that, today, the shortage of funds to add to Forest Preserve lands has run up against the need to preserve open space as well as to protect the forest products industry.

Additional legislation introduced that same year, 1922, at the insistence of the Association for the Protection of the Adirondacks, may not have been a serious attempt to pass new laws, but, however unrealistic it was, it indicated concern. It would have prohibited cutting on private tracts without permission of the Conservation Department. The expectation was that the department could then enforce appropriate forestry management.

Given all the problems faced by the forest products industry during the depression years, it is not surprising that even large industrial landholders were slow to adopt scientific forestry. It was not until 1943 that St. Regis Paper Company hired a forester.[48] Draper Corporation employed a forester at Sabattis in 1947, Elliott Hardwood Company in 1953. In 1956, *The Northeastern Logger* mentioned that the biggest area set aside for silviculture was the 10,000 acres owned by St. Regis Paper Company and known as the Northern New York Experimental Forest. Today, it is a part of the Higbie Tract and is accessible from Cranberry Lake.

By 1956, New York State's forests were increasing both in acreage and in the volume of trees per acre, mostly as a result of farmland returning to forest cover. The greatest increase, however, was among the less desirable trees and the rate of removal of the favored species still exceeded the rate of replacement.[49]

Foresters continued to lament their inability to improve the forests in their care. In 1962, Thomas W. Church, who had been employed as a forester at Whitney Park, noted changes in cutover hardwood stands which "have generally been high-graded [so] that there is little high-quality saw log material left."[50] He concluded that, unfortunately, market conditions determine the future condition of the forest and predicted that in the next twenty years, beech would take over the forest. In spite of the presence of beech die-back, that is exactly what has happened at Whitney and Litchfield parks and in many other areas, such as tracts south of Jerseyfield.[51]

A hundred years ago, foresters not only failed to convince landowners to follow scientific forestry practices, but, by their own later analyses, they showed that in fact it had not been economically possible.[52] Few land owners practiced scientific forestry, and those who did failed to reap the desired results. They found that the marketplace defined forestry, not scientific principles.

However, the belief that foresters were important was slowly advancing. Schools were being established, foresters were being trained. Prior to the late 1940s, *Lumber Camp News* referred to field managers as foremen, jobbers, or woods superintendents. After about 1950, they were all called foresters, independently of whether the title was self-proclaimed or indicated professional training.

To leap to recent times, it is obvious that little has changed, although many aspects of forestry are better understood now. Foresters are employed to advise all too few landowners, especially those with small holdings, on managing their land; excessive or unwise cutting is prevalent on tracts harvested without benefit of the advice of foresters. Rumored examples of overcutting abound even on big and supposedly well-managed forests--it has been said that International Paper Company's tract on the Raquette River may not recover to be harvested again for six or more decades. Current cutting to improve stands at Whitney Park is not expected to result in a good forest harvest for many years.

Historically, foresters sensed something was going wrong, that there were problems with every harvest carried out; but the science did little to assure the continued availability of the most desirable species, spruce. Even more troublesome than the fact that their recommendations were defeated by the marketplace is the fact that foresters did not foresee many of the problems caused by planned harvesting such as the dominance of hardwoods, and the later preponderance of beech.

On the other hand, the economics of the pulp and paper industry should have had a salubrious effect on forest management. The capital needed to construct pulp and paper mills is so great and the period over which their construction can be amortized is so long that they can only be built where there is adequate present and future supply of timber. As historian Stewart Holbrook noted,

> Little or nothing was done about forest management till the coming of the pulp wood industry. The sawmill outfits had cut out and got out; they either migrated or liquidated, but wood-converting plants could not pull up stakes and move on because they had large investments in site, power, water sources, buildings, and specialized equipment. A forest becomes the first essential to the capital structure of such an enterprise. It must be an immense forest, and it must be under management.[53]

Beginning with Churchill and Recknagel, Finch, Pruyn and Company has maintained that it has practiced good forestry on its company lands, even though insiders admit that most often the market still determines the company's forest policies. The company differs from other Adirondack paper companies in its continuous private ownership. This company appears to have been more successful than most for in 1993, Richard Carota, the company's president, said it needed no tax abatements or conservation easements because of its stewardship and good management. He suggested that companies presently seeking such relief or selling land were doing so to purchase mill improvements and that properly managed land could only rise in value and could thus in the future be used to leverage borrowing for capital improvements.[54] All this implied that Finch, Pruyn's superior management of both its business and its timberlands gave it an advantage over other such companies in the north country.

Most Adirondack timberland, however, is not under such beneficial management. In 1898, Ralph D. Nyland, a forestry professor at Syracuse College of Environmental Science and Forestry, wrote an appendix to the *Report of the Governor's Task Force on Forestry*, of which he was a member. He was very pessimistic about forest resources and their future productivity. He wrote:

> The widespread practice of extracting products rather than deliberately managing timber stands is usually equivalent to what the Society of American Foresters calls "selective cutting" or high-grading, a type of exploitation that removes only certain species ... above a certain size ... of high value, known silvicultural yields being largely ignored. ... [The forests] are cut for immediate market value without attention to the regeneration of replacement crops, nor the character of the growing stock left behind."[55]

In the same publication, Nyland expresses the belief that without markets for cull trees the practice of high-grading will become more prevalent. His prognosis is so bleak that he sees New York on the "threshold of the second great exploitation of the forest."

Selective harvesting has amounted to selecting against quality in a way that favors the poorest specimens and least valuable species. Past forest manipulation could actually destroy the value of the region's timberlands.

In some areas, only smaller and smaller trees are available for harvest, although a few virgin stands have been logged in the past few decades. The Johnston and Son harvest at Jerseyfield in 1940 was said to include virgin timber. Also in the 1940s, Johnson and Son cut a "fine stand of virgin spruce on the Jessup" on lands belonging to International Paper Company. First-cut spruce trees were harvested in 1943 on Dug Mountain. Gould was cutting virgin timber on Seventh Lake Mountain near Inlet in 1946.[56] The last significant cut of virgin timber was made by International Paper Company on lands swapped to the State in the 1970s to consolidate their holdings. The harvest yielded a volume of wood roughly equivalent to what the company harvests on its managed lands. Today there are few uncut, privately-owned softwood stands, such as the Gill Brook Valley belonging to Adirondack Mountain Reserve. There are, however, hardwood stands that have never been harvested, most notably in portions of Finch, Pruyn and Company's tracts on the south side of the Indian River and near the Blue Ledges.

# To the Present

Between 1939 and 1963, the number of active pulp mills in the State "dwindled from 42 to 18 and output, after rising to a peak of 711,000 tons of wood pulp in 1951, subsequently declined.'[57] As a result, the level of production in 1963 was thirty percent below that of 1939. During the same period, the number of mills in northern New York declined and those that remained were either among the larger ones or among those whose capacity had been greatly increased by new machinery. Today, only a few mills continue to produce paper, with production concentrated in a few large corporations. The continued need to upgrade and modernize pulp and paper machinery and the tremendous investments to do so are currently balanced by questions about whether the amount and condition of regional forests would support ever more costly equipment. Of the remaining paper mills, those owned by both International Paper Company and Finch, Pruyn and Company import part of their pulp requirements from outside the Adirondacks.

The lumber industry of northern New York has suffered an even greater decline; only a few large sawmills exist and there is very little manufacture of wood products. Logging after 1950 declined so that growing stock had a net increase of twenty percent between 1950 and 1968.[58] The number of sawmills decreased so that today two companies, International Paper Company and Domtar, Inc., ship their best spruce sawlogs to Canada to be sawn.

A dichotomy confronts commercial forestry in the Adirondacks. Market values of tree species change with the times, at intervals of a few years, while it takes a century or more to grow some trees to maturity. As a result, even foresters, who can convince owners of timber tracts to place stand improvement on an equal footing with the desire for profit, are less effective than they might be for they cannot predict what stands will be most valuable in the future.

The intent of this work is not to analyze the future of Adirondack timberland and forest production, nor to determine the validity of industry claims that New York provides a poor environment for timber production. Everyone admits that the tax structure could be improved and that forests in other locations are more efficient and economical producers of newsprint. On the other hand, the local industry has avoided over-regulation of their timberlands and environmental restrictions on mills are onerous but appropriate.

For those mills that are part of national or international conglomerates, local management practices are hostage to corporate accountants in an arena where the Adirondacks can barely compete. Industrial timberland owners look more and more to recreation revenue to balance the cost of owning Adirondack forests. Every large company has lease arrangements for hunting and other recreation. Lyons Falls Pulp and Paper Company has placed some of its holdings in conservation easements in hopes of lowering their tax burden.

Some companies like Lyons Falls Pulp and Paper Company are currently suffering; some like Finch, Pruyn and Company appear to be thriving. Some tracts are in position to produce good timber harvests for their owners; some have been so stripped it will be years before they yield much profit in either pulpwood or timber.

Many believe that the future of Adirondack private forests lies in the production of sawlog and veneer-quality hardwood logs. Some believe that tourism and recreation will soon overtake the wood products industry in economic importance in the region. Current trends seem to substantiate both propositions.

One thing seems certain, however. While it is not clear whether pessimistic views of the future forest are correct, there is no reason to believe from past experience that foresters will be able to predict or influence the future condition of the private portion of the great forest of the Adirondacks. The greatest change to Adirondack private forestland occurred thirty years ago, when the loggers ceased harvesting only a fraction of the species in the forest and began to cut all species down to small dimension. Today, regulations limit the degree of cutting, but the marketplace permits much more intensive harvests than those of earlier years. Furthermore, economic pressures will persist, making it ever more fortunate that a portion of the forest has been preserved in a way that forever prohibits logging.

### LARGE ADIRONDACK INDUSTRIAL TIMBERLANDS 1990

| | Acres |
|---|---|
| International Paper Co. | 205,714 |
| Finch, Pruyn & Co. | 154,476 |
| Champion International (St. Regis) | 118,265 |
| Domtar, Inc. | 88,744 |
| Whitney Industries | 50,937 |
| Lyons Falls Pulp & Paper Co. | 8,131 |

Map 12

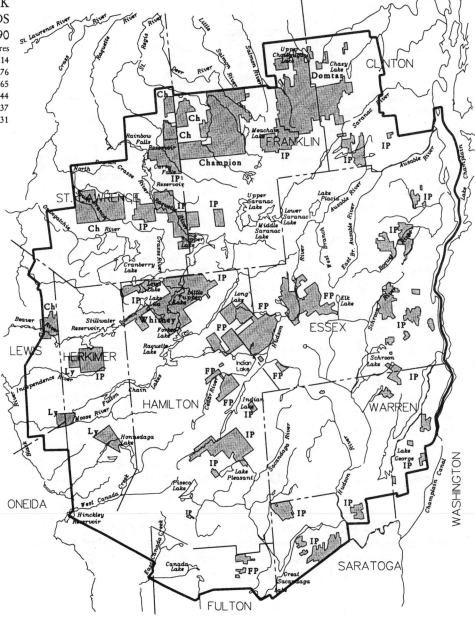

# IX

## Lessons from the Past

### Calls to Cut Timber on the Forest Preserve

The underlying theme that emerges from the history of Adirondack forests is, of course, how the Forest Preserve was created and given constitutional protection. However, one of the more intriguing ancillary topics arising from the preservation history has had great potential relevance for the forest, and apparently will continue to in the future. Attempts to change the State Constitution to permit logging of the Forest Preserve have occurred repeatedly, from the time of its creation until the present. These attempts sum up the conflict between public and private lands in the Adirondacks. Even though proponents of the opposing views change, the conflict does not go away.

At the time the Park was created, many professional foresters and lumbermen were convinced that the prohibition against cutting was wrong. They assumed that if excesses could be curbed, scientific foresters could and would someday direct cutting on State-owned forest lands. Professional foresters kept trying to get around the constitution. Bernhard Fernow was able to get the State to acquire land for the ill-fated Cornell experimental forest at Axton (see appendix). Gifford Pinchot in 1900 argued in favor of repealing the constitutional amendment and substituting a program of managed forestry on State lands. He said that amendment [Article VII, Section 7], "while probably fully justified by the circumstances which led to its enactment, is a direct confession on the part of the State of its inability to manage its forest lands."[1] Oddly enough he did not call for a forester to oversee the harvesting of timber on State lands, but rather someone with management skills. He thought the advice of the United States Department of Agriculture would provide sufficient safeguards.

This first generation of foresters succeeded in bringing to the rest of the country the values of "wise use" for the common good. Pinchot was particularly successful; witness his success in creating National Forests. Their idealism did not inspire New Yorkers. Foresters failed to convince the State to adopt measures that would permit controlled logging in the Adirondacks because they failed to convince the public that it could be done without further harm to the forest. The failure to adopt forestry principles for the Forest Preserve can be attributed to a combination of lumber barons, whose actions thwarted the conservation movement, and fledgling preservationists, who distrusted both the lumbermen and the foresters.

From its establishment in 1885, the Forest Commission, with its industry bias, never quite seemed to believe in the Forest Preserve. An 1887 Law (Chapter 475) gave the commission the ambiguously worded right to sell timber on "separate small tracts" of the Forest Preserve. During its existence, when disappearance of the last virgin tracts in the Park seemed a real possibility, the Forest Commission tried to generate support for harvesting virgin tracts--the over-mature forests so coveted by foresters.

The Forest Preserve Board established in 1897 did begin by giving serious consideration to its protection of the Forest Preserve, but the legislative climate had not changed. The 1898 Assembly Report continuing the investigation of what lands should be acquired in order to protect watersheds applauded the State's efforts to that date and stood ready to absolve lumbermen of past excesses. "It is highly gratifying for the committee to be able to testify to the growing interest that is being taken by the people of the forest counties in the care and preservation of the woodlands. Frequent testimony was given before the [Assembly] committee to the effect that the old haphazard way of lumbering, against which so much complaint has been made in the past, is fast being superseded by an intelligent treatment of forest property." This optimistic view led the committee to conclude "that the time is soon to come when the question of applying scientific forestry to the State Preserve will be an all important one."[2]

In 1901, the Forest, Fish and Game Commission asked the United States Department of Agriculture to prepare a study of the Adirondack Forest Preserve in order to "set before the people of the State, reasons why the above clause [now Article XIV] should be so modified that the forest might be properly utilized and administered."[3] The result was *A Forest Working Plan for Township 40, Totten and Crossfield*, carried out by two disciples of Gifford Pinchot. The Commission was so impressed with the plan that it requested funds from the legislature, which appropriated $3,500 to prepare working plans for adjacent virgin townships 5, 6, and 41.[4]

The Commission's introduction to the report for Township 40 was careful to note that timber harvesting and water conservation, the principal reason for the creation of the Forest Preserve, were not mutually exclusive. "Wisely lumbered, these Adirondack forests will continue to supply water in undiminished quantity to feed the streams, which rise among them, if fire is kept out." Both reports are careful to spell out logging practices that would not adversely affect the forest. They were summarized in fourteen rules for harvest such as use of saws not axes, care in felling and skidding logs and in cutting roads, attention to top-lopping, the height of stumps, and so on. There would be no logging on summits and upper slopes, the forest would only be slightly opened so as not to "disturb the bed of humus" or "invite erosion."[5]

Both reports attempted to dazzle the reader with elaborate statistics on the amount of timber that could be harvested. Buried in the first report was the call for funds for a permanent dam at the outlet of Raquette Lake, a structure that would be better adapted for driving logs. Funds were also needed to build roads, but with the amount of lumber available, provided the State guaranteed its price, these costs should be recovered. The first report suggests that it might be wise to build a lumber mill near the outlet of Raquette Lake and to extend the Raquette Lake Railroad from its spur at the southwest corner of the lake to the outlet.[6] No mention is made of cost; the report merely focuses on the desirability of a mill and the best way to locate it on the shores of Raquette Lake.

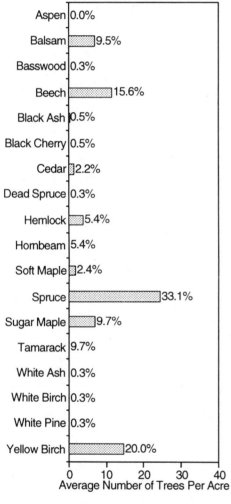

Distribution of tree species in Township 5, T & C

Average Number of Trees Per Acre

Figure 47
Sample made on 943-acre virgin tract in 1901

Forest, Fish and Game Commission,
*Sixth Annual Report*

The reports certainly did not bring about the desired constitutional amendment, but that did not stop the Forest, Fish and Game Commission from trying.

Both of the State's forestry schools advocated the cutting of the Forest Preserve. Cornell's school was founded on an experiment to do just that. The Syracuse school preached cutting as evidenced by calls to change the constitution in several theses written by graduate students who presumably were able to substantiate the benefits of cutting the Forest Preserve.

By 1910 harvest of Adirondack timber was on the decline; many writers had observed that the cutting in the late 1890s through 1905 had been at a rate greater than the forest was being regenerated. The Conservation Commission used the facts that the State's timber cut in 1912 was five times the rate of growth and that timber consumption was ten times the growth as the basis for recommending cutting on the Forest Preserve. The commission supported a bill introduced in the 1913 legislature that would have permitted such logging.[7]

Sensing the winds of change, or perhaps hoping to fan them, the Conservation Commission undertook a survey of timber on Forest Preserve lands in preparation for the Constitutional Convention of 1915. It used the information summarized in figures 46 and 47 to advocate cutting timber on Forest Preserve land. The survey substantiated the Commission's prediction that cutting the Forest Preserve under State supervision would yield the State a direct revenue of a million dollars a year. This would leave a surplus of $635,000 a year, after the State paid local taxes and carrying charges on bonds used to acquire the Forest Preserve. The report appears to be completely market driven and totally ignores the hindsight that was available to the commission. No mention was made of what was to happen when the State lands could no longer produce enough to compensate for increased cuts, something that would have inevitably occurred. That Forest Preserve timber would be rapidly depleted never occurred to the Commissioners.

The New York State Forestry Association devoted much effort to the repeal of Article VII, section 7 of the Constitution, as reported in its first two Bulletins of 1914. George N. Ostrander urged Association members to influence the 1915 Constitutional Convention to "guide the convention to a proper and wise solution," which would permit forestry on the Forest Preserve. Ostrander believed that the original provision was "plainly designed as a restraint on the power of the legislature to make enactments with relation to the forest preserve, and nowhere is it suggested that its consideration was had with regard to the principles of either forestry or economy."[8] The Committee on Forests of the Board of Trade and Transportation was opposed to repeal of Article VII. F. A. Gaylord argued against that group's stand, claiming they did not understand scientific forestry. He did, however, conclude that in spite of the need to change the constitution to prevent a timber shortage, if it could not be done without "the proper safeguards, it is much better to let it remain as it is."[9]

The Empire State Forest Products Association also advocated cutting the Forest Preserve in its 1914 bulletins. At an ESFPA meeting in 1915, Dean Baker of Syracuse University argued against the Forest Preserve on economic grounds: "Frankly, it is a question whether the

### Adirondack Forest Preserve timber cover classifications, 1912

Total 1,406,899 Acres

|  | Acres |  |
| --- | --- | --- |
| Water | 52,270 | 4% |
| Denuded | 94,313 | 7% |
| Non-merchantable Timbered | 201,747 | 14% |
| Merchantable Timbered | 1,058,570 | 75% |

Figure 48

Source: Conservation Commission, 1914

State can afford the luxury at the present time of nearly two million acres of idle forest land."[10]

Fortunately, none of the rhetoric was successful; the 1915 Constitutional Convention killed, for the time being, all proposals to log the Forest Preserve. However, the attempts very shortly began again. A constitutional amendment that would have permitted logging was offered in 1918 in the guise of a proposal to harvest fuelwood.

The pulp and lumber industries kept clamoring for regulated cutting on State land. One member of the group that since 1901 has styled itself as the "watchdog of the Forest Preserve" appears to have agreed. In 1930, Prof. E. R. A Seligman, a vice president of the Association for the Protection of the Adirondacks, told a conference of pulp and lumbermen that the constitutional clause was "antiquated." He thought that the tying up of the forests as tightly as we have done cannot be a permanent condition and ought not to be." He believed that when the lumberman subjected himself to control for the benefit of all, then the Association would "be willing to relax our rigid program, ... to relax our watch-dog policy."[11] The Association quickly disassociated itself from this view, and just a few years later, in 1934, castigated the lumber industry: "The inadvisability of permitting lumbering on Forest Preserve when private owners were cutting faster than their trees reproduce was made manifest when lumbering interests urged opening of the preserve."[12] The implication then, as now, seems obvious--no amount of forest would be enough.

In a 1942 report, the New York State Department of Commerce attributed the State's need to import more fifty percent of the pulp it consumed from other States and Canada to the fact that north country timber-using industries had not taken adequate care of their forests and to the "locking up of 2,000,000 acres of potential timber-producing land in the Adirondacks in the Forest Preserve."[13]

In recent years most calls to cut timber on the Forest Preserve have come from those who believe harvest would promote game (deer) and from those who look at downed trees and see waste, not natural renewal. The majority of these proposals have not been passed by the legislature.

For years it was easier to call for cutting more land than to husband what was available. Even if the lumbermen had been permitted to cut all of the great forest of the Adirondacks, it was still a finite resource and its reserves of desirable species would shortly have been exhausted if the lumbermen had continued as before.

It is ironic that all the while the State was engaged in constitutionally driven preservation efforts, opposition to those efforts was so strong from within the government itself.

The lumber industry seems to have veered away from the view that the Preserve should be cut, but only in the past decade; and some of its members continue to quietly support cutting on the Forest Preserve. The industry (though not all its individual members) has chosen to give up trying to gain access to the Forest Preserve and has supported the "environmental movement" in exchange for support from that movement for easements to protect the economic viability of the forest products industry in the Adirondacks. Today, logging for lumber or pulp is more marginal than ever, given the competition from the vast reserves of Canada and the plots of forests in the southern United States that produce pulp almost as if it were an agricultual

Adirondack Forest Preserve
tree-cover classifications, 1912

| | |
|---|---|
| Misc. | 3% |
| Maple | 13% |
| Birch | 15% |
| Beech | 10% |
| Hemlock | 11% |
| Balsam | 12% |
| Spruce | 36% |

Figure 49

Source: Conservation Commission 1914

crop. Some believe that only with easements or some form of tax abatement can the Adirondack timber industries become competitive.

The industries' shift has come at a time when practices are radically different from a hundred years ago; they come at a time when clearcutting and high-grading are very real, when the condition of many private tracts within the Park is not healthy.

It is frightening to view the history of the Forest Preserve in the context of these events. Consider the relatively short span since major agencies of the State stopped calling for an end to the constitutional amendment, the very few years since this policy has been advocated by the lumber industry, and cacophony of voices in the north country of those who still want cutting on the Forest Preserve. In that light Forest Preserve does not seem so secure.

Forests throughout the world are dwindling, being cut at a rate far greater than their replacement. The potential to cut Adirondack forests at that excessive rate exists. Echoing Hough, I can only ask, how long will supplies last and what next? And then I can add a prayer of thanks that so much of the great forest of the Adirondacks has been preserved. The struggle to keep it safe must continue.

# Exaggerations

An equally perplexing, though far less dangerous, aspect of the preservation movement surrounds the tactics of that movement. Throughout, advocates of the Forest Preserve have used exaggeration, hyperbole even, to win their points. The events leading up to 1892 are the epitome of this: Writers described the disasters left by charcoal manufacturing but assigned the devastation to lumbermen. Advocates for preservation protested that any railroad could produce views such as in the countryside surrounding the Chateaugay Railroad, which traversed charcoal lands. They equated all loggers' dams with the dam on the Raquette north of Tupper Lake, the one dam that caused highly visible and well-photographed forest damage. They ascribed the Hudson and Champlain valleys' denuded roadsides to lumbermen, when in fact they had been cleared for agriculture.

An 1891 article in *Garden and Forest* described the ride up the Champlain Valley and along the Chateaugay Railroad but reported the scene as if it were common throughout the Park: "At that early day much of the land had been stripped of its timber and had been abandoned by the owners after it had been removed, because it was not worth to them even as much as the taxes due on the wild land."[14]

Even Governor Flower, who signed the law creating the Adirondack Park, attempted to inflame support for forest preservation by claiming that the State has lost over a hundred thousand acres to those who claimed errors in the State's tax sales when in fact at that time the actual lost acreage was far less.

Advocates of the day, writing in journals that have been preserved and are most accessible for modern study, claimed that lumbermen were responsible for most forest destruction. That was not the case, but modern writers have found it easier to quote these journals than to seek the truth. As a result much that has been written for the centennials of the Forest Preserve and the Park claims that reaction to clearcutting was the principal cause of their establishment. No one today seems to look to the Forest Commission reports that noted that up until spruce was harvested for pulp, only the largest sawlogs were taken, that the forest was little disturbed, and that such lumbering did not affect the forest's ability to retain water and release it slowly.

Certainly, the potential for destruction of the forest was at hand. Threats were ubiquitous and very real; they came from the projected railroads and from the pulp manufacturers' ability to use smaller and smaller logs. But, lumbermen had not clearcut any portion of the great forest, and indeed would not until well into this century.

Lumbermen themselves added to the misconceptions--they bemoaned the fact that the timber was all gone, when they meant only that the merchantable timber was all gone, the accessible portion of the fifteen percent of the forest that had spruce. Yet it would appear from their writings that they had stripped the forests bare.

People not only believed these exaggerations at the time, they often still believe them today, because the writings containing them constitute the body of readily available information about what was happening in the Adirondacks. The writers were perpetrating an historical disservice at the same time they were rallying support for the Forest Preserve.

The recognition that the public is often moved only by such exaggerations seems to be a poor excuse for outright misstatements of facts. The events of the 1880s and 1890s parallel today's hyperboles about the destruction of the Park by overbuilding. Today, such destruction is neither rampant nor particularly visible over wide areas, but the potential does exist. The threats are real. In this time of public awareness, such tactics seem to be unfortunate. Might it not be wiser to be more factual? Don't such exaggerations invite inflamed retorts? It is easy to view one portion of the Park, say the area around Lake George, and see how severe the problem is locally. But anyone who drives Route 30 through the middle of the Park can see how much forest is preserved, how most settlements are benign supports for those who seek recreation in the Park.

We have in place strong, albeit imperfect, legislation that regulates the private portion of the Park; the State Constitution gives total protection to the public portion. The constitution can of course be changed, but it has proven difficult to do; and no amendments that would destroy the forever wild principle have succeeded. Vigilance is essential and will always be needed. Improvements must be made in the way private lands are regulated, not because things are so bad, but because it is possible to do a better job. So, is inflamed rhetoric necessary? I cannot believe it is, but then I ask myself if the movement to save the forest could have succeeded a hundred years ago without the exaggerations. Ultimately I question their value even as means to an end, and I cringe to think what misconceptions current rhetoric will breed a century from now. More importantly, I fear that the exaggerations will continue to fuel the conflicts surrounding the Park and the Forest Preserve. I believe it is time to continue the struggle for preservation with reason, not emotion.

# The Search for Remnants of the Great Forest of the Adirondacks

The search for remnants of the Great Forest of the Adirondacks--for those tracts that were never logged or were hardly touched by man--became for me a quest of Holy Grail proportions. In an attempt to approach the quest systematically, I sought to determine from the historical record which stands had never been logged, and this portion of the search yielded significant acreage, unequivocally at least 200,000 acres. However, delving into the historical record to determine how extensive are the tracts where man's intrusion has been minimal proved to be a lengthy process. It entailed applying all the historical knowledge I had gained to a multitude of individual tracts and lots. Further, it involved assessing those lots with respect to their relation to the great forest of a hundred years ago. This requires a rigorous description of great forest and man's minimal intrusion.

Today, scientists view remnants of great forest in terms of "old-growth," where by definition stands must show no signs of logging, no sawn stumps, no logging roads, no evidence of the presence of man such as charred stumps that point to man-caused fires. The term old-growth provides a way of describing forests that avoids the logical incongruity of the term "almost virgin." Old-growth forests must contain uneven aged stands with as many fallen giants littering the forest floor as there are giants standing and a wide variety of heights and diameters in each species. The dominant species must naturally reproduce themselves.

Recognizing stands that are old-growth is a challenge, even for biologists. One expert in spruce forests in the northeast has offered a definition of old-growth that can be tested scientifically, albeit with considerable effort. Dr. Charles Cogbill defines a stand as old-growth forest if the average age of the species present (computed from those over six inches in diameter) is at least half the life expectancy of that species.

An old-growth forest does not necessarily look impressive, as evidenced in the scrubby summit spruce and balsam stands of the High Peaks, which are certainly old-growth, but not as aesthetically pleasing as lower elevation pockets with their towering and majestic trees.

In the excitement of discovering that the historical record suggested there really might be many remnants of the great forest, I rushed to visit some of the tracts I first identified as having never been logged. Walking through Adirondack forests, as I have been privileged to do for so many decades, the visitor cannot but be aware of the many variations in existing stands. From the deep, impenetrable gloom of hemlock stands where all growth on the forest floor is shaded out to fresh cut stands with brambles and blackberry bushes and rampant new growth, Adirondack forests range a wide spectrum.

On my walks I try to notice everything--it has been my business to do so. But I never appreciated the variations in forest as much as when my forays were directed by historical information. It was instructive to compare those possible old-growth stands with earlier depictions of virgin forests. Two things focused my search. The first was the application of the knowledge gained from my study of logging history that spruce is the major indicator of old-growth forests and I

**Comparison between diameter and average age of red spruce**

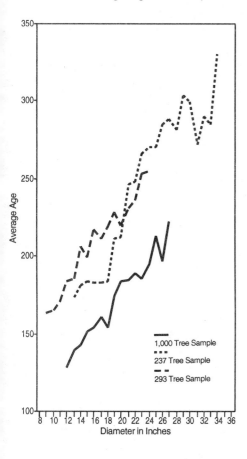

Figure 50

Information based on three historical studies made in the 1890s
1,000-tree sample, Twp 20, Franklin County, Fox, *The Adirondack Black Spruce*
237-tree sample, Twp 14, St. Lawrence County, Fox, *ibid*
293-tree sample, Nehasane, 1897, Graves, *Practical Forestry*

could limit part of my search to old-growth spruce stands or stands where the spruce present met the biological definition of old-growth. I would not have to examine the other species. The second was the realization, after countless hours spent tracing the ownership history of many lots, that the southern Adirondacks might contain the greatest percentage of the Adirondacks' old-growth forests. The fact that most recent studies of old-growth have focused on the northern Adirondacks explains why so little was known about the possibility of old-growth stands in the southern Adirondacks.

One reason there might be so much old-growth in southern areas was quickly obvious: Hardwood trees dominate the vast majority of southern Adirondack stands. These are the forests where spruce was confined to a few valleys or exposed ridges and sparsely scattered or totally absent from the hardwood slopes. That is why these tracts were never or only lightly logged. These were not forests from which spruce had been taken, but stands where it never grew in quantities sufficient to attract the lumbermen. This might account for the fact that these tracts were abandoned early on and returned to the State for unpaid taxes. If spruce and pine were so rare, and nothing but spruce and scattered pines was logged before 1890, then these stands might by definition be considered old-growth. Hence I could conclude that not only were there so many acres (upwards of 1.5 million) of uncut hardwoods, but many of these--the places where spruce do not grow--might be considered old-growth.

One aspect of the historical record had puzzled me all along. From 1850 to 1880, lumbermen had claimed that spruce occupied no more than fifteen percent of the forest, yet the studies of virgin tracts done by Graves, Pinchot and others showed concentrations of spruce as high as forty percent or more of the stands. It seemed reasonable that these studies should focus on spruce flats and lowlands where spruce was more prevalent, places the lumberman sought after the Hudson Valley sources were depleted. However, if spruce constituted no more than fifteen percent of the forest, then it is logical that some places had much smaller amounts. There is no proof, but experience tells me that the vast stands in the southwestern Adirondacks that were abandoned early really did have such small and inaccessible amounts of spruce that it was prudent to ignore them. Certainly seeing the dense spruce stands of the upper Hudson, Raquette, and Beaver River watersheds would be enough incentive for the lumberman to look to the northern and western Adirondacks. These observations led me to hypothesize that a large part of the half million acres abandoned before 1890 might be old-growth.

With my eyes raised (it is safer to walk looking down, so searching for forests can become a hazardous adventure) I wandered through a dozen areas where my historical research predicted there might be old-growth stands. Imagine my pleasure when I discovered on my first such foray that not only was I walking in great forest, I was finding spruce approaching 30 inches in diameter. I recalled that the largest spruce ever cut in the Adirondacks was 36 inches at breast height (the largest measurement, 41 inches, was of a stump). The spruce were intermingled with huge yellow birch; one giant old birch measuring 52 inches in diameter. I realized I was standing in the archetype of a spruce/yellow birch forest.

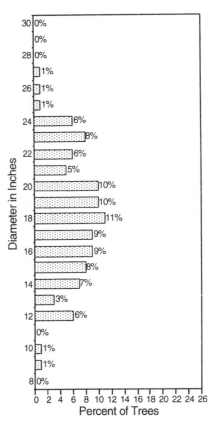

Diameter distribution of red spruce in virgin tract, 1990

**Figure 51**
123-tree sample, north of Stillwater Reservoir, measured by the author, 1993

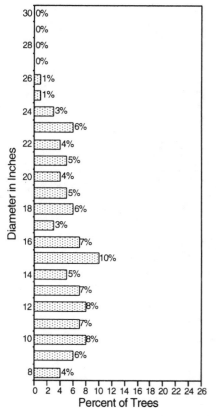

Diameter distribution of
virgin stand northeast of
Big Moose Lake

Figure 52

172-tree sample,
Measured by the author, 1993

State ownership of such isolated lots can be established for 128 years, back to 1871. Treks to see many such lots were equally revealing. They did contain big spruce--spruce of over 25 inches in diameter. The knoll south of Blind Man's Vly and north of Big Alderbed in southern Hamilton County lies in one such lots.

It was wonderful to walk through forests I had previously appreciated, only to discover how much I had to learn about them and how much more there was to see, now that my visits had a special purpose. Each trip to view old trees, carefully plotted by historical research, yielded a different forest. A magnificent stand of maples whose crowns thrust higher than a church steeple covers a cove in the slopes of Moose Mountain near Wells. I returned to Pine Orchard to view its giants, but this time I saw large spruce mixed in with the pines on the southern slopes of the knoll, huge hemlocks interspersed on the northern slopes. I found several stands of very large hemlocks, one of which was a fascinating mingling of stately white ash and white oak, all in lots in the southern Adirondacks on land owned continuously by the State for over a hundred years or more.

Friends joined me in the search. One party visited the Tefft Tract, south of Morehouse, and confirmed the presence of spruce big and old enough to confirm my theory that the tract was never logged before its sale to the State as records indicate. Its remote location, far from streams used to float logs ensures that trespass, if any, had minimal effect.

My first visits had been to tracts so far out of the way and distant from navigable streams that intense logging on them before 1870 into the early 1880s seemed a remote possibility. I thought, in order to test my thesis, I ought to revisit one site acquired early on by the State where logging was known to have occurred. The area on the West Branch of the Sacandaga south of Whitehouse has magnificent stands of spruce, which appear as they must have over a hundred years ago, right where they could easily have been dragged to the river. Here, some riverside lots were acquired through tax sales in the 1870s; some were purchased later by the State for $1.50 an acre, the low price indicating that the purchase was made after the forests had been logged of softwoods. Wandering back and forth across the Northville-Placid Trail heading south from the river, it was possible to go from lots that have been continuously in State ownership since 1871 (tax sales), to lots purchased in 1898 for $1.50, to one of the few that was purchased in 1897 for $6.00 an acre, with the claim that it was a virgin lot.

The first impression of this walk is that previous ownerships or methods of acquisition are not reflected in the forest. The forests, while not uniform by any means, responds primarily to changes in slope, humidity, and exposure. Today, the deep flatlands along West River are spruce flats at their most dynamic. Peppered with hardwoods of large proportion, dotted with fairly substantial hemlocks, the forest is nevertheless heavily mixed with spruce that average over eighteen inches in diameter. Significantly larger specimens are common. As the land sweeps uphill away from the river toward the slopes of Grindstone and Mud Lake mountains, the cover becomes increasingly dominated by hardwoods--again large trees. But the forest is never without spruce--and here isolated giants range up to the magical twenty-seven inches in diameter. These trees have to be over 200 years old.

Why was I finding such remarkable indicators of old-growth and minimal disturbance? First of all, before 1890, loggers had cut no hardwoods in the heart of the Park. No trucks or trains were available; spruce logs floated down the river were at least ten inches in diameter on the butt end. So, little damage was done and so much spruce was left that the forests not only recovered, they leapt forward, with the remaining spruce easily attaining near maximum size in the next hundred or hundred and twenty years.

How would such a previously harvested stand differ from stands where spruce had never been cut? Would I be able to detect the difference? It was not possible to determine the age of enough trees by coring them to confirm that the stand met the biological definition, although ages of 245 years and over were established. Was this old-growth forest? By the biologist's definition, probably. But now what? All of my test lots were surrounded by Forest Preserve stands that were equally notable for their long and continuous ownership by the State. My lots stood out because I had sought them out, not just because historical records indicated they might be old-growth, but because I remembered from past visits that their forest cover was special. Were there others that were equally notable? What of the intervening land? Why did the ones I visited seem to stand out?

A few were exceptional because of their remoteness, but that was not the common factor. No, common to all was also some element that permitted the stands to grow untouched by wind and storm as well as by man. They were enclosed by the shoulders of encircling mountains, in sheltered coves where whatever tree was natural there could attain its maximum growth. The forest floor beneath each site announced a profusion of fern and plant that indicated deep, rich soils. Each site could grow the best forest of the type most at home there.

And, the stands in between? They were only marginally less exciting. I recalled the biologists' caution that you cannot tell the age of a tree by its size. But size certainly does overwhelm, especially when so many magnificent sites exist. In most instances, neighboring sites had not been more logged, nor more subject to disturbance by man. The historical record shows that their pasts--at least as far as State ownership--were similar. The differences were only of location.

Isolated and remote stands everywhere were not touched, but whole stretches in between barely felt the logger's axe. Today, almost the entire Benson Tract south of Whitehouse and in many other localities in Hamilton and Herkimer counties, old-growth forests undoubtedly exist. From this it seemed plausible that, with the addition of the areas where no cutting ever occurred, there really might be something approaching a half million acres of old-growth.

Ruling out trespass on this part of the forest or extending my conjecture to places not seen loomed as an impossible given the haphazard way I had thus far made use of the historical record. Collating the amount of information available for the hundreds of Adirondack lots would be an insurmountable task. As I struggled to figure out a way to apply what I had learned to larger areas, I realized that the only way to begin would be with a map. Starting with a modern version of the Koetteritz map from which the color had been removed, I colored in every tax sale lot acquired by the State before 1900 with a scheme that showed the year of acquisition. Clusters of different-colored squares emerged in distinctive patterns of concentric

Diameter distribution of red spruce in stand logged before 1870

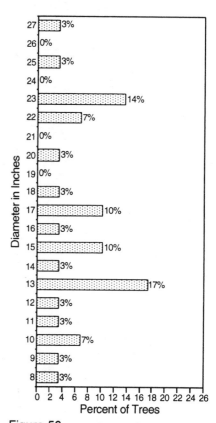

**Figure 53**
29-tree sample made in 1993 by F. Aldinger, south of Whitehouse on the West Branch of the Sacandaga

185

circles. They depicted large sections that had been continuously owned by the State, with the earliest acquired lots at the centers. This pattern led me to theorize that lumbermen had never reached the centers, that they had been abandoned before they were logged. The remoteness of the centers of the clusters from navigable streams tended to confirm this theory. Then I added different colors to show the known virgin lots and those whose appraisals by the State indicated little or no logging before they were purchased.

With trepidation, I checked these concentrations of acquisitions against the multitude of trespass records. It was quickly obvious that the largest thefts occurred close to the Hudson River or on lots where the State had been forced to grant timber reservations. The lots with the larger thefts were mostly in Warren County, in southern Essex County along the Hudson River Corridor, along the West Canada Creek just upstream from Hinckley, and along the East Canada Creek between Oregon and Stratford. Discovering that agents and later foresters had stopped thefts in the East Canada watershed south of the area with the wonderful spruce stands confirmed my speculations about their provenance. By focusing my search through trespass records on lots in the cluster areas, I was able to gain sufficient information to conclude that the hearts of the clusters had largely remained untouched.

Next I checked the clusters against the *1916 Conservation Fire Protection Map of the Adirondacks*. This proved to be an easy task. There were no fires in the areas that had been owned for so long by the State. They were too far from the railroads to have burned, even in the one year (1903) in which the greatest amount of uncut forests did burn. They have always had the dense canopy and moss-laden floors that make modern writers refer to them as asbestos, because they will not burn.

I did not rule out areas that showed up on the Map of the 1950 Blowdown because it depicts a natural phenomenon that destroyed the forest. However, I tried to eliminate from consideration tracts where there was significant harvest of the blowdown trees.

The map on the next page summarizes where to look for possible old-growth stands. Virtually all of the forests that had been owned by the State continuously for over one hundred years and where trespass was minimal or absent probably qualifies as old-growth. While a few stands are truly awe inspiring, the intervening forest is no less old and special.

The map record, however, remains incomplete; it is such a massive project that it will ultimately have to be computerized. But I was able to carry it far enough to satisfy my estimate of the amount of old-growth scattered in parcels around the Park. The tracts that more completely satisfy the criteria of old-growth both technically and emotionally are found in either of the modern land use classifications; wild forest and wilderness. The Silver Lake Wilderness, parts of the West Canada and Siamese Ponds wilderness areas, Ferris Lake Wild Forest, and Wilcox Lake Wild Forest contain the bulk of the southern Adirondack old-growth forests.

Diameter distribution of virgin red spruce in 1000-tree sample, 1890s

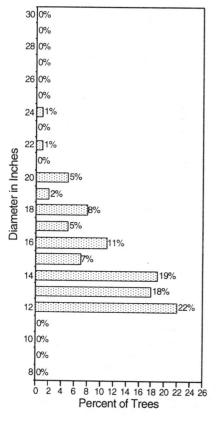

Figure 54

Source: Fox, Adirondack Black Spruce

# POTENTIAL OLD-GROWTH SITES
## Map 13

© 1994

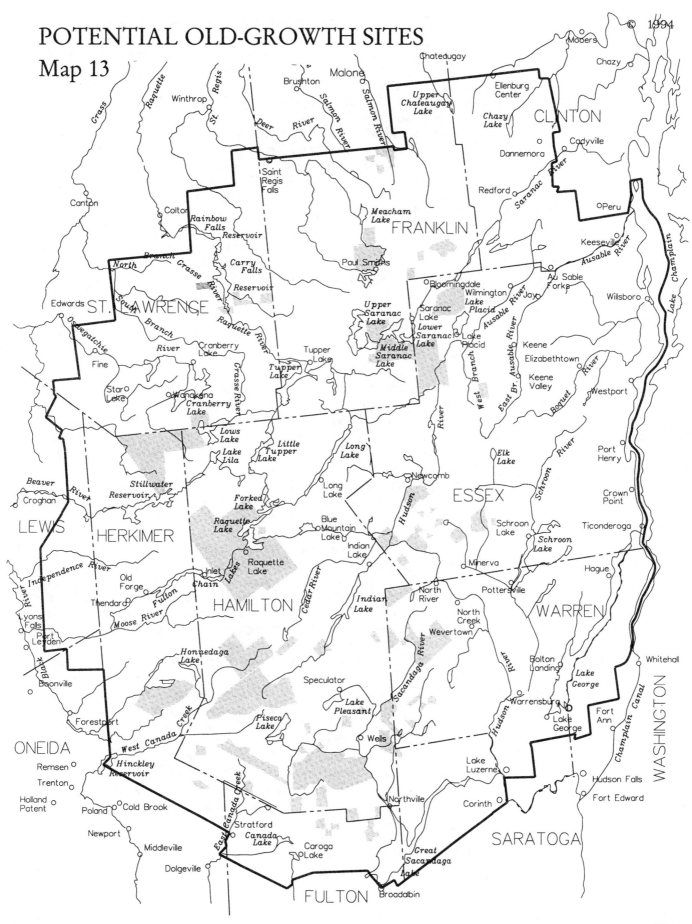

Visually confirming the old-growth stature of these parts of the forest, given their remoteness, presented formidable obstacles. Then I discovered another approach to examining forest stands. New York State still pays taxes on the Forest Preserve to local governments. In order to assess the State's tax burden fairly, the same methods are applied to State land as to private forested tracts. The type and quality of forest cover is determined, and such special features as water and streams are identified. Some of the tracts are visited by foresters from the State Department of Equalization and Assessment; most of the time these men study three dimensional projections of aerial photographs of the tracts to arrive at stand descriptions, only checking scattered plots to substantiate information gained from the photographic record.

When I learned of these photographs, I questioned how they could reveal so much detail. As I adjusted the pictures to bring my first stereoscopic view into focus (I had chosen the spot on the Powley-Piseco Road where I had seen giant spruce), the contours of the land revealed themselves, but the spruce appeared to thrust up so high above the canopy that they startled me. I used the photos to expand the area of search out from the road to the east, north, and west. My arm-chair visit approximated an aerial exploration equal to countless hours of hiking. Stands of spruce revealed their height and size as they thrust needle-like above the canopy and extended all the way to the Tefft Tract, confirming its history.

The other places visited yielded equally reassuring views. Each forest type appeared special and unique. Most astonishing and instructive were the views of tracts not yet visited. The virgin tracts north of Fawn Lake did look different. Moose River Townships 9 and 10 showed series of small hills rising from wetlands with spruce; the southern slopes were uniformly hardwoods, the northern slopes peppered with spruce which were sparse enough and sufficiently inaccessible that it is no wonder these tracts were sold to the State early on with the claims that they had been lightly logged, if at all. I expect visits to confirm that they contain old-growth.

After the initial visits to the several special sites and after identifying many more through aerial photographs, I returned to those which did have spruce with the intention of measuring all the trees in test plots and of determining the ages of some of the individuals by coring them. Most of my efforts were limited to measuring the diameters of the spruce. Even though a tree of a given diameter can have such a wide range of ages (see figure 13), stands measured in the 1890s clearly show a correspondence between size and average age (figure 50). This correlation only permits an approximation of the ages of the trees measured, but not cored. However, even assuming the minimum possible range of ages demonstrates that many of the stands measured in 1993 were remarkably similar to the virgin tracts examined a hundred years ago.

Again the Powley-Piseco Road, which traverses the Ferris Lake Wild Forest in the southern Adirondacks, offered the most accessible old-growth forest. There the forest is spectacular, undoubtedly old-growth. Just north of the trail to Ferris Lake, spruce stands border the road, with the largest spruce I have found, one that is 33 inches in diameter, standing almost at roadside. To the west of that giant, growing in sphagnum-covered wetlands, spruce constitute 65 percent of the forest; to the east, on slightly higher ground, spruce, even larger

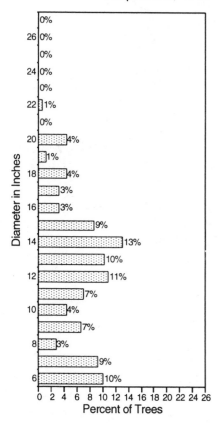

Diameter distribution of 735-tree virgin stand near Seward and Ampersand, 1900

Figure 55

Source: Forest Preserve Board

specimens become mixed with hardwoods so that spruce make up 45 percent of the stand. These figures and the profiles of the stands, shown in the accompanying charts are even more splendid that those identified by Graves and Fox. The spruce occur less frequently, still interspersed with hardwoods farther north along the Powley Road, and the proportion of hardwoods in stands near the road gradually increases. One sample site yielded a 30-inch spruce, 89 feet tall, with a dozen other spruces ranging down to 20-inch specimens in a seventy-foot circle. The oldest trees, approaching senescence, had rotten cores, making it difficult to determine their ages, but specimens at least 285 years old were found. The substantial yellow birch and maples in this circle constituted less than half the stand. This was as rich a site as any described by Fox and others a century ago. Farther north, as the ground rises slightly, there are fewer but still large--up to 27 inch-spruce. The predominantly hardwood stands are more open and hemlock intersperse. To the northwest in the lowlands along the path to Goldmine Stream waterfall are several giants measuring about 33 inches in diameter.

But what is truly amazing is the comparison of this stand with measurements taken at the Benson Tract site south of Whitehouse on the West Branch of the Sacandaga, where we know they logged the spruce. Here the spruce profiles show slightly smaller specimens, but the stand profile is comparable to some surveyed by Fox, where it was possible that natural disturbances had created stands of younger average age. The Whitehouse site may qualify as old-growth status, but more cores to determine age will be necessary to prove it.

One further method of investigating forest cover is available: satellite pictures of the Adirondacks give a rough sense of forest types. The information they provide was initially confounding. Conifers, primarily a spruce-fir mix, show up in the High Peaks regions, as would be expected. The next greatest concentration of spruce-fir appears in the southwestern and central Adirondacks. The areas with the fewest conifers are in the north. How could I rationalize the absence of spruce in the northwest, especially in areas where studies in the 1890s showed it dominated? I looked again at the modern land-ownership map. Those are the regions with the greatest amount of industrial timberland in the Park. The spruce was stripped from those stands. Further, it is obvious that spruce would not yet be able to reseed in the northeastern regions that were clearcut a century or more ago. I could only conclude that as poor as they seemed to be in spruce a century ago, the Forest Preserve tracts, which had been among the earliest to be abandoned for taxes, have today quite a lot of spruce. They were saved by their relatively small numbers as well as by their inaccessibility. Spruce would only be there today if disturbance had been minimal, suggesting one more argument for the possibility of their old-growth stature.

As might be expected the dark green areas denoting conifers on the satellite images correspond to the areas of the Forest Preserve that were among the first to be acquired.

Diameter distribution of old-growth spruce at two sites on the Powley Road, Arietta, 1993

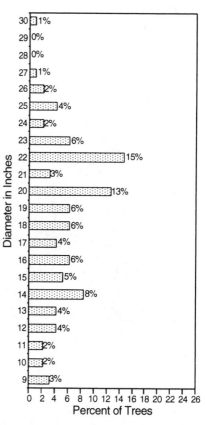

Figure 56, Site #1, spruce flat
95-tree sample

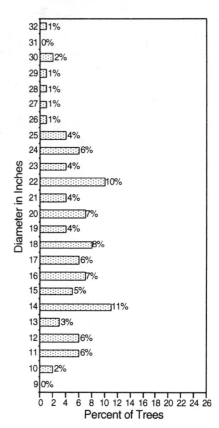

Figure 57, Site # 2, mixed forest
125-tree sample
Measured by the author

189

All this is the reasoning behind my present belief that a great deal of the land acquired by the State for taxes before the establishment of the Forest Preserve, lands where ownership was never challenged, is old-growth. In addition to these forests, the virgin tracts acquired by purchase in the next decade or so, were rarely subjected to trespass. Observations focusing on the condition of the spruce stands they contain or the absolute absence of spruce, which indicates rich hardwood sites, confirm the lack of intrusion by man predicted by the historical record. Finding so much information to corroborate my hypothesis concerning the amount of great forest has been the penultimate step in my proof. Others will have to examine and possibly core many more samples in diverse stands to complete the final step in the proof--the determination of the average age of species present--but for me that is not necessary. I feel confident now that the physical record will confirm the existence of at least a half million acres of old-growth forest in the Adirondacks. New York's great wealth of forest is found nowhere else in the eastern United States and New Yorkers can be proud that at least part of the Great Forest of Northern New York can still be found in the Adirondacks.

*The author with a noble spruce,
near Powley Road, Arietta.*

# Appendix

## Major Lumber and

# Major Lumber and Pulp and Paper Companies

The 383, 233, 257, and 337 Adirondack saw mills reported in the United States Census of Manufactures for 1850, 1860, 1870, and 1880 respectively is misleading. Almost all were small, sawing anywhere from a few hundred to a few thousand logs a year. A majority of saw mills could be classified as colonial operations, those that served the local communities. It has been demonstrated that the number of colonial saw mills shrank during this period. The rise in 1880 reflects the population expansions in southern St. Lawrence and Franklin counties, settlements north and east of the Black River in Lewis County. Elsewhere the trend to consolidation is more constant.

A few of the saw mills grew in milling capacity and in the amount of timberlands they controlled. They evolved into the large lumber companies and in each area, a few large companies dominated. Those charted below sawed a minimum of 10,000 logs in the Census years; those in the Glens Falls area in 1880 sawed over 100,000 logs a year.

**Number of larger mills or lumber companies**

|          | 1850 | 1860 | 1870 | 1880 |
|----------|------|------|------|------|
| Clinton  | 1    | 1    | x    | 1    |
| Essex    |      | 4    | 2    | 1    |
| Franklin |      | 1    | 1    | 2    |
| Fulton   |      | 1    | 2    | 1    |
| Hamilton |      |      |      | 1    |
| Herkimer |      |      | 1    | 2    |
| Lewis    |      |      | 4    | 6    |
| Oneida   |      |      | 2    | 2    |
| St. Law. |      |      |      | 4    |
| Saratoga |      | 1    | 4    | 4    |
| Warren   | 5    | 5    | 3    | 4    |
| Wash.    | 3    | 5    | 4    | 4    |

Total number of large mills as a percent of all mills
| 3.7% | 6.4% | 8.2% | 9.5% |
|------|------|------|------|

x indicates the missing Clinton County Census.

The towns chosen represent those in or touching the present Blue Line except that Malone is included in Franklin County to trace development on the Raquette River and towns around and south of Glens Falls are included to show the mills where the majority of Hudson River lumber was sawn.

Even the figures for the increasing percentages of large mills needs interpretation. The mills along the Hudson River near Glens Falls or along the Black River were growing in capacity that far exceeded that of all other mills. Many of this handful of lumber companies that grew in these two areas continued to grow. Their owners pooled mill sites and timberlands to fund expansions into paper mills after 1880.

Little additional information is available about the early large lumber mills discussed in the chapter on logging from 1850 to 1890, unless these mills converted to pulp and paper. Those that converted became the giants of the industry after 1890. The exception are the large lumber companies that sprang up in the Tupper Lake area and along the Raquette River, but this development did not get underway until 1890.

The following discussion deals with the larger companies where enough information exists to provide the company profiles.

In the 1880s and 1890s at the same time that wood fiber became dominant in the production of paper, so many pulp and paper companies were built nationwide that there was a glut of paper and significant problems in its pricing. In the Adirondacks as elsewhere, this led to a period of consolidation in the industry, the full effects of which were not felt until the turn of the century. From this consolidation came many of the industry's giants, whose birthplace can be traced to the Adirondack region.

## The Hudson Watershed

The two largest paper companies still active in the Adirondacks were formed as partnerships of men with roots in Glens Falls. Glens Falls' particularly advantageous location on the Hudson River at the edges of the great wilderness to the north guaranteed that city's dominance up to the present day.

At first forests around Glens Falls and Hudson Falls sufficed to feed the emerging mills, but gradually timber was taken from the north as far as Lake George. We know the timing of the first log shipments on the Schroon River. Speculate that logging moved first to branches of the Sacandaga River, then to the upper reaches of the Hudson River.

The New York portion of International Paper Co. was absorbed into this large multinational giant and much of its early history is lost. Finch, Pruyn and Co., on the other hand, remains a privately held for much of its existence a deep sense of its historical role in the Adirondacks. Its history has been far more easily recovered than that of International Paper Co.

## International Paper Company

Jones Ordway, owner of Totten and Crossfield Township 34, lumbered the area around the Rock River as early as 1854. His activities there have been described by Harold Hochschild in the book *Township 34*. He had as partner James Morgan, a Glens Falls lumberman. In 1865 the two men joined with A. M. Adsit and William McEchron to form the firm of Morgan, Adsit and Co.[1] Their holdings included Cheney Mills at Glens Falls. By purchasing or building they eventually had five mills, with a total capacity of forty million board feet a year, located on the south side of the Hudson River in the Glens Falls area.[2]

In 1871, Adsit's interest was sold to J. Underwood for $75,000 and the firm was renamed James Morgan and Co. After Morgan's death in 1873, his interest was bought by an Albany company and Morgan's son-in-law and the firm's name was changed again, this time to Morgan Lumber Co. Jones Ordway was its president. In 1874, Morgan Lumber Co. had five water-powered mills with seventeen gang saws and fifteen canal boats to ship its products. The mills employed 200 men and had a capacity to saw thirty million board feet of lumber cut from 150,000 standard logs.

The company expanded its partnerships and included the two owners of the Albany lumber yard, W. H. Weaver & Co.,[3] which sold much of the company's production. (W. H. Weaver and Co. had been formed in 1866 by William McEchron, Jones Ordway, and James Morgan of Glens Falls and A. M. Adsit and W. H. Weaver. Later James Underwood and Charles E. Van Zandt were added to the firm.) On Ordway's death in 1890, his interests in Morgan Lumber Co. were sold to the remaining partners, W. E. Spier and William McEchron, who later used their holdings to help form International Paper Co.

At the time of incorporation in 1898, International Paper Co. had over 60,000 acres in the Hudson River areas, including tracts adjacent to the Rock River; these lands belonged to its various incorporators or were purchased by the corporation.

The first ground wood paper mill was built in 1869 by the Hudson River Pulp and Paper Co. at Luzerne. It was quickly followed by a second mill at Palmer (Corinth) and this mill was among those added to IP in 1898, making it the oldest mill in the group that became International Paper Co.

The Glens Falls Paper Co., which also became part of International Paper Co. in 1898, had a contract for 15,000 cords of pulp to be shipped from Delaware and Hudson Co. lands in 1896.

Also incorporated into the company in 1898 was former New York Governor Roswell P. Flower's Piercefield Paper Co. mill, which had been built in 1892. The mill was situated on a virgin tract on the Raquette River[4] and near the New York Central Railroad, so softwoods could be floated to the mill and paper products shipped out by rail. The mill was designed to produce mostly wrapping and bag paper, 16,000 tons of it from a mixture of groundwood and sulfite pulp. To produce this amount the mill consumed over 28,000 cords of pulp and employed 240 men annually. The mill operated until 1933 when the supply of pulp wood in the area was exhausted. The mill's machinery was moved to other plants and the mill and all the buildings in Piercefield except for two churches were sold in 1946.

International Paper Co. swept into the Black River Valley in 1899, buying the Remington Mill and considering purchase of the Taggarts Paper Co. mill. By that year, International Paper Co. had mills at eight locations in the north country, with three mills in the Watertown area alone. The two largest mills were at Cadyville and Watertown. The Cadyville mill used pulp floated down the Saranac River and was second in size only to J. and J. Rogers' paper mill. Other mills were located at Fort Edward and Lyons Falls.

The Ticonderoga mill was not acquired until 1925. That mill began as a small groundwood mill in 1878, which became the Ticonderoga Pulp and Paper Co. in 1881. That company added a second paper mill at the base of the falls in Ticonderoga in 1884, which was rebuilt and expanded in 1891. These mills continued to operate for forty years, but were deemed obsolete after World War II. Because of the shortage of softwoods, International Paper Co. changed its paper process to making kraft paper and built a totally new plant, which opened in 1971.[5]

In 1899, the company's total consumption of wood was 103,000 cords of pulp per year, or almost 30% of the entire north country pulp consumption.

Shortly after it was incorporated, International Paper Co. also had mills in Massachusetts, Vermont, and New Hampshire, which added to the New York mills gave the company a total of twenty with a daily capacity of a thousand tons of newsprint or three-fourths of all newsprint produced in America.[6] Initially, over 90 percent of International Paper Co.'s production was newsprint. Needless to say International Paper Co.'s ability to set prices did not please newspaper publishers, whose papers labeled the formation of the new corporation a conspiracy.

The corporations first decade was a very difficult time. As an International Paper Co. publication noted, "the course of the company had not been a bed of roses. It was not a simple task to harmonize all of the different interests and perfect an efficient organization. ... The principal consumers of newsprint were united under an uncompromising and relentless leadership to force prices to a ruinous level."[7] Earnings dwindled until World War I.

By expansion and Canadian leases, International Paper Co.'s New York holdings in 1920 constituted only 10% of the company's total woodlands. Like other paper companies, International Paper Co. was forced to buy pulp from Canada after 1920 to keep its New York mills in operation. The company bought 125,000 cords of timber from the 30,000-acre Meacham and Everton Tracts, timber that was harvested between 1926 and 1931. The company cut pulp in the Perkins Clearing Tract in the war years (after 1942) and floated this wood down the Jessup River where it was boomed north on Indian Lake to a jackworks to be loaded on trucks.

During this period, International Paper Co. built big new, faster, and more efficient mills in Canada. Through sales and consolidation, International Paper Co. has reduced the number of its paper mills in the north country to two, Ticonderoga and Corinth. The Adirondack region supplies 60 percent of pulp wood consumed at the two mills. International Paper Co. began harvesting hardwoods for pulp in the 1960s and today the mills use a mix of hardwoods that varies from 60 to 75 percent.

An interesting sidebar to International Paper Co.'s wood's operations is the fact that the company used horses for logging as late as the 1960s.

When International Paper Co. swapped land with the State to consolidate its holdings in the Perkins Clearing area, the company received some virgin lots. They yielded a few very large trees; three pine logs filled one truck. The amount harvested averaged twenty cords per acre, the same as the yield on the company's managed tracts, but with a high percentage of valuable sawlogs. It is ironic that today the company sends its best spruce sawlogs to Canada to be sawn.

The company's forest lands are selectively cut and regenerate naturally; the company feels that economics of reforestation are marginal.

The two remaining Adirondack mills today represent only a small fraction of the corporation's production even though they consume annually 350,000 cords of groundwood (unprocessed pulpwood) and chips from sawmill waste. Both mills use older technologies, but remain competitive because of the high cost of building new mills.

## Finch, Pruyn and Company

The falls that have given Glens Falls its name were originally known as Wings Falls for Abraham Wing, a pre-revolutionary settler. After the revolution he built a sawmill at the falls. His grandson, Abraham Wing III, "initiated a custom of sluices, river drives and booms for floating logs into the Hudson River and thence to sawmills on or near the Champlain Feeder Canal,"[8] which was completed in 1832. Glens Falls grew as a lumber capital so that, in 1850, the Hudson River Boom Association replaced Wing's smaller river booms with the Big Boom at the big bend in the Hudson River just west of the city.

A portion of the Wing sawmill was acquired by J. W. Finch and his father in 1866. In 1850, they had purchased Township 15 of Totten and Crossfield Patent to secure timber on the Indian River tributary of the Hudson River.

In 1865, the partnership of Jeremiah W. Finch, Daniel J. Finch, and Samuel Pruyn purchased the Glens Falls Co., manufacturers of lumber, lime, and black marble. This company took over the balance of the Wing sawmill in 1876 consolidating ownership of all the mills on the north side of the river. J. W. Finch (1827-1904) had been a logger, cutting timber in the Town of Johnsburgh, and he managed the company's lumbering operations. Samuel Pruyn (1820-1908) ran the company's mills and other business, which at one time included 30 boats, on which the company's products, including lime, were shipped to New York and returned with coal, grain, and other materials.[9]

The company's records constitute a history of logging practices in the Adirondacks. Its lands and early logging operations were all located on the Hudson River and its tributaries, the Sacandaga, Boreas, Schroon, Cedar, and Indian rivers. The company was aided in its land acquisition by George N. Ostrander, who served as counsel to the company and served the company well in relation to its timberlands. (Ostrander's land speculation is discussed in Chapter V.)

Up until 1890, only merchantable sawlogs (pine and spruce) were harvested and only those of twelve or fourteen inches or more on the stump were taken. After 1890, spruce logs for pulp with diameters down to seven or eight inches were taken. The company started logging the Boreas Ponds area in 1891. (That area was logged again, heavily, in the 1930s and 1940s, and logged a third time, lightly, in the 1970s and 1980s.)

Finch, Pruyn and Co. pioneered in high country logging and experimented with the use of dry slides to deliver pulp logs to streams and rivers.

After 1915, the company began cutting pulp logs of four-foot length along with the 13' 4" saw logs and floated the last of the longer logs in 1924. In 1929, the last year of the Hudson River Boom Association, only Finch, Pruyn and Union Bag and Paper companies were driving logs on the river. That year was the last long log drive and the next year, Finch, Pruyn and Co. was the only company left driving the Hudson River. From 1929 to 1950, 667,000 cords of four-foot spruce and balsam pulpwood were sent down the Hudson River to the mill at Glens Falls.

Finch, Pruyn and Co. was incorporated in 1904. The corporation constructed a paper mill with two paper machines in 1905, added a third paper machine in 1910, and a steam sawmill in 1913.

One of the company's early logging operations was in the Stillwater area (Marcy Swamp) south of Panther Gorge; the company logged the region for under contract to the Adirondack Mountain Reserve. The company purchased the Blue Mountain Tract (in Totten and Crossfield Township 19) in 1903. Around 1905, the company was logging in the Cold River area. In 1910, the company owned 160,000 acres in the Adirondacks, all but 20,000 acres[10] of which had been cut over, albeit in most instances very lightly.

Also in 1910, the company hired a professional forester, Howard L. Churchill. Churchill surveyed all the company's lands and estimated their growth potential, concluding that there was "too small an annual increase to supply"[11] the company's mills. (A letter marked 'confidential,' written by a company vice-president in 1941, stated that Churchill's figures indicating stands of one and a half million cords of softwoods and an annual growth rate of 2.38% were probably low.)[12]

As part of the planned expansion, the company, in 1913, acquired the spruce stumpage on lands owned by the MacIntyre Iron Co. for $365,000 and the right-of-way for a railroad. It was estimated that the price equalled $2.00 a cord for the stumpage. The land was all in Essex County and involved some of the state's highest mountains, specifically Totten and Crossfield Townships 27, 45, 46, 47, the Gore East of Township 47, and the Gore around Lake Colden. The entire 70,000-acre area, with the exception of 10,000 of the highest acres, had been lumbered prior to 1913, but was ready to be logged again.[13] The MacIntyre company sold the Gore East of Township 47 and the Gore around Lake Colden in 1919 to the State before Finch, Pruyn and Co. had finished the job; a law suit followed with Finch, Pruyn and Co. claiming that it had been deprived of 117,000 cords of wood. The company won $750,000 from New York State and significant parts of the High Peaks remained uncut as a result.

In 1915, the company's saw mill handled 170,000 logs, of which 130,000 were spruce.

Logs sawn in 1917 by Finch, Pruyn and Co.

|            | board feet |
|------------|------------|
| Spruce     | 6,943,782  |
| Hemlock    | 2,898,223  |
| White pine | 1,081,121  |
| Cedar      | 151,041    |
|            |            |
| Total      | 11,074,227 |

To compensate for the shortfall in pulpwood, the company began to import pulp logs from its lands in Quebec (a 40,000-acre tract near the village of Henry River south of the St. Lawrence River).

The company gradually increased its land holdings to 230,700 acres by 1924. Of this the company had owned 20,000 acres since 1850. The company apparently added about 80,000 acres in the 1880s and the rest after 1910.[14] This land now included parts of Townships 7, 16, 18, 19, 20, 27, 33, 44, 45, 46, and 47, Totten and Crossfield.

In 1923, the company again assessed the potential of its lands under a study devised by A. B. Recknagel, a Cornell forestry professor. At that time, the company needed a sustained yield of 20,000 to 25,000 cords of wood to supply its paper mills. This study pointed out the extent to which "spruce and fir were overtopped by poor hardwoods that had no commercial value, could not be given away, could not even be cut down without heavy expense and also without a lot of damage to the softwoods."[15]

In 1927, the company reported to the Empire State Forest Products Association (ESFPA) that it held 225,000 acres, of which 15 percent was virgin territory. The company logged its tract in the Santanoni Mountains in 1929 and again in the 1960s through the 1980s, but never logged that range's steep northern slopes. The upper slopes of the Santanoni tract never produced spruce sawlogs, only pulp, although the adjacent lowlands were cut for spruce sawlogs sometime in the 1880s.[16]

The company began an extensive program of girdling hardwoods to "release" the growth of softwoods.[17] This step was considered necessary to fulfill the company's desire to deal with its lands on a "sustained yield basis." Hardwoods were girdled on approximately 12,000 acres.

In 1938, the company had 500 men working in the woods and hundreds of horses. Logging camps were located on the Cedar River and in the Newcomb area near the Boreas and Santanoni. In 1939, to satisfy its needs for pulp, the company was harvesting about 40,000 cords annually, of which 80% was spruce, the rest balsam. Logs were still floated to the Glens Falls mill, principally down the Boreas and Cedar rivers to the Hudson River, routes that were followed until 1950. The hundred-mile log drive could be accomplished in sixty days, thanks to dams on the upper Boreas (Goodnow River, Fishing Brook, Beaver Brook, O'Neil Flow, 34th Dam, Blackwells, Six Mile, County Line, Elk Lake, and the Branch.

In the 1940s, the company had twelve logging camps that produced 41,000 cords a year. The last logging camp was phased out in 1957, but jobbers continued to use horses to harvest a portion of the company's timber into the 1970s.

In the late 1940s and 1950s, there was a market for hardwoods. The harvest from Township 8 was sold to Oval Wood Dish Co. at Tupper Lake and Northern Lumber Co. at Riparius.

The 1000-acre tract around Clear Pond was logged just before it was sold in the 1950s and the rest of what is now Elk Lake Preserve was logged in the 1960s and sold before 1963.

In the 1970s the company changed its pulp mix to include hemlock, which it now imports from surrounding northeast states. Finch, Pruyn and Co.'s paper machines now consume between 250,000 and 300,000 cords of pulp a year.

Over the years Finch, Pruyn and Co. has sold much land to the state and also donated 85,000 acres to the state. The gift lands include Cheney Cobble and the North River Mountains in Totten and Crossfield Townships 45 and 46.

# Companies in the Western Adirondacks

## Gould Paper Company

In the realm of logging and paper making in the western Adirondacks, Gordias H. P. Gould (1848-1919) was the most colorful and successful individual. His story typifies the region; he did not appear on the scene until 1874, a date that marks the beginning of large-scale logging operations in the western Adirondacks. His company survives as a local paper mill, Lyons Falls Pulp and Paper Co., but during his long career, Gould's reach was extended internationally and to one of the largest companies to do business in the Adirondacks, the St. Regis Paper Co.

Gould's early partnership with the three daughters of Lyman R. Lyon (Mary L. Fisher, Julia L. deCamp, and Florence L. Merriam), brought his company valuable timberlands, most of which were accessible to the Moose River. Gould's drives on the Moose River[18] rivaled the lore and excitement of drives on the Hudson River, but never their size (see chart). In the early days, the company was supplied by drives down the North and Middle branches of the Moose and their northern tributaries; Gould's drives on the South Branch of the Moose through McKeever began later and continued until 1948.

Starting with a sawmill at Gouldtown near Lyons Falls at the junction of the Moose and the Black rivers, Gould enlarged that first mill and in 1880 added a pulp mill, capable of producing 780 tons a year. To this complex at Gouldtown, he added other sites along the Moose and Black rivers. He purchased small mills at Fowlerville, Shuetown, and Port Leyden and International Paper Co.'s mill at Kosterville. This last purchase, in 1892, marked the beginning of Gould Paper Co.

In 1895, the company erected a huge new paper mill at Lyons Falls and began construction of a new sulfite mill three years later. A third paper machine was added in 1907 and it was the first in the United States to use electricity.[19]

Gould continued to saw spruce lumber, averaging 8 to 10 million board feet a year throughout the 1890s.[20]

The company also acquired 55,600 acres in the Tug Hill area.

## Gould Paper Company Land Purchases

| Year purchased | Source | Location | Acres | Cost | Cost per acre |
|---|---|---|---|---|---|
| 1896 | G. H. P. Gould | Twp 1, Brown's Tr. | 10,000 | $35,000. | $3.50 |
| 1899 | Adk. Timber & Mineral | Twp 3, Moose River Tr. | 13,064 | | |
| | | Twp 4, Moose River Tr. | 14,120 | | |
| | | Twp 5, Moose River Tr. | 22,384 | | |
| | | Twp 4, T & C | 1,280 | $343,278. | $6.75 |
| 1907 | International Paper Co. | Twp 4, T & C | 16,543 | Stock | $12.90 |

Figure 59          Source: Gould Paper Co. papers at Adirondack Museum

At the same time, he began acquiring timberlands, starting in 1896 with the southern part of Township 1, Brown's Tract, originally part of the Lyons' tannery holdings. This land had been cut for tanbark and was logged by Gould, but a company timber cruise in 1947 reported that there were still uncut portions of the tract, that a disastrous 25,000-acre fire circa 1917 had stopped at the north boundary of the tract, and that the tract remained the "sole appreciable area of large, old growth timber within a short radius of Lyons Falls" with much spruce (60,000 cords) and hemlock and considerable hardwoods. In 1896, Gould purchased Townships 3, 4, and 5 of the Moose River Tract from Adirondack Timber and Mineral Co. These lands in Hamilton and Herkimer counties had been logged in a few places near the South Branch of the Moose, but were basically untouched. As late as 1940, the company was said to be cutting virgin forests near the upper Indian River (a tributary of the South Branch of the Moose) and several timber cruise reports made after the 1950 blowdown detail tracts that still had not been harvested.

Gould acquired large Tug Hill tracts in 1902 and the Glenfield and Western Railroad to bring their logs to his mill. He purchased Totten and Crossfield Township 4 from International Paper Co. in 1907 and that brought his Moose River holdings to 77,000 acres.[21]

The paper company also bought logs from the Adirondack League Club whose property was downstream from Gould's holdings on the South Branch of the Moose. Gould Paper Co. had to pay the League Club for the right to drive logs through the League Club's lands, an expense that amounted to about $5,000 a year.

When Gould acquired the four townships in the Moose River Plains, Gould built a number of logging dams and a series of logging camps. The 52,000-acre tract in the Moose River Plains was sold to the State in 1964 for $15.50 an acre. The company logged the tract continuously until it was sold and the timber reservation expired.

In 1923, Gould acquired part of Township 1, Moose River Tract from Iroquois Pulp and Paper Co. as well as that company's rights to drive logs on the South Branch of the Moose through that part of the township.

Until the late 1930, Gould Paper Co. espoused the principal of making modest cuts to preserve future production on his 100,000 acres and no softwoods smaller than 10 inches in diameter were taken. In the later 1930s, the company began taking smaller diameter spruce logs for pulp.

In 1909 he extended his interests to Canada and mills at the confluence of the Cartier and St. Lawrence rivers. He built a giant pulp mill at McKeever, which was later sold to Rice Veneer.

The company was the first to use mechanized vehicles for logging. In 1918, Gould Paper Co. acquired three of the newly invented Linn Tractors, gasoline-powered vehicles "propelled by tracks in the rear and guided on the road by steering runners in front." The purchase was made because Gould's supervisor of logging operations, John B. Todd, was convinced, and rightly so, that one tractor would haul as much pulp as twenty teams.[22]

The tractors were needed to haul pulp logs stored at North Lake (whose outlet flows into the Black River) north over the shoulder of Ice Cave Mountain and down to the South Branch of the Moose, in order to consolidate the company's river drives. The acquisition of tractors and the later introduction of trucks to haul logs to mills mark a significant change in what happened to the forests as a result of logging. Hard-packed, gravel roads were constructed. Even without further care, the roads in the Moose River Plains on the Gould Paper Co. tracts will remain for many years to come.

The 1950s blowdown was especially severe on Gould Paper Co.'s lands in the Moose River Plains. Co. records[23] show extensive loss, up to fifty percent of softwoods, as a result of the blowdown and that 18,000 cords of downed spruce was harvested.

Gould Paper Co. sold hardwoods (birch and cherry) to Rice Veneer between 1949 and 1957, although assessments made in 1954 indicate that the hardwood stands on about 90 percent of the Moose River Plains had never been cut.

The harvest that occurred in the Moose River Plains during the next decade was as complete as anywhere because not only spruce but hardwoods were logged for pulp. Although contracts called for cutting softwoods down to 10 inches and hardwoods to 12 inches, the timber reservation permitted cuts down to 8 inches and smaller cuts may have been made. Large areas are now filled with dense thickets of trees no bigger around than an arm--they look like jungle thickets of bamboo.

When cut for hardwoods, such tracts as those on Ice Cave Mountain, where yellow birch to 14 inches was taken, were found to be incapable of reproducing birch unless beech and maple were removed.[24]

The company was sold to Continental Can Co. in 1951, which in turn sold to Georgia Pacific in 1963. Today the company is again privately held and continues today as Lyons Falls Pulp and Paper Co.

## Forestport Lumber Company

Forestport was ideally located to become a major lumber center: it was close to both the Mohawk Valley and Adirondack timber resources. It is situated at the southernmost point of the Black River, the bend where the river changes flow from southwest to northwest. In 1868 there were ten water-powered and two steam-powered mills sawing over 8 million board feet.[25] Two of the mills were served by wooden-railed tram lines. Several large lumber companies were built in the vicinity, among them Denton and Waterbury, Syphert and Harris, and Forestport Lumber Co.

Forestport Lumber Co. logged Adirondack League Club lands in Moose River Township 6 in the 1890s. At that time, Albany lumberman Henry C. Patton was associated with the company. The interlocking of company ownership and boards is shown in the figure 25.

## Beaver River Lumber Company

Theodore B. Basselin, who became a member of the Forest Commission in 1885, started as a lumberman before 1880. His first mill, a gang mill, was located at Beaver Falls on the Beaver River. That mill sawed hemlock that Basselin bought from the Rice Tannery, which was upriver at Croghan.

Hemlock was very cheap as it would normally have been wasted after it had been stripped for bark. Two years later, in 1882 he bought an existing mill, just downstream from the first mill.[26]

With Henry C. Patton, Basselin formed the Beaver River Lumber Co.[27] He expanded into building boats for the Black River Canal and shipped from six million board feet of lumber in the 1880s to around ten million in 1900.

Fires plagued his mills and he rebuilt all but the last with the most modern equipment possible, shifting early to steam to compensate for the idle periods caused by low summer water on the Beaver River. When his mill burned in 1909, he built a modern pulp mill, which was sold to J. P. Lewis Co. before Basselin's death in 1914.[28]

Basselin owned between 17,000 and 25,000 acres of timberland in Townships 3, 4, 5, and 42 of John Brown's Tract.[29] His mills had contracts on 65 to 70,000 additional acres with Adirondack Land and Mineral Co.

Basselin served as one of the first Forest Commissioners, a role in which his activities were later questioned (see the Chapter VI).

## J. P. Lewis and Company

In 1881, James P. Lewis in partnership with his two brothers-in-law built a dam on the Beaver River at Beaver Falls and a mill to produce groundwood pulp. The operation was not a financial success and by 1883 Lewis was sole owner. He installed a new pulp mill with new equipment. In 1887 it was the second in the country to use the new grinding equipment (after Ticonderoga). In 1889, with a fourth brother-in-law, John Slocum, he built a paper mill, the first one erected in Beaver Falls. It was capable of producing 1,888 annually tons of pulp board and waterproof building paper.

This mill was expanded in 1892 by the addition of a 64"-machine to produce an additional 2,000 tons of carpet paper annually. In 1903, the mill began producing Beaver Board (a pulp board used in construction). All of J. P. Lewis Co.'s operations focused not on newsprint and paper, but on materials made from pulp that figured in building and construction.

Until 1890, the company's wood needs were met by local forests. He expanded the company's woods operations and from 1904 to 1923 used logs from the Mary Lyon Fisher Tract. The company shared a sorting boom on the Beaver River with St. Regis Lumber Co.

A new paper machine was added in 1917. In 1931, J. P. Lewis acquired the Lewis, Slocum, and LeFevre Co. which had produced beaver board, paper plates, and milk bottle caps. This company merged with the Latex Fiber Industries subsidiary of Uniroyal in 1973 and was acquired by Boise Cascade in 1977.

The company, with St. Regis Paper Co., bought Moose River Tract Township 6 from the Adirondack League Club in 1941, later selling it and part of Township 7 to Lyons Falls Pulp and Paper Co.

## Moose River Lumber Company, McKeever and Rice Veneer

The site known as McKeever on the Moose River was dammed to harness water power for a series of mills, which occupied the site until 1947 when the dam was washed out. The first sawmill was built by Lemon Thomson in 1891 and was known as Moose River Lumber Co. That mill burned and was rebuilt in 1895.

Also at the site was a pulp mill with four grinders that sent carloads of pulp to Thomson, NY.

During the teens, a new Moose River Lumber Co., of which former Governor Dix was part owner, milled selected birch and hard maple from McKeever along with railroad ties made from the hearts of the hardwood logs. The company apparently enlarged the mill built by Thomson. It maintained six camps of forty men each on tracts to the east of McKeever and used its standard gauge railroad to haul logs to the mill.

The untouched hardwoods yielded enormous specimens so that the company could produce 26" birch lumber, "clean as a hound's tooth."[30] The company and its woodlands were taken over by Iroquois Pulp and Paper, which in turn sold Township 1 of Moose River Tract, exclusive of the Wager Tract, to the State in 1918.

The pulp mill was expanded by Gould Paper Co., and in 1949, Rice Veneer bought Gould Paper Co.'s mill and began producing veneer from 100,000 board feet of lumber a week. Hardwood was cut on Gould Paper Co.'s Moose River Tract near Indian and Squaw lakes (4 million board feet) and on International Paper Co.'s Speculator tract, which supplied 3.5 million beet of hardwood.

*Interior of pulp mill at McKeever, H. M. Beach*

*Courtesy Adirondack Museum*

199

## Moose River Lumber Corporation was

formed in 1941 as a partnership between J. P. Lewis Co. and St. Regis Paper Co. in order to buy Township 6 and part of 7 Moose River Tract from the Adirondack League Club.[31] Heavy cutting by St. Regis and others depleted the area's wood supply and the resulting timber shortage was thought to have a profound effect on the region's paper industry.

## Patton and Co., Albany lumber merchants, had

put together a group of lumber companies that included E. C. Hargreave & Co. of Hinckley, the Forestport Lumber Co., and the Trenton Falls Lumber Co., and Beaver River Lumber Co. The January 1896 failure of Patton and Co. affected primarily the Hinckley firm.[32]

## Hinckley Fibre Co. grew out of a mill built

partly in Oneida County, partly in Herkimer County, on the West Canada Creek, in the 1850s by Gardner Hinckley, 2d and Theodore P. Ballou. This company had a "disastrous failure"[33], undoubtedly the one referred to above, in which the "creditors lost substantially." The company reorganization to produce pulp was aided by the arrival in 1890 of a rail line. Throughout the 1890s, Hinckley Fibre Co. produced 5 percent of all Adirondack pulp. It remained a producer of pulp into the 1920s. The Hinckley Division of the New York Central Railroad was virtually abandoned by 1930.

## Everton Lumber Company was

incorporated in 1888. Trustees were Henry Patton of Albany, George E. Dodge, David H. Patton. Associated with it were Thomas H. McGraw and Theodore B. Basselin of Croghan.

## Beaver River Lumber Company was

incorporated in 1890 with trustees Henry Patton, Thomas H. McGraw of Poughkeepsie, and Theodore B. Basselin of Croghan.

## Trenton Falls Lumber Company was

incorporated in 1890 with Thomas H. McGraw of Poughkeepsie, Henry Patton of Albany, David Patton of Albany, and Amos C. Hall of Albany, trustees.

# Logging and Lumbering in the Northern and Northwestern Adirondacks

Logging and lumbering in the northern regions differed from the rest of the Adirondacks in three ways: large scale activities started later than in other regions; much of the transportation of logs depended on railroads; harvest of hardwoods for the lumber industry on a significant scale began in this region.

Five communities grew up to support the industry: St. Regis, Santa Clara, Piercefield, Tupper Lake, and Cranberry Lake. Of these, Tupper was the largest.

## Tupper Lake Mills

Difficulties of floating logs down the Raquette River slowed the growth of the region's logging between the time the first dam was built in 1860 on the Raquette northwest of the future town and the arrival of Hurd's Northern Adirondack Railroad in 1890. Tupper Lake's growth accelerated quickly with the coming of the Adirondack and St. Lawrence Railroad in 1892 and the construction of a number of large mills. By 1907, Tupper Lake surpassed all other Adirondack towns (hence the entire state) in producing lumber (over 40 million board feet). That year Glens Falls fell to fourth place in lumber production with a little over a third as much. That year, two companies, A. Sherman Co. and Norwood Manufacturing, led the state in the number of board feet sawn, while Rich Lumber Co. at Wanakena was a close third.

## A. Sherman Lumber Company and Oval Wood Dish Company

The builders of the first sawmill on Raquette Pond sold the mill in 1888, shortly after it had been built, to A. Sherman Lumber Co. of Potsdam. A. Sherman Lumber Co. was founded in 1867 by George W. Sisson, a legendary lumberman from Potsdam. The company's holdings, all adjacent to the Raquette River, encompassed 90,000 acres. Sisson was also the first president of Raquette River Paper Co., a paper mill that was still active in the Potsdam area in the late 1930s as Sisson and White Co. (Stanley A. Sisson and Donald P. White)

The Sherman Lumber Co.'s Tupper mill burned and was rebuilt and operated by the firm until it was sold to Oval Wood Dish Co. in 1915. Oval Wood Dish became the largest lumbering firm ever to operate in Tupper Lake. This financially successful company moved to Tupper Lake when its Michigan forests were depleted. The company quickly enlarged the mill, brought in its equipment from the Midwest, and in 1918 began to produce veneers, fine flooring, and its signature oval wood dishes from the region's birch, beech, and maple.

To supply its mill, the company bought land and stumpage on tracts totally nearly 80,000 acres, much of it in Macomb Township 19 from Santa Clara Lumber Co., A. Sherman and Co. and Raquette River Paper Co. Much of the land near Kildare was accessible to the railroad and had been logged for softwoods in the past twenty years. Also included were the Turner and Iron Ore Mountain tracts.

The company's voracious appetite for hardwoods impelled logging operations north over nearly twenty miles of railroad corridor in seven years, with seven logging camps of forty to fifty men each active for those years. Beginning in 1920, tractors, trucks and trailers were used to bring logs from the company's tracts near Mount Morris.

The company's surveys of the forests, however, proved to be inadequate, for it was discovered that much of the hardwoods were in poor condition because of wood rot. "The forest management of the forest was conspicuous by its absence. Anything profitable was removed, felled haphazardly, leaving stumps averaging twenty-nine inches in height."[34]

The company experienced problems beginning in 1924, part of it traceable to competition from paper plates. However, the worst blow was the exhaustion of its wood supply after only seven years. Initial timber estimates had indicated there was twice as much lumber as the company was able to harvest. In quick succession the company bought stumpage on and exhausted the supply of hardwoods on the Rockefeller Tract (1926) and the Everton Tract (1933). Maple continued to come from the Santa Clara area, and later from the Whitney Tract. In 1941, Oval Wood Dish Co. acquired all the standing hardwoods on Santanoni Preserve for a quarter of a million dollars.[35] Prof. A. B. Recknagel estimated that the tract contained 35 million board feet of hardwoods.

Oval Wood Dish's need for hardwoods was so great that at the same time it negotiated for the stumpage at Santanoni, the company was using hardwoods from International Paper Co. land a few miles south of Indian Lake and from their holdings north of Speculator.

The company's business during World War II was so successful that it added new plants in Potsdam (1946) and Quebec (1948). In 1957, Oval Wood Dish Co., expecting such new products as bowling pins to sustain its growth, completely modernized the saw mill at Tupper Lake. The exhaustion of the timber supply and changing times caught up with the company in 1961, when it closed its Potsdam and Quebec plants and sold 20,000 acres of Adirondack timberland in 1964.

Adirondack Plywood Corporation was formed to buy the Oval Wood Dish plant in 1964, using Job Development money from New York State and other sources. This company was quickly sold to United States Plywood, and that corporation expanded the plant, investing about two million dollars to modernize the operation, which was already hampered by lack of rail service. Fire destroyed the plant in 1967 and although smaller companies later occupied the site, large scale manufacturing from hardwoods essentially ended.

## The Big Mill--The Hurd Mill-- Santa Clara Lumber Company

Santa Clara Lumber Co. had arrived in the Adirondacks twenty-five years before the Tupper region's explosive growth. It started as a partnership whose name ultimately became Dodge, Meigs & Co. for the two families involved. The partnership goes back to 1869 and had holdings in Georgia and Pennsylvania. George E. Dodge and Titus Meigs were put in touch with John Hurd in 1888 by the firm of Patton and Co., Albany lumber merchants.

John Hurd is an Adirondack entrepreneurial legend, whom Donaldson described as a "man of plunging, bulldog enterprise." He had organized the St. Regis River Lumber Co. and had built the Northern Adirondack Railroad from its northern connection with the Ogdensburg and Lake Champlain Railroad at Moira to Santa Clara in 1884. He had a large sawmill in St. Regis Falls and a huge tract (75,000 acres) to the south that was virgin forest. He pushed his railway into that tract "by gradually extending it to nowhere in particular and then creating a semblance of somewhere." That nowhere became the hamlet of Santa Clara, complete with mill, a store, where "it is said, he managed to diminish by credit unpaid wages they earned,"[36] and a community building that served as school and church. In 1886 his line reached Brandon, where Patrick Ducey had built a town and one of the region's best equipped sawmills to cut timber from his 28,000-acre tract.

By 1889, Hurd's railroad was completed to Tupper Lake. Hurd and Dodge, Meigs & Co. joined to form the Santa Clara Lumber Co. in 1888, with Dodge, Meigs & Co. holding controlling interest with 2,200 shares to Hurd's 1,800. Titus's son, Ferris J. Meigs, joined Dodge, Meigs & Co. in 1890. He later wrote a history of Santa Clara Lumber Co. that pays tribute to his father's business acumen while denouncing Hurd as being unreliable, constantly overreaching his business enterprise, and without good standing among his bankers and creditors. Meigs says the choice of company name was Hurd's, for his wife Clara, a saint to him.[37] Almost at once, Titus discovered that the timberlands brought to the company by Hurd, did not contain the amount of lumber, particularly pine, represented as being there.

According to Ferris Meigs "profits were supposedly made by the lumber company in the early years, but the timber was nearly exhausted in four years and the company's capitol stock was reduced from $400,000 to $100,000."[38]

In 1899, Santa Clara Lumber Co. built a mill to ross logs for pulp wood and a mill to produce paper board at Tupper Lake Junction. The latter mill burned two years later and the company closed the rossing mill when it acquired the Hurd's Big Mill.

Dodge, Meigs & Co., controlling Santa Clara Lumber Co., joined in partnership with George C. Sherman and David Anderson of Watertown to form St. Regis Lumber Co. in 1899. The disagreements among the partners led to the break-up of Dodge, Meigs & Co. Ferris reported that Dodge, after long years of close association with Titus, was seduced by a schemer from Watertown. Only George E. Dodge participated in the actual incorporation of St. Regis Lumber Co., while the Meigs, father and son, gained control of Santa Clara Lumber Co.[39]

In 1890, John Hurd started building his "big" sawmill at Tupper Lake to take advantage of his railroad, which was to reach Tupper Lake that year. (See Railroads). It was said to be the biggest sawmill in the state, producing chips for pulp and bark for tanneries as well as sawn lumber. Hurd's insolvency, which followed shortly after the opening of his railroad forced him to sell the big mill, which had a rapid succession of new owners: the Shepard-Morse

Co. of Boston, Export Lumber Co. of New York, several individuals, and finally Norwood Manufacturing Co. Norwood ran it until it was sold to Santa Clara Lumber Co. in 1913.

With other lumbermen, including Thomas McGraw, the firm of Dodge, Meigs & Co. joined in the formation of the Adirondack Timber and Mineral Co., which in 1889 acquired the Adirondack Co. lands held by William West Durant. According to contemporary newspaper accounts, the Durant Trust had purchased 390,000 acres of timberland, which it had been empowered to buy by legislation in 1862. (Durant's activities are discussed in the chapter on the Adirondacks from 1850 to 1890.) Durant's land was said to include 306,000 acres of virgin pine and spruce, plus hemlock and hardwoods.[40]

A tract of 35,000 acres (variously quoted as 39,000 acres) in Macomb Townships 26 and 27 of Franklin County was purchased for $4.50 an acre by the Santa Clara Lumber Co. from Adirondack Timber and Mineral Co. Santa Clara sent logs to its Tupper mill from these holdings for nearly thirty years, from the winter of 1890-1891 until 1919, when the supply of timber on it was exhausted.

The tract stretched from the Raquette River to the headwaters of its tributary, the Cold River; it encompassed the steep slopes and heights of the Seward Range. To log these heights, the company used techniques that were revolutionary in the Adirondacks. The logging operation extended south into the Gore North of Township 47, whose 2,270 acres the state claimed as "unappropriated lands belonging the state." The state sued Santa Clara Lumber Co. for half a million dollars, but the company was able to prove its original purchase gave it title to those lands.

In another dispute, this one with MacIntyre Iron Co., Verplanck Colvin was called in to settle the matter. The company logged lands down to the Preston Ponds and along the road (now trail) from Ampersand to Duck Hole. Ferris claimed, that when this territory was logged, the company selected only the larger trees, but was still able to harvest as much as sixty-six cords per acre.

With supplies of timber depleted, the mill closed in 1926, and it was torn down in 1930.

## International Paper Company

In 1899, International Paper Co. built the Underwood Mill at the foot of Raquette Pond and operated it until 1911, when it was closed. International Paper Co. at Piercefield was one of the largest paper mills owned by that company in the 1920s. It was located 5 miles west of Tupper Lake Junction, in a town that was owned by the company. Its specifics are included in the section on International Paper Co.

## Brooklyn Cooperage and Tupper Lake Chemical Companies

Brooklyn Cooperage Co. built a large barrel stave mill in Tupper Lake in 1900 at the urging of Bernhard Fernow. Details of its woodland's operations are given in the appendix on Fernow and the Cornell Forestry School at Axton.

Fernow envisioned the need for a market for the hardwoods to be cut on the Cornell Forestry School property. Barrel staves and heads were cut at this mill for twenty years.

Waste from the mill prompted the founding of another company to manufacture wood alcohol, charcoal, and acetate. That was taken over by Tupper Lake Chemical in 1915 and operated until the close of World War I. The company was able to stay open during the war because of the great demand for wood acetates used in explosives and a preparation that made cloth-covered airplane wings fireproof.

Brooklyn Cooperage Co. also built a mill to produce barrels and staves in Salisbury, on the southern edge of the Adirondacks, in 1910.

## Draper Corporation

One of Tupper Lake's later arrivals, after World War II, was a bobbin factory, built by Draper Corporation on the site of Brooklyn Cooperage Co.'s plant. To supply the mill, Draper purchased 70,000 acres from Emporium Forestry Co. in 1948.

## Cranberry Lake and Vicinity

It is hard to imagine how undisturbed the entire Cranberry Lake area was in 1889, given that the first dam on the lake had been built between 1865 and 1867. Few logs had been taken from the area, even though they could be floated down the Oswegatchie River. No logs from the drowned lands were saved when the lake was flooded and no logging was done on the shores of the enlarged lake until after 1890.[41] That year, Cranberry Lake village, which grew up at the outlet of the lake, consisted of only a few houses. There was a mill downstream near Benson Mines, but the area between Newton Falls and Cranberry Lake and to the north and south of the lake was untapped wilderness. Even Newton Falls downstream had no settlement before 1894, when its mill and dam were built. Clark and Squires began logging on an 8,000-acre tract north along the Grass River shortly after 1894. They bought the hardwood mill and logged all the lumber between Newton Falls and the mill. Tanbarking was also part of their operations, with barked shipped out at first to Harrisville, then later (until 1916) from Cranberry Lake mills to tanneries outside the Adirondacks.

When Rich Lumber Co. arrived at Cranberry Lake in 1903 from Pennsylvania to build their headquarters at Wanakena, where the Oswegatchie River flows into the lake, the only logging on the lake's shores was in the Sucker Brook vicinity. As one who saw it happen later described, the site of the future village of Wanakena was just a fisherman's camp in the original forest, far from any settlements. "In most of the township of Emilyville, the primitive forest of spruce and hardwoods covered the hills and valleys, many great pines towered above the prevailing forest of spruce."[42]

About the same time, a rossing mill was built near Cranberry Lake Village to debark pulpwood before it was sent down the Oswegatchie River. International Paper Co. logged the eastern shores of the lake for pulp and Emporium Forestry Co. arrived in 1917 to cut the hardwoods left by International Paper Co.

## Rich Lumber Company

Rich Lumber's short stay in the Adirondacks is a paradigm of the intensity of logging made possible by railroads. Chapter VII details the way the company built a railroad to reach the virgin spruce and pine stands of the Plains of the Oswegatchie, west of Cranberry Lake.

Rich Lumber Co. moved to the inlet of Cranberry Lake in 1902 and within a year had built the railroad, both the common carrier connecting Wanakena to the Carthage and Adirondack Railroad at Benson Mines and also the logging line that stretched almost to High Falls on the Oswegatchie River. The company also built the town of Wanakena with neatly laid-out streets, complete with houses with water and electricity, and a large mill. Seven hundred people quickly moved to a site where only fishermen and hunters had camped.

Rich Lumber Co.'s sawmills began operating around 1903; its logging railroad began running about

1905. The intensity of logging was so great that timber on the company's tracts was rapidly exhausted, causing the softwood mill to close in 1910, the last hardwood mill in 1912.

The trees on the 16,000-acre tract were impressive, and so was the lumber cut from them. Almost all the logs were sawn into dimension lumber; little pulp was taken. The majority of softwood logs were cut to a standard 20 feet. Seven years was all it took to strip the tract of its virgin timber. Railroad logging had permitted the clearing of 2,300 acres a year, although the company's departure was hastened by a disastrous fire in 1908 that swept a portion of the company's timberland.

## Emporium Forestry Company

As the leader in the manufacture of hardwood products, Emporium Forestry Co. was the Adirondack's most successful lumbering operation in the first half of this century. Well-run, innovative, careful to use every scrap of wood, the company was the last of the large lumber companies to come to the Adirondacks, joining the group of other mills centered in nearby Tupper Lake. For all its apparent success, the operation still appears to have been barely profitable.

A 1916 Cornell report predicted the company's policy toward the large tract of land the company acquired. "No attempt is made by this company to aid reproduction on a commercial basis and it is expected that the lands will revert to the State in twenty or twenty-five years, when the merchantable timber has been removed."[43]

William L. Sykes, with thirty-five years experience as head of his Emporium Lumber Co. of Pennsylvania, began buying land in St. Lawrence County in 1905, first purchasing an 18,000-acre tract near Clare. In 1910, Emporium purchased a large tract closer to Conifer from the Grasse River Paper Co.[44] That year, a mill under construction at Conifer was purchased and its layout altered to resemble the Pennsylvania mill and to install circular saws. Saws from A. A. Low's operation at Horseshoe were also added to the Conifer mill, which ran for thirty-seven and a half years.

The Emporium Lumber Co. was established in Pennsylvania in 1882, incorporated in 1892, and incorporated in New York State in 1912. Sykes built a small town surrounding the Conifer mill, which grew to include a hotel and become the home for nearly three hundred people. Sykes' three sons assumed management of the company's New York interests. George was general manager, becoming president on the death of his father in 1941; Clyde was treasurer; Roy was sales manager and superintendent of the railroad.

For the first two years of operation, the mill sawed logs from adjacent tracts. In 1913 track and locomotives from Pennsylvania were sent to Conifer. The company began to reach north and west, buying land and laying track, until its operations eventually reached all the way to the Clare Tract, which had been its first Adirondack purchase.[45]

The railroad, incorporated in 1915 as the Grasse River Railroad,[46] was first built a mile to the east to connect Conifer with Childwold Station on the New York Central Railroad, then sixteen miles west to Cranberry Lake. As more of the company's Pennsylvania mills closed for lack of timber, a second mill was built on a small lake near the outlet of Cranberry Lake in 1917. Its capacity was twice that of the Conifer mill.

In 1920, the company purchased a 22,000-acre tract for just under $20 an acre; International Paper Co., the previous owner, had removed all the pulp wood from the tract. Steamers pulled rafts carrying hardwood down Cranberry Lake to the mill, which cut 200 million board feet of hardwood before closing in 1927. In a little over a decade the hardwoods as well as the softwoods were gone.

The company built a logging railroad, the North Tram, forty miles north and west from Cranberry Lake Village to the Clare Tract. With all its spurs, the line reached a total of close to one hundred miles of track.[47] The line brought hardwoods to the Cranberry mill and pulp to be dumped into the Oswegatchie River, where it floated downstream to Newton Falls Paper Co. mill. Railroad construction continued as needed up to 1937; the North Tram was closed in 1941.

Suffering financial problems and internal dissension, the company, in 1941, sold 72,000 acres of cut-over land to the Draper Corporation.[48] It is amazing that a buyer could be found for the company's files indicate that the hardwoods were exhausted. They are full of correspondence dealing with tracts that might have enough hardwoods to keep the mill running, but few were found. Emporium Lumber Co. was able to stay in business a while longer, bringing hardwoods to the Conifer mill by rail. Finally, in 1949, Heywood-Wakefield, the furniture manufacturing company from Massachusetts bought the mill, rebuilt it, and operated it until it was destroyed by fire in 1957.

Two aspects of Emporium Lumber Co.'s operations stand out. One, the innovative way the mills were run, is beyond the scope of this summary, except to note the economical methods the company employed and the way everything from the forest was used. Spruce logs were cut into lengths for dimension lumber and small logs were sold for pulp. In the early years, hemlock logs were shipped to A. Sherman Co. Hemlock bark was sold from 1913 to 1917, bringing $7.75 a cord. Hardwood flooring was always the company's principal product. The company also made doors, barrel staves, lath, and boxes, shipped gun stocks, stove wood, maple syrup, sawdust and even ferns. Scrap wood which had no other use was burned to provide steam power for the saws, and the ash from the furnaces was turned to potash. To improve its profits, the company also leased tracts to sportsmen's clubs, notably the Grass River Outing Club, Massawepie Club, and Stillwater Club.

The second aspect is the size of the company's land holdings and what the company had to pay for them. Various figures, averaging 80,000, are stated for the company's acreage. A company document giving both land and stumpage lists tracts totalling 110,000 acres, which includes also land obtained from International Paper Co. For the 110,000 acres, Emporium paid $1,455,572 or $13.22 an acre. Since most of this land was acquired before 1920 and had been cut for pulp, this seems a high price (see discussions on the value of land), especially in light of the fact that the company also had to develop a railroad to extract its timber.

Not all of the land acquired was covered with timber, some correspondence says only about two-thirds was, and that fire had reached the rest.[49] However, the company had virgin hardwood stands on at least 60,000 acres and 17,000 acres had never been cut for either hard or softwoods at all, including the 7,000-acre Railroad Lot and 7,000 acres in the Clare Tract.

For all the land that was cut and all the burning of wood at the mill, it is exceptional that the company never suffered a fire of any significance.

The company was liquidated between 1968 and 1970, but its production had declined steadily after 1940. During its tenure, Emporium Lumber Co. sawed some 2.7 million hardwood logs, producing 194 million board feet.[50] With an average of ten million board feet of lumber sawn every year, it is easy to see how the company's forests were depleted by 1940. Its cut-over lands were worth but $2 to $2.50 an acre in 1943, and then had value only for the State. Assuming a harvest of 3,000 acres a year to supply the company's mills, then Emporium, which did most of the hardwood logging in the region, only cut at a rate

that was less than half the rate of cutting for charcoal production in the second half of the nineteenth century.

## St. Regis Paper Company

Although the St. Regis Paper Co.'s first mill was located outside the Adirondacks, it initially drew its timber from within the Park. The corporation was born late in the era of consolidation as a partnership of five men with very different backgrounds. David M. Anderson of Watertown, the manufacturing expert of the group, had joined several ventures in the papermaking industry before becoming general manager of Taggart Paper Co. George C. Sherman's background was financial and he had served as vice-president of the American Pulp and Paper Association's News Division. These two men began buying parcels of land along the Black River. In the last two years of the century they acquired a mill site with power rights on the Black River and began planning to build a paper mill.

In their search for timberlands to supply their mill, the men approached the firm of Dodge, Meigs and Co., which had three north country lumber mills (St. Regis Falls, Santa Clara, and the Santa Clara Mill at Tupper Lake) and timberlands stretching from Canada to Georgia to serve those mills. The company's railroad would make possible the shipment of logs to the mill planned by Anderson and Sherman. The three men responsible for Santa Clara Lumber Co., George E. Dodge, Titus B. Meigs, and Ferris J. Meigs, completed the partnership that incorporated the St. Regis Lumber Co. in 1899.

A stock transaction secured the needed timberlands for the new corporation. Sherman and Anderson proceeded to build their paper mill capable of producing 50 tons of paper a day, a rate which would exhaust St. Regis timberlands in twenty years. Plans were made to double the mill's capacity, apparently without considering that it would increase the rate of depletion of the company's timber supply. Dissension developed between the partners over costs associated with building the larger mill, delays and added expenses grew out of the problems of blasting out a diversion canal beside the Black River to supply power, and questions arose about the actual amount of timber on the company's lands.

To settle concerns, Sherman and Anderson had to borrow to pay for the enlarged mill, the Meigs' sold their stock to Dodge and pulled out of the partnership, and Dodge assumed control of the stock. The Meigs were then accused by Sherman and

Anderson of fraud in misrepresenting the amount of spruce on the tract. Financial problems affected the company and by 1902 Dodge had withdrawn as president. Litigation among the former partners continued through most of the first decade of the century.

To raise money, St. Regis sold 22,000 acres to William Rockefeller and arranged for the sale of hardwoods on its remaining land. Other problems slowed the building of the canal; but finally, in March 1901 all four paper machines were operating at the new Deferiet mill.

St. Regis Paper Co. won a quarter-million dollar settlement against Santa Clara Lumber Co. because that company could not supply the promised timber, but that did solve the basic problem of timber supply. The company then bought the 80,000-acre Mary L. Fisher Tract, which bordered on the Black River so logs could be floated to the mill.[51] With timber rights to additional acreage, St. Regis Paper Co. became the north country's third largest forest land-owning paper company. Despite this, the company, like others, depended heavily on growing imports from Canada.

But dissension among the remaining partners and the board continued. Gordias H. P. Gould (see Gould Paper Co.) became president in 1909. In August 1914, Anderson sold his stock to Gould. A week after that sale Sherman was accused of conduct injurious to the credit of the company and was forced to resign as treasurer and secretary. Gould, the entrepreneur, did not have Anderson and Sherman's management skills. Opposed to a closed shop, he fought the growing union movement. St. Regis suffered a strike from 1915 into 1916, when Gould was voted out. Late in 1916, after failing to sell his stock to the Pulitzer's *New York World*, Gould sold out to a group of Watertown businessmen, one of whom was David Anderson.

The new owners gradually expanded the company, rebuilding its machinery, acquiring other firms and timber tracts along the east coast and into Canada. Rapid expansion after World War II made St. Regis Paper Co. one of the largest paper companies in America.

## J. and J. Rogers Company

The J. and J. Rogers Co. spanned 140 years of Adirondack history as a leader in the two largest industries of the region. The company's role in the iron industry is discussed in the chapters on Iron and Charcoal and on Railroads. The family's role in the iron industry is discussed in detail by Philip J. Hardy,[52] and although fascinating, it is too complex to be summarized here.

The company's role in the pulp and paper industry began at the close of the company's iron era, when the company had approximately 100,000 acres. (A foreclosure sale of April 10, 1893 describes company holdings totalling over 90,000 acres.)[53] The company continued to add to its forest land and at one point, according to family recollections, the company owned as much as 250,000 acres, making it one of the largest privately-owned timber tracts in the Adirondacks.

Even during the period before 1888 in which the company primarily harvested its lands for hardwoods for charcoal, the company also harvested softwoods, shipping the best logs to company-owned saw mills. About 1.5 million board feet were shipped from the Black Brook region alone.

Between 1866 and 1882, the company shipped 88,000 tons of iron ore.[54] This would have required over 43,000 cords of wood a year, so the company was clearcutting hardwoods on 1,000 acres a year. Little wonder that the First Annual Report of the Forest Commission for 1885 said the company's kilns were leaving the "country bare."

In 1893, the company faced not only the economic upheavals of the period and reductions in tariffs on foreign iron and steel but also competition from new open pit iron mines in the Midwest and from the new Bessemer process which could produce iron more cheaply than the company's forges. The company was reorganized, the forges and rolling mill dismantled, and a new sawmill and pulp mill were built near a dam on the West Branch of the Ausable River at AuSable Forks. "Ultimately the Rogers paper enterprise would become more extensive than iron."[55] Triggering this expansion was the developing shortage of spruce and fir in the Adirondacks combined with the abundance of those species on the company's tracts, from which mostly hardwoods and mature spruce had been taken during the previous sixty years.

The company's sulfite pulp mill, which began operation in 1894, was the first sulfite mill built in the Champlain valley. It had the largest capacity of any mill in the Adirondacks, rivaled only by International Paper Co.'s mill at Cadyville, near Plattsburgh.[56]

A spur of the Delaware and Hudson Railroad was extended to the mill in 1895 to make it possible to ship pulp to other paper mills. In 1902 the company began building a paper mill, which consumed half the output of the pulp mill. In 1905 the company bought the Alice Falls Pulp Co. with its 50,000 acres of timberland.[57] In the next few years, forestland or timber rights were acquired on upwards of 100,000 acres. To harvest sufficient wood for its mills, the company began logging spruce on virgin tracts it owned on the slopes of Whiteface and Esther and on other high peaks near Keene and Keene Valley. The company logged the slopes of Mt. Marcy and the northern portion of Indian Pass, the Johns Brook Valley, and the slopes of the Giant-Green Mountain complex.[58]

With consumption of 50,000 cords per year, the company built lumber camps up to twenty miles away from the mill at AuSable Forks. Some logs were brought to the mill by sleds pulled over iced roads in winter, most were floated down the Ausable River. Flumes were built to carry logs to the river, an 8-mile one along the East Branch, a 2.5-mile one that carried four-foot logs from Whiteface Mountain. To supplement the Whiteface source, the company bought pulp from the Adirondack Mountain Reserve lands near Elk Lake or adjacent to the North Fork of the Boquet. It also began logging on a company-owned tract in the Johns Brook Valley. (The section on High Peaks logging gives additional details of the engineering feats that made such logging possible.)

J. and J. Rogers' mill consumed so much that by 1920, most resources were exhausted. The last log drive occurred in 1923,[59] and after that the mill imported pulp wood from Canada. The mill ran for forty-eight years, closing in 1942.

It is difficult to assess the extent of regrowth that occurred during the seventy-five years in which the company harvested its lands. However, in the thirty years that production depended on pulp from its holdings, it is safe to conjecture that 8,000 acres of pulp a year were harvested.

# Land Holding Companies

The interlocking nature of the companies described below is discussed in Chapter VI.

## Adirondack Timber and Mineral Co.

This company was variously referred to as Adirondack Mineral and Land Co. in Basselin's 1891 testimony before the assembly and sometimes called Adirondack Mineral and Timber Co., but its official name was Adirondack Timber and Mineral Company. It was formed by R. K. Hawley of Cleveland, Thomas H. McGraw, Henry Patton, and Dodge, Meigs & Co. It appears to have been formed to buy land from the Adirondack Co. or William West Durant and to sell that land. The two principal timber tracts sold by Adirondack Timber and Mineral Co. were lands sold to Santa Clara Lumber Co. and Moose River Tract Townships 3, 4, and 5 sold to Gould Paper Co.

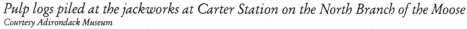

*Pulp logs piled at the jackworks at Carter Station on the North Branch of the Moose*
Courtesy Adirondack Museum

# Forest Parks and Preserves

The thirteen large private preserves, whose history can be documented, have experienced different fates in modern times. Santanoni Preserve and Webb's Nehasane Park are now part of the Forest Preserve. Huntington Preserve, Pack Forest, and Paul Smiths are owned by colleges or universities; part of their lands are not cut and part are harvested as demonstrations of scientific forestry and for education. The fourteenth tract described, Axton, is the only Forest Preserve land on which forestry has been practiced.

Parts of Whitney Park, Litchfield Park, Brandreth, and Jerseyfield have been sold to the State or to paper companies, but all four are still held by individual family groups. Cutting Preserve is now either State land or timber company owned.

The Adirondack Mountain Reserve is considerably smaller than it was originally and the current club members eschew logging. The Adirondack League Club is also smaller, but it continues to log its property as it has done almost from its formation.

Though smaller than originally, the Delaware and Hudson Tract remains industrial forest land.

## Nehasane Park[1]

Nehasane Park was part of the original 115,000 acre tract purchased in 1890 by Dr. William Seward Webb, builder of the Mohawk and Malone Railroad. Part of the tract was in Hamilton County, Totten and Crossfield Townships 37 and 38, and the rest in Herkimer County, Townships 42 and 43, and the parts of John Browns Tract Township 8 and the eastern third of Township 5. A dam built on the Beaver River, which enlarged the Stillwater Reservoir, flooded much of the Webb lands and according to Webb made it impossible to log them. He sued to recover damages for the flooded lands and the loss of timber. In the settlement of his suit against the State and the State's counterclaim to the titles to portions of his land, Webb sold much of his land to the State. The tangled lawsuit, settled in 1895, determined the value of the land and established the fact that the dam made it inaccessible and made harvest of timber impossible.

The price paid set a record for sales up to 1895. The northern portion, most of Townships 42 and 43, which went to the State, had never been cut. Webb retained a timber reservation on the rest. Webb received $600,000 for the 75,000 acres that included both virgin and reserve lands.

The 40,000 acre tract that he retained was known as Nehasane and encompassed the headwaters of the Beaver River, including Lake Lila. The tract is hilly with low swampy areas near lakes and streams and low knolls and ridges extending in a northeast-southwest direction, in other words, fairly easy to log. Its greatest asset was the fact that it was crossed by Webb's railroad, which by 1895 was owned by the New York Central Railroad and known as the Adirondack and St. Lawrence Division or, more commonly, the Mohawk and Malone Railroad. (See Railroad chapter for details of the railroad's construction.)

Gifford Pinchot surveyed the land in 1893 and found that it contained 22% swamp, 10% spruce flats, 42% hardwood stands, and 26% spruce slopes. He thought that the swamp lands contained 48% spruce, the spruce flats 45% spruce, the hardwood stands 37% spruce, and the spruce slopes 48% spruce. This high a proportion of merchantable spruce made the tract a valuable timberland.

Pinchot felt a 12"-diameter limit cut would leave sufficient seed trees.[2] He recommended that the forest should be studied and a management plan prepared for logging it. He proposed that it be managed for the future and observed that "lumbering yields a slightly larger revenue than forest management, but in the end falls far behind it."[3] Pinchot suggested that his protege, Henry S. Graves, prepare the actual plan for cutting.

Graves' study, indicating the tract contained more than 43% spruce, is chronicled in his *Practical Forestry in the Adirondacks* as well as in Gifford Pinchot's *The Adirondack Spruce*. Graves reported the tract was covered with "virgin forest, much of which is very old and on the decline. Here, as in any original forest, the growth of the trees is just about equalized by the loss through decay and wind or other destructive natural agencies."[4]

The first cut at Nehasane, made under Graves' plan, called for selective cutting of spruce and pine over ten inches in diameter on the stump, leaving two seed trees of at least the same size to guarantee reproduction. No hardwoods or balsams were to be cut. The yield turned out to be only thirteen standards per acre (2630 board feet), a smaller than expected harvest that Pinchot attributed to windfall loss.[5] The 1896 cutting of the southeast side of Lake

Lila and the 1898 cutting of the northwest side yielded even less, about 2,400 board feet per acre.

Graves' plan responded to Webb's desire "to cut as much timber as possible without injuring the productive power of the forest." However, he was unable to accomplish a number of things considered essential to practical forestry, such as the removal of dead and unsound trees and the maintenance of a sustained annual yield.

The southeast portion was recut in 1915 when current markets permitted the cutting of balsam (above 6") as well as spruce (above 9") At this time hardwoods were also cut (any tree yielding at least one 16-foot log 12" at the small end). The 1915 cut removed between 75 and 85% of the volume of the standing timber.

After the first cut, a fire took nearly a third of the stand. Webb had a modern fire-fighting train available as pictured in the Forest, Fish and Game Commission Report. The remainder of the unburned part of the tract was cut again between 1913 and 1918. This time both hardwoods and softwoods were taken, yielding about 8 cords of pulpwood and 1,000 feet of hardwoods per acre. Areas which had predominantly softwood stands were found to be reproducing spruce at a reasonable rate. However on the hardwood ridges, which constituted the bulk of the tract and where spruce had only occurred scattered through the hardwoods, the spruce yield for the second cut was significantly reduced. "The hardwoods have taken advantage of the openings; they have reseeded themselves in large numbers; the crowns of older trees have already spread out over the unused spaces, and the spruce factor is dwindling."[6] Areas that contained 36.8% spruce in the first cut in 1898 had only 16.4% spruce available for the second cut.[7] At the observed rate of decrease in spruce, it was projected that by 1934, spruce, still the most valuable species, would constitute only about 7% of the stand available for a third cut. Graves' goals for a twenty-year cutting cycle that took only the larger trees was undermined by unexpected growth of hardwoods.

Forestry literature is full of criticisms of the forestry practiced by Graves and by F. A. Gaylord who succeeded him as forester at Nehasane. Principally, there was objection to the fact that with the selective cutting, the forest did not reproduce itself, that the second cut was too severe, that the diameter restrictions were also too severe, that the second cut was no different from an ordinary logging operation, that the forest still contained an abundance of cull trees, and that the burned lands were not returned to productivity.

In 1920, Ralph C. Hawley of the School of Forestry at Syracuse discussed the various criticisms of Graves' plan and tried to justify it. "Graves' cutting [at Nehasane], while failing to stimulate growth to increase the percentage of softwood, or to replace an over-mature, decaying forest by a healthy young forest, was the best possible considering the market conditions of that time and the sentiment in favor of very conservative cutting on private preserves." Hawley, however, failed to refute the most damaging charge that the "cutting was not distinguishable from that of a logging operation where forestry receives no consideration."[8]

A timber cruise, made in 1978 in conjunction with the sale of Nehasane's remaining 14,644 acres to the State, showed that there was little spruce left and that there were only 3,000 acres or so where the hardwoods had not been cut. The State purchased that acreage, which included the prized Lake Lila for $100 an acre.

## Whitney Park

Henry S. Graves also devised the plan for the first cut of Whitney Park, a 68,000-acre tract in Hamilton County, townships 35, northwest part of 36, part of 23 and the triangle east of 23, and a few lots in township 21. The tract is characterized by a large number of lakes and ponds, many of which flow into the Raquette River.

Between 1896 and 1898, William C. Whitney and lumberman Patrick C. Moynehan assembled Whitney Park from many small parcels. The purchases were made under an agreement in which Whitney furnished most of the financial backing. The two shared the expenses and profits of the first lumbering, and Whitney was to succeed as sole owner in 1914, after the lumbering was completed. A logger's saw of a different kind held that, at the outset, Moynehan had the experience, Whitney had the money; at the end, Whitney had the experience and Moynehan had the money. Moynehan also profited by selling land to both Robert Pruyn and Archer Huntington for their preserves.

Whitney Park was mostly virgin territory, though some small amount of spruce had been taken from selected areas. Graves, who did not study the tract with the same thoroughness he used at neighboring Nehasane, thought that Whitney Preserve had a smaller proportion of spruce than Nehasane. Whitney Preserve's long, low ridges produced mostly hardwoods, and the spruce on the preserve had been further reduced by disease in the early 1880s.

In the first harvest, which occurred between 1898 and 1909, only spruce ten inches or larger and pine were taken. It was predicted that an equal amount of spruce could be cut after 36 years. The second harvest began in 1934; both balsam fir and spruce were logged for pulp, then hemlock and the hardwoods were logged. In both logging operations, the softwoods were skidded by horse, then dragged by sled to waterways for driving down the Raquette River to Tupper Lake. This method gave the best protection to the trees left. Hardwoods and hemlocks were skidded by horse to landings and taken by truck to Tupper Lake. No significant fires followed the first cut. About 1.5 million markets were floated to the Santa Clara Mill during the first cut (the equivalent of 250,000,000 board feet). A roughly equal amount of trees over 10 inches in diameter was made in both cuts (5.8 and 5.2 cords per acre respectively) though the second harvested an additional 3.2 cords per acre in spruce down to 5 inches.

No trees were taken within 200 feet of the shores of lakes and ponds. A 1000-acre tract was left untouched, but the blowdown of 1950 took so much of the pine and spruce that the "timber on the reserved areas is of little better quality today [1966] than on the remainder of the forest."[9]

It was anticipated that a good third cut could be made about 1970, after another thirty-five year interval. Actually, logging resumed in the 1950s and continued through the 1960s with hardwoods being sent to Elliott Hardwood, pulp wood to Finch, Pruyn and Co., and spruce fir to Champion. Horses were used until the 1960s, when logging became totally mechanized. This mechanization led to high-grading, which was exacerbated by the fact that through the 1970s, local mills only wanted high grade sawlogs and were taking little low grade lumber for pulp.

The cut that continued through the 1970s to the late 1980s appears to have been a disaster because of the failure to supervise the loggers who carried it out. Even a part of the shorelines, which were to have been spared, were logged. The diameter limit failed to work. Up until the late 1980s, eleven logging crews cut Whitney's forests at a such a rate that if it had continued for four more years, no further harvest at all could have been made for another twenty-five years.

Currently Wagner Woodlands has created a thirty-year plan for a fourth cut. It will permit Whitney to continue timber operations on a reduced scale. Only two logging crews continue to harvest timber and each crew is supervised by a forester who marks individual trees for harvest.[10] Timber management is said to be the family's principal interest in the tract.

With the sale of 8,630 acres north of Sabattis Road to International Paper Co.(for $81 an acre), Whitney Park is smaller that it was. Lease arrangements on half the property are necessary to balance tax costs on that portion of the Park. Representatives of Whitney Industries express the belief that it can remain as a Park, owned by the fourth generation of the family, which comprises a hundred individuals, and dedicated to timber management.

## Santanoni Preserve

Santanoni Preserve encompasses part of the western headwaters of the Hudson River. Its initial acquisition by a lumber syndicate in 1868 is indicative of how remote northern timberland, adjacent to the tributaries of the Upper Hudson River, was sought out by lumbermen. The syndicate which acquired the 5,695-acre tract surrounding Newcomb Lake, included Albany lumberman Lemon Thomson, his father-in-law and Albany banker William A. Sherman, and William Weed, also of Albany.

In 1892, Robert C. Pruyn began to create the 12,900-acre preserve by accumulating numerous parcels. With Newcomb Lake as its centerpiece, the preserve stretches from Newcomb settlement to the slopes of Santanoni and also includes Moose Pond and several smaller bodies of water. Pruyn purchased land from such diverse sources as Finch, Pruyn Lumber Co.,[11] various lumbermen, the MacIntyre Iron Co., William West Durant, and the State, through tax sales. Patrick Moynehan, the lumberman later associated with Whitney Park, and his wife sold Pruyn the Parallelogram Tract for $18,000 in 1892. Moynehan retained a timber reservation on the Parallelogram Tract, which had been owned by the syndicate. Pruyn later purchased Moynehan's reservation and it appears that Moynehan never logged the tract.

In 1892 the spruce was logged from the lower portion of the tract, a cut down to only 10" in diameter. In 1917, Finch, Pruyn and Co. was offered the tract's softwood stumpage at $4.50 a cord, but the company rejected the offer. In 1918 International Paper Co. bought all the softwood stumpage greater than 8 inches, principally spruce, which was still considered the only major merchantable timber.

International Paper Co. cut nearly 100,000 cords of spruce and fir, from which Finch, Pruyn and Co. earned $6 per cord. The logging operation left "no softwood of merchantable size on the property except for the reserve strips of 100 feet on either side of the principal roads, lakes, and trails."[12]

Recknagel, writing in 1939, thought the cut had been about 83,000 cords, based on the fact that the "softwood stumpage brought a round half-million dollars."[13] Actually Finch, Pruyn and Co. earned $481,000 for the harvest from 1920 to 1923, and $247,000 from the 1924 cut. During these years, Finch, Pruyn and Co. also derived income from a sugarbush located near Moose Pond.

No hardwoods were cut initially on this tract, which a 1923 Cornell report stated contained 60% hardwood. A few years later Emporium Lumber Co., the region's major buyer of hardwoods, estimated that there was little valuable hardwood because of the blowdown caused by a storm of January 1930.

Pruyn died in 1934 and in 1941 his estate negotiated a contract for sale of hardwoods to Oval Wood Dish of Tupper Lake. The contract called for cutting an average minimum of five million feet of lumber at $6.50 a thousand board feet. The contract was amended to include all merchantable spruce and fir over 10 inches in diameter at $8.25 per thousand. It specified summer cutting of all trees close to roads and winter cutting of trees that could be skidded to the roads. Recknagel estimated there were 35 million board feet of hardwoods on the preserve. According to the *Watertown Daily Times*, all the hardwoods on the Preserve were purchased by Oval Wood Dish Co. for a quarter of a million dollars; but the actual yield was much less, under $100,000.

Rice Veneer built a road to Moose Pond that could accommodate trucks in 1946 and harvested some veneer logs in the northern part of the Preserve.

The Melvin family of Syracuse acquired Santanoni Preserve in 1953 for $72,250. To help pay taxes, which were increasing, the Melvins contracted with Finch, Pruyn and Co. and others to harvest softwood pulp in the 1950s. Northern Lumber Co. cut hardwoods on the property throughout the 1950s and 1960s, rebuilding the Harris Lake bridge to facilitate transportation of logs by trucks. The harvest yielded enough ($35,000) to cover taxes, and although at least one lumberman believes the revenues were considerably higher, there is no evidence that they were.

The property was sold by the Melvin heirs to the Nature Conservancy in 1972, with a simultaneous sale to the State. The State acquired a magnificent tract with ancient cedars ringing the shores of Newcomb Lake. The casual visitor who walks to Newcomb Lake or paddles its shores is totally unaware of past logging, though a walk down the road/trail toward Moose Pond or north of Newcomb Lake reveals the severity of past logging. Patches are only slowly being reforested and the preponderance of beech is obvious; but despite two hardwood harvest periods and two softwood harvest periods, most of the tract is well-forested and its future secure.

## Jerseyfield

Jerseyfield is a relatively small (29,000 acres) tract in the southern Adirondacks. Originally owned by Alfred Dolge of Dolgeville, it was first lumbered to produce veneers and sounding boards for his piano factory. In 1898, he offered the tract to the State in connection with the State's plans for a demonstration site for the Cornell University College of Forestry. In his letter offering the lands to the State, Dolge said he had owned them since 1876 and had "practised forestry on them ever since."[14] The German forester, George Seibel, hired by Dolge to survey his property, reported that the land contained 5% hemlock, 25% spruce, 30% beech, 20% birch, 15% maple. Softwoods only above 12 inches had been cut, and almost no hardwoods had been cut.

Whatever cutting Dolge did, it must have been conservative, for during the years of World War II, the next cutting, after an interval of forty years, produced 69,000 cords of pulp for West Virginia Pulp and Paper Co. of Mechanicville. The jobber for the logging was the prominent lumberman, John E. Johnston. The trees were mostly spruce with some hemlock (one of diameter 52") and balsam, with some fine hardwoods. Finch, Pruyn and Co. also participated in the logging operation at Jerseyfield. At the beginning of the logging operation in 1939, the tract was described as containing virgin spruce, "one of the finest stands in the Adirondacks,"[15] according to *Lumber Camp News*.

The rail line from Little Falls through Dolgeville to the edge of the tract facilitated logging in the first part of the century. The northern extension had been taken up by the time of the last logging, but it still existed into Salisbury Center where logs were carried by trucks to the train for shipment to mills.

Portions of the tract were sold. Julius Breckwold, who acquired the Dolge factory, retained the 5,000-acre core of the tract, which is still privately owned.

FELT & SOUNDING-BOARD FACTORIES AT DOLGEVILLE.

*Alfred A. Dolge Factory relied on spruce from Jerseyfield*

*Courtesy Adirondack Museum*

## Frank A. Cutting Tract

This 8,000-acre virgin tract was purchased in 1892 by F. A. Cutting to provide a continuous supply of hemlock bark for his railroad shipping business. Cutting was primarily an exporter of bark to tanneries in the southern tier of the State and in western states. He had forest land in Maine and Canada, and bought bark from other Adirondack tracts, but this eponymous tract, located on the border between Franklin and St. Lawrence counties, was his largest in the Adirondacks.

In 1896 Cutting sold all the stumpage on the tract for 27 cents per thousand board feet on the stump. The contract for $45,000 covered all white pine, spruce, hemlock, ash, and cherry on the 9,000-acre tract. The contract specified an 8"-minimum-diameter cut, but did not specify the height at which that diameter had to be measured. As a result, the logger measured trees at ground level and was thus able to cut such small specimens that he was actually clearcutting the tract. Cutting saw what was happening, was appalled, and tried to obtain an injunction to prevent the abuse. A clause in the contract, permitting the logger to harvest hemlock only after it was peeled, enabled Cutting to stop the logger's abuse. Cutting simply stopped peeling the logs, even though this deprived him of both bark and revenue from the logs. This accounts for the fact that

in 1916 there were many fallen hemlocks decaying on the tract. Cutting resumed hemlock harvest and did not stop shipping bark from his lands until 1926.

Fire in 1908 burned only brush and small trees on 2,000 acres of the tract. Cutting sold hardwood to Brooklyn Cooperage for barrel staves after 1916. To facilitate hardwood harvest, the railroad spur was extended through the tract along Stony Brook. A sawmill on Stony Brook produced railroad ties from maple and birch logs. A second spur reached Lake Ozonia in 1917. At the same time, softwoods were sold to St. Regis Paper Co. John E. Johnston logged the tract again between 1926 and 1931.

A 1916 report concluded that the logging had been so heavy as to preclude adequate regeneration.[16] Cutting reforested the tract extensively with white pine.

The tract was sold to Gould Paper Co. for $23,000 in 1926 and resold to St. Regis Paper Co. in 1929.[17]

## Brandreth Park

In 1851, Township 39, Totten & Crossfield, was purchased for $3,000 by Dr. Benjamin Brandreth of Ossining. He was the grandson of the founder of a patented pill that had made the family's fortune.[18] The tract contained about 26,000 acres, part of which is still owned by the family.

212

The tract was not logged until 1912, when stumpage for all trees 10 inches or more in diameter was sold to the Mac-a-Mac Lumber Corp. Branches from the New York Central Railroad station at Brandreth spread out to haul 310,000 cords of pulp wood and 84,000,000 feet of pine and hemlock (or 365,000 cords of 16 foot peeled wood or 220,000 cords, depending on who is to be believed).[19] The sale of the stumpage brought $650,000.

Mac-a-Mac Lumber Corp. was not the first to consider bidding for the timber. Albert Hosley of Norwood Manufacturing Co. "spent a month on the tract but did not bid on it as he considered the virgin timber overripe."[20]

Mac-a-Mac Lumber Corp. was incorporated to carry out the logging operation, which took seven years. Among the incorporators were lumberman John MacDonald and Benjamin McAlpin, a member of the Brandreth family. MacDonald had cruised the tract and estimated it contained upwards of half a million cords of spruce. He secured a contract with St. Regis Paper Co. for pulpwood delivered in 16-foot lengths to the Brandreth station for $10.75 a cord.[21]

In 1949, Brandreth negotiated to sell to Gould Paper Co. stumpage for $3.60 a cord, but the blowdown of 1950 intervened before the cut could be made. Windfall spruce was harvested, but because of the glut of storm-damaged trees, it brought a lower price, as low as $2.50 a cord. Timber contracts for 1957 were negotiated at $4.00 a cord.[22]

In the early 1970s, International Paper Co. purchased parcels totalling 15,523 acres at an average of $84 per acre; with Brandreth reserving recreation rights on them for 99 years.

## Huntington Forest

The area presently occupied by Huntington Forest was first settled in the early 1800s and abandoned by 1830 by a farmer named Catlin. The tract straddles the Hamilton-Essex County line north of Newcomb. A series of ponds and lakes, of which long, thin Catlin Lake is the largest, drains into Rich Lake and thence into the Hudson River. Logging began to reach the upper Hudson River about the middle of the nineteenth century, and it reached stands around Rich Lake shortly after; a dam built for logging was already in disrepair by 1866 when Lossing described it. At that time there was the typical harvest of the largest and best spruce, with nothing else touched. More intensive logging began around 1883 in an area within a mile and a half or two miles of Rich Lake. The area around Catlin Lake

was logged by Dennis Moynehan in 1883[23] In 1890, a part of the tract was owned by lumberman Lemon Thomson. The Caughnawaga Club purchased the northern part of the future Huntington Preserve from Moynehan in 1894. Archer Huntington was a member of that club and after his marriage in 1895, he began accumulating land in the southern portion, purchasing the Arbutus and Goodnow Mountain preserves from William West Durant and land east to the Finch, Pruyn and Co. border (presumably from Lemon Thomson). In 1911, Huntington purchased the 8,000 acre Caughnawaga Club lands.[24]

There was no logging between 1883 and 1900, when softwoods were again harvested in a cut with a relatively high diameter limit. Fire burned the northwest shore of Rich Lake and northeastern shores of Catlin Lake around 1900. The last commercial softwood cut (14,750 cords) was made during 1928 by Finch, Pruyn and Co., which owned the timber rights to the land east of Trout Brook. No hardwoods were cut, but this time all spruce and balsam were cut down to six, sometimes four, inches in diameter. This small diameter cut severely limited softwood reproduction. Further, the area cut was left in a hazardous condition, which made it prone to fire.[25]

All but the 2,000-acre tract around Camp Arbutus was given to Syracuse University in 1932 by Anna and Archer Huntington as a laboratory for both wildlife and forest management. The University received the Arbutus parcel in 1939. It is believed that a thousand-acre reserve of pure hardwoods on ridges on the west shore of Catlin Lake was never logged. Between 1937 and 1941, small plots were cut and replanted to study the effects of deer browse.

Since 1943, with the Huntingtons' permission, commercial logging has been practiced and studied for its effects on wildlife and the forest.[26] In the mid 1960s, "constraints in funding and philosophical differences" led to the "harvest of larger areas of economically viable timber stands. ... As a result of the accelerated harvest, the volume removed went well beyond what the property could support on a sustained yield basis, and limited the type of forest diversity desired for some research programs." While net growth increased, "nevertheless, during the 1970s and 1980s, harvest slowed as a result of the redirection of the program and changing market conditions."[27] In other words, financial considerations had taken precedence over the school's scientific research and forestry management plans. It is little wonder that finances and the marketplace dominated almost all other Adirondack timber stands.

## Pack Demonstration Forest

This 2,200-acre tract north of Warrensburg is the dream of Charles Lathrop Pack, son of a Michigan lumber baron, George Willis "Clearcut" Pack.[28] The son studied forestry in Germany and became a national figure in the conservation movement, serving as president of the American Forestry Association from 1916 to 1922. He wished to establish demonstration forests around the country to promote forestry ideals. In 1927, he purchased the Warrensburg tract and deeded it to Syracuse University to be used as a working forest. The land was mostly abandoned farms with cut-over woodlots. The one exception was the Woodward lot of 250 acres which contained some of the finest old growth stands of pine and hemlock in the area, with trees whose ages ranged up to 400 years. While experiments in forestry proceed on most of the tract, this virgin stand has been left in its natural state.[29]

Cutting plans, drawn up at the time the tract was acquired, call for the harvest that is below the replacement level, with attention given to culling diseased and deformed trees, practices that improved the stand, but which are not financially possible on most commercial lots.

A sawmill on the property produces 25,000 board feet a year at present, down from the quarter million board feet at the peak of cutting years before. The forest not only serves as a model, as Pack envisioned, it is a laboratory for students of forestry.

## Paul Smiths Experimental Forest

In 1859, Paul Smith, one of the Adirondacks' most successful entrepreneurs, settled in the area where a hamlet and a college now carry his name. He gradually enlarged his land holdings into a tract of 32,000 acres and he built a sawmill and a branch of the steam railroad (later electrified) from the Mohawk and Malone Railroad line.

Part of the tract had been cut lightly for spruce and hemlock and part was virgin forest, which had exceptional stands of pines. He harvested only mature timber and by 1952, the tract had been cut for pulp three times, with a fourth cut due shortly after that year.

Paul Smith consulted foresters Gifford Pinchot and Clifford Pettis (Pettis later became Superintendent of Forests for the Conservation Commission, 1910-1927). Twenty-thousand acres of

the original tract became the experimental forest associated with Paul Smith's College. That tract contains virgin forest, plantations, and second-growth. The college faced the same problems related to the expense of timber management as on other private forests.[30]

A 2,300-acre portion of the tract became one of the U. S. Forest Service's Northeastern Forest Experiment Stations in 1948. That year a series of experiments with different chemicals was begun with the goal of finding the most efficient and economical methods of killing cull hardwood trees to promote softwood growth.[31]

## Delaware and Hudson Adirondack Forest

The Chateaugay Ore and Iron Co. was organized in 1873 to mine and produce iron, and that history is summarized in the chapter on Iron and Charcoal. To supply the company's needs for charcoal, the company accumulated upwards of 100,000 acres. The narrow gauge Chateaugay Railroad reached the company's forge near Lower Chateaugay Lake in 1878. The railroad was extended to Standish in 1885, where the company built a large furnace. An extension of the railroad to Loon Lake in 1886 took the line and its spurs deeper into company tracts. At Chateaugay and all along the line at such places as Upper and Middle Kilns, the company erected beehive kilns, which ultimately numbered 101.[32] From its woodlands near Lyon Mountain and along the railroad near Loon Lake, it was estimated that one and a half million cords of hardwoods were harvested between 1873 and 1903.

The company also sold 15,000 cords of spruce and fir pulpwood in 1896 to Glens Falls Paper Co., which was soon to become part of International Paper Co. Between 1896 and 1915, when the merchantable timber ran out, 300,000 cords were harvested from the Chateaugay Ore and Iron Co. lands. Sawlogs were shipped to large mills at the outlet of Lower Chateaugay Lake and at Bradley Pond.

In 1903, when the Delaware and Hudson Railroad acquired the Plattsburg-Lake Placid Railroad, it also acquired control of the Chateaugay Ore and Iron Co. The Delaware and Hudson Railroad recognized the extent to which the Chateaugay's tracts had been cut-over, and began a survey of the lands. This showed 18,000 acres of virgin spruce and hardwoods; 17,000 acres of virgin hardwoods with some spruce; 10,000 acres second-growth hardwoods; 23,000 acres second growth hardwoods ready for cutting; 28,000 acres denuded or brush lands. Agricultural or mining lands constituted the rest. Three-fourths of the company's tracts were burned in the fires of 1903, but the tract was further damaged in the fires of 1908, 1911, and 1915, the latter because of continuing failure to lop the tops of harvested softwoods. Salvage operations and harvest of timbered lands continued until 1918, when all the old-growth timber was exhausted.

The company began a program of reforestation in 1906 by building a nursery at Wolf Pond, which proved unsuccessful because the climate was too cold. Some white pine was planted on company tracts, but most of the planting was done with exotic species such as Scotch pine, Norway spruce, and European larch. A second nursery was built at Rouses Point near Plattsburgh. Experimental plantings of Douglas fir, Austrian pine, western yellow pine, white willow, Norway poplar, Engelmann spruce, Colorado spruce, and others. At the beginning of the reforestation program, it was estimated that there were 50,900 acres of burned and denuded lands to be planted. "Natural changes converted 38,400 acres of this to brush land unsuitable for planting, so upon completion of the program in 1927, 12,500 acres had been restocked with nearly 15 million trees."[33] About a million trees were set out on lands belonging to the railroad before 1917.

The Delaware and Hudson Railroad continued acquiring land until it held 150,000 acres. The company remained committed to forestry management, but at the same time was concerned that it might not be economical. "The fixed charges of interest and taxes can be computed but the value of the material from a planted forest and the time when it will reach commercial maturity are unknown. There will have to be much higher values for new wood being grown if its production is to prove good business."[34]

The company and its tracts continued under a series of successive ownerships and different names including Chateaugay Pulp and Paper Co. and Republic Steel Co. It was sold to Diamond International, who sold part of the timber tracts to Sherdom Associates and some to Lassiter Corporation. Domtar acquired the Adirondack timber tracts in 1963. That company has been harvesting its lands since then and is currently cutting the areas that were burned; the intervening eighty years has produced significant timber growth on the company's land, which now covers 105,000 acres in Franklin and Clinton counties. Hardwoods make up 84% of the company's timberlands and tracts thinned in the 1970s are producing a good percentage of sawlogs, primarily some valuable hard maple.

## Adirondack Mountain Reserve

The Adirondack Mountain Reserve, founded as a private club in 1887, grew through a series of acquisitions so that the reserve encompassed approximately 40,000 acres in 1910.[35] The Reserve covered the High Peaks slopes and summits above the Ausable Lakes with the exception of the summit of Mount Marcy. A sale in 1923 to the State of the northeastern flanks of Mount Marcy and the northern slopes of the Great Range, including the summits of the all the peaks in the Range except Mt. Haystack, reduced the holdings to 16,300 acres; a further 9,100 acres was sold to the State in 1978.

The lower slopes of the future reserve were logged for softwood sawlogs. The area between the present-day Ausable Club and the Lower Ausable Lake, was clear cut to furnish wood for making charcoal before 1878. A forester's survey in 1890 (made by the State as part of a study to determine the condition of private lands in the Adirondacks) noted that most of the tract contained virgin timber.

To finance the original purchase, Adirondack Mountain Reserve's founders allowed Finch, Pruyn and Co. to log the area south of Panther Gorge in the 1890s. Between 1901 and 1918, land north of Elk Lake, around Marcy Brook, and the northern slopes of Wolf Jaws was logged under contract to J. and J. Rogers Co. There has been no logging on the remaining 7,000 acres since 1978, and it is thought that no logging occurred between 1918 and 1978.[36]

Whatever logging occurred, it is clear that the area around Gill Brook and up toward the valley between Nippletop and Colvin was never logged and is virgin forest.[37]

## Adirondack League Club

The Adirondack League Club was founded in 1890 as a hunting and fishing preserve, with the purchase of the 91,000-acre Anson Blake Tract. The club accumulated a total of 128,000 acres plus 63,000 acres of leased land before selling off some of its land and contracting to its 53,000-acre size today.[38] In its first prospectus, the club boasted that its land had been "untouched" by woodsman's axe. About half of the club's original land was in the drainage of the West Canada Creek, the rest in the Black River watershed, with the South Branch of the Moose River bisecting the club's land from east to west.

Forester Bernhard Fernow was among the club's charter members and his assessment of the club's tracts was the first plan for scientific management of private timberlands in this country. (See discussions of Fernow under Scientific Forestry and under Tupper Lake Mills.) The club's claim of virgin forests was substantiated by Fernow's 1891 report, which contained one of his most eloquent statements on forestry. Because a private preserve offered a measure of permanent ownership and would be able to spend part of its income for improvement of the existing forest, he believed a private preserve was the proper place to demonstrate forestry principles. He saw the club lands as a place to blend technical and financial considerations, a place where "wise curtailment of present revenues [would] secure permanent and increasing revenues for the future."[39]

The club sought to finance its acquisition of the Wager Tract (Moose River Tract Township 1) and some of its activities such as road and clubhouse building, by logging its lands. The club attempted to heed Fernow's advice by limiting the cutting to a 12" minimum. A contract, which Fernow believed was far-sighted, had been negotiated with Henry Patton, Albany lumber merchant, and Thomas H. McGraw, just before the club purchased the Blake Tract. Patton and McGraw immediately resold the timber rights to Trenton Falls Lumber Co., Forestport Lumber Co. and to the Gould Paper Co.

Included in the logging contract was all the spruce and pine on the tract except within 80 rods of Jocks (Honnedaga) and Little Moose lakes and within 20 rods of Panther Lake and the West Canada Creek Stillwater. The exclusion of cutting on lake, river, and stream shores and the borders of roads mark this and all other contracts that Adirondack League Club negotiated with lumbermen. (Such reserve rights were common to logging contracts on most private preserves. See Santanoni, for instance.) The Gould Paper Co. contract gave the lumbermen the right to build logging roads and to use and improve all waterways but the two large lakes for the driving of logs to mills.[40]

The club anticipated a constant revenue of $30,000 a year for fifteen years from spruce sawlogs and a further amount from sale of tops and unhealthy spruce for pulp. The contract called for top-lopping to reduce fire hazard.[41] To oversee forestry on its lands, the club, on Fernow's recommendation, hired

Edward Rausch, Ph. D., a professional forester from Germany. Fernow estimated that the merchantable spruce and pine constituted 25% of the club's lands, which he appraised at "a round million dollars."[42] He told the club's trustees that they could increase the harvest to yield $60,000 a year without destroying the forest.

Patton and Co.'s bankruptcy in 1896 upset the club's anticipated harvest plans, but does not account for the trustee's misgivings with the logging contracts. "Each year brings us nearer to the end of our relations with those lumber companies."[43] While logging was deemed undesirable from an esthetic perspective, from a sportsman's point of view, it was thought to be beneficial for the propagation of deer. Part of the revenues had to be paid to Patton and McGraw's assignees. The club bought out parts of the sub-contracts, including the "two great dams on the West Canada Creek, and a lot of unattractive looking booms, chains, etc," erected by Trenton Falls Lumber Co.[44] Annual reports indicate that the lumber companies were cutting beyond the terms of the contract. Besides concern with contract abuses, club members thought that logging was detrimental to trout fishing and they just did not like the looks of the slash left by the logging. Whatever the reasons, the trustees resented suffering the "annoyances which the work and presence of the lumbermen bring."[45]

In spite of the club's problems with its first lumber contract, the club purchased the 12,000-acre Wager Tract in 1894 and financed that purchase by the sale of the tract's spruce, pine, and hemlock to Gould Paper Co. The trustees could only hope that "the methods employed in taking off this timber ... will prove less objectionable" than the contract with Patton and McGraw. "The time is far distant, no doubt, if it ever comes, when the club will even consider a proposition to again utilize the value of this forest growth, and suffer the annoyances which the work and presence of the lumbermen bring."[46] This marked a bitter ending to the club's initial foray into the realm of scientific forestry. In spite of all the club earned from the sale of timber, it mortgaged its property in 1903.[47]

In 1897, the club sold to the State for $3.33 an acre the Adgate Tract, which had been logged between 1890 and 1897. The club's hunting and fishing lands were increased in 1899 by the lease of hunting, fishing, and hiking rights on Township 5 of Moose River Tract from the Gould Paper Co., land Gould had purchased that year from Adirondack Timber and Mineral Co. In 1900 the club sold its portion of Township 8 and the south part of

Township 7 Moose River Tract. The West Canada Creek flows through these tracts.

Because of Forestport Lumber Co.'s non-compliance with the original contract, the club voted in 1900 not to enter into any further logging contracts. The prohibition continued until 1913, although some logging did occur in the interval under earlier contracts.

In 1904, the club negotiated a contract with Gould Paper Co., which had acquired most of three townships upriver from the club. Gould was given the right to float logs down the South Branch of the Moose River through the club's lands, paying tolls of between $5,000 and $6,000 a year, depending on the number of logs, to drive them down Limekiln Creek and the South Branch of the Moose River. (Gould's last drive on the Moose occurred in 1948.)

A 1913 contract with Gould Paper Co., which was negotiated with the help of Gifford Pinchot, called for the harvest of all the softwoods on two of the club's townships. To oversee this new logging, the club hired forester R. E. Hopson on Pinchot's recommendation. Hopson supervised the club's forests from 1914 until his retirement in 1955.

The trustees thought the outlook for receipts during the first years of this Gould contract were "favorable beyond our most sanguine expectations."[48] The income from logging on townships 2 and 6 remained high through 1919 with softwoods bringing $2. and $2.75 a cord. Despite negotiating a contract in 1926 to sell Gould the timber on Township 7 for $4. and $4.50 a cord, the club mortgaged its property again in 1927. In 1921, the club contracted to sell Hinckley Fibre Co. pulp at $10 a cord, but that contract collapsed.

The Gould Paper Co. contract was to run through 1937, but Gould was able to cut only 20,000 cords between 1927 and 1932, because by 1932, the market for pulp dropped so low that Gould could harvest very little more. Instead of the anticipated $100,000, the club realized less than half that from the Gould contracts. The sporadic logging that occurred during the 1930s and 1940s could not make up the club's deficits, so the club turned to land sales. Township 6 and the south half of township 7 were sold to the Moose River Lumber Corporation, an enterprise formed by J. P. Lewis Co. and St. Regis Paper Co. to buy the land. The club leased the hunting and fishing rights from the corporation.

The club's motive for lumbering continued to be its need for cash.[49] Gould Paper Co. cut softwoods through 1950, and as elsewhere, the depletion of softwood stocks and the discovery of ways to use hardwoods for pulp led the club to begin harvesting hardwoods after 1950. Logging methods on the club's lands as elsewhere in the Adirondacks were changing: Lumber camps were phased out and although most logging occurred in winter, gradually roads were built to accommodate summer logging. Plagued by non-payment by or the bankruptcy of loggers, the club realized at most $25,000 to $30,000 a year through the 1960s, amounts even less than revenues earlier in the century.

In 1978, the club, its lands reduced to 51,000 acres (currently the club owns 53,000 acres) surveyed its lands and determined that beech predominated. Until recently, most trees were cut for pulp. As the club struggled to create a "sound cutting policy," the loggers had to cut smaller diameters to compensate for the increased expenses of building roads. The goal of cutting hardwoods above 18" in diameter on a twenty-year cycle proved difficult to maintain. To achieve its goals, the club decided it had to limit the areas logged annually to an acreage that could be supervised by its forester.

In the early years at least, successful scientific forestry proved more difficult to achieve than the club's desire to turn its forests into income. With a good forester, the club appears to have been able to ensure that logging was usually carried out properly, but rarely on a level to assure expected income from its lands. In fact, if the club's timberlands had been held only for the production of lumber, the profits realized would not have permitted the level of forestry practices the club has maintained.

## Litchfield Park

Litchfield Park occupies the southern third of Totten and Crossfield Township 25; it has been owned by the Litchfield family since 1893. The tract had been owned by Samuel Gilchrist and at the time of Litchfield's purchase, the tract was being logged for pine, spruce, and hemlock in the last year of a five-year contract to deliver logs to the Norwood Mill at Tupper Lake. The contract specified thirty cents a market for spruce over 9" and pine or cherry over 11" and all logs were driven to Tupper Lake by sled and floated down the lake to the mill.

Edward H. Litchfield purchased the tract during the last year of the contract and it was said that he paid Albert Hosley, a logger for Norwood, five dollars apiece to leave the virgin white pine standing around some of the lake shores; some of them are still standing.

No further cutting was done until 1911 when a number of local lumberjacks were hired to cut spruce and run a sawmill to furnish scaffolding to use in building the eighty-foot towers for Litchfield's Chateau or Castle as it is sometimes known. In 1920, Litchfield hired the James W. Sewall Co., a consulting forestry firm from Maine to cruise the tract. The report identified 9,633 loggable acres with about 70,000 cords of mature softwood pulp and 17.5 million board feet of hardwoods with only 6% beech. According to John Stock, who later became the park's forester,[50] the forestry firm prepared "skeletal management plans but there is no evidence that anyone paid any attention to them."[51]

In 1924, Litchfield incorporated the tract under the name Litchfield Park Corporation (Liparco) and he and his son E. Hubert, Jr. decided to derive some income from the park which had been nothing but an expense for the family. The senior Litchfield said that "in the thirty years we have owned the Park our only income from it has been the sale of a puppy for five dollars." On the advice of William Read, their neighbor to the north who had been selling stumpage in 1922 and 1923, they hired a self-taught Tupper Lake forester, Floyd Hutchins whose approach was to cut half the mature trees and half the younger trees over a certain diameter. Hutchins contracted for such a cut at Litchfield; from 1924 to 1928, this softwood pulp was sold to the McCarthy Brothers who were brokers for St. Regis Paper Co.

From 1924 to 1931, Liparco also sold mangle blocks taken from maple and birch logs over 16" in diameter to Elliott Hardwood Co. (mangles, or cylinders of sapwood, were used to extract water from clothes in early washing machines).

The softwood cut continued until 1929 when the depression brought the price of stumpage down. By then, 63,000 cords of spruce and balsam, 12,000 cords of hemlock, and 115,000 lineal feet of boom logs or sawlogs destined for Tupper Lake's various sorting booms had been harvested. By 1931, 11 million board feet of hardwoods had been cut.

There was no further cutting until 1942 when a new contract with Elliot Hardwood Co. called for cutting trees over 17" in diameter. The program, under the Timber Production for War Purposes, or TeePeeWeePee, failed at first because of the shortage of manpower, but by 1943 nearly a million board feet was harvested.

No further harvesting was done until 1950 when Liparco contracted with Draper Corporation to cut a half million board feet in the area between Tupper Lake and NY 30. Draper continued by cleaning up after the 1950 blowdown. With the

contract extended, Draper harvested about 6 million feet of hard and soft wood through 1957.

Due to income tax problems, Liparco decided to cut up to half a million more board feet in the northeast corner of the park at the rate of a thousand board feet per acre; this cut of over-mature hardwoods was actually high grading. In 1961, under John Stock's supervision, timber stand improvement was started. It entailed chemically peeling small beech and junk hardwoods for use in a Heartwood charcoal plant purchased by Liparco to deal with the oversupply of unmerchantable hardwoods.

Litchfield bought Elliott Hardwood Co. in 1963; Elliott bought North Creek Dry Kilns in 1965. The State shut down the Heartwood plant because of air pollution. In 1965, Liparco purchased 14,000 acres from Whitney to insure log supply for a new mill planned for the park. This new mill was designed to cut 20 million board feet a year of hard and soft woods; its specialized equipment could handle any tree from the woods that was 50% sound with no regard for size or shape. In other words, it could deal with the big old cull trees. This might have been a good idea, except for the decline in the lumber and pulp markets and rising interest rates. Liparco sold the mill to Elliott, the Whitney lands to International Paper Co., and the park's uncut Tupper Lake shoreline to the State. This reduced the park to its present 11,000 acres where a fourth generation member of the family oversees the continued selling of stumpage with advice from a Tupper Lake forester.

## Axton--Bernhard Fernow and the Cornell College of Forestry

The strangest saga involving professional foresters in the Adirondacks juxtaposed Bernhard Fernow, the Cornell College of Forestry, Axton, Brooklyn Cooperage Co., and Tupper Lake Chemical Co.

The Cornell College of Forestry was established by the New York State Legislature in March of 1898 to educate future foresters and demonstrate practical forestry on a tract of timberland in the Adirondacks. Fernow, in testimony before the Senate Industrial Committee gave his interpretation of forest history:

In 1888 the Sstate possessed a property of some 600,000 acres of timberland, acquired by tax sales, mostly culled and more or less maltreated, and a Forest Commission was instituted for its management. Although the Commission had the power to do whatever was necessary to institute technical forest management, it failed to secure expert advice and to formulate a coherent plan. It exercised the power to cut timber by selling stumpage to lumbermen who continued to cull the woods of the valuable spruce and pine in the same manner as before,[52] and as a consequence those who saw that this method of treating the woods as a danger to their continuance and to their effectiveness as protectors of the watershed, brought about the insertion of a clause into the Constitution, which forbids the cutting of any trees on State lands, as well as the building of railroads over State lands. By these clauses the application of forestry to the State lands was effectively prevented.

At that time, the public and the advocates of forest preservation were still ignorant of the fact that forest preservation and forest utilization do not exclude each other; that the forest is preserved and continued in the same way as the human race, by harvesting the old crop and reproducing it.[53]

Fernow thought he could prove that forestry could be carried out on public lands and thus influence the State to carry on forestry on the Forest Preserve. In order to avoid the strictures of the state constitution, Fernow had to find a suitable tract of private land to demonstrate the efficacy of his forestry plans.

Governor Black established at Cornell University the College of Forestry and plans were put forward for the state to buy such a tract to be run by the new forestry school. Fernow looked about for land on which to establish an experimental forest. Among the tracts offered for the demonstration forest were 14,000 acres in southwestern Hamilton County and adjacent Herkimer and Fulton counties[54] with access to a sawmill, land held in the western Adirondacks by Taggart Paper Co. of Watertown, and the Jerseyfield Tract, on which the owner, Alfred Dolge had practiced scientific forestry since 1876. Dolge, the owner of a piano factory in Dolgeville, had, in 1881, hired a German forester, who "laid out the course by which the forests would be continually improved. ... A natural consequence is that the forest is now worth more than when I bought it." One of Dolge's German foresters claimed that the 29,000 acre tract contained 25 percent spruce. Dodge, Meigs & Co. offered lands in the southern part of Franklin County.[55] The company claimed that although the tract had mostly been cut over for spruce and pine,

leaving the hardwoods still standing, "a large portion of the tract is 'strictly virgin.'"[56]

None of these tracts appealed to Fernow as much as the 30,000-acre tract at Axton, offered to the state by the Santa Clara Lumber Co., which had logged all the softwoods from the tract. The state acquired the tract for Cornell; it was to revert to the State after thirty years. The State also appropriated $30,000 to start the experiment, $20,000 short of the amount Fernow requested. According to Fernow, "the first step necessary was to find a market for the hardwood, which did not exist locally." He had also to find a market for the "debris of logging," which he claimed exceeded by three or four times the volume of the available sawlogs.

Fernow interested Brooklyn Cooperage Co. in the production of wood alcohol and persuaded it to establish a plant at Tupper Lake to produce hardwood barrel staves and wood alcohol.[57] The company agreed to take all the hardwoods harvested from experimental forest for a period of fifteen years (not thirty years as Fernow wanted).

A six-mile-long railroad spur was constructed from Tupper Lake to the tract to facilitate the shipment of the hardwoods, which otherwise would have had to be hauled to the Raquette and transported downstream on rafts, though the north end of the tract was accessible to the existing line.

Several companies indicated interest in buying the hardwoods and were even willing to locate factories near Tupper to take advantage of yields on the experimental forest. Among them were a lumber and lime company from St. Albans, Vermont; a lumber dealer in Hamilton, Ontario; the Penn Match Co. of Scranton, Pennsylvania; and the Studebaker Wagon Co. of Great Bend, Indiana, which considered locating a wagon-hub factory in the Adirondacks.[58] Selling his hardwoods would not turn out to be one of the obstacles Fernow encountered. Fernow's problems began almost immediately after the Tupper factories opened and the chain of events led to the state taking the College of Forestry away from Cornell and later placing it at Syracuse. Fernow claimed his difficulties stemmed from the short cutting cycle and the insufficient state appropriations for the forestry experiment. Fernow never received from the legislature the funds he had estimated were necessary, but his plans would never have worked. Even Fernow later observed, harvesting hardwoods and leaving the young spruce was not feasible:

A satisfactory natural reproduction, however, requires that the old crop be removed gradually, while a young crop is gradually developing, giving light to it as the different species require. But such a procedure-repeated logging over the same area-is costly; the scanty allowance of working capital has prevented it in the first season. Besides, nearly all of the hardwood trees, even the small or young ones, are defective and unpromising, ... while the spruce which might be left as seed trees, being shallow rooted, are readily thrown by winds, ...hence it appears in many places preferable, less expensive and surer of results to artificially secure the young crop by planting.

Fernow established nurseries for softwoods on the experimental forest and began to reforest the area. Fernow cloaked his espousal of reforestation with noble intentions. In an article paradoxically titled "Civilizing the Wilderness," Fernow described his experiment as setting an example, "how the wilderness may be civilized and made to grow better, and more trees per acre retaining its beauty and yet becoming more useful and furnishing continuous supplies of valuable wood material, now to cover up the scars and bruises which charcoal burner and lumberman followed by fire have inflicted upon the woods." Ironically, the 1903 fires swept along the railroad to Axton, burning the college's lands and leveling its lumber camps. The fire threatened Tupper Lake Village and destroyed thousands of cords of wood piled near Brooklyn Cooperage Co.'s mill.

Logging began nearest the existing railhead, on the northern portion of the tract. The proximity of the logging to Upper Saranac Lake alarmed the lake's wealthy estate owners. The loggers quickly denuded the area and it looked every bit as bad as any commercial logging operation of the day. The landowners tried to overturn the title to the experimental forest tract. Lieutenant-Governor Woodruff testified at a public hearing that he, as a member of the Forest Preserve Board when the tract was bought, never considered that "denudation" had been contemplated by the legislature. The Forest Preserve Board decried the cutting. An appeal to the State's attorney general, however, left Cornell on firm legal ground.[59]

Fernow's utilitarian approach did not help matters. Whereas he had expected to market sufficient hardwoods to pay for the improvements on the tract,[60] he now declared that forestry "is engaged in utilizing the soil for the production of wood crops, and thereby of the highest revenue obtainable."[61] In practice, he was cutting so much so as to earn enough money to maintain the experimental station.

A Special Committee of the Legislature made a brief tour of the Adirondacks during the summer of 1901, focusing their attention on the Tupper Lake area, where they heard complaints "deprecating the destruction of the forest on the tract." The committee concluded, after talking to Fernow, that "the college has exceeded the original intention of the State when the tract was granted the university for conducting silvicultural experiments."[62] A second Legislative committee examined the tract in 1902 and concluded, "We deeply regret that our careful investigation of the experiment leaves us unable to approve of what has been done and obliged to condemn both present and prospective results."[63]

Fernow was no politician; he "alienated nearly everyone in sight on the political horizon,"[64] including the newly elected Governor Odell, who in 1903 vetoed the annual appropriation for the College of Forestry. Cornell did not try to replace the funds from private sources, so the College of Forestry ceased to exist.

The fact that there was no longer a manager of the Axton project left unanswered many questions about the status of the experimental forest as well as those concerning the status of Brooklyn Cooperage Co. as a private manager of state lands. Litigation concerning Brooklyn Cooperage Co.'s right to continue harvesting hardwoods from the tract dragged on for a decade. In the end, Cornell's operation of the experimental forest was not declared unconstitutional, although legitimizing its existence retroactively did nothing to revive it. Later appeals questioned whether Fernow's approach had been appropriate and although the State Supreme Court held that the initial permit allowed the clearing of the land, that court ruled that Brooklyn Cooperage Co. could not continue logging.

Unanswered in all the controversy were questions about what scientific forestry methods were appropriate. Less that fifteen years later a professor at Yale School of Forestry concluded that Fernow was wrong because "in mixed forests satisfactory softwood reproduction cannot be secured after cutting except by means of planting." However, the plantations were a different matter: "There is no better vindication of Dr. Fernow's policy than the present condition of the logged-off areas near Wawbeek. All plantations, made under twelve different [experimental] conditions, have proved entirely successful."[65] Like many of the reforestations made early in this century, the forest at Wawbeek, with its hiking and ski-touring trails, is a beautiful addition to the Forest Preserve.

# Bibliographic Essay

Because this book was written to refute the many misconceptions about logging in the Adirondacks in the nineteenth century that exist in today's literature, research for it relied primarily on known statistical information. The New York State Census for the years 1820, 1835, 1845, 1855, 1865, and 1875 provide population and industrial information. Records of all the individual lumber mills and paper mills, given in the United States Census of Manufactures for the years 1850, 1860, 1870 and 1880, give raw material and production details that were tabulated by town and county. To these totals were added information available in the reports of the New York State Forest Commission and its successor agencies. For the years 1890 to 1910, they are a particularly rich and detailed account of forest use in the Adirondacks.

As Adirondack logging declined, shifting to other parts of the country, and as logging in the rest of the State increased through farmland returning to forest, State tallies shifted from its Adirondack focus to State-wide reports. Statistics relating to pulp and paper became spotty and inconsistent, with no clear picture of how much pulp was actually produced in the Adirondack region and how much was imported from elsewhere. To bring the analysis forward from 1910, records of the Empire State Forest Products Association provide some of the missing data.

*Lumber Camp News*, edited by Frank A. Reed, began publication in 1939. It was called *Northern Logger* briefly in 1952, then renamed *Northeastern Logger* that same year. Its issues contain invaluable accounts of the amount of logging, insight into World War II problems in the industry, and background on almost every logging operation, lumber mill, and pulp and paper company in the region. Historical articles trace the origin of the principal companies and form the basis of the company and tract profiles in the Appendix. Its anecdotes on logging operations from 1939 to 1960 include tallies of logs harvested and these were totaled to complete the harvest picture through 1960.

Over the years, *Lumber Camp News* and its successor traced the development of most of the innovations in machinery and transportation in the Adirondacks. These articles form the basis of those discussions in this book.

As the Adirondack lumber industry shrank, the magazine expanded to cover the entire northeast. The magazine's shifting focus is a most telling indication of the Adirondacks' declining role in the wood products industry.

General industry information and particular company backgrounds are found in the vertical files and collections of the Adirondack Museum and of the libraries at both Cornell University and the State University of New York, College of Environmental Sciences and Forestry at Syracuse. Particularly helpful were numerous graduate students' reports, theses, and dissertations from these libraries.

Here also, the shifting pattern of research subjects reflects the industry's evolution. Initially, almost all papers dealt with the regrowth of spruce and its diseases and problems. Questions of how to harvest for more spruce were debated. Then, quite suddenly, the realization that spruce was almost gone turned researchers to discovering just how much might be left. This was followed by a shift to broader industry perspectives--those outside the immediate region. Finally, scientific research replaced studies on practical aspects of forestry. Buried in the larger themes are bits and pieces of information on almost all the companies in the industry. Forest conditions and evolution have been the subject of a number of recent papers, representing a new depth of research; the seminal papers and researchers have been quoted.

Among the more valuable archival papers at Mann Library were the bound pamphlets of the Pettis Collection. The Kroch Library has Bernhard E. Fernow's papers and a collection of documents from the Empire State Forest Products Association.

The Adirondack Museum's collections include the records of a number of companies: Santa Clara Lumber Co., Emporium Lumber Co., and Gould Paper Co. The land holdings of William West Durant are available in ledgers and maps.

John Stock, forester for Litchfield Park, and Tim Schlechter, Vice-president of Whitney Industries, have information on their respective tracts. Richard Nason of Finch, Pruyn Co. has files on that company's history as well as all the records covering the almost century-long operation of the Hudson River Boom Association (the Big Boom Association).

The history of logging in the Hudson River watershed is well-documented in regional histories. Books have been written on the Tupper Lake region and the St. Regis Lumber Company. Newspaper accounts from the *Boonville Herald* and the *Watertown Times* supplemented local histories on logging in the Black River watershed.

Research on other industries dependent on Adirondack forests has varied with the available sources. My own history of the tanning industry details how much of the forest was cut for bark and where and how much hemlock remained when the industry disappeared from the Adirondacks by 1890. The amount of clearing for agriculture can be extrapolated from census records for cleared land. Several doctoral dissertations describe facets of the iron industry, but none are specific on the amount of wood cut for charcoal and where it was harvested. This has to be inferred from the theses and from published statistics of the industry.

Background on railroads is found in a number of well-researched histories, which have been cited in the text. While they do document railroads designed for the logging industry, they do not relate their impact on the forest.

Tracing the effects of political history on the forest begins, of course, with the annual reports of the Forest Commission, the Fisheries, Game and Forest Commission, the Forest, Fish and Game Commission, and the Conservation Department. Early records of the Land Office are housed in the Office of General Services in Albany. Later ledgers and printed records of the Land Office are found in the Real Property Office of the New York State Department of Environmental Conservation in Albany. That office also has the reports of the Forest Preserve Board and ledgers detailing all trespasses on State land.

The State Engineer and Surveyor's reports, laws affecting the Forest Preserve, and numerous Attorney Generals' opinions complete the record.

Supplementing these formal agency records are a number of legislative hearings and the reports of special commissions. Assembly Hearings during the 1890s and early 1900s make fascinating reading; they make the actions of the legislature and the commissions seem remarkably fresh and exciting and convey a real sense of the period's turmoil. The 1891 Assembly Committee Report of its hearings is particularly enlightening with respect to State policies and problems. The 1910 Moreland Commission Report and its Abstract give much history of the problems of early land acquisition. (That report also contains details of the condition of particular parcels purchased by the State.)

The New York State Archives houses a collection of records from the Comptroller's Office and the Department of Taxation and Finance. The file containing letters from agents appointed to serve notice on illegal occupants of State lands, 1881-1893, to the Comptroller's Office, offers an invaluable and never before published account of how the State began to protect its lands. These led to an acquaintance with one of the more colorful agents, John B. Koetteritz, who is today almost unknown, even within the Department of Environmental Conservation.

Accounts of unpaid taxes on non-resident lands and registers of bids and payments for non-resident lands exist in mind-numbing completeness. They were briefly consulted with respect to limited geographical areas. The records are so voluminous as to make synthesizing them difficult; however, it is suggested that they could be used as the basis of a study of nineteenth-century tax policies and further investigation of the relation of tax policies to the creation of the Forest Preserve.

The Proceedings of the Albany Institute contain the speech by Lemon Thomson.

Forestry magazines are a major resource. They were culled for all articles pertaining to the Adirondacks; the *Journal of Forestry* summarized almost all of the works of early foresters. *Garden and Forest* had a series of articles, almost all written by Charles Sprague Sargent, that urged the formation of the Forest Preserve and the Adirondack Park. These familiar environmental writings stand in sharp contrast to the little known Assembly hearing records, which give the other side of the drama and conflict of the time. Among the most useful of newspaper articles were those of the *Boonville Herald*, which were especially valuable in filling in the logging history of western Adirondacks.

Finding what foresters thought about the Forest Preserve was easy, discovering what lumbermen thought proved difficult. A speech by Lemon Thomson before the Albany Institute proved seminal and focused my search through different hearings on his testimonies. The Moreland Commission's spotlight on George N. Ostrander similarly focused research on him, although his persona remains illusive. Biographical writings exist for such men as Gould and Basselin. Among the material that is still missing, I feel most deeply the inability to discover additional details on the lives of Ostrander, Thomson, Moynehan, and other lumbermen who profited from the Great Forest.

# Footnotes

## Chapter I

1 The map was created in 1884 for the *Sargent Commission*. See details in Chapter VI.

## Chapter II

1 New York State Climatological Records, *Maps of the State of New York Showing Total Precipitation for 1895, 1903, 1904, and 1908* Northeast Regional Climate Center, Cornell University, NY.

2 Edwin H. Ketchledge, Ph. D., "An Interpretation of the Adirondack Landscape" (Paper delivered at the Fall Symposium of the Association for the Protection of the Adirondacks, Keene Valley, NY, 1989).

3 The summary of post-glacial vegetation and the chart showing the advance of species after glacial recession are based on: Stephen T. Jackson, "Late-Glacial and Holocene Vegetational Changes in the Adirondack Mountain: A Macrofossil Study" (Ph. D. diss., Indiana University, 1983); Stephen T. Jackson, *Postglacial Vegetational Changes along an Elevational Gradient in the Adirondack Mountains*, New York State Museum Bulletin No. 465 (Albany: University of the State of New York, 1989); Donald R. Whitehead and Stephen T. Jackson, *The Regional Vegetational History of the High Peaks*, New York State Museum Bulletin No. 478 (Albany: University of the State of New York, 1990); Donald J. Leopold, Carol Reschke, and Daniel S. Smith, "Old-Growth Forests of Adirondack Park, New York," *Natural Areas Journal*, 8, no. 3 (1988): 166-188.

4 Conversations with Charles Cogbill, expert on spruce in the northeastern United States. He defines old growth to mean a forest where the average age of the trees over six inches in diameter of all species present is at least half the life expectancy of the species.

5 F. H. Eyre, ed., *Forest Cover Types of the United States and Canada* (Washington: Society of American Foresters, 1980).

6 This phrase was first used by Verplanck Colvin.

7 Forest, Fish and Game Commission, *Sixth Annual Report* for 1900 (Albany: J. B. Lyon Co., 1901), 239-240.

8 William F. Fox, *The Adirondack Black Spruce* (Albany: J. B. Lyon Printer, 1895); Nathaniel Wheeler Coffin, *The Forest Arcadia* (Boston: T. O. H. P. Burnham, 1864).

9 Forest, Fish and Game Commission, *Sixth Annual Report*, 239-240.

## Chapter III

1 The descriptions of the patent, tracts, and purchases are taken from the *Annual Report of the Forest Commission for the Year 1893*, Vol. I (Albany: J. B. Lyon Co., 1894), 73-149.

## Chapter IV

1 To make these computations from the 1855 Census, some estimating was needed because of the number of towns with acreage both in and outside the Park. There is no real way of knowing how much of the cleared land in those split towns was actually inside the future Blue Line.

2 Ulysses Prentiss Hedrick, *A History of Agriculture in the State of New York* (New York: Hill and Wang, 1933), 140.

3 Floy S. Hyde, *Adirondack Forests, Fields, and Mines* (Lakemont, NY: North Country Books, 1974), 106-108.

4 Sackets Harbor, the town and the proposed railroad to it were originally spelled with one t, although the battlefield is spelled Sacketts.

5 Hedrick, *Agriculture*, 140.

6 Franklin B. Hough, *Report Upon Forestry* (Washington: Government Printing Office,1878), 440. Hough reported a steam mills in Glens Falls and along the Champlain Canal in 1877.

7 Frank A. Reed, *et al.*, "Early Lumbering in New York," *Northern Logger*, April 1964, 62.

8 *Ibid.*, 63.

9 The only statistical records found come from the 1820 Census, which gives the number of pine logs sawn. The author could find no records of the shipment of logs.

10 William F. Fox, *History of the Lumber Industry in New York State.* 1901. Reprint. Harrison, NY: Harbor Hill Books, 1976, 28.

11 This calculation assumes the logs were standards and that an acre could produce 15 standards. Standards are defined in Chapter V.

12 Fox, *Lumber Industry*, 35-36. H. P. Smith, *History of Warren County* (Syracuse: D. Mason and Co., 1885), 621. Smith attributes the beginning of this form of river driving to Abraham Wing III, grandson of the founder of Glens Falls, who was also instrumental in the formation of the Hudson River Boom Association.

13 The 1820 Census lists two gang mills in the Town of Northumberland, Saratoga County, with 20 and 22 saws. This information appears to predate the mills reported by Fox, 58ff.

## Chapter V

1 The map was compiled by A. Robeson and printed by Julius Bien & Co., NY.

2 Charles S. Sargent, *Report on the Forests of North America* (Washington: Tenth Census of the United States, Vol. 9, 1884), 501-505. The account of forest conditions in the Adirondacks also confirms the fact that most logging on the Raquette before 1884 was along its downstream portions.

3 Forest Commission, *Fifth Annual Report* for 1890 (Albany: J. B. Lyon Co., 1891), 109; see Chapter VI for discussion of the Forest Commission.

4 Barbara McMartin, *Hides, Hemlocks and Adirondack History* (Utica, NY: North Country Books, 1992).

5 John Richard Moravek, *The Iron Industry as a Geographic Force in the Adirondack-Champlain Region of New York State, 1800-1871*, (Ph. D. diss., University of Tennessee, 1976), 1-3.

6 Bruce E. Seely, "Blast Furnace Technology in the Mid-19th Century," *Industrial Archeology*, n.d., 27-49.

7 "Iron Making in Northern New York-Catalan Forges," *Bulletin of the American Iron and Steel Association*, 9 (August 20, 1875): 250.

8 Moravek, *Iron Industry*, 108.

9 This figure is widely quoted in the literature and was confirmed by the author by computations from census reports.

10 William G. Neilson, *Charcoal Blast Furnaces, Rolling Mills, Forges and Steel Works of New York in 1867* (n.d.: The American Iron and Steel Association, 1867). Statistics for 1864 are taken from this document.

11 Carlin Walker, "Bessboro Beginnings," *Valley News*, September 2, 1987.

12 J. R. Linney, "A Century and a Half of Development Behind the Adirondack Mining Industry," *Mining and Metallurgy* (November 1943): 480-487.

13 Moravek, *Iron Industry*, 48-49.

## Chapter V continued

14 Neilson, 259-264. Of the total 132 forge fires listed, only 112 were being used in 1864.

15 *Essex County Republican*, August 25, 1870, 3.

16 Moravek, *Iron Industry*, 116.

17 Linney, 483.

18 E. A. Sterling, "Forest Management on the Delaware and Hudson Adirondack Forest," *Journal of Forestry* 30 (May 1932): 569-574.

19 Ross F. Allen, James C. Dawson, Morris F. Glenn, *et al.* "An Archaeological Survey of Bloomery Forges in the Adirondacks," *Industrial Archeology* 16, no. 1 (1990): 3.

20 "Circumnavigating the Adirondacks," *Forest and Stream*, August 27, 1891, 104-105.

21 Forest Commission, *Annual Report* for 1891 (Albany: J. B. Lyon Co., 1892), 162.

22 *Ibid.*, 169.

23 It should be noted that even after coke became the source of fuel for making iron, the region continued to export modest amounts of charcoal. Perkins Coville, "Silvicultural Problems in Management of Forests of Adirondack Hardwood Type" (M. A. thesis, Cornell University, 1920), 6.

24 Henry S. Graves, *Practical Forestry in the Adirondacks*, U. S. Dept. of Agriculture, Division of Forestry, Bulletin No. 26 (Washington: Government Printing Office, 1899); see also Gifford Pinchot, *The Adirondack Spruce* (New York: Critic Co., 1898).

25 Fox, *Black Spruce*, 13.

26 Sargent, *Forests of North America*, 503. By the 1880s, logs were being driven down streams so small, steep and rocky that they came down with their ends badly battered and often filled with gravel and fragments of rock. They had to be 'butted' or cut at the ends to protect saws and still provide the standard 13-foot log.

27 *Ibid.*, 79.

28 Fox, *Lumber Industry*, 57. "Logs are all measured, and in counting them each log is reckoned according to the ratio that the square of its diameter bears to the square of the diameter of the standard or nineteen-inch log. This is obtained by dividing the square of the diameter of each log by the square of the diameter of the standard." On the Saranac River, lumbermen used a 22-inch diameter as standard.

29 *Ibid.*, 58.

30 *Testimony Taken Before the Assembly Committee on Public Lands and Forestry Concerning the Administration of the Laws in Relation to the Forest Preserve by the Forest Commission, Etc.* (Albany: J. B. Lyon Co., 1891), 413. [Hereafter 1891 Hearings.]

31 Most early accounts hyphenate the name: Ne-ha-sa-ne.

32 Pinchot, *The Adirondack Spruce* (New York: Critic Co., 1898).

33 Graves, *Practical Forestry*, 29.

34 *Ibid.*, 30.

35 State Engineer and Surveyor, *Annual Report for 1884*, (Albany: 1885), 26.

36 T. C. Hennessey, P. M. Dougherty, C. G. Tauer, "Forest Decline: Assessing Impacts of a Changing Environment on Forest Productivity," *Tree Physiology* 3 (March 1987): 37.

37 Arthur H. Johnson and Thomas G. Siccama, "Acid Deposition and Forest Decline," *Environmental Science and Technology*, 17, no. 7 (1983): 304A.

38 Forest Commission, *Annual Report* for 1891, 203.

39 Fox, *Black Spruce*, 12.

40 Verplanck Colvin, *Report on the Topographical Survey of the Adirondack Wilderness of New York for the Year 1873* (Albany: Weed, Parsons and Co., 1874), 270.

41 Franklin B. Hough, *Report upon Forestry 1877*, (Washington: Government Printing Office, 1878), 162-163.

42 This yield is roughly two-thirds the oft-quoted standard of fifteen markets per acre.

43 Sargent Commission Hearings, *Proceedings before the Forestry Commission at Saratoga Springs, NY*, July 23, 1884, 72. Typescript, Adirondack Museum Library. [Hereafter Sargent Commission Hearings].

44 Forest Preserve Board, *Second Annual Report* (Albany: Brandow Printing Co., 1899), 52-53.

45 Philip G. Terrie, *Wildlife and Wilderness* (Fleischmanns, NY: Purple Mountain Press, 1993), 55.

46 Duncan McMartin, Jr. "Field notes for Oxbow Survey," 1830, Survey for lots 252-256, manuscript and microfilm, NYS Archives, Albany.

47 Albert Fowler, *Cranberry Lake from Wilderness to Adirondack Park* (Syracuse, NY: Syracuse University Press, 1968), 19-34.

48 Verplanck Colvin, Adirondack Survey Notebook no. 295 for 1879, 67, Real Property Office, DEC, Albany; *State Land Survey* for 1883, Twelfth Report (Albany: Weed, Parsons and Co., 1884), 145.

49 Forest Commission, *Annual Report* for 1891, 114.

50 Graves, *Practical Forestry*, 28.

51 The Ely map of 1867 and the Stoddard map of 1874 showed approximate locations of roads, lakes, rivers, and larger streams. Neither gives a real indication of the topography of the land and neither shows tracts, patents and lots. The first to show the some of the latter is the B. C. Butler map of 1879, entitled *New York Wilderness, Hamilton County and Adjoining Territory*, which also gives a fair approximation of natural features. However, it, along with the 1884 Sargent Commission map, was considered inadequate by the Forest Commission, which commissioned the Koetteritz map. See Chapter VI.

52 *The Lumber Trade of Albany: Its History and Extent* (Albany: Argus Co., 1872).

53 *Ibid.*, 40.

54 Hough, *Forestry*, 442ff.

55 The counties are grouped according to districts that are used in later Forest Commission reports so that the results will be comparable with data from these later dates. Only those townships are included in the county figures that are in the Park or would have derived lumber for milling from the Park.

56 Laws of 1849, Chapter 406. Forest Commission, *Annual Report* for 1893, vol. 2 (Albany: J. B. Lyon Co., 1894), 128-9.

57 The Raquette was variously spelled Racket and Rackett in nineteenth-century legislation.

58 Forest Commission, *Report for 1893*, vol. 2, 85.

59 *Ibid.*, 89-05.

60 Fisheries, Game and Forest Commission, *Second Annual Report*, 1896 (Albany: Wynkoop, Hallenbeck, Crawford Co., 1897), 385. Testimony in the Webb lawsuit.

61 Records of the Hudson River Boom Association are in the custody of Richard Nason of Finch, Pruyn and Co. He has shared yearly data showing the amount of logs in the river for more than one year.

62 Fisheries, Game and Forest Commission, *Second Report*, 396.

63 Fox, *Lumber Industry*, 40.

64 The source is "A Relative Comparison of Logging Methods," a series of articles sent to H. P. Gould, Lyons Falls, NY, by H. A. Maine in July 1922. Another copy was sent to the Ranger School at Wanakena, NY. Whether these articles were written by Maine or his brother is unclear, but the author did spend time in logging camps in the southern and southwestern Adirondacks in the early part of this century. Gould Paper Co. Papers, AM Library.

## Chapter V continued

65 *Ibid.*, 22.

66 J. S. Bulkeley, *Leading Industrial Pursuits* (Ballston, NY: Waterbury and Inman, 1877; Glens Falls: Chapman Historical Museum, 1982), 9.

67 Hudson River Boom Association, *Articles of Agreement*, 1862, AM Library.

68 Bulkeley, *Pursuits*, 14.

69 *Ibid.*

70 Information on the Glens Falls' mills and the chart are from Bulkeley's *Leading Industrial Pursuits*.

71 A mulay saw was a variation on the up and down saw patented by Israel Johnson of the Town of Moriah in 1826. Roger Mitchell, *Clear Pond* (Syracuse: Syracuse University Press, 1991), 110-111.

72 State Engineer and Surveyor, *Annual Report for 1888* (Albany, 1889), 17.

73 Watson B. Berry, "Early Logging Days on the Black River," *Farm and Garden*, February 4, 1956 and December 31, 1955.

74 State Engineer and Surveyor, *Annual Report for 1889* (Albany, 1890), 20-21. Similar remarks appear in the *Annual Report* for 1884.

75 State Engineer and Surveyor, *Annual Report for 1884*, 17-25 details evidence of lower levels of canal waters in 1834-36, 1841, 1850, 1858, 1861, 1865, and 1867, all caused by local droughts.

76 *Ibid.*, 15.

77 *Boonville Herald*, May 22, 1879.

78 State Engineer and Surveyor, *Annual Report for 1898* (Albany, 1898), 526.

79 Sargent Committee Hearings, 28.

80 1891 Hearings, 68, 71.

81 *Ibid.*, 376.

82 The exceptions were Townships 9 and 26, Totten and Crossfield purchase.

83 This figure has been calculated from the Census of Manufactures and from Forest Commission reports.

84 State Engineer and Surveyor, *Annual Report for 1884*, 26.

85 1891 Hearings, 376.

86 Craig Gilborn, *Durant* (Sylvan Beach, NY: North Country Books, 1981), 10.

87 Printed property lists (Adirondack Museum Library) confirm that Durant owned 658,245 acres directly or through interconnected companies or through joint ownership. Unfortunately, this list is undated and untitled, but it does contain all of the lots given on a second list which totals 394,598 acres and which is entitled "Adirondack Railway Company Lands, 1887." It may be that Durant used the smaller list to minimize his holdings when sued by his sister for her share of their father's estate. It is more likely that the difference represents land acquired through tax sales by the Adirondack Co. Records of these bids may be found in Land Office Minutes, vol. 15 at the Office of General Services, Albany.. Also at the Museum is a presentation copy of the Butler map which its maker gave to Durant, who colored in the townships he owned. The map reflects tracts totaling the larger acreage.

88 1891 Hearings, 104-106.

89 Richard Nason of Finch, Pruyn and Co. believes the company owned about 35,000 acres in 1890; he questions the larger figure, which nevertheless was taken from tax records.

90 1891 Hearings, 600.

## Chapter VI

1 The Forest Preserve amendment adopted in 1894 and signed by the governor in 1895 was identified as Article VII, Section 7 of the State Constitution. It was renumbered during the Constitutional Convention of 1938, but not changed. For simplicity, it will be referred to as Article XIV, as it is most commonly known today.

2 Forest Commission, *Annual Report for 1891* (Albany: J. B. Lyon Co., 1892), 115

3 Forest Preserve Board, *First Annual Report*, (Albany, NY: Brandow Printing Co., 1898), 5.

4 Laws of 1890, Chapter 8.

5 VanValkenburgh, Graham, *et al.*

6 Commissioners of State Parks, *First Annual Report*, May 15, 1873 (Albany: Weed, Parsons and Co., 1874).

7 Franklin B. Hough speech, quoted by Edna L. Jacobsen, "Franklin B. Hough," *New York History*, 15, no. 3 (July 1934).

8 Commissioners of State Parks, *First Annual Report*, 12.

9 Special Assembly Committee, *Investigation as to what Lands Should be Acquired within the Forest Preserve in order to Protect the Watershed*, Assembly Doc. 47, February 15, 1897, 106, 133.

10 Lemon Thomson, *An Address before the Albany Institute on the Adirondack Wilderness*, March 18, 1884 (Albany: Weed, Parsons and Co., 1884), 15.

11 *Ibid.*, 16-17.

12 1891 Hearings, 68, 71.

13 Sargent Committee Hearings, 62.

14 *Ibid.*, 50.

15 Thomson, *Adirondack Wilderness*, 17.

16 Only a small acreage of land was acquired through mortgage default.

17 Norman J. VanValkenburgh, *The Adirondack Forest Preserve* (Blue Mountain Lake, NY: Adirondack Museum, 1979), 303.

18 Conservation Commission, *List of Lands in the Forest Preserve* (Albany: J. B. Lyon Co., 1920).

19 Colvin, *Report* (1884), 28.

20 Special Assembly Committee, Doc. 47, February 15, 1897, 43.

21 Colvin, *Report* (1884), 30.

22 *Ibid.*, 112.

23 *Ibid.*, 19.

24 Verplanck Colvin, *Seventh Annual Report, Topographical Survey of Adirondack Region of New York to Year 1879* (Albany: Weed, Parsons and Co., 1880), 141.

25 Land Office, *Minutes*: Book 14, 1864-1869; Book 15, 1870-75; Book 16, 1876-1884, Office of General Services, Albany.

26 Lot 34, Township 27, Totten and Crossfield.

27 Land Office, *Minutes*: Book 16, January 1877 Meeting, Office of General Services, Albany.

28 Lots 23 and 24, Schroon Tract, *Land Office Minutes*, Book 16, 541. These 160-acre lots each cost the State $305.05 in 1877, and were assessed at $900 in 1878.

29 Thomson, *Adirondack Wilderness*, 11-18.

30 John R. Curry, *A Study of the Growth of Spruce and Balsam in the Adirondacks* (M. A. thesis, Cornell University, 1924). This paper summarizes the study done by A. B. Recknagel of Cornell and H. L. Churchill, forester for Finch, Pruyn and Co. of growth statistics on a 19,000-acre tract owned by that company.

31 1891 Hearings, testimony by Theodore B. Basselin, 161.

32 George Leavitt, letter to Comptroller, November 25, 1882, Comptroller's Office Records, Box 21, Letters from Agents, NYSA. Another Leavitt letter, June 4, 1883, concerns his

# Chapter VI continued

appraisal of the Tefft Tract and notes it had never been cut. Further letters attest to the fact it was never logged and describe the way agents kept thieves from this lot. While not easy to find, this information is typical of the history of particular lots. Leavitt appraised lots in the interior of Oxbow and Benson tracts and noted that many had good stands of spruce, "were well-timbered but quite a distance to where it can be floated."

33 Leavitt, letter. to Comptroller, March 24, 1882, NYSA.

34 Koetteritz was employed by Alfred Dolge to stop trespass on the Jerseyfield Tract. It appears that Koetteritz reported a wrongdoing on the part of Dolge and expected to lose his "best customer" as a result. Letter to the Comptroller, May 11, 1884.

35 Leavitt letter, March 24, 1882.

36 Verplanck Colvin, Adirondack Survey, Annual Report for 1883 (Albany: Argus Co., 1884) 33.

37 Obituary, John B. Koetteritz, *Little Falls Evening Times*, March 12, 1928.

38 All quoted Koetteritz letters are in the Comptroller's Office Records, Box 21, Letters from Agents, NYSA.

39 Koetteritz, letter to Ira M. Davenport, Comptroller, June 1, 1883.

40 Koetteritz, letter to Comptroller, March 14, 1884.

41 E. G. Stokes, letter to Comptroller T. E. Benedict, Jan. 1, 1886 NYSA.

42 Koetteritz, comp., "Catalogue of Maps, Field-notes, Surveys, and Landpapers of Patents, Grants, and Tracts Situate Within the Counties Embracing the Forest Preserve of the State of New York," in Forest Commission, *Annual Report for 1890* (Albany: J. B. Lyon, Co., 1891), 165-315.

43 *Ibid.*, 1890, 165.

44 J. B. Burnham, "Errors in the Official Map," *Forest and Stream*, October 22, 1898, 523.

45 Norman J. VanValkenburgh, *Land Acquisition for New York State* (Arkville, NY: Catskill Center, 1885), 14.

46 Commissioners of the Land Office, *First Annual Report for 1884* (Albany: Weed, Parsons and Co., 1884), 4. The Commissioners were a distinguished group: the Lieutenant Governor, Speaker of the Assembly, Secretary of State, Comptroller, Treasurer, Attorney General, and State Engineer and Surveyor.

47 This involved land that had been bid in by the State for taxes in 1871 and subsequent years, but for which the title was questioned; the State did not obtain a clear title until the Webb purchase of 1896-97.

48 Sargent Committee, *Assembly Report*, Doc. 36, January 23, 1885, 11.

49 Thomson, *Adirondack Wilderness*, 14. The writer of Thomson's obituary characterized this speech as one of the "ablest papers read before that body," and noted that Thomson was "especially well posted in the history of lumbering and was an expert in the study of forestry." *Albany Journal*, undated clipping supplied by Winthrop Aldrich.

50 *Ibid.*, 18.

51 1891 Hearings, passim.

52 *Ibid.*, 387.

53 Forest Commission, Records of Trespass, Ledger, Real Property Office, Department of Environmental Conservation, Albany.

54 1891 Hearings, 113-114.

55 Records of Trespass, 236-259.

56 Special Assembly Committee, *Report to Conduct an Investigation as to What Lands Should be Acquired Within the Forest Preserve, in Order to Protect the Watershed,* Doc. 46, February 15, 1897, 136.

The repeated remarks about the paucity of pine in the heart of the Adirondacks make it appear that pine was always really rare in that area.

57 Records of Trespass, 169, describes a trial in which the jury disagreed with the fine imposed for the theft of fiddlebutts.

58 1891 Hearings, 298.

59 *Ibid.*, 590, testimony of a deputy comptroller..

60 *Ibid.*, 424.

61 *Ibid.*, 434-5.

62 *Ibid.*, 34ff.

63 *Ibid.*, 95.

64 *Ibid.*, 348.

65 *Ibid.*, 143-151.

66 *Ibid.*, 16.

67 *Ibid.*, 402-403.

68 *Ibid.*, testimony by Basselin and others.

69 *Ibid.*, 60.

70 Roswell P. Flower, *Message Relating to Preservation of Forests on State Lands*, Assembly Doc. 79, 1893.

71 Laws of 1892, Chapter 707. Its provisions for sale of land outside the Blue Line were consolidated in Chapter 332 of the Laws of 1893, which also created a five-man commission to replace the three-man commission.

72 Verplanck Colvin, *Topographical Survey of Adirondack Region*, Report for 1896 (Albany: Wynkoop, Hallenbeck, Crawford Co., 1897), 308.

73 Attorney General, *Opinion, Forest Commission, Timber Sales*, February 6, 1894.

74 Campbell W. Adams.

75 The American Forestry Association is the oldest, continuing conservation organization. It was founded in 1875 for the purpose of "protection of existing forests of the country from unnecessary waste." John A. Warder, a trained physician like Franklin B. Hough, was its first president. In the 1880s, the organization merged with the American Forestry Congress, which had been formed in 1882. Bernhard E. Fernow drafted the constitution of the joint organization. William G. Robbins, *American Forestry* (Lincoln: University of Nebraska Press, 1985), 4-6.

76 Land Office, *Records for 1894*, Real Property Office, DEC, 91.

77 *Ibid.*, 92.

78 *Ibid.*, 93.

79 *Ibid.*, 99.

80 Governor Flower noted in his 1894 message that "the standing spruce timber above twelve inches in diameter has already been sold on 17,468 acres of State land." No records of those sales have been found in Land Office Minutes.

81 Forest, Fish and Game Commission, *Eighth and Ninth Reports, 1902 and 1903* (Albany: J. B. Lyon Co. 1894), 383. "The forest on these townships has, with the exception of a few very limited areas, never been cut over."

82 Land Office, *Records for 1895*, 237; VanValkenburgh, *Land Acquisition*, 35.

83 Fisheries, Game and Forest Commission, *Second Annual Report for 1896* (Albany: Wynkoop, Hallenbeck, Crawford Co., 1897), 130.

84 Assembly Committee, *Report of 1895 Committee to investigate certain depredations on Adirondack Timber lands*, Assembly Doc. 60, February 27, 1896.

85 Records of Trespass for 1894, Real Property Office, DEC.

86 Assembly Committee, *Report on 1895 Committee to investigate certain depredations on Adirondack Timber lands*, Assembly Doc. 60, February 27, 1896, 21.

## Chapter VI continued

87 Verplanck Colvin, *Topographical Survey of the Adirondack Region, Report for 1895*, (Albany: Wynkoop, Hallenbeck, Crawford, Co., 1896), 18.

88 Amendment to the Revised Statutes, May 7, 1889, as reported in Treadwell Cleveland, Jr. "The Forest Laws of New York," *Forester* 7 (April 1901): 81-85.

89 "The Plunder of the Adirondack Reservation," *Garden and Forest*, March 11, 1896, 101-102.

90 1895 Assembly Committee, 8.

91 Special Committee of Assembly, *Report on Lands to be Acquired to Protect Watersheds* (Albany: Wynkoop, Hallenbeck, Crawford Co., 1898), 19.

92 Laws of 1885, Chapter 448.

93 "Moreland Commission Report, 1910," unpublished microfilm copy of typescript, title page missing, NYS Library, Albany, *passim*. [Hereafter 1910 Moreland].

94 1891 Hearings, 162.

95 Attorney General, *Report for 1897*, "Supreme Court of the United States, No. 41, October Term 1897," 12-16, 404-408.

96 Fisheries, Game and Forest Commission, *Second Annual Report*, for 1896, 131.

97 Assembly Hearing, 1896, 372.

98 *Ibid.*, 373.

99 Forest Preserve Board, *First Annual Report* (Albany: Brandow Printing Co., 1898), 5-7. The Forest Preserve Board consisted of Lieutenant Governor Timothy L. Woodruff; Fisheries, Game and Forest Commissioner Charles K. Babcock; and State Engineer and Surveyor Campbell W. Adams.

100 Sales were completed on 69,380 acres at a cost of $249,903.

101 Webb sold the softwood timber on Township 8, Brown's Tract to Thomson and Dix for $6.00 an acre. This sale was for the trees only (technically for the "stumpage") and only those greater than 10" in diameter.

102 Forest Preserve Board, *First Annual Report*, 19.

103 These totals have been calculated from Forest Preserve Board reports and are based on the price paid for the land. Eliminated from the totals were tracts where it was later established (by Moreland Commission and other information) that inflated prices had been paid for the land, given its actual condition.

104 Forest Preserve Board, *Fourth Annual Report* (Albany: J. B. Lyon Co., 1906), 6.

105 *Ibid.*, 11-12.

106 The company was founded in 1899; its first president was R. K. Hawley. Chauncey Truax was later named president.

107 1910 Moreland, 89.

108 *Ibid.,* 70.

109 *Ibid.*, 93.

110 Raymond S. Spears, "Adirondack Timber Thefts," *Forest and Stream*, April 4, 1908; "Adirondack Timber Stealing," February 8, 1908, 219.

111 Special Assembly Committee, February 15, 1897, 154-155.

112 1910 Moreland, 50.

113 *Ibid.*, 130.

114 *Ibid.*, 162.

115 The rights to cut for ten years the spruce greater than 8", pine greater than 10".

116 With John Anderson, Jr. and Albert Newcombe.

117 1910 Moreland, 231-233.

118 *Ibid.*, 181ff.

119 *Ibid.*, 188.

120 Moose River Tract Township 9, lots 121, 123.

121 Roger C. Thompson, "The Doctrine of Wilderness: A Study of the Policy and Politics of the Adirondack Preserve-Park" (Ph. D. diss., State University College of Forestry at Syracuse, 1962). Thompson shows that principal land speculators sold the State 300,000 of the 800,000 acres purchased by the State between 1892 and 1909. By tying Ostrander to Harris and to the other companies where Ostrander was a principal, the estimate of between 400,000 and 500,000 acres becomes plausible.

122 Testimony in Marsh and Ostrander vs. Nehasane Park Association, 1895, 41, AM Library.

123 1910 Moreland Commission, *Abstract of Report of Commissioners Roger P. Clark and H. Leroy Austin, Appointed on February 16, 1910, by Governor Hughes to Investigate the Management and Affairs of the Forest, Fish and Game Commission* (for publication October 5, 1910), 36. [Hereafter Moreland *Abstract*].

124 1910 Moreland, 132.

125 *Ibid.*, 33.

126 Moreland *Abstract*, 11. Whipple and B. H. Davis acquired "an interest in iron ore deposits in Cayuga County. Among those who subscribed for stock were George R. Ostrander, George R. Finch and Walter C. Witherbee, all operators in Adirondack timberlands; James B. Lyon, State Printer, several employees of the Forest, Fish and Game Commission, including Colonel William F. Fox."

127 Moreland *Abstract*, 47.

128 *Ibid.*, 32.

129 Forest Commission, *Special Assembly Report*, Doc. 22, January 16, 1894, 13.

130 Special Assembly Committee, *Report to Continue Investigation as to What Lands Should be Acquired Within the Forest Preserve in Order to Protect the Watersheds Therein*, March 31, 1898 (Albany: Wynkoop, Hallenbeck, Crawford Co., 1898), 6.

131 Moreland *Abstract*, 29.

132 1910 Moreland, 132.

133 To arrive at these numbers, an attempt was made to analyze all the large trespasses and to review all the published reports of forest conditions of land acquired by direct purchases. This was carried out as far as was logistically possible, well beyond what was needed to substantiate these assertions.

## Chapter VII

1 The Fourdrinnier had been patented in France by Nicholas Louis Robert. The patent was sold to Francois Didot who took the patent to England, where the first Fourdrinnier was erected in 1803.

2 George W. Rafter, *Hydrology of the State of New York*, New York State Museum Bulletin 85 (Albany: University of the State of New York, 1905), 868-869.

3 Although the process was used experimentally in 1854, it was little used in the Adirondacks until after 1910. Even then this process was employed sparingly, and produced only 10% of the region's pulp in 1920. Use of the process, which was primarily employed to make pulp from soft maple or poplar, gradually increased. Bernard Frank, "The Utilization of Beech, Birch, and Maple in the Pulp and Paper Industry of the Northeastern United States" (M. A. thesis, Cornell University, 1927).

4 Rafter, *Hydrology*, 686.

5 *Ibid.*

6 *Paper Trade Journal*, February 22, 1917.

7 The history of Adirondack paper making was taken from two very similar articles: Thomas Good, A.B. Recknagel, and Frank A. Reed, "The Growth of the Paper Industry in

## Chapter VII continued

Northern New York," *Northeastern Logger*, April 1964, 18-65. The second article has no author listed, but was presumably written by Reed, editor and publisher of *Northeastern Logger*. "Paper Making in Northern New York" was printed in the May 1956 issue, 18-19, 58-59.

8 Fisheries, Game and Forest Commission, Second Annual Report, (Albany: Winkoop, Hallenbeck, Crawford and Co., 1897) 342-3.

9 *Ibid.*, 387.

10 Henry Vettel, "The Location, Supply and Management of the Chief Pulpwood Species in the United States" (M. A. thesis, Cornell University, 19210.

11 Lee J. Vance, "Lumbering in the Adirondacks," *Godey's Magazine*, March 1896.

12 Stewart H. Holbrook, *Yankee Loggers* (New York: International Paper Company, 1961).

13 Louise A. Halper, "'A Rich Man's Paradise': Constitutional Preservation of New York State's Adirondack Forest, a Centenary Consideration," *Ecology Law Quarterly* (1992): 256.

14 This may explain in part the anomaly of the decline in sawmills in 1860, then the increase in 1870 that was noted in the earlier chapter.

15 Jacobsen, "Franklin B. Hough," 311-325.

16 *Ibid.*, 316.

17 Commissioners of State Parks, *First Annual Report*, 1874, 16.

18 Alfred Dolge, letter to Board of Trustees, Cornell University, April 5, 1898, R. S. Hosmer Papers, Cornell University Library.

19 Frank Graham, Jr., *The Adirondack Park* (New York: Alfred A. Knopf, 1978), 134.

20 R. H. Campbell, "An Adirondack Forest Experiment," *Journal of Forestry* 13 (1917): 1384-88. Campbell was impressed with the regrowth of Fernow's forests, concluding that removing hardwoods to encourage conifers was appropriate and that Fernow's plan of management was well justified.

21 Fox, *Black Spruce*, 1895, 79.

22 Graves, *Practical Forestry*, 15.

23 George S. Meagher and A. B. Recknagel, "The Growth of Spruce and Fir on the Whitney Park in the Adirondacks," *Journal of Forestry* 33 (May 1935): 499-502.

24 John R. Curry, "The Management of Whitney Park," *Northeastern Logger*, July 1957. He states that the original Whitney cut was only for "standard" trees, i.e. those 19" and over dbh. This may not be true.

25 Fox, *Black Spruce*, 78.

26 *Ibid.*, 79.

27 Edward F. McCarthy, "Observations on Unburned Cut-over Lands in the Adirondacks," speech delivered to the Society of American Foresters, January 22, 1919. *Journal of Forestry* (April 1919): 387.

28 Adirondack League Club, *Yearbook*, 1891, "Report of Professor B. E. Fernow," 50.

29 Special Assembly Committee, *Report*, Hearing of 1898 (Albany: Wynkoop, Hallenbeck, Crawford Co., 1898), 39.

30 Special Assembly Committee, *Report*, Hearing of 1896, Assembly Doc. 46, (Albany: Wynkoop, Hallenbeck, Crawford Co., 1897), 25.

31 Nelson A. Brown Scrapbook, *The Adirondack Hardwoods*, c. 1914, article unsourced, Cornell University Library.

32 Railroads, real and phantom, occupy a large part of Adirondack literature. Books by Allen, Donaldson, Harter, Hochschild, and Kudish have been used for the railroad summary presented here.

33 Thomas A. Rumney, *Post-Frontier Adjustment in Regional Settlement Structure* (Ph. D. diss., University of Maryland, 1980), 104.

34 "Railroads in the Adirondacks," *Garden and Forest*, June 10, 1891, 265.

35 Alfred L. Donaldson, *A History of the Adirondacks*, (New York: Century Co., 1921) vol. 2, 137.

36 "Adirondack Echoes," *Boonville Herald*, Oct. 2, 1890.

37 Donaldson, *History*, II, 138.

38 Henry A. Harter, *Fairytale Railroad* (Utica, NY: North Country Books, 1979). This wonderful account of the building of the railroad makes good reading, even for those who are not railroad buffs.

39 *Garden and Forest*, June 10, 1891, 266. The writer was undoubtedly the editor C. S. Sargent.

40 *New York Times*, May 27, 1891.

41 *Forest and Stream*, August 27, 1891.

42 A second narrow-gauge Adirondack railroad designed primarily to carry passengers was built from Moose River Settlement to Minnehaha on the Middle Branch of the Moose River, where passengers could board a steamer for Old Forge. This "peg-leg" railroad only operated during the summers from 1889 to 1892, when Webb's line made it superfluous.

43 The syndicate included ex-Senator Warner Miller, who brought the pulp and paper industry to the Adirondacks, see Chapter V; Henry Patton, lumber merchant from Albany, and Mills W. Barse of Olean. These three men were also charter members of the Adirondack League Club.

44 Donaldson, *History*, II, 135.

45 Charles H. Burnett, *Conquering the Wilderness* (Norwood MA: Privately printed, 1932), 26.

46 Ward claimed that the sale should be overturned because the original assessment was placed on the entire township, not individual lots, which he said involved both resident and non-resident owners. The sale was set aside by Comptroller Weller for what today appear to be legal but questionable reasons. The Forest Commission did not object to the sale, a further questionable act.

47 The station called Saranac Junction in 1892 was renamed Lake Clear Junction in 1893. Correspondence from Michael Kudish.

48 Robert Langlotz, letter to B. E. Fernow, Nov. 7, 1901, B. E. Fernow Papers, Cornell University Library.

49 Colvin, *Report for 1883*, 27.

50 Michael Kudish, *Where Did the Tracks Go* (Saranac Lake, NY: Chauncey Press, 1985) 33-34.

51 *Ibid.*, 97.

52 Donaldson *History*, I, 60; Kudish, *Tracks*, 96.

53 Kudish, *Tracks*, 12.

54 *Ibid.*, 12.

55 Richard F. Palmer, "Logging Railroads in the Adirondacks," *Northern Logger and Timber Processor*, March 1970, 15.

56 Richard S. Allen, William Gove, *et al.*, *Rails in the North Woods* (Sylvan Beach, NY: North Country Books, 1978) 6. This is a fine source of information on logging railroads.

57 *Ibid.*, 32.

58 Franklin B. Hough, *History of Lewis County, New York* (Syracuse: D. Mason and Co., 1883), 547.

## Chapter VII continued

59 Lucinda M. Parker, *Into Salisbury Country* (Brookfield, NY: Warden Press, 1987).

60 Fisheries, Game and Forest Commission, *Second Annual Report*, for 1896, 399.

61 H. J. Mols, "Hardwood Utilization in the Adirondacks" (M. A. Thesis, Cornell University, 1937).

62 Sargent Commission Hearings, testimony of Lemon Thomson, William McEchron, and "Mr. Finch."

63 *New York State Climatological Records*, Northeast Climate Research Center, Cornell University, Ithaca, NY.

64 Forest, Fish and Game Commission, Eighth and Ninth Annual Reports, 102.

65 Records of the Hudson River Boom Association, courtesy of Richard Nason.

66 Sargent Committee Hearings.

67 No Finch is listed as appearing before the Committee and no initials are given. George N. Ostrander, who worked for Finch, Pruyn, and Co., is listed as being present. Whether it was Finch or Ostrander who testified is not clear. Whoever he was, there is much testimony from "Finch."

68 Sargent Committee Hearings, 21-22.

69 *Ibid.*, 23.

70 *Ibid.*, 83.

71 Department of Agriculture, Bureau of Forestry, Map: *Adirondack Mountain Region, State of New York*, "Showing Approximately the Areas Burned by Forest Fires During the Spring of 1903," copy in AM Library.

72 Forest, Fish and Game Commission, *Annual Report for 1907, 1908 and 1909* (Albany: J. B. Lyon Co., 1909), 35-38.

73 Reed, "Gould's Old-Time Logging," 9.

74 Donaldson, II, 144. Richard Nason believes the 1891 date for the introduction of the crosscut saw is correct, however.

75 Special Assembly Committee, *Report on Lands to be Acquired to Protect Watersheds* (Albany: Wynkoop, Hallenbeck, Crawford Co., 1898), 10.

76 James Goodwin, "Lumbering in the Town of Keene," unpublished typescript, n. d., author's collection, 4.

77 Edith Pilcher, *Up the Lake Road*, (Keene Valley, NY: Adirondack Mountain Reserve, 1987), 49.

78 Goodwin, "Lumbering in Keene," 4.

79 *Boonville Herald*, December 12, 1901.

80 "Adirondack Rivers and Lumbermen," *Albany Journal*, June 7, 1899, as quoted in *Forest and Stream*, June 17, 1899.

81 State Engineer and Surveyor, *Annual Report for 1896*, 515.

82 *Boonville Herald*, June 7, 1900.

83 *Boonville Herald*, April 11, 1901.

84 Forest Commission, *Report* for 1893, vol. I, 151.

85 *Ibid.*

86 Special Report of the Forest Commission, Assembly Doc. 22, 1894, 10.

87 Special Assembly Committee, *Report* for 1896. Doc. 47, 11ff.

88 1891 Hearings, 474.

## Chapter VIII

1 Goodwin, "Lumbering in Keene," 6.

2 Ferris J. Meigs, "Santa Clara Lumber Co.: 1888-1938," unpublished typescript, n. d., 90-91, AM Library.

3 Goodwin, "Lumbering in Keene," 9.

4 Conservation Commission, Karl Schmitt, comp., *Fire Protection Map of the Adirondack Forest*, "Based on Field Work of State Forest Rangers and on the United States Geological Survey" (Albany: J. B. Lyon Co., 1916).

5 Goodwin, *Lumbering In Keene*, 5.

6 *Lumber Camp News*, December 1949.

7 *Northeastern Logger*, December 1952, 31.

8 P. T. Coolidge, "The Beginnings of Mechanical Traction," *Northeastern Logger*, April 1956.

9 C. W. Mason wrote that the fact such a tractor could haul both team and loaded sled out of a ditch, while pulling a load of logs, was the deciding factor. Actually several versions of Gould's Woods Superintendent John B. Todd's acceptance of the tractor survive. The fact that there were so many stories, some undoubtedly apocryphal, about the coming of the tractor, testify to the excitement surrounding its arrival. This version comes from C. W. Mason, "The Coming of the Tractor," *Lumber Camp News*, May 1949, 12.

10 Nelson C. Brown, "The Use of Tractors in Logging," *ESFPA Bulletin 12*, December 1921, 25.

11 Stanley H. Sisson, "The Use of Tractors in Winter Log-Hauling," *ESFPA Bulletin 12*, December 1921, 27-28.

12 Edgar E. Moore, "A Ride With Walt Wagner," Newsletter of the Salisbury Historical Society, Fall 1993.

13 *Free Press and Herald*, Tupper Lake, series of nine articles on Emporium Lumber Co., vertical files, AM Library.

14 *Lumber Camp News*, February 1940.

15 Kling, Nelson, and Reed, "Growth of Lumber Industry," 59.

16 *Northeastern Logger*, December 1952, 31.

17 Wallace, Oliver P. "Is your horse pulling his load on the logging job?" *Northeastern Logger*, September 1954.

18 Kling *et al.*, *Northeastern Logger*, April 1964, 59.

19 Fred C. Simmons, "Mechanized Logging Increases in Northeast," *Lumber Camp News*, March 1947.

20 Conversations with Richard Nason.

21 *Lumber Camp News*, 2d Anniversary Edition, 1941, 5.

22 E. F. McCarthy, "Observations on Unburned Cut-over Lands in the Adirondacks," *Journal of Forestry*, April 1919, 393.

23 Frank A. Reed, *Lumberjack Sky Pilot* (Old Forge, NY: North Country Books, 1965) 79.

24 Coville, "Silvicultural Problems," 9.

25 *Ibid.*, 12.

26 Mols, "Hardwood Utilization," 12.

27 Meigs, 51-55.

28 *Lumber Camp News*, April 1942.

29 Avi Cohen, "Technological Change as Historical Process-United States Pulp and Paper Industry 1915 to 1940," *Journal of Forest History*, September 1984, 775-800.

30 A. B. Recknagel, "Pulpwood Stands and Consumption," *Paper* 24, no. 5, 38. An ESFPA report for 1920 states that "imported spruce exceeds the amount of domestic spruce used in the ratio of 5 to 4."

31 It is ironic, but fairly typical, that shortages of pulp continued to prompt calls for harvest of the Forest Preserve even at the State's schools of forestry. See Willard H. B. Hine, "The Pulp Mills of New York State, With Special Reference to the

## Chapter VIII continued

Available Supplies of Pulpwood" (M. A. Thesis, Cornell University, 1921).

32 Division of Commerce, *The Paper and Pulp Industries of New York State*, Albany, 1942.

33 Committee of the NYS Section, Society of American Foresters, 7, Fernow Papers.

34 *Ibid.*, note 32.

35 Pulpwood production in the Adirondack region: 1939, 140,000 cords; 1940, 170,000 cords; 1941, 220,700 cords; 1942, 192,000 cords. These figures are in issues of *Lumber Camp News*, November 1939, June 1940, October 1941, and 2d Anniversary Edition, 1941.

36 George R. Armstrong, "An Economic Study of New York's Pulp and Paper Industry" (Ph. D. diss., SUNY College of Forestry at Syracuse, 1965) 14.

37 Conversations with Richard Nason about Finch, Pruyn and Co.'s experience.

38 Armstrong, "Economic Study," 121.

39 Conversation with D. T. Schlachter, Vice-president of Whitney Industries. Nason of Finch, Pruyn and Co. claims this did not happen.

40 Thomas J. Considine and Thomas S. Frieswyk, *Forest Statistics for New York, 1980*, (USDA, Forest Service, Northeastern Station, NYS DEC Resource Bulletin NE-71, 1982) 22, 104.

41 ESFPA, *Tenth Annual Report*, 45.

42 H. C. Belyea, "A Suggestion," *Journal of Forestry* 20 (December 1922): 867.

43 Proposed Sale, signed Karl Kornmeyer, Gould Papers.

44 A. B. Recknagel, ESFPA, *Bulletin 15*, 1922.

45 *Ibid.*, 5

46 A. B. Recknagel, "How far have we come in Industrial Forestry?" *Northeastern Logger*, May 1956, 19.

47 Theodore S. Woolsey, Jr., "Public Forestry on Private Land," *Journal of Forestry* 20 (February 1922): 130-134.

48 Amigo and Neuffer, *Beyond the Adirondacks*, 113.

49 George K. Armstrong, "The Forest Resources of New York State," *Northeastern Logger*, May 1956, 74.

50 *Northeastern Logger*, January 1962.

51 Conversation with John Stock.

52 A. B. Recknagel, writing in the *Journal of Forestry* 27, no. 10 (October, 1939), concluded that managing for sustained yields would cost $.20 a cord more than any recorded pulpwood sale in the Adirondack region.

53 Holbrook, *Yankee Logger*, 1961.

54 Richard Carota, president of Finch, Pruyn and Co., letter to Senator Ronald Stafford, *Hamilton County News*, March 30, 1993, 16.

55 Ralph D. Nyland, *The Forest Resources of New York, Their Condition and Productivity*, Appendix 8, Report of Governor's Task Force on the Forest Industry, 1989, 86-88

56 *Lumber Camp News*, September 1940; July 1942, 4; June 1943; May, 1946.

57 Armstrong, "Economic Study," 15.

58 R. H. Fergusen and C. E. Mayer, *The Timber Resources of New York* (USDA Forest Service, Northeast Forest Experimental Station, Resource Bulletin, NE-20, 1970).

## Chapter IX

1 Pinchot in *New York Sun*, February 25, 1900; also "To Preserve the Adirondacks," *Boston Transcript*, March 6, 1900, vertical files, AM Library.

2 Assembly Report, Transmitted to the Legislature, March 31, 1898 (Albany: Wynkoop, Hallenbeck, Crawford Co., 1898), 3-12.

3 Forest, Fish and Game Commission, *Sixth Annual Report for 1900* (Albany: J. B. Lyon Co., 1901), 168.

4 Forest, Fish and Game Commission, *Eighth and Ninth Annual Reports for 1902 and 1903* (Albany: J. B. Lyon Co., 1904), 377.

5 *Sixth Annual Report*, 170, 234-235.

6 *Ibid.*, 212-216.

7 Conservation Commission, *Fourth Annual Report for 1914* (Albany: J. B. Lyon Co., 1915), 43.

8 George N. Ostrander, "A Discussion of Article VII, Section 7 of the State Constitution," *Bulletin of the New York State Forestry Association*, June 1914, 11-12.

9 F. A. Gaylord, "A Reply to Certain Statements Relative to the State Forest Preserve," *Bulletin of the New York State Forestry Association*, October 1914, 39.

10 ESFPA, "Report of Tenth Annual Meeting," *Bulletin*, 1914, 58.

11 E. R. A Seligman, "Sane Conservation Proposals;" Speech before New York State Development Association, *Up-Stater*, September 1930, 9, 20.

12 Association for the Protection of the Adirondacks, *35th Annual Report*, 1936..

13 Division of Commerce, *Paper and Pulp Industries*.

14 "Railroads in the Adirondacks," *Garden and Forest*, June 10, 1891, 265.

## Appendix, Lumber and Pulp and Paper Companies

1 Harold Hochschild, *Lumberjacks and Rivermen* (Blue Mountain Lake: Adirondack Museum, 1962), 4-5.

2 Reed *et al.*, "Growth of the Lumber Industry," 53.

3 *The Lumber Trade of Albany*, 27.

4 Part of this tract was given in December 1992 to the State, part sold to the Conservation Fund to manage.

5 "Ticonderoga Dedication Issue," *Inter/Com*, October 21, 1971.

6 Amigo and Neuffer, *Beyond the Adirondacks*, 18.

7 W. E. Haskell, *Newsprint* (New York: International Paper Co., 1921) 69.

8 Robert N. King, *Bridging the Years, Glens Falls, New York, 1763-1978* (Glens Falls: Glens Falls Historical Association in cooperation with the Crandall Library, 1978.) 15.

9 *Lumber Camp News* 10, no. 12 (April 1949), 1, 10

10 Howard L. Churchill, "An Example of Industrial Forestry in the Adirondacks," *Journal of Forestry* 27 (1929). Churchill said that the company's lands contained about "20,000 acres virgin."

11 *Ibid.*, 24.

12 Letter to Ovid Fisher, editor *American Forests*, ESFPA Papers.

13 Manuscript, *Schedule A, Purchases and Sales of Land and Merchantable Timber*, Parties: MacIntyre Iron Company to Finch, Pruyn and Co., Hosmer Papers.

14 These published acreages and intervals at which they were acquired have been questioned by Richard Nason.

15 Churchill, "Industrial Forestry," 25

16 Conversation with Richard Nason.

## Appendix, Lumber and
## Pulp and Paper Companies continued

17 M. J. Plice and G. W. Hedden, "Selective Girdling of Hardwoods to Release Young Growth of Softwoods" (Graduate report, Syracuse School of Forestry, 1930). This paper describes Finch, Pruyn and Co.'s study of the effects of girdling and describes the process.

"Girdled trees require from two to five years to die and several more years before they cease to function as a windbreak. During this time the taller softwoods become more windfirm and the smaller growth has a better chance to survive because it has a longer time to adjust itself to its subsequent complete exposure. Root competition and shade gradually decrease and, with more light, moisture and warmth reaching the forest floor, the litter and humus matter decompose more readily, thus furnishing an extra supply of available nutrients. Thus the proportion of softwoods in a forest stand may be increased."

18 Matthew J. Conway, *Port Leyden "The Iron City"* (Woodgate, NY: Tug Hill Books, 1989), 212-232. Conway quotes newspaper accounts that give locations of drives, logs transported, and several mishaps to log drivers.

19 Howard W. Palmer, "Development of the Gould Paper Company," *Watertown Daily Times* Archives, Scrapbook 74, n.d.

20 Gould Testimony in the deCamp Case, Court of Appeals, Herkimer County, 1897.

21 The 1899 purchase from Adirondack Timber and Mineral Co. was at $6.75 an acre. Less than a decade later, the company paid $12.90 an acre for the lands acquired from International Paper Co. The history of Gould Paper Co. comes from articles in *Lumber Camp News*: 2, no. 4; 8, no. 5; 10, no. 5; and 11, no. 2; *Boonville Herald*, December 15, 1887; and Gould Papers, AM Library, in particular a summary "Timberlands Owned by Gould Paper Co."

The state paid $15.50 an acre for the bulk of the Moose River land acquired in 1963.

22 Reed, "Gould's Old-Time Logging Operations," *Northeastern Logger*, February 1953, 8-25.

23 These records have been given to the Adirondack Museum.

24 Robley W. Nash, "Survey of Utilization, Cull, and Residual Stands, Hardwood Operations, South Branch Moose River," December 1955, Gould Papers.

25 Thomas C. O'Donnell, *Birth of a River* (Boonville, NY: Black River Books, 1952), 62.

26 Kenneth R. Proulx, *The Life and Enterprise of Theodore B. Basselin* (Castorland, NY: KMAJ Books, 1980).

27 1891 Hearings, 406.

28 Lewis S. VanArnam, *Beaver Falls Cavalcade* (Beaver Falls, NY: By the author, 1979).

29 1891 Hearings, Basselin's testimony, 19.

30 Edwin M. Kling, "McKeever in the 'Teens,'" *Lumber Camp News* 2, no. 9, (September 1949).

31 Terrie, in *Adirondack League Club*, 92.

32 "Patton and Company Short," January 1 and "Patton & Company Fail," January 22, 1896, *Boonville Herald*.

33 *History of Oneida County*, 448.

34 Mols, "Hardwood Utilization."

35 *Watertown Daily Times*, August 1, 1941.

36 Donaldson, *History*, II, 138-9.

37 Meigs, *Santa Clara Lumber Co.* 9.

38 *Ibid.*, 108.

39 Amigo and Neuffer, *Beyond the Adirondacks*, 21.

40 *New York World*, June 29, 1889; *New York Herald*, July 3, 1889; and *New York News*, July 2, 1889, vertical file AM Library.

41 Fowler, *Cranberry Lake*, 35ff.

42 "Otto Hamele Tells Wanakena History," *Lumber Camp News*, June 1940, 4.

43 C. W. H. Douglass, *Report on Lumbering to the Emporium Forestry Operation at Conifer* (Graduate Report, Syracuse School of Forestry, n.d.), 4.

44 Thomas T. Taber III, *Whining Saws and Squaling Flanges*, no. 6 in the Series, *Logging Railroad Era of Lumbering in Pennsylvania*, 634-641.

45 *Ibid.*

46 The Grasse River Railroad was chartered as a common carrier, meaning it carried passengers as well as freight.

47 Fowler, *Cranberry Lake*, 102.

48 Letters dealing with the search for more land indicate Emporium's interest in tracts east of Harrisville, the Walker property, Whitney Park, tracts near Long Lake (including the property belonging to Henry S. Harper, New York publisher and friend of B. E. Fernow, with its long shoreline on the lake, which had not been cut for fifty years), the Underwood and Low properties, Mt. Arab Preserve, Sabattis, and the Raquette River Lumber Co. In 1942, the company spent considerable money bringing hardwoods to the mill from other tracts. Emporium Lumber Co. Papers, AM Library.

49 Emporium Papers.

50 Vertical files, Emporium Lumber Co., AM Library.

51 Amigo and Neuffer, *Beyond the Adirondacks*, 40.

52 Philip J. Hardy, "The Iron Age Community of the J. and J. Rogers Iron Company, AuSable Valley, New York, 1825-1900" (Ph. D. diss., Bowling Green State University, 1985).

53 A printed copy of this foreclosure sale, obviously taken from a newspaper, was loaned to the author by James Rogers III.

54 "Editorial Notes: Black Brook," *Plattsburgh Republican*, June 3, 1882, 1.

55 Hardy, 247.

56 Forest Commission *Reports for 1897, 1898, and 1899*.

57 Hardy, 254.

58 Some of these tracts were owned outright. J. and J. Rogers Co. owned only the timber rights on the rest.

59 Hardy, 289.

# Appendix, Parks and Preserves

1 This book adopts the modern spelling of Nehasane, which was hyphenated as Ne-ha-se-ne in early discussions of the tract.

2 Pinchot, *Adirondack Spruce.*

3 Pinchot quoted in an unsigned article in *Garden and Forest* 6 (April 12, 1893): 168-9.

4 Graves, *Practical Forestry in the Adirondacks*, 17.

5 Pinchot, *Adirondack Spruce*, 64

6 B. A. Chandler, "Results of Cutting at Ne-ha-sa-ne, in the Adirondacks," *Journal of Forestry* 17 (April 1919): 378-385.

7 *Ibid.*, 380.

8 Ralph C. Hawley, "Forestry at Nehasane Park," *Journal of Forestry* 18 (November, 1920): 681-692.

9 John R. Curry, "The Management of Whitney Park," *Northeastern Logger*, July 1957, reprint, 4.

10 Conversations with D. T. Schlachter.

11 Robert was a distant relative of the Glens Falls' Pruyns and not financially connected with them. Winthrop Aldrich has accumulated much information on Santanoni Preserve for DEC's Unit Management Plan for the property and the historic structures. The profile of Santanoni Preserve was prepared using the documents in this file.

12 Recknagel letter, 1938, Santanoni File, DEC.

13 *Ibid.*

14 Alfred Dolge, Letter to the Board of Trustees of Cornell University, April 7, 1898, Fernow Papers.

15 *Lumber Camp News* 1, no. 6.

16 Thomas Patrick Malloy, "Treatment of Cutover Forests in the Adirondacks with Particular Reference to the F. A. Cutting Tract" (M. A. Thesis, Cornell University, 1916).

17 Paula LaVoy Trim, *Looking Back Upstream: St. Regis Falls and Its Past* (Privately printed, 1989), 94-102.

18 Donaldson, I, 60.

19 Donaldson, *ibid.*, gives one figure, the two others are in the state study of land sales: Schedule A, 1921, Brandreth Estate to Mac-a-Mac Corporation and attached letters, H. A. Castle to George N. Ostrander, and F. L. Carlisle to Rufus L. Sisson, ESFPA papers, Cornell University Library.

20 George N. Ostrander, President ESFPA, undated letter, Schedule A, ESFPA Papers.

21 A letter from Ostrander in Schedule A, page 4, explained that there were different interpretations of measurement because of the 16-foot logs and that if the trees had been cut into 4-foot lengths, the price would work out to $3.00 a cord, about standard for the times.

22 Contracts and letters pertaining to them are in the Gould Papers, Adirondack Museum, gift of Lyons Falls Pulp and Paper Co.

23 Raymond D. Masters, *A Social History of the Huntington Wildlife Forest* (Utica, NY: North Country Books, 1993), 40.

24 *Ibid.*, 55.

25 Carl Hammarstrom, "A Management Plan for the Archer and Anna Huntington Wildlife Station at Newcomb" (M. A. Thesis, Syracuse University, 1936).

26 Masters, letter to the author.

27 Masters, *Huntington Forest*, 70, 80.

28 Andrew Shanley, "A Forest for the Trees," *Adirondack Life*, 21 no. 3 (May/June 1990) 83.

29 "The Pack Demonstration Forest," *Lumber Camp News* 10, no. 11 (March 1949).

30 William Rutherford, "Timber Management at Paul Smith's," *Lumber Camp News*, January 1952, 3, 16, 25.

31 Francis. M. Rushmore, "The Adirondack Research Center," *Northeastern Logger*, June 1956, 20-21, 50.

32 E. A. Sterling, "Forest Management on the Delaware and Hudson Adirondack Forest," *Journal of American Forestry* 30 (May 1932), 570.

33 *Ibid.*, 574.

34 *Ibid.*

35 Pilcher, *Up the Lake Road*, 39, 52. Pilcher states that a total of 45,000 acres was acquired, but because of sales the Reserve never exceeded 40,000 acres.

36 James Goodwin, letter to author.

37 *Ibid.*

38 Edward Comstock, Jr., ed., *The Adirondack League Club 1890-1990* (Old Forge, NY: Adirondack League Club, 1990), 12.

39 Adirondack League Club, *Yearbook*, 1891, 43-59.

40 "Transfer of Timberlands," *Boonville Herald*, August 28, 1890.

41 Adirondack League Club, *Yearbook*, 1891, 32-33.

42 *Ibid.*, 35.

43 Adirondack League Club, *Yearbook*, 1899, 11.

44 *Ibid.*,

45 Adirondack League Club, *Yearbook*, 1901, 13.

46 *Ibid.*, 12.

47 Adirondack League Club, *Yearbook*, 1903, 30.

48 Adirondack League Club, *Yearbook*, 1915, 41.

49 Philip G. Terrie, "'The Grandest Private Park': Forestry and Land Management," Chapter 2, *The Adirondack League Club, 1890-1990*, 85.

50 John Stock, letter to the author, June 1992. Stock is former Litchfield Park forester and member of the Adirondack Park Agency.

51 *Ibid.*

52 Chapter VI generally disputes this. Logging continued exclusively on private land.

53 B. E. Fernow, Testimony before the Senate Industrial Committee, typescript, Fernow Papers.

54 These lands are of interest because the offering letter from J. C. Livingston and Co. of Stratford, NY, April 27, 1898 (Fernow Papers) claimed that 4,000 of the 14,000 acres were virgin timber on which no spruce had been cut. As far as can be determined, the land was sold to the State without further logging on those 4,000 acres, which figure in the last chapter's discussions of virgin lands.

55 Letter, April 27, 1898, Fernow Papers.

56 *Ibid.*

57 A May 5, 1901 document between Cornell University and Brooklyn Cooperage Co. spells out the terms of the agreement, which apparently became effective a year earlier. The company agreed to build the mills. Fernow Papers.

58 *Ibid.*, four letters.

59 State of New York Annual Report of the Attorney General for 1902, 435-441.

60 B. E. Fernow, *Civilizing the Wilderness*, 5, Fernow Papers.

61 Thompson, "Doctrine of Wilderness," 144.

62 *Report of the Special Committee of the Assembly Appointed to Investigate as to Certain Matters Pertaining to the State Park and Forest Preserve*, March 24, 1902, Assembly Doc. No. 40, 3-7.

63 Report of the Adirondack Committee of the Assembly of 1902, April 16, 1903, 5.

64 Thompson, "Doctrine of Wilderness," 149.

65 R. C. Bryant. "Silviculture at Axton and in the Adirondacks Generally," *Journal of Forestry* 15 (1917): 801-810.

# Index

Barbara McMartin has a Ph. D. in mathematics and she has spent most of her life concerned with the Adirondacks. From her experience writing thirteen Adirondack guidebooks, she knows intimately its forests, lakes, mountains, and rivers. She has written two previous histories: *Caroga*, the history of a town, and *Hides, Hemlocks and Adirondack History*, an economic study of the tanning industry. She has also written public information material for the Adirondack Park Agency. As a member of several boards and advisory committees dealing with Adirondack issues, she has been most concerned with recreation in the Forest Preserve. In 1992, she served as Chairman of the New York State Committee for the Adirondack Park Centennial.